Working in Tourism

The UK, Europe & Beyond

for seasonal and permanent staff

Working in Tourism

The UK, Europe & Beyond

for seasonal and permanent staff

Verité Reily Collins

REVISED BY
Munira Mirza

Distributed in the U.S.A. by Peterson's Guides, Inc.,
202 Carnegie Center, Princeton, N.J. 08543-2123
Web site http://www.petersons.com

Published by Vacation Work, 9 Park End Street, Oxford
Web site http://www.vacationwork.co.uk

WORKING IN TOURISM

by Verité Reily Collins

Editor Munira Mirza

First Edition 1995

Second Edition 1999

ISBN 1-85458-218-6 (softback)

Cover Design by Miller Craig & Cocking Design Partnership

Illustrations by John Taylor

Publicity: Roger Musker

Typeset by WorldView Publishing Services (01865-201562)

Printed by William Clowes Ltd., Beccles, Suffolk, England

Contents

PART I THE JOBS & HOW TO FIND THEM

PART II   COUNTRY BY COUNTRY GUIDE

PART III   DIRECTORY OF PLACEMENT AGENCIES AND TRAVEL COMPANIES

PART IV   APPENDICES

Preface

Tourism is fast becoming the world's largest industry and every year more and more people join the millions already employed in this exciting sector. Working in tourism provides a unique opportunity to experience the lifestyle of the rich (and possibly famous) on ordinary wages, stay in top hotels, meet interesting people and visit the wonders of the world – all as part of your job. In addition, helping people to enjoy the holiday they have been dreaming of is a source of great job satisfaction.

Consumer legislation, which has thankfully resulted in greater protection for the holidaymaker, has also brought changes for those working in the industry. Companies have been forced to adopt a more professional approach or risk going out of business, and the days when tour operators would employ staff for a season with no training at all are long gone. Today there is a whole range of courses which will improve your chances of finding a job in tourism, and details are given in the following pages.

Although it helps to speak another language, probably 80% of the world's tourism business is conducted in English. The annual pilgrimage in search of sun and sand, so popular in the 1970s and 1980s, is changing. People's horizons have expanded, and the public's awareness of conservation issues is subtly altering the nature of holidays that people want. Be it activity holidays, gourmet wine and food tours or learning a new skill, special interest holidays are currently all the rage and the operators involved in this, the fastest growing sector of tourism, are looking to recruit specialists in a whole range of very diverse activities.

When the first edition of *Working in Tourism* came out, kind readers sent me letters about how the book had helped them find work. It has found its way into classrooms and public libraries as a store of useful information about the ever-growing industry. I am confident that this new, updated and revised edition will continue to provide practical and realistic advice about where and how to find work in the industry, as well as helping newcomers and those hoping to build a career in tourism to avoid the rough introduction so many of us experienced in our first jobs. Most will agree that the advantages far outweigh the frustrations.

Bon voyage to both you and your future clients.

Verité Reily Collins
London
December 1998

Acknowledgments

Colleagues (who are usually friends, unless I have stretched the bounds of their goodwill too far) helped by passing on their expertise, information and tips, as well as giving permission to publish their stories. To all of them a heartfelt thank you.

Many people have helped, including the Press Officers of the National Tourist Offices. I would particularly like to thank: Steve Fletcher of the Employment Information Unit (236 Grays Inn Road, London WC1X 8HL), Alan G. Bowen, Head of ABTA's Legal Department, Corinna Croft, Bob Crossey, Allen Evershed (Tourism & Hotel Security Consultant and ex-Head of Diplomatic and Royalty Protection Group, Metropolitan Police), Alan Fluke (Federation of Tour Operators), Michelle Ramsay, Jim Rowe and the team in Eurostar's Press Office, the staff of Kensington & Chelsea Library, Peter Worger of the Association for Conferences and Events, and Donna Bridgeland.

We would also like to thank the following for supplementing our research and providing first-hand accounts of their trials and triumphs working in the tourist industry: Nicky Brown, Heidi Brisley, Rhiannon Bryant, Carolyn Edwards, Xuela Edwards, Charlotte Jakobsen, Jane Labas, Eric Mackness, Jayne Nash, Christine Pennington and Matt Tomlinson, Annabel White.

Finally, a special thankyou to Nelly Gentric from the Travel Training Company and Enzo Paci of the World Tourism Organisation, for their invaluable assistance.

Telephone area code changes.
On April 22nd 2000 there are to be a number of changes to certain area telephone code prefixes in the UK. The most important of these is that the current 0171- and 0181- prefixes for London will be replaced by the prefix 020-, followed by 7 for current 0171 numbers and 8 for current 0181 numbers. Also affected will be Cardiff (numbers will begin 029 20), Portsmouth (023 92), Southampton (023 80) and Northern Ireland (028 90) for Belfast; contact directory enquiries for other numbers in Northern Ireland).

In addition, as from the same date the numbers for various special services including freephone and lo-call numbers will begin with 08 and all mobile phone numbers will begin with 07. Telephone operators are planning to ease the transition by running the current 01 numbers in parallel with the new 02 numbers until spring 2001.

Note: Companies and organisations mentioned in the text in italics and without an accompanying address or cross-reference may be found in Part III, the alphabetically organised Directory of Travel Companies.

PART I

The Jobs and How to Get Them

INTRODUCTION

The World Tourism Council estimates that by the end of the twentieth century the tourism industry will be the world's largest employer. Even at the moment, it has been estimated that travel and tourism employ one in every 15 workers worldwide. Once only the rich travelled, but now the proliferation of hotel and resort accommodation together with the affordability of air transport and the increase in leisure time mean that travel is commonplace.

Whenever the topic of international tourism crops up, statistics involving tens of millions are always bandied about and it is not always easy to understand how these statistics are compiled. How can anyone count all those people who move away from their homes in search of novelty and entertainment? Of course the tens of thousands of Britons who take a package holiday abroad and their counterparts in North America who go south in the winter are tourists. But so are the daytrippers who go on a cross-Channel shopping spree, a day trip to the seaside, a theme park or a National Trust property, and so are the business people and scientists who regularly attend conferences away from home. All these travellers require an army of people to service their needs.

SOME DEFINITIONS

The tourism industry is so diverse that job definitions are not always precise. In this book we have adopted a very broad definition of tourism, though in some contexts we have necessarily dealt with a narrower view.

Although the great majority of tourists stay in hotels and eat in restaurants, the hotels and catering industry is not always considered to be part of the tourist industry. Typically, the Careers & Occupational Information Centre, part of the Department of Employment in the UK, publishes separate booklets on 'Working in Tourism' and 'Working in Hotels & Catering'. Certainly someone who trains to be a chef will follow a very different career path from someone who works as a guide or rep. Yet some of the key areas of tourism, such as cruise ships or ski resorts, require both. They always have vacancies for cooks and assorted hotel staff as well as for more mainstream tourism personnel. Therefore this book also contains some advice for people who are interested in this aspect of the tourist business.

The classic tourism job is that of guide or representative (formerly known as couriers), the person who looks after holidaymakers. Guides work in a town, city or area and usually return to base each evening whereas tour managers/directors travel round with their clients staying in a different place most nights. Travel is generally by coach but can be by rail, plane, private car or limousine or any of these in combination.

A tour operator puts together the components of a holiday package or tour, booking accommodation, travel and services. The people who work in the office in charge of the bookings, budget, etc. are 'destination managers', most of whom were once reps or guides themselves. A ground handler is the term for a company which looks after visitors at a destination.

Travel agents (or consultants as they prefer to be called in the US) have the job of selling the packages created by tour operators. Travel agencies are like any high street store rather than designer studios. They are retail outlets which, like high-street stores, are often part of a national chain. Contrary to popular belief, working in a travel agency does not lead directly to jobs in other tourism sectors, though it is useful training for other things.

Tourist information centres (TICs) employ a vast number of people. There are more than 800 in the UK alone. Tourist boards are generally a government or local authority funded organisation which promotes an area, region or country to visitors and local people.

Incentive conferences serve as bonuses to the high-achieving staff in big companies, and provide a surprising amount of work within the industry. For example a multinational electronics company might organise a luxury island holiday for those employees who have been responsible for increasing turnover in the previous financial year.

Before turning our attention to the scope of employment opportunities available, it is worth pausing to consider the wider issues. Arguably, package tourism has been guilty of harming local economies, particularly in developing countries. From the point of view of the locals in the tourist destination, foreign tour operators employ foreign staff to look after foreign holidaymakers who pay for most of their holiday in foreign currency. There is some trickle down to the local community but not nearly as much as there would be if the locals themselves provided the services to travellers and tourists. On the other hand, packaged tourists can be better controlled, and if the company looking after them is sensitive to local concerns, this can be less intrusive than a mass invasion of independent travellers.

SCOPE OF OPPORTUNITIES

The range of jobs subsumed under that all-encompassing heading 'Tourism' is staggering, from fourth pursers on cruise ships to children's reps on European campsites, guides in national parks to ski chalet cooks. Of course tourism provides holiday jobs, but it also provides careers in marketing, promotions, public relations, etc. and for people with degrees in archaeology, business administration, history of art or a host of other subjects.

There is no clear line of demarcation between seasonal and permanent jobs in the world of tourism. Although many companies offer employment for only six months of the year, they are not necessarily looking for drifters and dabblers. In many cases they are seeking professionally-minded candidates who intend to make a career in the industry. A substantial percentage of those filling administrative jobs in tour operations started as reps or guides and worked their way up, often by accepting part-time or badly paid admin work over the winter for the first year or two. The large tour operators employ an army of people in accountancy, personnel, marketing, brochure production, design, contracting, reservations, etc. At one time the major UK tour operators were all based in London. But when a small company set up in a village in Lancashire and grew to become the giant company Airtours (which is still in the village though in somewhat larger premises), other companies moved out of London too.

There are very few countries which are not on the tourist map. Recently Vietnam, Myanmar (formerly Burma), Albania and all the Central Asian Republics have opened their frontiers to tourism, and Thomas Cook says there is a waiting list for the first trips to the moon. There is plenty of opportunity to work in another country, and with the free movement of labour within the European Union (at least in theory), it is becoming easier to cross European boundaries in the job hunt (see section *Red Tape* below).

There are jobs in tourism for young and old, male and female, school leavers and university graduates, people of all nationalities. An ability to crack jokes and solve practical problems knows no limits of age, nationality, gender or background. It is one of the few industries where sex discrimination is minimal. Many heads of companies are women, particularly in conference organising and the only jobs which women don't seem to want are those as coach drivers with Japanese or American clients, since lifting their enormous suitcases can be a challenge.

Opportunities exist for people working from home (see separate section *Working for Yourself*), for people who want to work part-time and for people with disabilities. For instance, being partially sighted or dyslexic may not hinder a guide. People with wheelchairs may have trouble getting insurance for jobs which require mobility and the ability help evacuate passengers, but there are suitable jobs in hotels and museums.

It doesn't matter what nationality you are. Dutch people take Australians and Americans flying around Europe, British staff look after American cruise clients in the Canaries, Germans look after Asian coach tourists in Italy, Australians and North Americans are highly prized as having the right attitude to look after trekking expeditions. etc. What matters is that you have the right kind of personality and what one tour operator calls 'stickability',

The biggest change recently has been an increased demand for people with training. At one time tourism companies employed untrained people who sat at the elbow of an experienced guide or staff member until they were deemed ready to go it alone. With the arrival of the single European market, EU consumer legislation has meant that many companies will no long employ staff unless they have been trained (see chapter *Training*).

Standards are improving and today companies can afford to be more selective when hiring staff. There are jobs for untrained people, but those who want to climb the career ladder should consider investing in one of the many tourism courses available lasting from a few days to several years.

WHAT EMPLOYERS ARE LOOKING FOR

Anyone who enjoys looking after people, has stamina and the will to work hard even under pressure has a good chance of finding work in tourism. Everyone involved with the travel industry agrees that personality is more important in this sector than in most others, and in many cases even more important than qualifications and experience. Although there are behind-the-scene roles, most travel industry employees deal with the public face-to-face, especially those who work overseas, and employers are looking for bright, enthusiastic and well-organised individuals to look after their clients. The literature from ABTA (the Association of British Travel Agents) addresses the issue of what skills and qualifications are needed and how to get them: 'It is vital that you have *or develop very quickly* a pleasant personality, presence and bearing, commonsense and positive motivation' – quite a tall order in some cases.

Knowledge of a foreign language is becoming more valued, though a great many people employed in the industry are still monolingual. People who speak with a pronounced accent (regional, foreign, etc.) are not normally disadvantaged, provided they speak clearly and can be easily understood by other people.

Basic emergency aid training, perhaps a health and hygiene certificate, plus any specialist qualifications will get you more interviews and will help you to give a better service to clients. For certain jobs a background in conservation, history, architecture or other professional qualification is more useful than general tourism training. Many attractions need local guides with specialised knowledge; for example, anyone with a background in marine biology has a good chance of being hired as a guide when they approach dive cruise firms from Queensland to Belize.

Returners (those returning to work after having children) and early retirers will find plenty of work. For example one British firm (see entry in Directory of Travel Companies for *NSS Riviera Holidays*) runs a holiday village in the south of France staffed exclusively by mature couples. Mothers with young children can often find part-time opportunities in their local tourist organisation.

Recent years have seen a welcome and growing awareness of the damage that mass tourism can do. Groups which were once allowed to rampage through tourist destinations with no regard for the feelings of the locals or the preservation of the local environment (both natural and cultural) are being better controlled. Nowadays tourism bosses are beginning to realise that tourism has been destroying the very thing it seeks to promote, though there is still a great deal of scope for progress in this area. A more mature and sensible attitude prevails today, and applicants for many posts will be expected to show sensitivity to these issues. Anyone with a background in conservation or who can demonstrate an ability to interpret sympathetically the culture of foreign countries will have an advantage. For a list of 'green' companies see *The Independent's Guide to Real Holidays Abroad*, by Frank Barret.

Extensive travelling experience impresses prospective bosses, as in the case of Xuela Edwards who spent more than a year roaming around Europe filling temporary vacancies in hotels and other jobs. When she returned to England in the month of February, she got several interviews with tour operators, despite the lateness of her applications, on the strength of her work abroad. She ended up working as a rep for Olympic Holidays on Corfu.

One or two less publicised talents can come in very handy, including a talent for acting, which goes hand-in-hand with an ability to bluff. The last thing a punter wants is a dithering, angst-ridden leader. Although speaking the language is not essential for directing holidaymakers to their acommodation, clients will expect you to speak some of the language.

REWARDS AND RISKS

The vast majority of people who turn to tourism as a career option want to meet and work with people. Many come from desk jobs and the variety and sociability of many jobs in tourism appeal strongly. Motivations for joining the industry vary from wanting simply to find a paid summer job (and tourism and hospitality are by far the greatest providers of this kind of seasonal employment), to gain experience or learn a language, to be paid to travel and work abroad, or to make a career in the world's most exciting industry, either at the beginning of their working lives or later on when a career change is called for or the stagnation of retirement needs to be avoided.

However reality doesn't always match dreams. It is necessary to think carefully about the drawbacks of the job you may be considering. Obviously the potential problems of becoming a ski guide in the Alps are completely different from those associated with leading overland trips through Africa. Yet there are some recurring issues. In the world of tourism, the client may have feet of clay, but he/she is still a god. The obligation to tolerate all sorts of obnoxious behaviour and the strain of non-stop smiling can become unendurable in some circumstances, whether coping with the incessant whinger on a cruise or the gang of lager louts in a resort. The firm of Thomas Cook runs an annual Round-the-World luxury tour and one might have expected the job of a tour manager on this month-long trip to be the kind to which any tour guide would aspire. But freelance tour director Valerie Forster expresses a different view:

> *After two weeks people start to get tired and pick holes in the tour and each other. Having to look after the same group for 32 days is not my idea of fun. I really enjoy the 14 to 17 days trips when people are still expectant at the end of the tour.*

Turn to the chapter on *Problems* for useful tips on how to anticipate and cope with specific problems which recur in the world of tourism.

Having to be sickeningly nice can take its toll very quickly

Some people do not realise how much of a guide or rep's earnings derive from tips. Often the non-stop smiling is not disinterested, and some people find this aspect of the job demeaning. Even worse is the pressure put on employees in certain jobs (especially reps) to sell excursions in order to boost company profits and incidentally increase their wages with commission.

Other potentially serious drawbacks to be taken into consideration are the discrepancy between the amount of responsibility most guides and reps must shoulder, often in very trying circumstances, and the low pay. The feeling of isolation when confronted with a problem can be daunting since, of course, you must maintain the fiction in front of the clients (whenever possible) that there are no problems. Long absences from home may sound romantic but almost always give rise to varying degrees of homesickness and can put a great deal of strain on any relationships you may have intended to preserve. On a more mundane level, the mechanics of collecting mail, doing your banking and laundry become more complicated.

Finally the insecurity of many jobs in tourism can come as a shock. Only a handful of the people taken on for the summer season (i.e. April to October) can be employed by the same company over the winter and, since summer wages are seldom enough to last for the rest of the year, an alternative has to be found. The majority of jobs in tourism, at least initially, are contract jobs, even in a year-round activity like cruising. This means that many employees in the field miss out on the benefits enjoyed by people in permanent jobs (and there is almost no union representation in the industry) and any downturn in business due to a war, hostage scare, transport strike, etc. inevitably means the overnight loss of jobs. Rhiannon Bryant was astonished by the difference between Crete in 1990 when jobs were plentiful and 1991 during the Gulf War and world recession when 'the resort of Malia was absolutely dead and workers were wandering around in crowds looking for work'. Similarly a fever of hiring in a ski resort one year may be utterly absent the next if the snows don't fall on cue. Tourism is a fickle business.

It is not so long ago that reps working for tour operators which went bankrupt might have found themselves thrown into jail as security for debts. Today there is less chance of companies going bust, thanks to efforts by associations like ABTA in the UK and counterpart organisations in the US, Australia, etc. and their bonding scheme for members. The European Union Package Travel Directive has put the onus on tour operators to safeguard their clients' money. In the UK, it is worth enquiring about whether the employer for whom you may be considering working has an ATOL (Air Travel Organiser's Licence) from the Civil Aviation Authority (CAA). A free leaflet about ATOLs may be requested by phoning 0171-832 6353.

On the other hand it is not unknown for staff in the field to be left in the lurch by dodgy tour operators. When Hannah Start spent a summer in France working for a major camping tour operator (since taken over), she was faced with a client with appendicitis and couldn't get any useful advice or support from the head office in England. Valerie Forster worked for such a company (since closed down) for 16 weeks:

> *I felt sorry for their clients and spent hours trying to sort out problems (and incidentally neglecting my health) because no one at head office had bothered. This was rather stupid of me, since my company had been offering cheap tours to people who didn't care about the quality. At the end of the season, I had to threaten them with solicitors' letters before I was paid the money owed me.*

Try at all costs to avoid paying for expenses out of your own pocket, since there is no guarantee you will be able to recoup the outlay.

The risk of outlining all the risks is that readers will be discouraged from pursuing their idea, which is not the point at all. One of the unexpected pleasures of the job for some people is the buzz they get from sorting out a difficult problem. Every day will be different and in many respects you are your own boss. Although you have to work hard, some of the clients always appreciate your efforts. One guide reports how gratifying it was when an eight-year old on her coach tour would shush everyone up whenever she picked up the mike and another remembers with great fondness the time she was taking an old soldier around Europe. In the British War Cemetary near Assisi he burst into tears when he found the grave of a comrade whom he had been told had no known grave.

Other pluses probably need no emphasis since it is the chance to travel the world, eat in marvellous restaurants without paying, escape the drudgery of making your bed or doing the washing up which prompted you to read this book in the first place. You can snatch some off-duty time to swim or ski, to watch a superb sunset over the Aegean or sit in the best seat for a performance of *Aida* at the Caracalla Baths. Even those who stay behind in a tour operator's office or tourist board may have perks (e.g. meals in restaurants with clients) but will also have to work long hours and weekends.

Clients often decide to buy their rep a present rather than give a tip

Coming Home

Working in tourism is addictive, and once you are in, it is easy to find other jobs. However there comes a time when you may wake up in the middle of the night and not know which hotel or town or even country you are in, and furthermore not even care. Eventually people get burned out and go stale. If you find yourself agreeing with the Rev. Kilvert whose famous Victorian diary claims that 'of all noxious animals, the most noxious is the tourist', then it is time to head home, perhaps to work in the company's head office.

At some point most people in the field decide it is time to trade in the Mediterranean grapevine for the job-hunting grapevine at home which usually turns up some interesting offers. With a good CV, some administrative experience and possibly fluency in another language, you are in an excellent position to build a successful career. Tour operators, conference organisers and tourism companies need people with that kind of experience. Working back at base need not spell the end of travelling. But this time you will be in charge, fly business class instead of tourist, stay in hotels you choose and, within reason, plan where and when you want to go.

TYPES OF EMPLOYMENT

REPS

Acting as a company rep in a foreign country gives you a unique chance to meet locals and become part of the local scene. The pay is not fantastic to put it mildly, but as your company often pays your salary into a bank account at home you are cushioned from currency fluctuations and can usually save.

The peak recruitment time starts the preceding September, though strong candidates can be interviewed as late as February. Most companies will not send anyone under the age of 21 abroad, since the responsibilities are just too great. Most employers want staff who will stay for the whole summer season April to October inclusive and normally hold back a range of bonuses and commissions to guarantee that you honour your contract.

Personality and maturity are what count most. As noted later in the relevant section, interviews can be fairly gruelling as they try to weed out the candidates who will crack under the pressure of holidaymakers' complaints and problems, or who may not cope well with the homesickness of being isolated for extended periods. It is estimated that only one in forty applicants gets a job.

The most important thing a company needs to know about new reps is whether or not they will fit in with the profile of a team. For many of the larger UK tour operators, the appropriate language comes very far down their list of priorities, even though knowledge of a European language is always requested. But even if the language requirements are not very rigorous, candidates should show that they are at least interested in learning about foreign cultures including the language. As you progress up the company ladder and are offered jobs as a senior rep or manager, then you will need to speak the local language. Reps from other European countries must be able to speak foreign languages, principally English.

A tour operator needs staff who can be flexible. Junior reps do not have any say in the resort to which they are posted, and six months in a place you hate is a very long time. Telling the tour operator you want to work in X in order to be near a partner will guarantee that you are sent to the opposite end of the Mediterranean. No company wants their staff to have outside interests which might interfere with their work. Once trained in the company ways, e.g. to send in correct company paperwork, sell the company excursions and work the way the company wants, a rep can be transferred from one resort to another, sometimes one country to another, at short notice. Once you have a season or two of experience you should be given a say in where you go (a tip: try to choose a resort which does not have runway lights as this means that there will not be any night flights and therefore no sleepless nights). Note that it is normally necessary to work several seasons in Spanish and Greek resorts before having a chance of being sent to a long haul destination such as Florida, Thailand or India.

Reps are expected to work six or seven days a week between seven and fourteen hours every day depending on whether transfers, hotels check-ins, welcome meetings, excursions, client visits, hospital visits, etc. are scheduled. Time off is seldom enough to do much independent travelling. Most reps spend their day off catching up on sleep or flopping on a beach. The industry demands total dedication. If there is a strike and 40 clients are suddenly rerouted to another airport, you will just have to miss the party to which you had been looking forward. If there is a crisis, you could end up working up to 36 hours at a stretch, and are expected to be smiling at the end of it.

Considering the rigours and pressures of the job of package tour company representative, wages are low, though of course accommodation, travel and some other perks are provided. The accommodation can be anything from a small dark room with only a bed and a shower to a room in a five-star hotel. Note that sometimes reps have to share accommodation with other reps. On more than one occasion male reps have been expected to share with females, but this is unusual. And the free travel may have its drawbacks too. Don't be surprised to be put on a flight that arrives in the capital at 2.30am with a connecting flight to the resort at 5.30am. Wages can be truly appalling, starting at £50 a week. When Xuela Edwards was a rep on Corfu, a salary of £160 per month was paid into her UK bank account and was subject to deductions for National Insurance and income tax. Since your salary is usually paid in sterling into a bank account at home, be sure to take enough cash to see you through the first month and a supply of Eurocheques to give you access to your salary. Meagre wages will be supplemented with commissions from restaurants, shops and car hire as well as selling company excursions.

It is self-evident that reps looking after holidaymakers, must remain aware of the consequences of giving bad advice. According to EU Package Travel regulations which came into operation in 1993, the tour operator is responsible for the holidays they provide. Some companies have become so cautious in the face of possible litigation, that they now prohibit their reps from recommending a local restaurant in case the punter gets food poisoning.

Obviously medical emergencies are the most serious problem which reps may face, for instance if an elderly client has a heart attack or a young tearaway has a serious accident on a hired moped. The situation becomes even more difficult if your employers have told you not to do anything apart from summon help for fear that relatives may later sue if the rep is deemed to have taken the wrong steps. In the opinion of at least one major insurance company, a rep who did nothing could be shown not to have offered a 'duty of care' as set out in EU regulations. For your own peace of mind, try to take a reputable lifesaving course before taking on a rep's responsibilities.

Another part of the rep's job is to look after the locals. If a small group of clients party noisily into the wee small hours, the rep is the one who has to placate the irate locals whose sleep has been disturbed. If those same troublemakers damage their apartment, the rep has to placate the villa owner and arrange compensation. In the words of journalist Sue Arnold who shadowed a company rep in Crete for a feature article, 'Amazing as it may seem, repping does not require commando training, a Berlitz language course, a St John Ambulance diploma and a background in the diplomatic service; all you need is guts... and a big smile.'

As must have become obvious by now, the life of a resort rep is not as glamorous as it may sound. An apt headline appearing in *The European* newspaper once read 'Fun-in-sun image belies hard graft of the tour rep.' When you're not sorting out some crisis or other, smoothing the ruffled feathers of some disappointed punter or irate local or struggling to achieve your sales target, you will be wading through your paperwork for the company. When your group implores you to join them in a tour of local nightclubs, you must have the discipline to wave them off and go upstairs to fill out the daily reports and plan for the next day. Even if you report to a resort manager, it is up to you to sort out your daily routine.

You will need to employ all your powers of diplomacy when faced with a group of mixed ages and interests

Yet the job retains enough appeal to attract many more candidates than there are jobs. Charlotte Jakobsen, who has worked for a Danish tour operator as a rep and guide in Spain, Tenerife, Turkey and Thailand, concludes:

> *I can only recommend this job. You learn a lot, not only about the world and the people in it but also about yourself. Being a tour rep is never a holiday but very hard work, often for little pay. But also a great job. You get to travel a lot and you never do the same one day as the next.*

Like any job, it takes years of experience before most people are really good at being a rep.

New reps often have to work a one month trial period, after which the contract can be terminated. Many tour operators provide a uniform, though there is normally a returnable deposit (say £60) for its return at the end of the season (so try not to spill red wine on it).

Commission rates for reps are very important, so pay close attention to the terms of your contract. Usually you earn a certain percentage 'on liquidation' (i.e. when the punters pay) and a bonus commission if you complete your contract. Anyone whose contract is terminated or who resigns before the end of the contract period forfeits all additional end-of-season commission payments. One rep explained the importance of being part of a good sales team:

> *At first I was embarrassed standing up to talk in front of clients, but now the the other reps and I know enough to run a good double act together, with a lot of laughs. This is important. Our basic salary is very low so we need to earn commission from the sale of excursions. The team pools commission, so if I do badly, they won't be very pleased.*

Typically the rep might expect to receive 4% of income generated from excursions or local car hire plus a further 4% of sales beyond the set target, both paid at the time, plus a further 2% paid on successful completion of the contract. Do not be surprised if local taxes are deducted from these amounts. The most lucrative commission rate (say 10%) is paid for arranging local lets.

The two banes of every rep's life are sales targets and customer questionnaires. Often the questionnaires given out by tour companies to clients are crudely worded (e.g. was your rep's appearance excellent, good, adequate or poor?). The results are taken very seriously and can be soul destroying.

Meet-and-greet Guides

Meet-and-greet representatives stay in one place and accompany groups of tourists or conference-goers, often from an airport to a city-centre hotel. It is possible for temporary residents of a holiday resort, for example young people spending the summer season on a Greek island, to find this kind of transfer work with a tour operator by asking around at the local travel agencies which act as the headquarters for overseas reps. The work is intermittent and paid on a piece-work basis (which may not take into account whether the flight you are meant to meet and greet is delayed).

Working for Ground Handlers

The company which looks after the clients on the ground is not normally based in the tour operator's own country but rather in the country where the holiday takes place. They service the incoming market, i.e. tours coming in to their area. The area may be defined rather broadly, and so the ground handler may be located in a third country. For example, an American group flies into Paris, tours France, Switzerland and Italy and flies home from Rome. The tour operator in the US will have contracted with a ground handler for all their European tours, who might well be based in the UK. This ground handler does not want the expense or bother of flying in tour guides from across Europe so draws their staff from people available for interview in Britain. The tour guide who is booked for the tour may well have to meet the group outside the UK, at the ground handler's expense. Therefore some of the best jobs in tourism are allocated in the ground handler's country.

Ground handling companies servicing American, Canadian, Australasian, Asian and Japanese markets are also based in the main European countries and some smaller ones like Luxembourg too. For the large segment of Scotland-only tours, ground handlers are based in Edinburgh and Glasgow. For the huge South American market, ground handlers are based in Spain and Portugal, and again they tend to interview and select local staff.

If you find yourself in a resort and would love to stay and work then it is worth approaching local ground handlers. They may be contracted by smaller operators, especially those with the more upmarket tours (which may mean the work is scarce or intermittent). Furthermore, ground handlers tend to employ locals. However if you have some experience and/or training and are persistent there is work. There may also be some last-minute work with ground handlers in resorts, usually only available to foreigners in the event of a sudden and unexpected vacancy. Therefore we have included the names and contact numbers of some ground handlers in the country-by-country guide. Note that ground handlers pay local wages which are unlikely to be less than a UK wage, however without all the attendant perks like free travel, accommodation, etc.

Ground handlers employ people on a permanent basis. Such companies need office staff who are good at administration and able to work on their own initiative.

This can be extremely interesting as you have to visit the hotels and venues to find out whether they are suitable for your company's clients. If you speak a foreign language fluently, look through the BITOA (British Incoming Tour Operators Association) list of members and approach those companies which handle visitors from the country whose language you speak.

Tourism professionals working for big companies may not get to travel much as part of the job. However staff are often eligible for free or heavily subsidised trips when there is space on company flights.

TOUR PERSONNEL

The person who accompanies a group of holidaymakers on a packaged tour is variously known as tour manager, director or leader. The job title 'courier' has largely been superseded in the industry. The tour leader may be an employee of the tour operator, a freelancer or (less usually) someone who is operating (i.e. designing, marketing and leading) his or her own tour. Company employees are expected to project the company image, so someone who looks like they would win a wet T-shirt competition is unlikely to find work with Swan Hellenic and similarly an archaeological scholar need not apply to an 18-30s style tour operator like Contiki.

Officially the job of tour manager consists of representing the company, meeting and/or accompanying a group (usually on a coach), providing commentary, reconfirming accommodation and activity arrangements (which should have been put in place by the employing tour operator), helping with baggage, sorting out problems and generally creating an enjoyable atmosphere for the clients. This is quite a tall order and the scope for disaster is huge (see chapter on *Problems and How to Cope*).

The rewards are those which attract most people into the tourism business in the first place, the chance to travel, a desire to work with people and the chance to take responsibility. Many prominent members of the tourist industry started out as managers or reps as their first step on the career ladder. Recently, EU countries have tightened up on requirements and insist that personnel leading a tour have a recognised qualification. In some countries, staff have been hauled off coaches and taken to the local police station if they cannot produce a certificate. Make sure that you have an internationally recognised qualification (not just one issued by a local authority), and carry photocopies certified by the relevant Consul and translated into the language of the country you are visiting.

Although nationals of non-European countries do find work as tour managers, moving from one country to another with their groups, it is much more difficult to arrange to stay in one country because of the lack of a work permit. One possibility is to work with student groups based at a university campus.

Eventually when you have worked for three years as a tour manager, you can apply to become a member of the International Association of Tour Managers (IATM). Those who have completed a recognised tour manager training course, or have completed one season working as a tour manager, may apply for Affiliate status. (IATM, 397 Walworth Road, London, SE17 2AW; 0171-703 9154/fax 0171-703 0358; e-mail: iatm@iatm.co.uk; website:www.iatm.co.uk).

Tour Guides

Someone who knows a great deal about a single town, building, museum, park or other attraction can become what is known as an on-site, local or (US only) step-on guide. This normally corresponds to the individual's field of particular interest.

People passionate about anything from railways to butterflies can often find an outlet for their expertise in allying themselves to a tourist attraction. This is an excellent way to accrue experience which would be viewed favourably by any employer looking for local guides.

Guides accompany a group of people for a day or less and are normally found in big cities. (Note that it is illegal in Europe including the UK, for a coach driver to guide whilst a vehicle is moving, as is guiding whilst standing up on a vehicle.) Some countries require tour operators to book and pay for a local guide who is a national of the country. In the UK it is possible to become a Registered Guide by undertaking a rigorous training course monitored by one of the regional tourist boards (see chapter on UK). The director of any tourist information office would be able to offer advice on where to train as a local guide. Both clients and tour operators like including 'the local's inside view' and it may not be too difficult to persuade the people who design a tour that you can offer a personalised service.

Sometimes it is possible to do this on a more casual basis by making yourself known to the local excursion-organising tour operator and suggesting you could organise a specialist tour, e.g. birdwatching, local embroidery, etc. Although the official local guides won't want you to take away their work, they don't normally mind specialist walking tours, perhaps in the evening. You might also offer to pay commission to the local guides for suggesting your tour to their clients, which can result in a harmonious relationship with the official guides and their tour operators.

Longer Itineraries

Most tour managers aspire to accompany groups on longer and more varied itineraries, at least those who don't mind the idea of staying in a different place each night and who do not suffer from motion sickness. Coach tour operators put together an itinerary, sell it through travel agencies or directly, and then employ someone to lead the tour. If you have had no training, there are companies that will take novices, but they may charge a training bond of between £200 and £400 which be non-refundable if you are considered unsuitable.

Most coach tour routes are along well-worn lines and the stop-overs, restaurant and hotel stops are long established ones. Still, the arrangements do often go wrong (the longer the tour, the more scope for hiccoughs) and it is essential that the tour manager continually check and confirm reservations. Sometimes the manager is with the same group from their point of origin; sometimes they join the group once abroad.

Much of the work for tour managers is freelance. A coach company will ask you to take a short two or three day tour. You make a success of it, and they ask you back. However, the amount of work (from Britain) is circumscribed by the coach industry's calendar. There tend to be bursts of between two and eight weeks of work with not much available between: Dutch bulbfields in April/May, Edinburgh Tattoo weekends in August, weekend shopping trips to Calais in November/December, etc., interspersed with longer tours to Austria, Italian Lakes, etc. in June/July.

The most lucrative trip is the complete European circuit (of the 'if it's Tuesday it must be Belgium' variety) when clients do not have time to organise their own excursions and are happy to sign up for those that are laid on. Experienced freelance tour guides have been known to make £400 for half a day's work in Rome or Paris, especially if they are not working with Britons (to whom it is difficult to sell anything) or Australians (who aren't in the habit of tipping).

Whatever the kind of tour you are leading, one of your main roles is as trouble-shooter. Inevitably at some point the hotel or restaurant on the itinerary will have lost the group reservation, the coach will break down, a tour member will go missing or (less drastically) his suitcase will, someone on the trip will get sick (perhaps you) and all of these problems must be dealt with efficiently and cheerfully. As we have seen in the case of resort reps, the scrapes into which holidaymakers can get are almost limitless, and may involve serious problems such as being robbed, offending local customs or even breaking local laws.

There is usually a chronic complainer whose complaints, in some cases, are justified if the itinerary has not been well worked out ahead of time. Very occasionally there is a know-it-all who makes it his or her business to catch the tour guide out on minor mistakes. There is always a bore. And on a long trip, there is no escape, unless the client is so disruptive that you undertake to remove him from the tour. Many problems can be avoided by taking a firm hand at the beginning. Lay down the rules for punctuality, seat rotation, etc. at the beginning and make sure everyone complies and understands that it is in everyone's best interests. Sometimes you must be uncharacteristically strict. For example the group may express an interest in going to see a venue which is not on the itinerary and if you agree, you will be made late for another, for which you will (irrationally) be blamed. The only chance of surviving all this is to hear compliments from tour members who have had the time of their lives just because of you.

Your first coach commentary may not be an overwhelming success

Cross-References

In Britain, the appropriate training for tour guides is the one leading to the NVQ Field Services (Guiding) Level 2 or the RSA Coach Tour Guides Certificate. After gaining some experience, guides can work up to Tour Manager (NVQ Level 3 or RSA Diploma) and Tour Director (NVQ Level 4). In the US, the premier training is available from the International Tour Management Institute (see chapter on Training) though many local colleges offer short courses in tour leading.

See the chapter on *Getting a Job* for information on how to break into the world of tour guiding, including what preliminary steps you can take to improve your marketability, apart from formal training.

See the chapter on *Problems and how to Cope* for specific advice on how to prepare for and deal with the problems which tour leaders encounter.

See the following section on *Overland Expedition Leaders* if you are interested in this type of tour.

CAMPING HOLIDAY TOUR OPERATORS

UK camping holiday operators hire very large numbers of people with language skills to remain on one family campsite on the Continent for several months. The Eurocamp Group alone recruits about 1,500 campsite couriers and children's couriers. These companies provide self-drive, self-catering holidaymakers with fully-equipped tents and mobile homes. The courier's job is to greet clients and deal with difficulties (particularly illness or car breakdowns), clean the tents and caravans between visitors and introduce clients to the attractions of the locality or even arrange and host social functions and amuse the children. All of this will be rewarded with on average £80-100 a week in addition to free tent accommodation and travel to the site for those who complete their contracts). The season lasts from March to October, though some companies offer half-season contracts. Setting up and dismantling the campsites in March/April and September/October (*montage* and *démontage*) is often done by a separate team. This work is hard but the language requirements are nil.

Campsite Couriers

The advantages of the job of campsite courier are that you meet lots of people, are continually in a holiday atmosphere, get to know one area really well, improve your language skills and often manage to cultivate an enviable tan and a higher level of fitness into the bargain. Successful couriers make the job look easy, but it does demand a lot of hard work and patience. It can often be tedious and frustrating to have to clean out six family-sized tents in 90 degree weather or hang around all day waiting for just one family to arrive. Occasionally it is very hard to keep up the happy, smiling, never-ruffled courier look.

However most seem to end up enjoying the job and find their fellow couriers lively and congenial company. Alison Cooper described her job with on a site in Corsica as immensely enjoyable, though it was not as easy as the clients thought:

> *Living on a campsite in high season had one or two drawbacks: the toilets and showers were dirty, with constant queues, the water was freezing cold, the campsite was very noisy and if you're unfortunate enough to have your tent in sunlight, it turns into a tropical greenhouse. Of course we did get difficult customers who complained for a variety of reasons: they wanted to be nearer to the beach, off the main road, in a cooler tent with more grass around it, etc. etc. But mostly our customers were friendly and we soon discovered that the friendlier we were to them, the cleaner they left their tents.*
>
> *I found it difficult at first to get used to living, eating, working and social-ising with the other two couriers 24 hours a day. But we all got on quite well and had a good time, unlike at a neighbouring campsite where the couriers hated each other. Our campsite had a swimming pool and direct beach access, though nightlife was limited. The one disco did get very repetitive.*

Despite all this, she highly recommends that people who have never travelled or worked abroad before apply to a company like Eurocamp which provides accommodation, a guaranteed weekly wage (normally paid into a UK bank account) and the chance to work with like-minded people. Although the wages are not high, customers often leave food and drink behind and invite couriers to join them for meals.

Caroline Nicholls' problems at a campsite in Brittany included frequent power failures, blocked loos and leaking tents:

> *Every time there was a steady downpour, one of the tents developed a leak, and I would appear, mop in hand, with cries of 'I don't understand. This has never happened before.' Working as a courier would be a good grounding for an acting career.*

"I can't understand it; this has never happened before"

Campsite couriers have to contend with frequent floods in the tents, power cuts and blocked loos

She goes on to say that despite enjoying the company of the client families, she was glad to have the use of a camp bicycle to escape the insular life on the campsite every so often. Some companies guarantee one day off-site which is considered essential for maintaining sanity. The companies do vary in the conditions of work and some offer much better support than others. For example a company for which Hannah Start worked ignored her pleas for advice and assistance when one of her clients had appendicitis.

Supervisors

All these couriers need area supervisors, which is a challenging role for which a week's training is arguably not enough. Area supervisors are sent out to their respective regions of Europe with a couple of 'squaddies' (who are drivers as well as tent erectors) to welcome couriers as they arrive. One supervisor is in charge of up to 30 couriers. Often it is a race against time as pre-season preparations can be hampered by bad weather, late deliveries, temperamental campsite owners and general exhaustion.

Once all the sites are up and running, the supervisor visits each in turn every 10-14 days to sort out problems, deliver equipment (a never-ending chore), butter up the local campsite owners, etc. The closing down of the site at the end of the season is much more relaxed though harder work as there are usually fewer people left to help. Despite all the problems, Jayne Nash had a great season with Canvas:

> *Overall is was a great experience livng and working the holiday spirit. At times things were dire but this was compensated for by the good times. I had an amazing summer living in a tent in the orchard of a chateau. It is definitely not a job for the faint-hearted: be prepared for accidents, deaths, robberies, floods and storms that whisk tents away. Have a solution to everything or at least be willing to try anything.*

Supervisors are paid a salary plus bonus, modest daily living allowance and given the use of a vehicle. Winter opportunities are few. The major campsite operators may be able to offer a job in the office, but probably at a lower salary.

Other Employment

Most companies employ their own drivers who must be over 21 and have held a clean driving licence for at least a year. The season is longer than for the couriers, starting in mid-February. The company *Trans Sure (UK) Ltd* (see Directory entry) employs HGV drivers to distribute and return camping equipment from central depots in France throughout Europe on behalf of British camping tour operators.

Montage assistants normally work only for four to six weeks from early April and *démontage* assistants are needed for a minimum of four weeks, usually in September. Campsites which offer watersports facilities need a waterports courier to book out the equipment to customers, and instruct, carry out repairs, etc. A professional canoeing or windsurfing qualification is preferred.

Applying

Most of the major camping holiday and tour operators based in Britain begin recruitment in November and have finished most of their interviewing by the end of February or even January. But there is a very high dropout rate (over 50%) and vacancies are filled from a reserve list, so it is worth ringing around the companies as late as April for cancellations. Despite keen competition, anyone who has studied a European language and has an outgoing personality stands a good chance if he or she applies early and widely enough. Although the majority of couriers are aged 18 to 25, the big companies are keen to receive applications from mature applicants including couples. According to Carla Mitchell, not having too posh an accent helps when applying to companies based in the North; with her Surrey accent, she was given a job without too much 'client profile'.

Most companies provide a few days of training in the destination country before starting work.

Unexpected high season vacancies with companies like Club Cantabrica and Carisma Holidays are occasionally filled on location. English speakers based in holiday areas can ask the area supervisor about this possibility.

Directory References

For camping holiday tour operators based in the UK which operate in a range of European countries, see: Canvas Holidays, Club Cantabrica, Eurocamp, Eurosites, Haven Europe, Trans Sure (UK) Ltd and Venue Holidays.

Other companies operate in one country only (mainly France) and are listed in the relevant country chapter.

ACTIVITY HOLIDAYS

Many specialist tour companies employ leaders and reps to run their programmes of hiking (such as *Ramblers Holidays*), canoeing holidays (see *Headwater Holidays*), sailing flotillas (see *Sunsail*) or cycling holidays (see relevant entries in the Directory such as *Susi Madron's Cycling for Softies*).   Outdoor   activity centres are another major employer of summer staff, both general domestic staff and sports instructors. One of the biggest is *PGL Travel* which recruit for about 3,000 seasonal vacancies at their holiday centres mainly in Britain and France, primarily for activity intructors, group leaders and support staff. The norm seems to be to pay low wages but to allow lots of free time and access to all the holiday facilities. The basic weekly rate of pay is £36, with higher rates being paid to those who can start between February and May.

Children's Camps

The practice of sending children to summer camps used to be uniquely North American. However, the idea is catching on in Europe and large numbers of young people are needed to work on these camps, such as *Village Camps* which hire a range of staff for their camps in Switzerland, Austria and elsewhere. For detailed information about becoming a counsellor at an American summer camp, see the chapter on the USA. Anyone who has a connection with the YMCA-YWCA should enquire about international summer camp possibilities.

Sports Instructors

Any competent sailor, canoeist, diver, climber, rider, etc. with relevant instructor's certificates should have no difficulty marketing his or her skills either at home or overseas. Since the canoeing tragedy of 1993 in which several young people were drowned at an activity centre on the south coast, directors have been looking for higher standards of training and experience. Do not apply for an instructor's job unless you have the proper qualifications and know what to do in the event of an emergency. Association initials are printed in brackets after the sport (and if you don't know what the initials stand for should you really be looking after kids taking part in these sports?)

Many local colleges run courses in outdoor leisure including sports instruction, for example Bicton College (East Budleigh, Devon EX9 7BY. Tel 01395 568 353) and Pencoed College (Pencoed, Bridgend, Mid Glamorgan. Tel 01656 860 202). The Institute of Leisure and Amenity Management (01491 874800) produce a free booklet explaining the qualifications and where to obtain them.

The Youth Hostels Association can advise on short courses around the country. For example, it is possible to obtain the British Hill Walking Leaders Certificate after three weekends of training in the Lake District (at a cost of less than £110 per weekend); contact Summitreks, 14 Yewdale Road, Coniston, Cumbria LA21 8DU for details.

Finding amusements which will appeal to children of all ages can be tricky

Qualified divers and guide/leaders can find work in a range of exotic locations from the Philippines to Eilat in Israel, Queensland to Belize. Often the American PADI system of certification is more familiar than the one used by the British Sub-Aqua Club. Wages in developing countries would be subsistence levels, but the pleasures of the job for divers are enormous.

The following are the governing bodies of major sports which oversee qualifications in the UK: send an s.a.e. for more information.

British Canoe Union, John Dudderidge House, Adbolton Lane, West Bridgford, Nottingham NG2 5AS. The BCU Level 2 Coach Award is recognised by the Department of Education as the minimum standard for instructors.

British Horse Society, Stoneleigh Deer Park, Kenilworth, Warwickshire CV8 2XZ (01926 707707).

British Mountaineering Council, 177-179 Burton Road, Manchester M20 2BB. The representative body for climbers can provide details of instructing courses. The basic qualification is the MLTB Single Pitch Supervisors Award.

British Snowboard Association,First Floor, 4 Trinity Square, Llandudno, North Wales LL30 2PY (01492 872 540). Snowboarding is the fastest growing sport in Europe.

British Sub-Aqua Club, Telfords Quay, Ellesmere Port, South Wirral, Cheshire L65 4FY (http//www.bsac.com)

Royal Yachting Association, Romsey Road, Eastleigh, Hants. SO50 9YA (www.rya.org.uk). Instructor qualifications available in sailing, windsurfing and motor cruising.

Sailing

Flotilla sailing refers to a fleet of yachts which set off together, usually sailed by the holidaymakers but under the guidance of a lead boat with skipper, engineer and hosts. The concept started in Europe but has now caught on in the Caribbean as well. Boats go out exploring the local area, meeting up in the evenings for barbecues and restaurant meals. Skippers need the RYA Yachtmaster qualification or equivalent experience. The engineer needs knowledge of diesel engines, electrics and pumps, ropes and rigging. Hostesses must be personable, good at organising and (often) able to cook.

The chartering business is booming in holiday resorts and many are owned by companies or individuals who need crew, hostesses and cooks. Pauline Power, an experienced sailor from Ireland, noticed a beautiful four-masted tall ship called *Sea Cloud* while she was in the Canaries. *Sea Cloud* is the world's largest private yacht with 3,000 square metres of sail which sails around the Mediterranean in summer and the Caribbean in the winter. When Pauline later applied to work for the Hamburg-registered charter ship (Vorsetzen 50, D-2000 Hamburg; 040-369 0272) she was given one of the 80 contracts. Similarly Perry Morton from the States was so smitten by the vessel he saw moored in Livorno harbour that he asked to come on board and was hired on the spot as a deck hand. Pay is negligible but tips can be good. (Perry stayed on to study for his Mate's ticket and is now Third Officer.)

Take copies of any sailing certificates when job-hunting or, if possible, a letter from a boat owner saying you are a useful crew member. Ask around when you are in a marina. Harbour masters can often tell you if there are yachts looking for crew.

SKI RESORTS

Skiing and all the employment it generates is by no means confined to the Alps. There are skiing centres from Geilo in Central Norway to Mount Hermon in Israel, from the Cairngorms of Scotland to dormant volcanoes of New Zealand. And there are many ski resorts in North America, in addition to the most famous ones such as Banff in the Canadian Rockies, or Aspen in Colorado. The standard ski season in Europe and North America is roughly Christmas until late April, whereas in the southern hemisphere (the Australian and New Zealand Alps, Chilean Andes), it lasts from late June until early October. Between Christmas and the New Year is a terrifically busy time in European ski resorts, as are the middle two weeks of February during half-term.

Reps working for ski tour operators tend to be skiers themselves though this is not a requirement. Often tact is more important than athletic skill, especially when snow conditions are less than ideal. The rep who tells a group of clients on the way from the airport that the resort has no snow, and ski cannon have been banned so there isn't any artificial snow either, is not doing their job well. It will be up to the rep to give a sympathetic explanation of the reasons for the ban, how the local farming community can't survive without alpine pastures, which won't develop properly if buried under artificial snow, and so on. And then to get the group enthused about all the other sports and activities they can indulge in instead.

Winter tourism offers some variations on the usual theme of reps and tour guides, hotels and catering. Staff are needed to operate the ski tows and lifts, to be in charge of chalets, to patrol the slopes, to file, wax and mend hired skis, to groom and shovel snow, and of course to instruct would-be skiers. If you are lucky you might get a kitchen or dining room job in an establishment which does not serve lunch (since all the guests are out on the slopes). This means that you might have up to six hours free in the middle of the day for skiing, though three to four hours is more usual. However the hours in some large ski resort hotels are the same as in any hotel, i.e. eight to ten hours split up inconveniently throughout the day, and you should be prepared to have only one day off per week for skiing. Because jobs in ski resorts are so popular, wages can be low, though you should get the statutory minimum in

Switzerland (see chapter). Many employees are (or become) avid skiers and in their view it is recompense enough to have easy access to the slopes during their time off.

Snowboarding has become the fastest growing sport in the world, and anyone able to instruct this activity will find themselves in demand from the European Alps to New Zealand. Snowboard instructor courses are offered on dry ski slopes in the UK and on the Kaprun Glacier in Austria. Further details on all aspects of the sport can be obtained from the British Snowboarding Association, First Floor, 4 Trinity Square, Llandudno, North Wales LL30 2PY (01492 872540).

Either you can try to fix up a job with a British-based ski tour company before you leave (which has more security but lower wages and tends to isolate you in an English-speaking ghetto), or you can look for work on the spot.

Ski Tour Operators

In the spring preceding the winter season in which you want to work, ask all the ski tour companies whose addresses you can find for an application form. Their literature will describe the range of positions they wish to fill. These may vary slightly from company to company but will probably include resort representatives (who must be bilingual), chalet girls (described below), cleaners, qualified cooks, odd jobbers and ski guides/instructors. An increasing number of companies are offering nanny and creche facilities, so this is a further possibility for women with a childcare background. Most staff have been hired by mid-June, though there are always last minute cancellations.

The following ski tour operators are listed in the Directory of Travel Companies: Crystal Holidays, Ski Esprit, PGL Ski Europe, Simply Ski (see Simply Travel), Ski Olympic, Ski Scott Dunn, Ski Thomson (see Thomson), Ski Total and Ski World. There are dozens of others. Some have a limited number of vacancies which they can fill from a list of people who have worked for them during the summer season or have been personally recommended by former employees. So you should not be too disappointed if you are initially unsuccessful.

The book *Working in Ski Resorts* (Vacation Work, £10.99) contains many other addresses of ski companies and details of the job hunt in individual European and North American resorts. In response to the thousands of enquiries about alpine jobs which the Ski Club of Great Britain receives, it now distributes an information sheet; send £2 and a S.A.E. to the SCGB, The White House, 57-63 Church Road, Wimbledon, SW19 5SB. You can find other ski company addresses by consulting ski guide books, magazines and travel agents. Another good idea is to attend the *Daily Mail* Ski Show held each November at Earl's Court in London where some ski companies actually hand out job descriptions and applications. Call (0181 5152000) to find out more details.

Rhona Stannage, a Scottish solicitor, and her husband Stuart applied to all the companies they could find addresses for:

> *Only one company (Skibound) gave us an interview. No one else would touch us because we were too old (i.e. 28), married and had no experience in the catering trade. Skibound gave us both jobs as chalet girls (yes, Stuart signed a 'chalet girl' contract) working in a four-person chalet with a manageress and a qualified chef. The wages were as expected – dire (£48 a week) but we got free ski passes, accommodation in our own apartment and food. Stuart was a bit worried about the uniform but it was only a purple T-shirt.*

Another way of fixing up a job in advance is to go through the London-based agency *Jobs in the Alps* (see entry in the Directory). They recruit a variety of staff for Swiss ski resorts, for which good German or French is usually required. You must arrange to be interviewed by the end of September and be prepared to sign a contract for the whole season. They do not interview male school leavers unless they have had a full-time job for at least two months or are willing to do 'hard-slog backroom jobs' for up to six months. Wages are £550 a month net for a five-day week. Under the name Alpotels, the agency carries out aptitude tests on behalf of German and French hotels for the winter season. There is an agency fee of £30 plus £20 per month of the contract up to a maximum of £110.

Applying on the Spot

The best time to look is at the end of the preceding winter season though this has the disadvantage of committing you a long way in advance. The next best time is the first fortnight in September when the summer season is finishing and there are still plenty of foreign workers around who will have helpful advice. The final possibility is to turn up in the month before the season begins when you will be faced with many refusals. In November you will be told you're too early because everything's closed, in December you're too late because all the jobs are spoken for. Some disappointed job-seekers reckon there must be a 24-hour window between these two, and if you miss it, you're out of luck.

Assuming you can afford to finance yourself for several weeks, arrive as early as you can (say early November) so that you can get to know people and let them get to know your face. Weekends are better than weekdays since more shops and other tourist establishments will be open. Apply directly to hotels, equipment rental agencies, tourist offices, etc. It is also an idea to travel to the ski resorts out of season to look for work repairing or redecorating ski chalets, for instance, and then move on to a ski tow or bar job once the season begins. If you miss out on landing a job before the season, it could be worth trying again in early January, since workers tend to disappear after the holidays.

Mary Jelliffe gives an account of opportunities in the French resort of Méribel:

> *At the beginning of the season there were many 'ski bums' looking for work in Méribel. Many found something. People earned money by clearing snow, cleaning, babysitting, etc. for which they were paid about F30 an hour. You do need some money to support yourself while looking for work but if you are determined enough, I'm sure you'll get something eventually. One group of ski bums organised a weekly slalom race from which they were able to make a living. Another set up a video service; another made and sold boxer shorts for F100 a pair.*

Chalet Staff

Many of the ski tour operators active in France and Switzerland accommodate their clients in chalets which are looked after by a chalet girl or boy (but usually the former). The chalet maid does everything (sometimes with an assistant) from cooking first-class meals for the ten or so guests, to clearing the snow from the footpath (or delegating that job). She is responsible for keeping the chalet clean, preparing breakfast, packed lunches, tea and dinner, providing ice and advice, and generally keeping everybody happy.

Although this sounds an impossible regimen, many chalet girls manage to fit in several hours of skiing in the middle of each day. The standards of cookery skills required vary from company to company depending on the degree of luxury (i.e. the price) of the holidays. Whereas some advertise good homecooking, others offer cordon bleu cookery every night of the week (except the one night which the chalet girl has off). In most cases, you will have to cook a trial meal for the tour company before being accepted for the job.

Pandora Balchin, who got a job as a chalet maid on the strength of her catering degree, described her job this way:

It was a fantastic experience though it was very hard work. Although I had never skied before I went, I have to admit that I am now completely hooked, as are all the others who worked there. The spirit of comradeship in the resort was amazing, and also typical of other resorts I'm told.

"I don't eat meat and I'm allergic to vegetables"

Dietary restrictions must be given due consideration.

The pay will be £50-70 per week, with lots of perks. Your accommodation and food are free. Also you should get a season's ticket to the slopes and lifts (called an *abonnement* and worth several hundred pounds) and free ski hire. Recruitment of the 1,000+ chalet girls needed in Europe starts in May so early application is essential.

Ski Instructors

To become a fully-fledged ski instructor, qualified to work in foreign ski schools, takes time, commitment and a great deal of money (some estimate £2,000) and even then, competition is extremely stiff for jobs in recognised alpine ski schools. There are no short cuts to gaining qualifications for those who wish to make a career out of ski or snowboard teaching, however once fully qualified there are excellent opportunities to work in Europe and and America, with considerable demand for

English speaking instructors (though in France there is still a great deal of resistance to foreign instructors). Freelance or 'black' instructors – those who tout in bars offering a few hours of instruction in return for pocket money – are persecuted by the authorities in most alpine resorts.

As the head of one French ski school explained, avalanches are an ever present danger. One way to avoid these is to be able to read 'local' weather conditions. This forms part of the training his guides are given. British staff who have gained the coveted French qualifications say they received much help and encouragement when taking the course. The main legitimate opportunities for British skiers are as instructors for school parties or as ski guides/ski rangers.

The most practical way to gain a qualification is through the British Association of Ski Instructors or BASI (Glenmore, Aviemore, Inverness-shire PH22 1QU; 01479   861717/fax   01479861718/e-mail   basi@basi.org.uk/website www.basi.org.uk). BASI is the national body responsible for the training and grading of snow ski and snowboard instructors. It is a member of the International Ski Instructors Association and European Ski Instructors group. BASI currently has over 2,000 members but only 200 hold the highest qualification and international licence: National Ski Teacher. On average, this takes around 5 years to achieve. Qualified members work in 22 different countries and BASI qualifications are continuing to gain a worldwide reputation.

Courses tend to be either 5 or 10 days duration. Training fees for the longer courses are around £35 per day. This includes 5 hours training on the snow, followed by review groups, seminars, video analysis and lectures. Candidates receive course workbooks but are expected to purchase the regularly updated BASI manual (published 1996) price £25. A video called *The Central Theme* (£10) is also available or it is possible to access the two products on the new BASI CD rom which can be used with PC or Apple Mac computers (produced 1997, cost £30). The most junior instructor's qualification is a Grade III (Ski Instructor) which is awarded by BASI after a five-day assessment followed by a two-week training course in the Continent, America or in Aviemore. BASI also run Nordic ski instructor courses as well as the alpine ones. Most instructors teach from two to six hours a day depending on demand. Pay can vary from as little as £150 a week, but this often includes accommodation. Some participation in the evening entertainments is expected. It is of course much easier for Ski Teachers (Grade II) and National Ski Teachers (Grade I) to find lucrative work in Europe or beyond.

Prior to any training courses, candidates are required to be paid up members of the Association. All membership fees are annually renewable on the first of October. Full membership benefits include regular newsletters which are a valuable source of job advertisements for ski instructors. Other benefits include free contingent liability insurance when ski teaching and equipment discounts.

Obtaining work in the US and Canada is dependent on first obtaining a work permit. This is not normally a problem for National Ski Teachers in the US but lower grades may find it easier gaining work in the eastern states. Obtaining a work permit to teach as a ski instructor in Canada is difficult.

Ski Resorts Worldwide

In conclusion, there are plenty of jobs in ski resorts cooking, guiding, selling, cleaning and so on. If you do end up in a resort looking for a job, try the ski equipment hire shops which may offer you very short term work on change-over days when lots of skis need prompt attention, or the ski-lift offices preferably in the autumn. You might even find that the tourist office in the big resorts like Zermatt and Val d'Isère may be able to help. Outside the EU you will encounter work permit difficulties (details in individual country chapters), though when there is a labour shortage, there is usually a way round the difficulties. Unfortunately the drifting population looking for jobs in ski resorts can be much greater in one area than the number of jobs available. You should therefore try as hard as you can to sign a contract ahead of time.

For a thorough list of ski resorts in Europe, consult the *Good Skiing Guide* in a bookshop. Some major ski resorts are listed below:

France	*Switzerland*	*Austria*	*Italy*
Chamonix	Davos	Kitzbühel	Cortina d'Ampezzo
Les Contamines	St. Moritz	Söll	Courmayeur
Val d'Isère	Zermatt	Lech	Sestriere
Courchevel	Gstaad	Badgastein	Bormio
Méribel	Champery	St. Anton	Campitello
St. Christoph	Saas Grund	Mayrhofen	Canazei
Flaine	Wengen & Mürren	Lermoos	Livigno
Avoriaz	Crans-Montana	Alpbach	Abetone
Les Arcs	Kandersteg	Brand	Folgarida
La Plagne	Adelboden	Kirchberg	Forni di Sopra
Tignes	Verbier	St. Johann	Sauze d'Oulx
Montgenèvre	Grindelwald	Solden	Asiago
	Arosa	Obergurgl	S. Stefano di Cadore
	Saas Fee	Zell am See	Alleghi

Spain	*Germany*	*Norway*	*Scotland*
Sol y Nieve	Garmisch-	Voss	Aviemore
Formigal	Partenkirchen	Geilo	Glenshee (Glenisla)
Cerler	Telemark	Carrbridge	Glencoe
		Lillehammer	
Andorra		Gausdal	
Arinsal		Synnfjell	
Soldeu			

New Zealand	*Australia*	*Canada*	*USA*
Queenstown	Falls Creek (Vic)	Banff	Aspen, Colorado
Coronet Peak	Mount Hotham	Lake Louise	Copper Mountain
Mount Hutt	Mount Buffalo	Waterton	Steamboat Springs
Mount Ruapehu	Baw Baw	Ottawa	Vail
	Mount Buller	Huntsville	Winter Park
	Thredbo (NSW)	Collingwood	Alpine Meadows, Calif.
	Perisher	Barrie	Lake Tahoe
	Mount Field (Tas)		Mount Batchelor, Oregon
	Ben Lomond		Mount Hood
			Timberline
			Park City, Utah
			Sun Valley, Idaho
			Jackson Hole, Wyoming
			Sugar Mt. Resort, NC
			Waterville Valley, NH
			Stowe, Vermont
			Sugarbush Valley
			Dore Mountain, NY

OVERLAND EXPEDITION LEADERS

While the participants on long-haul overland trips are paying about £100 a week for the chance to visit safari parks, drive across sand dunes and shop for weird and wonderful vegetables in exotic markets, their leader/driver is being paid up to £150 for the same pleasures. The only difference is that he or she, along with one other crew member, will be responsible for keeping about 18 paying passengers as happy as possible.

Adventure travel companies which conduct small groups around the continents of Africa, Asia and the Americas require leader/drivers to escort these tours which last between three and 28 weeks. Most of the major overland companies are looking for experienced travellers with proven mechanical skills and of course good people skills. Other useful attributes include a knowledge of French (for Africa) or Spanish/Portuguese (for Latin America) and a first aid certificate. Most will consider only candidates who have a Passenger Carrying Vehicle (PCV) licence or a Heavy Goods Vehicle (HGV) licence. Most experienced drivers need five to seven days of tuition from a specialist driver training centre (at a cost of between £450 and £650) before trying the PCV test. People without a specialist licence or knowledge of mechanics may be able to find a support position such as cook or tour leader.

Most companies use Mercedes or Bedford trucks which have been stripped and rebuilt to their specifications to withstand rugged transcontinental trips. The cooking is usually done communally and nights are spent in campsites or in modest rest houses, normally along a well worn overlanders' trail. Many of these trips are not as off the beaten track as the clients fondly imagine. If a vehicle breaks down in the Sahara, the head of an urchin usually pops up over a sand dune within 30 seconds.

There will be one or two crew members (often the second is a trainee) who have to contend with vehicle breakdowns, border crossings, black market money exchanges and awkward social dynamics. One old hand, writing in the *Traveller* magazine published by WEXAS, claims that to be a good tour leader you have to be 'a cross between a Butlins redcoat and Scott of the Antarctic'. According to Brett Archer, who spent eight months in Africa as an expedition leader, one of the worst trials is coping with the chronic whinger (who in his experience, is usually a calculator-wielding female from New Zealand). Like all tour work, the job is unremitting but with the added challenges of dealing with sometimes frustrating bureaucracy in emergent Africa and difficult terrain over a much longer period of time. Most aspiring expedition leaders feel daunted to say the least at the prospect of being in charge of 20 adventure-seekers in the middle of the African bush or the Amazon rainforest. Full expedition leaders are paid at least £60 per week in addition to expenses and up to £150 including the inevitable commissions which leaders earn.

Procedures vary for choosing and training leaders. Requirements vary but normally expedition leaders must be at least 23. After getting past the interview stage, the tour leader without extensive first-hand knowledge of the continent to be toured is usually invited to join a training trip of six to twelve weeks at their expense (at least several hundred pounds) with no guarantee of work at the end. If successful, however, this money is generally returned after completion of an agreed term of work.

Training for driver/mechanics usually includes time in the company's vehicle workshop. Trainee leaders with some companies are paid a small weekly allowance in sterling, as Guerba explains in its standard reply to applicants:

The pay for this arduous job is a miserable £35 per week. However, being accepted for this position does give you the opportunity to see Africa. All incidental expenses such as visas, passports, air tickets, etc. are paid for. Guerba will also pay your kitty contributions and will cover any compulsory money changes that may exist en route. Although it is hard work being a trainee tour leader on one of our trips, I can only say that it is hard to imagine a more interesting or exciting job.

There's always a whinger, usually a middle-aged woman with a calculator

Applying

Competent expedition staff are greatly in demand by the many overland companies and youth travel specialists based in London and the southeast which advertise regularly in the London magazine for the Australasian community *TNT* published every Monday. (Distribution boxes can be found in selected locations throughout London, e.g. outside travel agencies, tube stations, certain pubs around Earls Court, etc.). Specialist travel agencies such as Trailfinders (42-50 Earls Court Road, London W8 6EJ) act as agents for the major operators. Study the brochures carefully and attend the informal video evenings which many of them hold to get a feel for the company and the kind of back-up they are likely to offer to their staff (which varies significantly between companies).

Readers in Europe and the US who wish to contact adventure tour operators based in their countries can find other addresses from the following specialist agencies:

Peregrine Adventures, 258 Lonsdale St., Melbourne 3000, Australia.
Divantoura, 176 Bagattenstraat, B-9000 Ghent, Belgium.

Trek Holidays, 8412-109 St, Edmonton, Alta.T6G 1E2, Canada.
Albatross Travel & Safaris, Kultorvet 11, 1175 Kobenhavn K, Denmark.
Council Travel, Graf-Adolf Str. 64, 50210 Dusseldorf 1, Germany (211 36 30 30).
Suntrek Tours, Bellerivestrasse, CH-8084, Zurich, Switzerland.
Adventure Center, 1311 63rd St, Suite 200, Emeryville, CA 94608, USA.

In addition to the companies with entries in the Directory of Tour Operators listed below, other smaller operators which may have occasional openings include:

Absolute Africa, 41 Swanscombe Road, Chiswick, London W4 2HR – (0181-742 0226).
Acacia Expeditions, Lower Ground Floor, 23a Craven Terrace, London W2 3QH (0171-706 4700/ http://www.acacia-africa.com).
Adventure Overland 3 Arcade Road, Littlehampton, West Sussex BN17 5AP (01903 884112).
African Trails 3 Flanders Road, Chiswick W4 1NQ (0181-742 7724).
AmeriCAN Adventures Inc., 64 Mount Pleasant Avenue, Tunbridge Wells, Kent TN1 1QY.
Australian Pacific Tours, 2nd Floor, William House, 14 Worple Road, Wimbledon, London SW19 4DD.
Bukima Africa, 55 Huddlestone Road, Willesden Green, London NW2 5DL.
Economic Expeditions 29 Cummington Street, Chiswick W4 5ER (0181-995 7707).
Hinterland Travel, 2 Ivy Mill Lane, Godstone, Surrey RH9 8NH.
The Imaginative Traveller, 14 Barley Mow Passage, Chiswick, London W4 4PH.
Trek America, 4 Water Perry, Middleton Rd, Banbury, Oxon. OX16 8QG.

Note also that if you have the required skills, it is possible to fill a vacancy on-the-spot. While travelling the length of Africa, J. M. Rapp noticed that all the overland companies in East Africa were looking for mechanics to be drivers.

Directory References

For overland adventure operators see the entries for: Africa Explored, Dragoman Overland Expeditions, Encounter Overland, Explore Worldwide Ltd, Guerba Expeditions, Journey Latin America, Kumuka, Top Deck, Tracks and Truck Africa.

CRUISE SHIPS

Not only was the luxury cruise liner business not affected by the recession but it is booming. Over one thousand liners sail the world's oceans at present, with more new ships on order each year, including the two recent additions from the Disney Corporation. Each ship requires a full range of staff, just as a fancy resort does. The largest ships sail with a crew of more than 1,000. With a very high turnover of staff, hiring takes place year round. Most recruitment takes place through specialist agencies or 'concessionaires', all of whom say that they are looking only for qualified and experienced staff. But in many cases it is sufficient to be over 21 and have an extrovert personality and plenty of stamina for the very long hours of work on board. Wages tend to be low but can be supplemented with tips and by the tax-free status that working at sea enjoys. A further advantage is the absence of red tape. People working at sea do not require a work permit so even if your employer is American, no US visa is required. However, workers aboard most passenger ships require a C/D-1 seaman's visa issued by the United States Embassy which is given only through an employer or agency presenting a confirmed letter of appointment.

Range of Jobs

Musicians, medics and masseurs are all employed by cruise lines. However the largest number of personnel work in catering, dining room and bar services, as cabin stewards, assistant pursers and shop personnel. Croupiers and beauticians, nannies and entertainers are all in demand. In many cases it does not take long to acquire enough land-based experience in a casino, restaurant, hotel or shop to make your CV more attractive to hiring agents, particularly if you are free to travel at very short notice. It is not unusual for a long silence after an interview to be broken by a phone call asking whether you can meet a ship in the Caribbean in less than a week.

On the majority of ships there are three categories of employee and this hierarchy creates a marked class system: officer, staff and crew. Officers (from fourth pursers up) are free to make use of all ship facilities and enjoy superior living quarters. 'Staff' consist of shop staff, hairdressers, beauticians and casino staff. The lowest rung is 'crew' whose leisure activities are severely circumscribed and whose living quarters are often little better than grim, four sharing a small cabin in the noisiest dirtiest part of the ship. Often the only recourse is to the crew bar where the (duty-free) drink is very cheap and employees are tempted to overindulge, especially unwise when the seas are choppy.

According to Jane Roberts, who crossed the Atlantic from Venezuela to Estonia as a cruising croupier, not all employees are experienced professionals:

I worked in the casino department of four different cruise ships and met many people doing jobs as waiters, bar tenders, stewards and stewardesses. These jobs are very easy to come by. In fact 80% of all crew members are people who have never done that particular job in their lives. The turn-over of staff is high, even when people sign year-long contracts, since few people complete them. It is difficult to live and work with the same people 24 hours a day. Crew don't get days off, perhaps just the odd breakfast or lunch off once a month. Patience levels have to be extremely high, since people who take holidays on cruise ships seem to think that they own the damn ship. Having to be sickeningly nice can take its toll very quickly.

Cruise companies and by extension their employees are expected to treat the clients as gods (no mere mortal could afford up to £10,000 for a holiday).

Anyone who wants to become a croupier needs to be at least 18 years of age with no criminal record. It takes one or two months to train with a casino and obtain a licence from the Gaming Board of Britain, preferably for both blackjack and roulette. Casino companies normally offer in-house training; try London Clubs Ltd, Golden Nugget, 22-32 Shaftesbury Avenue, London W1.

Those who are interested in work as a deck engineer might make enquiries about the training available from Clyde Marine Training Ltd (209 Govan Road, Glasgow G51 1HJ; 0141 4276886).

Finding a Job

Most libraries subscribe to the quarterly *ABC Cruise & Ferry Guide* which provides useful background information on the world's cruise lines, with specifications of their vessels and routes. Their head offices should be willing to tell enquirers who is responsible for hiring various categories of staff.

The hiring channels can be confusing. In some cases all recruitment is centralised in the head office which may be in Florida, Southampton, Helsinki, etc. In other cases, agents in various countries recruit their nationals for the international crew. For example Epirotiki Lines based in Piraeus, Greece have offices in New York, London, Hamburg, Paris and Rome which can handle job applications. The world's largest cruise company, Royal Caribbean Cruise Line, carries out its North American hiring through its headquarters in Miami (1050 Caribbean Way, Miami, FL 33132) where it operates a Job Hot Line with recorded messages about current opportunities (305-530-0471). In Europe, it makes use of agencies such as *Crewsline UK* (14 Cardiff Close, Great Sutton, South Wirral L66 2GR; 0151 3392278) and *International Services* in Paris.

But the majority of the major international cruise lines farm out their recruitment requirements to specialist agencies. Note that in most of Europe, agencies are not permitted to charge the candidate a fee for securing employment; however US agencies may charge a consultation fee and you wil be expected to provide proof of purchase of your own open return air ticket if working out of Miami, the world's cruise ship capital. You cannot use cheap charter flight tickets and currently, British Airways quote £1,036 (inc. tax) for this type of ticket. Some UK agencies which recruit for the most prestigious liners (like Logbridge in Southampton which has the concession for Cunard Lines, including the QE2) do recruit only professional hotel and catering staff through advertisements in the specialist press like *The Caterer and Hotel Keeper*.

The following companies recruit cruise ship personnel:

Berkeley Bureau, (0181 6533665/e-mail BerkBur/nt@aol.com). Casino staff with at least one year's experience on land.

Fred Olsen Cruise Lines, Fred Olsen House, White House Road, Ipswich, IP1 5LL.

Lawson Marine Services Ltd, Royale House, 2 Palmyra Place, Newport, Gwent NP9 4EJ (01633 254515). Experienced management personnel for the hotel and purser departments on worldwide cruises. College graduates with no practical work experience cannot be considered.

Logbridge Ltd (see entry).

Norwegian Cruise Line/Royal Cruise line/Royal Viking Line, 1 Derry Street, Kensington, London W8 5NN.

Nuance Global Ships Ltd., 84-98 Southampton Road, Eastleigh, Hants., SO5 5ZF (01703 673299). Preferably perfume, jewellry, fashion or photo electric sales experience.

P&O Cruises (Fleet Personnel Department), Richmond House, Terminus Terrace, Southampton SO14 3PN; 01703 534200. For information on working on P&O ferries, see next section of Introduction.

Quest Resort Recruitment, Binning House, 4-6 High St, Eastleigh, Hants. SO50 5LA (01703 644933). Member of FRES. Hotel Management and Supervisory Personnel, Chefs, Chefs De Rang, Sommeliers, Guest Services and Reservation Staff in South Africa, Carribean, Middle East, USA. Opportunities only available for personnel who can demonstrate relevant experience within hotels of 4/5 star quality.

Steiner Group Ltd, 57-65 The Broadway, Stanmore, Middlesex HA7 4DU. Beauty therapists, hairdressers, massage therapists, etc. for over 50 ships.

Supersearch International Ltd, (see entry).

VIP International (see entry).

Among major cruise line offices and concessionaires in America, try:

Apollo Ship Chandlers, 1775 NW 70 Ave., Miami, FL 33126, USA.

Norwegian Cruise Lines, 95 Merrick Way, Coral Gables, FL 33134, USA.

Odessamerica Cruise Lines, 170 Old Country Road, Minncola, NY 11501, USA.
Renaissance Cruises Inc (see entry).
Sea Chest Association, 3655 NW 87th Avenue, Miami, FL 33178, USA.
Windjammer Barefoot Cruises Ltd., 1759 Bay Road, Miami Beach, FL 33139, USA (305-672 6453).
In Europe try the following:
Maritime Management Services Ltd, Kristen 20, A-6094 Axams, Austria. Shop staff.
Silja Line, Mannerheimintie 2, 00101 Helsinki, Finland.(358-9-18041; web site www.silja.com.).
Paquet Cruise Line, 5 Malesherbes, 75008 Paris, France.
Hapag-Lloyd Cruises, Ballindamn 25, 20095 Hamburg, Germany.
Dolphin Hellas Shipping (see entry).
Büro Metro, (see entry).
In some cases cruise ships do fill urgent vacancies on-the-spot. When Stephen Psallidas was working on the Greek island of Mykonos, he noticed that several Aegean cruise ships were looking for staff. Many shipping offices are congregated in one street in Piraeus, Akti Miaouli (see *Greece* chapter).

Do not be misled by advertisements which read 'Cruise Ships are Hiring Now.' These are almost always placed by someone trying to sell a book about employment on cruise ships, and these are of varying quality. If you have £22.50 to spend on a specialist book, then the book from Innovative Cruise Services (36 Midlothian Drive, Waverley Park, Glasgow G41 3QU; 0141-649 8644) is worth considering because they receive monthly updates from an agent in Florida and will send these to purchasers of their book free of charge on request. Alternatively ask Vacation Work Publications (9 Park End St, Oxford OX1 1HJ) about their title *Working on Cruise Ships* which costs £9.99. Available in the USA at $15.95 from Seven Hills, 1531 Tremont Street, Cincinnati OH 45214.

Conditions of Work

The hours worked by crew members are staggeringly long in almost all cases. It is normal practice to have no days off for the three-month duration of a contract, only a few snatched hours after everything is cleaned up.. On ships with two meal sittings, dining room staff would standardly work from 6.30-9.30am, 11.30am-2.30pm, 5.30-8.30pm and again on the midnight buffet 11pm-1am. More luxurious ships have only one sitting and commensurately shorter working hours. Staff who work under customs regulations, for example in the on-board duty-free shop, boutiques and casino, do not work while the ship is in port and are free to disembark. Then it is possible to see, albeit briefly, some of the great cities of the world from Havana to Hong Kong.

Contract lengths, wages and conditions vary from ship to ship, and it is worth finding out as much as possible beforehand, preferably from a former employee. Contracts can be as short as four months but are normally six, nine or twelve months. Some ships pay straight wages and ban tipping, others operate a wages/tips system and other jobs are paid on commission. Wages for the most junior cabin crew can start as low as $50 a week, though junior officers would make eight times as much and the average crew wage would be about $100. Everyone gets free meals and accommodation. Expenses on-board are minimal, causing many crew employees to deposit their wages directly into a bank account at home.

To escape their minute cabins, cruise ship crew repair to the bar, where they unwisely overindulge even in choppy seas

Competition is so keen among cruise lines for good staff that many are now offering free travel from the point of origin including taxi transfers and hotel accommodation. If you complete the contract, they will pay for your return as well. On other lines, it may be the case that crew are expected to pay for their own travel expenses to the point of embarkation, though officers are not. Some companies have an arrangement by which air fares are deducted in instalments from employees' wages, which also encourages people to complete their contracts.

Because of the claustrophobic nature of the job, the crew's social life is of critical importance, and most people (at least the type who gets hired for the job) relish the party atmosphere. Kathleen Ager sums up the experience of working in the catering department of a clipper operated by Windjammer Barefoot Cruises in the Caribbean:

The ship, not being as stable as larger ones, was thrown about on long passages and on the first day nine-tenths of the passengers were extremely sick and it was impossible to set tables without things being thrown off again. I sometimes found I'd been working 16 hours non-stop. Our cruises were interrupted by strikes and riots on one island which had just become independent. But we had to keep the customers relaxed and happy despite the trouble. Altogether the work was very hard and poorly paid but I stuck it out for four months and have never been so miserable as I was when I left that ship. It really was a great experience and the mainly West Indian crew were all like my brothers.

TRANSPORT PERSONNEL

Airlines

Scheduled airlines are constantly recruiting new staff from the thousands of unsolicited applications for the position of cabin crew which they receive. Every airport has a list of the airlines operating out of that airport, so contact the one to which you have easiest access. At one time, airlines hired only young people as cabin crew and compelled them to retire at an early age. That is no longer permitted, though older candidates will have more difficulty being hired in the first place. Most airlines have a career structure and it is possible to progress through the ranks to purser and flight supervisor, or join the ground administrative team that organises each flight. Passenger service agents to work at the airports and of course telephone sales agents are needed for the reservation office (see entry for *Air France* for instance).

All airlines undertake their own intensive cabin crew training programme which concentrates on onboard safety and covers first aid, health and hygiene as well as cabin service (see *Training: Airlines* section).

Charter airlines often need cabin crew on a seasonal basis, for example not long ago Caledonian Airways were looking for candidates of either sex aged 21 to 33, who had to be at least 5ft 2in tall and not overweight, and also live within reach of Gatwick Airport. Similarly *Air 2000*, one of the top three charter airlines, encourages applications for cabin crew positions from suitable people.

Competition for jobs as flight crew (pilots) is intense. Some airlines will train you, but most entrants come already trained by the military or privately (flying courses are cheaper in the US than in Europe). See the directory for *Air 2000* and *Air France*, as well as the job centres at Heathrow and Gatwick. Also try the following;

Airtours International, Cabin Service, Parkway 3, 300 Princess Road, Manchester, N14 7QU (0161 2326600).

Britannia Airways, London Luton Airport, Luton, Beds LU2 9ND (01332 680146). World's largest charter airline.

British Airways, BA Resourcing, Meadowbank, PO Box 59, Hounslow TW5 9QX (0181 5641450).

British Midlands, Unit 3, Bulcan, Argosy, East Midlands Airport, Castle Donington, Derby DE7 2SA (01332 853000).

Caledonian Airways, Caledonian House, Gatwick Airport, West Sussex, RH6 OLF.

Debonair Airways, 146 Prospect Way, London Luton Airport, Luton, Beds., LU2 9BA (0541 500146).

KLM UK, Stanstead House, Stanstead Airport, CM24 1AE (01279 660400).

Ryanair Personnel Office, Corporate Head Office, Dublin Airport, Co. Dublin (353 1844 4400).

United Airlines, People Services, United Airlines, United House, Southern Perimeter Road, Heathrow Airport, Middlesex TW6 3LP (0181 7509403).

Virgin Airways, 01293 562345.

Coaches

There are more than 3,000 touring coach companies in the UK, over 6,000 in Germany and thousands more in France, Italy, the Netherlands, etc. To contact coach companies look in Yellow Pages or the weekly *Coach and Bus Magazine* (01733 467000) which also publishes *The Coach and Bus Guide* for £25 which lists all major UK companies. (Similar publications are available for other countries.)

A handful of coach companies train drivers but most accept only drivers who have had at least a year's bus or coach experience. EU qualifications are recognised in all countries, but there may be extra requirements, for example coach drivers working for German companies must have a first aid certificate. Some coach companies try to ask their drivers to work as driver/couriers, i.e. giving commentaries as they drive. As noted elsewhere this is illegal under the Conduct of Drivers Regulations which say 'a driver shall not, when a vehicle is in motion, speak to any person either directly or by means of a microphone'.

Since the tachograph was introduced (a clock which records how many hours a driver works) conditions have improved for drivers. There are still some cowboy companies around, but the better ones (particularly on the Continent) insist in their contracts with operators that the driver be given a single room with bath and, in the longer term, pension and other rights.

Part of the driver's job is to keep the coach clean, to wash down the outside and tidy the inside. If the coach has a loo, it is the driver's responsibility to clean and empty it, and therefore it is not unknown for drivers to hang up a sign 'Toilet out of use' to avoid this chore.

The Channel Tunnel

The most glamorous jobs on European railways are with Eurostar which operates a rail service London (Waterloo) to Paris (Gare du Nord) in three hours and London to Brussels in a quarter of an hour longer. Eventually there are plans to run eight trains an hour (four in each direction) which will obviously generate many new jobs both on the trains and at the stations. Each train carries approximately 30 staff to look after up to 800 passengers. Train managers, catering staff and receptionists are needed at the arrival stations. The primary requirement is a good knowledge of a second language. Each train needs bilingual staff: a driver plus train managers and on-board service staff. They join a crew operating out of one of the three stations but can transfer to one of the others if they wish to change their base. From 1996, direct services should be running to the Continent from Edinburgh, Manchester and Birmingham where teams of staff will also be based.

Train managers are on board to look after the 800 passengers, especially disabled passengers, to help with connections and answer queries about onward travel. They must also be able to take over from the driver in an emergency. Their station-based counterparts in customer services work at Waterloo, the Gare du Nord and Brussels Midi marshalling and assisting passengers. *Eurostar* welcomes applications from anyone who can speak French, Japanese or another European language as well as English and who has experience of working with the public. Eurostar has its own language laboratory, but new recruits must be linguists. Eurostar's training programme includes courses on group travel psychology, emergency and first aid and cultural awareness.

The franchise for serving food and drink on Eurostar belongs to the *Cross Channel Catering Company* made up of British, French and Belgian partners. Again, all trainees must be bilingual and most already have extensive experience in the industry, since this is one of the most sought-after glamorous jobs in catering today. All EU nationalities are eligible; of a recent intake, six were French, one was Irish, one was Portuguese and one was British. New recruits start with a four-week training course at CCCC's headquarters in Wimbledon which concentrates on delivering a better quality of service than can be found on airlines. A recent newspaper article called Eurostar rail stewardesses the 'crack troops of charm' who are rigorously trained in every detail. This month-long training is followed by a five-day course on tunnel safety and evacuation procedures.

CVs should be sent to the Personnel Department (EPS House, Waterloo Station, London SE1 8SE) or for on-board catering work to the Cross Channel Catering Company (Waterloo International Terminal, London SE1 7LT).

Ferries

The opening of the Channel Tunnel has decidedly not spelled the doom of the ferry companies which operate between England and France, and there are employment possibilities on all three. There are also job opportunities on routes in the Irish Sea, the North Sea and around the Scottish islands. The expected range of service staff and, increasingly, child carers is needed by the ferry companies on a seasonal basis between April and September with a very much reduced staff over the winter. According to Rhiannon Bryant, who spent a year working as a stewardess for P&O European Ferries, the essential quality being sought at interview was a smile:

Applying for a stewardess post on the ferries proved relatively easy. I sent my CV in January to Quest Resort Recruitment (4-6 High St, Eastleigh, Southampton SO50 5LA) and was invited to a group interview at Southampton. I was offered a place within a week, and was requested to attend various training sessions at my own expense, including basic sea survival in Poole and fire fighting in Portsmouth. This was followed by a day's on-board induction where behaviour is monitored. A couple of 'lads' who were confident that their jobs were secure were never seen again after larking around (possibly thrown over-board!)

Rhiannon began her job on the last day of March and after a week of moving between jobs (main lounge, cafeteria, restaurant and cabins) was assigned her summer location, the duty-free shops where the hourly wage was then £3.60, 30 pence more than non-cashier stewards. A further advantage was that few shoppers ventured to the shops when feeling seasick so (unlike the children's play areas) there was less cleaning to do. Note that duty-free shopping within Europe is to be phased out over the next few years and abolished completely by mid-1999. This may seriously damage the ferry business.

Depending on what company you work for, you may be working seven days or 14 days on, followed by seven days off. It is not unusual to work over 100 hours in those seven days on duty. The work is exhausting but it is reassuring to know that a full week's rest and relaxation is in the offing, which makes the experience completely different from working on a cruise ship. And the work is much more seasonal than cruise ship work. Even if you are kept on into October, your job may disappear at any time. Of the hundreds of temporary employees placed that year by the ferry recruitment specialist, Quest Marine Services, Rhiannon was only one of five who stayed on for the winter. Another difference which Rhiannon mentioned was that alcohol was forbidden by P&O.

As with all offshore work it is possible, though difficult, to reclaim tax. Permanent ferry staff can be given an official printout of sailing times by the purser's office, though it is wise to keep your own records for the purser to authorise. It is sensible to ask your local tax office what information and documents they will need.

When looking for a job, do not ignore the obvious of asking in Jobcentres in port towns. For the names and addresses of other ferry operators across the Channel and beyond to which you can send a speculative application, consult the quarterly *ABC Cruise & Ferry Guide* in public libraries. Here are the main operators between Britain and the Continent:

Eurotunnel, PO Box 2000, Folkestone, Kent CT18 8XY
Brittany Ferries UK Ltd, Brittany Centre, Wharf Road, Portsmouth PO2 8RU.
Caledonian MacBrayne Ltd, The Ferry terminal, Gourock, Renfrewshire PA19
1QP.
Color Line, Tyne Commission Quay, North Sheilds, Tyne & Wear NE29 6EA.
North Sea Ferries, King George Dock, Hedon Road, Hull HU9 5QA.
P&O European Ferries, Richmond House, Terminus Terrace, Southampton, Hants.
SO14 3PN. Also Peninsula House, Wharf Road, Portsmouth PO2 8TA (01705
827 7677) for Portsmouth-based vacancies.
Sally Line, Argyle Centre, York St, Ramsgate, Kent CT11 9DS.
Stena Sealink, Charter House, Park St (PO Box 121), Ashford, Kent TN24 8EX.

Hovercraft

Hoverspeed Ltd. run services between Dover and the continent. Each summer they
employ between 150 and 200 reservation clerks, cabin crew and staff for the duty-
free outlets (see Directory entry). Recruitment requirements and training are similar
to that described above.

HOTELS & CATERING

The hotel and catering industry is often treated separately from the tourist industry,
and certainly the training for both is very distinct. Yet its primary function is to
provide tourists with accommodation and (to a lesser degree) food, and so it is
worth considering the range of employment available in what is often referred to
(especially in North America) as the hospitality industry.

The marked hierarchy among hotel staff is most noticeable in large hotel
complexes or resorts:

Proprietor/Manager

Administration	Chef	Maitre d'hotel	Housekeeper
Secretary/	Sous-chef(s)	Bar Staff	Room Staff/
Receptionist	Kitchen Assistants	Waiting Staff	Chambermaids
Desk Porter	Kitchen Porter	Commis Waiters/	Laundry
Night Porter	Dishwasher	Busboys	
Doorman/Bell-hop			

Of course the majority of hotels are too small to support such a staff and you may
find yourself hired as a 'general assistant' in a small family-run hotel which means
doing everything from washing dishes to checking in guests.

Opportunities for People with Qualifications

Qualified people in the field of hotels and catering have a great deal of mobility since
good cooks and managers are needed throughout the world. Making contact with a
range of hotels or restaurants from any appropriate directory or guide book may well
produce results, especially if the applicant can write in (and speak) the appropriate
language. General guidance my be available from the Hotel, Catering & International
Management Association (HCIMA, 191 Trinity Road, London SW17 7HN;
Hospitality Hotline 0891-443322; website http://hcima.org.uk). For some specialist
recruitment agencies, see the chapter *Finding a Job: Recruitment Agencies*).

Although many luxury hotels belong to worldwide chains (Best Western, Hilton, Holiday Inn, Hyatt, Sheraton, etc.), most hiring is done independently by each hotel. The number of employees is staggering, for example the Hyatt Corporation (200 W Madison, Chicago, IL 60606) alone employs nearly 100,000 people worldwide. Some hotel groups operate management training programmes, especially in the US where trainees are recruited from universities.

Hotel and catering students may be able to take advantage of various exchanges which are run to provide training in other countries whether through EU-funded bodies or otherwise. For example, see the chapter on the US for details of the Hospitality Tourism Exchange Programme administered by the Council for International Educational Exchange (0171-478 2000). The Association for International Practical Training (10400 Little Patuxent Parkway, Suite 250, Columbia, Maryland 21044-3510, USA) runs a Hotel/Culinary Exchange programme with Australia, Austria, Germany, Finland, France, Ireland, Japan, Malaysia, Netherlands, Switzerland and the UK.

The American Hotel & Motel Association's Educational Institute (1201 New York Ave NW, Washington, DC 20005-3931) can send professional job-seekers a short list called 'Employment, Placement, Recruitment & Search Firms' which are primarily executive search firms operating at a very high level. For example Hospitality Associates (12 West 37th St, New York, NY 10018, with offices in other US cities/website http://www.yoursintravel.com) is one of the largest travel and hospitality industry recruitment agencies for the US, placing directors and managers in all hotel departments across 50 states as well as 4 continents.

OTHER TYPES OF EMPLOYMENT

Conferences and Events

Full-time organisers known as PCOs (Professional Conference Organisers) are employed as well as freelance staff to manage congresses, seminars, exhibitions, outdoor events, etc. The PCO will promote the conference, take bookings from delegates, liaise with the venue, possibly organise accommodation and menus, book speakers, arrange a spouse programme, and look after many other aspects of the meeting. Information technology skills and a highly professional demeanour are essential. The Association for Conferences and Events (ACE, Riverside House, High St, Huntingdon PE18 6SG) offers students a reduced membership fee of £41 which gives access to useful job contacts.

An important issue for conference work is access for disabled participants. Information for and about working with disabled people is available from RADAR (12 City Forum, 250 City Road, London EC1V 8AF). It produces a range of publications and operates in conjunction with an affiliated network of around 500 local and national organizations.

Tourist Offices

Tourist Information Centres normally employ local people who have a proven ability to communicate, preferably in more than one language. Experience in marketing, PR, administration, media work or advertising is useful. More than 800 TICs are scattered throughout the UK in places of visitor importance. Some are seasonal, some operate year round, and range in size from a small kiosk to high street shop frontage. Fired with enthusiasm, Mark waited for his first customer, only to be asked where the toilets were (apparently the most popular question). The other standard questions are where is the best place to eat or the best hotel, questions TIC staff are not permitted to answer, since they must not show favouritism. However there are lots of other problems that need solving, some of the most interesting of which come from locals. Otherwise the job consists primarily of replenishing the racks of literature (free leaflets always seem to walk out the door), selling books, booking beds and so on. Applications should be made to your local Regional Tourist Board's Personnel Department.

National Parks

With a growing awareness that the world's natural resources need better management, more people are being employed all the time to manage them and their visitors. Within this sector there are full-time jobs in management, plus the legal, planning, press and promotional departments, as well as jobs for wardens, trail guides, stewards, park attendants and shop stff. The basic requirement is a love of the outdoor life and a willingness to be outside in all weathers (more a consideration in the Peak District than Western Australia).

Leisure Centres and Theme Parks

Theme parks, visitor attractions, museums and sports centres are normally considered part of the leisure business, though again distinctions are hard to draw. A day trip to a theme park is a leisure visit, whereas a visit by people who have rented accommodation on-site or in the neighbourhood is considered tourism. The great theme parks of the United States and Europe create a huge demand for labour which cannot be filled by local people. Some American amusement parks employ up to 3,000 staff, and *Disneyland Paris* employs 12,000 in total. For information on specific theme parks, see the country chapters.

Leisure centres are an expanding market, both individual sites and those developed in conjunction with a hotel. Sports qualifications are often necessary for advancement up the career path. The magazine *Leisure Management* (Portmill House, Portmill Lane, Hitchin, Herts. SG5 1DJ) contains a good selection of job ads; a student subscription costs £20 per year.

Travel Agencies

Many people are attracted to the idea of working in a travel agency to 'meet people' when what they really mean is that they would like to look after people on holiday, i.e. a rep's work. Most job openings in agencies are geared to the 16+ age group who work on an apprenticeship scheme combining college and on-the-spot training (see *Training* chapter).

Apprentice pay scales are very low. Trawling through a sample of adverts, salaries start at around £6,000 for a junior travel clerk. However this can rise to £22,900 plus bonus and commission for a branch manager with five years' experience. If the low starting rates do not deter you, check job adverts in *Travel Weekly* and *Travel Trade Gazette*.

Business travel houses offer better pay, but of course competition for jobs is fiercer. Some business travel agents work in-house in big companies. A good knowledge of geography is essential.

CASUAL WORK

Tourism creates a wealth of opportunities for casual work, both directly and indirectly. Your average tourist wants someone to sell him ice cream on the beach or croissants in his ski chalet, someone to mend the roof of his holiday villa before the season begins, someone to look after his children on a campsite, to sell him a souvenir sachet of Ardeche lavender or a Texan 10-gallon hat, to entertain him at the local disco or teach him to windsurf. His wife wants to keep up appearances so a freelance hairdresser's services are very welcome. And so it could continue. The point is that casual jobs usually proliferate in tourist centres.

The seasonal nature of tourism often discourages a stable working population, and so hotel and campsite proprietors, resort and hostel managers, etc. are often forced to employ people from outside the vicinity during the busy season. Also, many tourist destinations are in remote places where there is no local pool of labour. Travellers have ended up working in some of the most beautiful corners of the world from the South Island of New Zealand to Lapland.

Of course there are also many opportunities at the budget end of tourism, in travellers' hostels and so on. Dustie Hickey describes the way she went about getting a job in the Avignon Youth Hostel:

> *I checked out all the hostels in Avignon and found someone to help me write a letter in French. Then I telephoned because I did not get a reply. The hostel could not promise me any work till they met me. Before I left the farm in Brittany where I was working, I telephoned again to remind them I was on my way. When I arrived, the hostel was very busy. For free B & B, I just had to keep the dormitory clean, but I pitched in and helped with cleaning, laundry, breakfast, etc. The manager was pleased and gave me a little money. At the end of July the paid assistant left so I was given her job, and eventually I had a room to myself.*

Many private travellers' hostels worldwide from the Greek islands to the Mexican mountains employ long-stay residents to act as PR reps at railway and bus stations, trying to persuade new arrivals to patronise their hostel. A free bed is always given and usually a small fee per successful 'convert'.

Even with the increasing value of a training qualification, the industry still respects somebody who has actually gone out into the world of work and experienced the trials and tribulations of tourism for themselves. Dealing with holiday-makers, solving unforseen problems, and working busy, unsociable hours, are all vital aspects of training in themselves. A summer doing a casual job can often benefit the CV of someone trying to break into a career in tourism.

Pubs and Clubs

Bars and night clubs should be included in any list of likely employers. Some globetrotters even carry a set of 'black and whites' (black trousers/skirt and white shirt) in case they pick up a job as a bartender or waiter. If you have no experience, it can be worthwhile volunteering to work at your local pub before you leave home for a week and then ask for a reference. Once you are abroad, ask at English style pubs which are found from the Costa del Sol to the Zamalek district of Cairo, from Santa Monica California to Austrian ski resorts and try to exploit the British connection. Irish people are at an even greater advantage since there is a Guinness pub around most corners of the world. In ordinary bars on the Continent you may be expected to be proficient in the prevailing language, although exceptions are made, particularly in the case of glamorous-looking applicants. Girls can find jobs from Amsterdam to Hong Kong, but should be sure that they can distinguish between bars and brothels.

Places like the Canaries, Ibiza, Corfu and the Caribbean islands are bursting at the seams with 'nite spots' of one kind or another. Not only is there a high turn-over of staff but there is a rapid turn-over of clubs too, and you may not have much job security. As long as you investigate the establishments in the place you want to work before accepting a job, you should not encounter too many unpleasant surprises. Handing out promotional leaflets for bars and discos is a job which travellers frequently do, especially in Spain.

Special Events

Great bursts of tourist activity take place around annual festivals, major sporting events like the Adelaide Grand Prix, trade fairs and World Fairs. For example, the Oktoberfest in Munich takes place each year during the last two weeks of September and you should be able to get a few days or weeks of work either helping to set up the facilities or to dismantle them. It is not possible for an event to host over 6 million visitors without a great deal of extra labour being enlisted to prepare the 560,000 barbecued chickens, 346,000 pairs of sausages and to dispense the 1,000,000 gallons of beer consumed. Or you may be able to offer a peripheral service. At least one enterprising mechanic with tools and spare parts has made a killing in the car park at Oktoberfest, fixing and adjusting the thousands of travel-weary vans and cars which congregate annually. The main problem with this sort of work is that affordable accommodation will be very difficult to find.

Casual Work in Hotels

Assuming you have not fixed up a season's work in a hotel or restaurant through the approved methods (see *Hotels and Catering*), it is very possible to find such work once you've arrived in a foreign country. All but the most desperate hoteliers are far more willing to consider a candidate who is standing there in the flesh than one who writes a letter out of the blue.

If you secure a hotel job without speaking the language of the country and lacking relevant experience, you will probably be placed at the bottom of the pecking order, e.g. in the laundry or washing dishes. Some hotels might confuse you by using fancy terms for menial jobs, for example 'valet runner' for collector-of-dirty-laundry or 'kitchen porter' for *plongeur*.

Reception and bar jobs are usually the most sought after and highly paid. However the lowly jobs have their saving graces. The usual hours of chamber staff (7am-2pm) allow plenty of free time. Some people prefer not to deal with guests (particularly if they are shaky in the language) and are happy to get on at their own speed with the job of room cleaning, laundering or vegetable chopping. The job of night porter can be excellently suited to an avid reader since there is often very little to do except let in the occasional late arrival.

Even the job of dish-washer, stereotyped as the most lowly of all jobs with visions of the down and out George Orwell as a *plongeur* washing dishes in a Paris café, should not be dismissed too easily. Nick Langley enjoyed life far more as a dish-washer in Munich than as a civil servant in Britain. Simon Canning saved enough money in five months of working as a dish-washer in an Amsterdam office block to fund a trip across Asia. Benjamin Fry spent a highly enjoyable two weeks washing dishes at the Land's End Hotel in Alaska and earned more per hour than he ever had in England.

When you are asking door-to-door at hotels, it is often a good idea to show up bright and early (about 8am) to impress prospective employers. Perseverence is necessary, especially midway through the season. It also might be necessary to return to the same hotel several times if you think there's a glimmer of hope. Kathryn Halliwell described her job hunt in Les Gets in the Haute Savoie of France:

> *I had to ask from hotel to hotel for three days before finding the job, and experienced what I have come to know through experience and others' reports is the normal way to hire a casual worker. The boss told me blankly that he had no work. As I was leaving he said, what sort of work? I told him anything. He said I could come back the next day in case something came up. I did and was told he was out, come again tomorrow. I eventually did get the job and realised he had just been testing my attitude as he had every other employee when they first applied.*

When going door to door, you should start with the biggest hotels. Try to get past the receptionist to ask the manager personally. If you are offered a position (either in person or in writing) try to get a signed contract setting out clearly the hours, salary and conditions of work. If this is not possible, you should at least discuss these issues with the boss.

Another way to get a foothold in a resort is to cultivate the acquaintance of the reps from the big travel firms. Not only will they know of immediate openings, but they can establish your position with local hoteliers who normally know and respect the reps. This is a job-finding ploy which has to be used with care since reps are constantly being asked for favours. You might volunteer to help them, meeting a group or standing in for someone who is ill. Lisa Brophy from Australia got to know a British rep in an Austrian ski resort who soon introduced her to a restaurant manager with a staff vacancy.

Although Kathryn Halliwell was forced to share a windowless room which had an intermittently working light and water streaming down the roof beams into constantly overflowing buckets, she still enjoyed her time working at a hotel in Corsica, simply because of the conviviality of her 'fellow sufferers'.

Hotels represent just one aspect of the tourist trade, and there are many more interesting venues for cooking and serving, including luxury yachts, resorts, holiday ranches, safari camps and ski chalets. Railway stations and airports often have catering outlets which employ casual labour at busy times.

Fast Food Restaurants

People with a background in catering often find it easier to transfer their skills to other countries than people with no relevant training or experience. Yet there are opportunities for the unskilled. You might find a job cooking hamburgers in a chain such as McDonalds or Burger King, which can be found from Tel Aviv to Toronto. Anyone who is not confident communicating in the language of the country can still hope for employment in a fast food kitchen. Pay is low, hours unreliable or inconvenient and the attitude to discipline more worthy of school children, however it is a good way of earning while you familiarise yourself with a new place and are in a position to move onto something better. When you are applying for jobs like this, which are not seasonal, you should stress that you intend to work for an indefinite period, make a career of fast food catering, etc. In fact staff turnover is usually very high. This will also aid your case when you are obliged to badger them to give you extra hours.

GLAMOROUS JOBS

The object of this book is to present a realistic picture of working in tourism. Therefore considerable space is devoted to puncturing illusions about the sun and fun image of working abroad in tourism. And yet cruising the world's oceans or crossing continents in a converted jeep are exciting and glamorous occupations, and a great many people would swap their office job any day for the unpredictability and variety of many jobs in the tourist industry.

People at a senior level, whether as chefs or conference organisers, may well get to move in glamorous circles; people working in incentive or upmarket tourism may have a chance to stay at some of the world's top hotels or go into some of the least visited corners of the world. Senior jobs in tour operations often involve familiarisation trips, familiarly called 'fam' trips, to inspect new destinations and work out the logistics. It may be hard work – assessing a dozen hotels in a day, checking the facilities thoroughly, dining with the agent, making notes about the restaurant, filling out reports, etc. – but it does make a change from working in the office. The new emphasis on responsible tourism has created new and interesting jobs like the one Rory has. He works as a conservation officer for a major tour operator, which involves monitoring the practices of the hotels used by his employer. Now the company uses recycled paper for its brochures, issues turtle watch leaflets to clients holidaying in Florida and is generally on the lookout for ways to help the environment.

The exciting and glamorous jobs do not come to the newcomer but to those who have made tourism their profession. A sample career structure is demonstrated by Bob Crossey who took a training course for tour guides. He speaks Norwegian, but at first found that this wasn't much help to him. His course finished in December, and he found work for two weekends before Christmas taking coach groups over the Channel on Christmas shopping trips. The Winter Olympics were due to take place in Norway, and he was provisionally booked by a British operator. A week before the job was due to start, Bob was told that due to lack of bookings his services would not be required after all. Meanwhile he had been making scores of phone calls and things suddenly looked up when coach companies began phoning him with offers of tours: OAPs to Bournemouth, weekends in Paris, London theatre weekends and so on. Bob found that he was getting regular work from three different companies. One paid well, but there was no opportunity to make commission on excursions; another paid badly but offered lots of lucrative excursions, and the third company had a short season to Norway which gave Bob the chance to use his Norwegian and show off the superb scenery to appreciative passengers.

At the end of the summer season Bob took out his diary and tried to make the companies book him up in advance so he knew what was happening. Although it was not possible to confirm bookings for the entire year, he was offered work month by month instead of day to day, so he began to see a pattern developing. Two years after completing his course, he is well satisfied. He has been all over Europe and one of his companies was so pleased that they offered him three coach tours through the Canadian Rockies. Bob loved these, but finds that long-haul trips take a lot out of you, and reckons to do no more than four a year, preferring to stay in the UK and Europe the rest of the time.

If you want to stay in one place there is glamorous work at the top level for registered guides. Kathleen is employed by the Foreign Office to meet guests of the British Government at the airport, take them around, look after them at lunch, introduce them to their hosts, interpret on official visits and be present at formal dinners. Eventually Kathleen was offered a promotion, to work in Brussels where she does a similar job with better pay and a small staff to help her. In jobs like these, you get to stay in lovely country house hotels, occupy the best seats at the opera or theatre (though one gets blasé about seeing the latest smash hit for the tenth time) and travel in chauffeur-driven limousines.

If you want to be a chalet girl with a difference try working as an assistant to the Chatelaine or *jeune fille* at the Chateau de Saran in France. Owned by Moet et Chandon Champagne, this is where important visitors from pop stars to politicians are entertained. You have to be able to speak impeccable French and talk about art, history or topics of the day, know how to arrange flowers and have an extensive smart wardrobe (something different for breakfast, lunch, tennis and dinner). The pay is about £120 a week for working from 9am-3am. As a past *jeune fille* says, 'it was a once-in-a-lifetime job, but you couldn't go on burning the candle at both ends for too long.'

Several small companies specialise in taking visitors to stay in castles and manor houses. The doyen of such companies is Take-a-Guide which has a team of personable staff who are good drivers and knowledgeable guides. They meet and look after clients, most of whom are wealthy and cultivated Americans, even ex-presidents and their families (whose visits are supposed to be secret, though there is little chance of this given how many secret servicemen come in their wake). The guides have to be experts at mugging up information, since each visitor's particular interests have to be catered for. One guide said, 'no sooner had I become an expert on Elizabethan embroidery than the next client had come to London to buy an Apostle spoon, so I had to make the acquaintance of silver dealers'.

Hotel booking/representation agencies in most major cities employ people to inspect hotels and look after the administration. Tired of being an interpreter at exhibitions and then a guide, Barbara Wenger de Po joined the company Leading Hotels of the World, an agency that represents exactly what its name suggests. After working briefly in their London office, Barbara was sent to France and Germany to visit the hotels which belonged to the consortium such as the Ritz Hotel and Le Bristol in Paris and Schloss Fuschl in Austria. She now runs the Spanish office and heads a team of staff who visit companies and travel agencies to promote their hotels. She is constantly on the go, flying to the States, organising smart dinners during exhibitions and speaking to the media, including doing the occasional television interview.

Smaller hotel marketing consortia such as Grand Heritage Hotels specialise in a certain kind of hotel. Some hotel groups such as Thistle and Sheraton have their own marketing offices which are staffed by people with language and IT skills and who like meeting people. Here are some of the relevant agencies and hotel groups:

Leading Hotels of the World – 212-838-3110 (New York), 3-5210 2058 (Tokyo), 0171-290 1000 (London), 69-13885120 (Frankfurt), 1-326 4535 (Buenos Aires).

Grand Heritage Hotels – 0171-376 2004.

Forte and Meridian Hotels – 0800 404040.

Consort – 01904 643151 (York, UK), 2-931 7711 (Sydney), 11-880 8624 (Johannesburg), 617-581-0844 (Boston).

Thistle Hotels – 0113 243 9111 (Leeds).

Relais et Chateau – 0171-828 9474.

People at the top of their profession have to be able to take the high life in their stride. Chris has a company which looks after the top horse riders when they compete in international events, supplying everything from horse boxes to hotel rooms for the riders (who can be more temperamental than the horses). Drinking tea in the sumptuous Ritz Hotel in Paris, Chris broke off to phone his wife to ask her to take his dinner jacket to the cleaners since he would be needing it the next day when he and his group would be in Windsor and were invited to have dinner with Prince Philip.

Similarly Valerie, who started out by taking overnight coaches to Italy, has been to Buckingham Palace (and not just when it is open to the public), met French Presidents and maybe an American one too, though he was so surrounded by bodyguards she couldn't be sure whose hand she shook. She now organises VIP receptions for CIPs (Commercially Important Persons) who are guests of top manufacturers. During events like the Paris Air Show she may stay in a suite in the exclusive Crillon Hotel which has to be booked and kept in readiness for any unexpected clients. She is often involved in organising programmes for the spouses of conference delegates where she might organise a private lunch in a stately home with the owner taking the guests around afterwards or other themed lunches and visits, the most popular of which seems to be when she books a restaurant and gets the chef to give a demonstration cookery lesson.

Anyone with certain skills may have the chance to transfer them to exotic locations and glamorous settings. Just about any job in tourism has a glamorous side; even an overstressed rep on a Greek island can take time out to admire a beautiful sunset or share a bottle of wine and a joke with friends on a taverna terrace, which beats a pizza in a rain-soaked town back home any day. Or as your coach climbs up into the Austrian Alps and your group sits back silent in admiration, you think how lucky you are to be paid to do this.

Even Saudi discos can go on into the wee small hours

There can be a tremendous amount of job satisfaction, from the game park warden who manages to get his group in exactly the right place to see wild animals at play to guiding children around little-known areas of London. There is satisfaction in nurturing a new hotel so that it becomes a favourite with clients, and helps the local economy by providing jobs. And if you like driving you can be paid to do this in some of the world's most beautiful scenery as a coach driver. There are always exciting moments in the tourist industry.

DJs & Entertainers

The idea that Britons know their way round the music scene better than other nationalities is fairly widespread, and anyone who knows how to use a turntable has a chance of finding work abroad as a DJ. Experienced DJs who want to work abroad should request details from a specialist agency like Juliana's Leisure Services (15/17 Broadway, West Ealing, London W13 9DA) which also has an office in Dubai. This company supplies entertainment packages to 5-star hotels and other clients. Juliana's DJ/Music Coordinator, distributes notes on how to become an international DJ.

Entertainers are also in demand abroad in a variety of roles for the tourist industry, from the actors who dress up in period costume at museums, like the Museum of the Moving Image in London, to musicians in Spanish resorts. A recent advert placed by a ski tour company (Les Chalets de St Martin, 1-3 Vine Lane, Christchurch, Dorset BH23 1AB) invited demo tapes for the position of piano entertainer in the French Alps.

WORKING FOR YOURSELF/FREELANCE

As many as a third of tourism companies operate from home. Many famous companies, especially specialist tour operators, started out using the kitchen table. Until you have tested the market for an unusual tour from birdwatching to white water rafting, you don't know if it is going to work. The recession has hit so many small businesses that a rent-free office makes sense, provided you are disciplined enough to settle down to a working day in your home. Loneliness is seldom a problem since in the tourism industry it is necessary to get out and about, visiting sites, venues and going on familiarisation trips.

Small companies that offer services for the tourist industry from meet and greet services at ports and airports, translations and brochure design, training courses, coach brokering, etc. are often home-based. Working from home has advantages for many people, including working mothers. Betty thought that if she worked from home (arranging homestays for visiting student groups) she could look after the 'unexpected' twins. Fat chance. She soon discovered that it did not make for a professional approach if a little voice could be heard in the background, 'Mummy, mummy, I need a wee' and the children were too major a distraction. So she sorted out childcare for four hours a day, and switches on the answering machine for the rest of the time.

Although most people who work for themselves do so in their home communities, it is also possible to work in an independent capacity abroad. Long-term residents who can speak authoritatively about the area and the local culture may well be preferred as guides to locals.

Conferences

Conferences are held all over the world, at conference centres, hotels, universities, sports centres, etc. and many need people to supplement the programme for accompanying family members. If you want to find out about freelance work in the conference, meetings and events industry which includes exhibitions, outdoor events such as pop concerts and incentive travel, then the relevant source of information is ACE (Association for Conferences and Events, Riverside House, High St, Huntingdon PE18 6SG; 01480 457595). Because they are inundated with enquiries about this 'glamorous' section of tourism, they only reply to queries from ACE members. The current student fee is £41. ACE publish a Suppliers' Directory in which you can be listed if your service is appropriate. Their *Buyer's Guide* costs £6.

Networking can be carried out at the World Travel Market in November and Confex in February (both at Earls Court in London) and at the Meetings and Incentive Travel Show at Olympia in July. Those interested in working for an incentive company or at an exhibition should consult the *Hollis Directory* (see below).

Running your own Tours

If you have money and/or time and/or expertise to invest there are plenty of opportunities in tourism, provided that you go about it in a sensible fashion. The fastest expanding tour market is for specialist tours from battlefield tours (which were started by ex-Army officer Tony Holt) to visits connected with hobbies such as gardens, railways, etc. To take one example, Jim had been in the Navy and travelled much of the world. He and his wife had frequently hosted visiting VIPs and their families. They had enjoyed organising tours for these visitors and thought they would like to do this professionally when he retired. His service gratuity set him up with a small office, paid for him and Betty to take a course in business admin skills and one in tour guiding, and also to join ACE. At their first ACE meeting they met a PCO who was organising a conference for 1,000 midwives in London, and wanted someone to set up a programme for the accompanying spouses. Jim and his wife produced a programme and asked a tour operator (a fellow member of the local tourist board) to advise on costings and details like coach parking. After a few hiccups, their first programme went well and now they run a small but successful business offering similar programmes for conferences in the UK and in places where they served in the Navy such as Malta, where they use a local agent as ground handler.

Anyone with a novel idea for a tour should try to interest the local tourism authorities or conference organisers with it. Judy is a registered guide who began to feel angry with the way visitors were thrust onto the same milk-run tours, all visiting the same places at the same time. Talking to a conference organiser at a Tourist Board function, she was asked to put up a proposal and three months later heard out of the blue that the conference organiser liked her idea (of a day out at a herb garden with a talk by the gardener and lunch with the owner) and wanted Judy to organise it for twelve people (conference spouses). The day was a big success and she now has a thriving business. She belongs to ACE and the Tourist Board, so uses both their logos on her headed paper to inspire confidence in enquirers.

To start your own small company, the basic tools of the trade are a telephone, word processor and fax machine. Word processors and faxes are only as good as their helplines, so be sure to invest in one which offers a good back-up service on their PhD equipment (Push here, Dummy). Be careful about giving out your fax number. Junk fax mail has become a menace and you may find your machine blocked by useless 'special offers'. The same caution applies to E-mail.

While companies have advertising budgets, one-man companies cannot afford this luxury. Networking backed up by efficiency seems to be the recipe for success. Try to meet as many relevant people as possible often at official functions like promotion evenings, Association get-togethers, Tourist Board functions, etc.If you are organising a highly unusual tour, try approaching the editors of relevant publications to persuade them to print a feature story or small announcement. *Willings Press Guide* in any library contains the addresses of about 10,000 magazines and newspapers.

Magazines and trade journals can help by sparking off ideas. In particular look at *Group Travel Leisure* (free from 9 Vermont Place, Tongwell, Milton Keynes MK15 8JA) which is aimed at the small tourism tour operator and is a mine of useful information. ACE has its own monthly magazine and also a *Job Spot* newsletter with information about functions (often free) where it is possible to make contacts. Subscribe to specialist magazines to find out well in advance about forthcoming sports matches, races and other events which might interest local clubs. Company directories can be very useful when trying to make relevant contacts or to market your services. In particular, look at the *Hollis Directory* which lists the PR contacts of thousands of companies. The cost is £82.50 but out-of-date copies are sometimes available for less (ring 01932 784781).

As mentioned in the section on Tour Personnel, there can be lulls in the working year. Bob fills these by organising short trips through his local pub, e.g. a trip on Eurostar, a kid's day out at half term. The publican helps to promote about four of these trips a year. It was hard work at the beginning, with one trip making a loss but Bob decided to go ahead with it for the sake of publicity. Now pub regulars are confident in the arrangements and are happy to book well in advance, which helps with cash flow.

Apart from pubs, any clubs or societies are a good place to look for groups of clients, especially if you can tailor the tour to their interest whether it is art and antiques, history, flower arranging, beekeeping, tiddlywinks or any of a thousand others. If you are going to offer tours to sporting events, then membership of your local golf, tennis, football club is important. It doesn't matter if you don't play or take part. They will be especially keen to welcome you if you undertake to give back a portion of your profits.

If you are uncertain about what kind of coach to book for your tour, you can seek advice from the Coach Tourism Council (c/o Gaia Communications, 28 Church Road, Tunbridge Wells, Kent TN1 1JP). On the whole, you get what you pay for, so beware an operator who undercuts. When choosing, visit the garage and see if it seems clean and efficient. Have seats been crammed in at the expense of legroom? Do the coaches have headrest covers and footrests? Do the drivers wear uniforms? Do they give commentaries? (This is against the law, but the driver may try to do this to get a tip; a giveaway is the position of the microphone.) Do you really need a toilet (which can get smelly) if there are going to be frequent stops?

INVESTING IN PROPERTY ABROAD

Mature people who, for whatever reason, want to change career or return to the workforce and have a substantial amount of money to invest might want to consider running a holiday villa or upmarket B & B. If thinking of investing in a villa, chalet or gite, you should do thorough market research (thinking of different seasonal possibilities, whether there is access to an annual festival, etc.), become a member of every tourist board and association that might be able to give information and go and stay at a similar property owned by expatriates to find out how it's done. Suitable training for such a business venture might include a health and hygiene certificate, a cookery course and a marketing and business administration course such as those run by tourist boards.

Today business people who are used to staying in hotels are looking for somewhere different when they go on holiday, and have taken enthusiastically to the chalet or villa holiday. However the accommodation has to meet very high standards of comfort and luxury, preferably with extra features like nannies and gourmet meals.

It is essential to start in an area that will welcome you. At present Bulgaria, Romania and Albania are all welcoming investment in small-scale tourist operations from campsites to luxury hotels. The cultural attractions of painted churches in Moldavia, wildlife attractions in the Danube Delta and the monastic heritage of Bulgaria are largely unknown, mostly because of the shortage of decent accommodation in these regions. Yet there are some beautiful old houses and farms which could be converted with skilled local labour (thereby providing much needed employment). The upmarket specialist tour operators are all keeping an eye on these countries but are waiting until there is enough accommodation of a high enough standard. Anyone with money to invest should consult the appropriate embassy.

The Savoie in France is an area in which foreigners have invested heavily (see chapter on *France*) and where the local *communes* are only too happy for foreigners to reclaim derelict farmers' cottages. Many of these take paying guests for winter sports, rent out their properties in the summer and welcome paying guests. One British couple say:

> *In these parts many houses still have outdoor loos and animals winter on the ground floor. But we have been pleased with the local services. The plumber and builders come at the time they say they will (we can't understand the problems Peter Mayle had with his Provencal builders). There are few local restrictions; you are simply expected not to do anything your neighbours won't like. There is nothing much that can't be sorted out over a glass or two.*

Once settled on a property you must place a deposit of 10% after which there is no backing out. It is vital to enlist the services of a good local accountant and solicitor.

People who own sizeable properties in the Alps can try to let them out to British chalet ski tour operators for the winter season. Nick Lunn does this and grosses £21,000 for the five-month season.

Wolsey Lodges (01449 741297) are a collection of privately owned houses offering luxury B & B accommodation to paying guests. Although initially all the properties were in the UK, they have expanded to Europe. The first to join was Casa Aloha (952-495 440), a property right on a secluded sandy cove in Mijas-Costa, Spain which has easy access to Malaga Airport. If Wolsey Lodges agree to market your property (after paying an initial inspection fee), they will include it in their guide which is distributed to upmarket travel agencies, business houses, journalists and so on. The annual membership fee varies depending on the number of rooms in the house and how much you charge (£700-800).

It helps to have a unique selling point. For example an exclusive hotel called the Sea Club (71-563310) integrates guests and English-speaking locals around a huge dining table. To publicise your property it is a good idea not only to become a member of the local tourist board but also to join ACE which makes networking with potential clients much easier.

TRAINING

THE VALUE OF QUALIFICATIONS

It is not essential to have a qualification to work in the tourism industry, but with today's consumer protection legislation, companies find that many of the jobs which used to be offered to students for the summer are better filled by people who have had training. There is a widespread recognition that the tourist industry would benefit from a better trained workforce. Training to become a representative, for example, can be as short as two weeks; but if the grounding is good, this training will help you to get a job and then to do it well. Maria Bertorelli of the Personnel Department of Thomson Tour Operations (one of the top ten tour operators in the world) says 'we like people who have invested in themselves', i.e. shown their seriousness about the job by enrolling in a training course. A qualification is not a magic passport to a job, but it certainly makes it easier to obtain an interview, after which is it up to you and your personality. Remember that no training in the world can teach you how to get on with people. You must feel confident in yourself that this is what you want.

Traditionally, the ability to get on with people was much more important than academic credentials or specific tourism training. However, though it is still crucial to be able to get on with people, this is no longer enough to guarantee a job in the industry. Training and experience are what employers look for so if you take a Gap year, take some time for training so that you improve your prospects in the long run. This 'investment' looks good on your CV and shows that you have an eagerness to learn. Of course, casual work is valuable because it shows you are a hard-working individual (see *Casual Work* section earlier) but today, many employers are not impressed with just stints as washers-up or 'bumming around'. If the applicant has not used their time wisely in trying to gain more specialised experience, it can look as if they have very little career motivation. The training which some tour operators do offer is usually in company procedures, not in the actual job.

The training period often gives the employer the chance to assess the suitability of the individual for the job and it is commonplace for trainees in these circumstances to be dropped before they even start the job. Jayne Nash describes her experiences with Top Deck:

The lucky applicants were invited to take part on a training trip. This involves completing a 'dummy' tour of central Europe in around three weeks, along with 50 other hopefuls (potential couriers and drivers) aboard a convoy of double decker buses. The cost of this was £300 plus a lot of homework, swotting up on the history, geography and culture of the ten countries to be visited. The training trip alone was the experience of a lifetime. We had to take our turn at being courier under the critical eyes of our two trainers, which was at times a terrifying experience. Throughout the tour unsuccessful candidates were dropped off by the side of the road; we lost one in Barcelona. If you made it through without losing your driver, your fellow passengers or your head, you were taken back to London and eventually given a trip to lead on your own.

Hilary Sanger was excited to be offered training by a winter ski tour operator until she was told to go home half way through the course. Very despondent she thought she should provide herself with a qualification that didn't depend on any one company, so she enrolled on a training course for the RSA Diploma for Coach Tour Guides. After obtaining the Diploma, her teacher gave her a list of companies to contact and she found a good job with *Sunsail*, for whom she is now a senior rep in Greece. Doing some training before applying boosts confidence and provides inside information about how the industry works, which will be invaluable during subsequent job searches. Course tutors may well have established contacts in the industry and can often help with job placement. Improving your marketability is not the only reason to take a training course. The assumption that just because you like dealing with people you can work in tourism is false. You must know the basics of administration, law and safety. A good course will give you confidence to handle all the problems that inevitably arise. (If there weren't any problems, there would be no need for your job.)

It often seems to be the case that a spell in charm school would be the best training for a job which will require becoming an intermediary between obnoxious or discontented holidaymakers and tetchy locals. Before proper training was widely available, a typical exchange between a new recruit and his employer might have resembled the one reported by Louis Weston:

> *My employer told me my first tour was to be to Italy. I told him I had never been to Italy, to which he replied there is no time like the present. When I pleaded that I knew nothing about Italy, he replied 'Now is the time to learn.'*

Off Louis went and, luckily, he found his coach driver a mine of information. But many colleagues were not so fortunate and gave up after their first tour.

But things have changed. Standards and expectations have risen. A holiday is one of the most expensive items in anyone's annual budget and holidaymakers rely on holiday staff to ensure that their dreams come as near to reality as possible. Not only will you derive little job satisfaction from just muddling through, but you may feel guilt for having given a poor return for people's precious time and money.

Nowadays it is most unwise to subscribe to the old school which said 'In my day we just bumbled along' or 'the best training is to sit by Betty', i.e. shadow an experienced guide or rep. Competition for tourist jobs within Europe is much more intense than it was fifteen years ago. Quality control means that structured training is more important than formerly. EU Directives which insist on good customer care mean that you must know what you are talking about. Furthermore, slipping standards of general education in the UK, especially in the study of modern languages and geography, mean that British nationals are often at a disadvantage when competing with their multilingual continental counterparts.

Tourism training seldom means a three-year degree course. Many courses do not need pre-entry qualifications. Fees vary enormously from one-day seminars for less than £50 on how to become a resort rep to tens of thousands of pounds at prestigious schools of hotel administration in Switzerland. The vocational qualifications which the government have newly introduced in the past few years have a weak reputation in the eyes of many employers. There have been complaints about the inadequacy of this training, so before signing up for any course, ask employers if they will tell you what qualifications they look for. You do not want to spend months on a course and then find out that no employer is interested.

Getting a Grant

Britons who need help funding a training course in the UK may be eligible for a government-funded Career Development Loan. Write for details to CDL, Freepost, Newcastle-upon-Tyne X NE85 1BR (0800-585505). These loans can help pay for vocational education or training, and are available through Barclays Bank, the Cooperative, the Clydesdale and the Royal Bank of Scotland. It is possible to borrow between £200 and £8,000 to cover up to 80% of course fees, and some extra for living expenses may also be forthcoming. Repayments are not due until after the course is finished and can in some cases be deferred for up to five months.

Americans can obtain details about financing their courses from the National Tour Association (NTF, 546 E.Main St., Lexington, KY 40508; 606 226 4275). Peterson's *Study Abroad* ($29.95) also offers valuable advice and information about financing a course overseas.

RANGE OF COURSES

As noted in the previous chapter, the tourist industry is so diverse that there is an enormous range of training possibilities for joining it. It is important to have a clear idea of the kind of work which interests you and for which you want to prepare yourself. For example, people often make the mistake of signing up for ticketing or travel agency courses, when they really want to train for a job that will enable them to get out and meet people, perhaps as a tour guide or representative. Those who want to go on to work for a tourist board, in tour operations or in incentive travel and conferences often find that a good business-oriented course covering marketing, promotion and sales is more useful than a basic travel and tourism course. Similarly a background in conservation, history, architecture, etc. can be more useful in some jobs than general tourism training.

Many, if not most, colleges of further education and higher education offer courses in travel and tourism at various levels. Unfortunately the structure and accreditation of these courses is confusing in the extreme with different award-making bodies using different systems. Furthermore additional courses are coming on-stream all the time. Start by contacting the Education and Industry Service Department at ABTA's Travel Training Company, mentioned below (01483 727321). They will send you a list of approved centres offering Travel Services National/Scottish Vocational Qualifications. Other lists of tourism training centres are available from the Institute of Travel & Tourism (113 Victoria Street, St. Albans, Herts AL1 3TJ; 01727 854395 - send an s.a.e. and a cheque or postal order for £3) and the NLG (addresses below) which is the professional body to which many tourist workers belong and which monitors academic courses in the field.

For advice on training in hospitality, leisure and tourism in the London area and the South, including East Anglia, contact Springboard UK (3 Denmark St, London WC2H 8LP; 0171-497 8654). They provide details on training courses, CV advice and the qualifications needed for the various careers in the industry. It is a national organisation with centres in Glasgow (0141-552 5554) and Wales (01222-484 899). Centres in the North and the Midlands are planned to be opened in Autumn 1999.

To become a registered guide in the UK, i.e. someone who works and is expert in a single city or region takes from 300 to 500 hours and can cost over £2,000.

There are also many short or long commercial courses which offer specific training in everything from how to apply to an airline to training in hotel administration. Many industry associations run useful short courses for their members, and will often allow non-members to join, though the fees may be higher. Not only do participants learn something on these courses, but they often have the chance to talk to prospective employers.

ABTA

The Association of British Travel Agents or ABTA is the trade association for the travel industry in Britain (68-71 Newman Street, London W1P 4AH; 0171-637 2444). Its subsidiary, the Travel Trading Company, produces the invaluable *Guide to Working in Travel* (£6.99 inc. p & p), which details job descriptions and opportunities, qualifications and useful contact addresses. The *Travel Training Company* (TTC) is responsible for designing courses and drawing up syllabuses. ABTA-accredited courses are run at about 100 accredited colleges (plus other colleges) and are also offered by distance learning programmes. Contact TTC on 01483 727321 to obtain leaflets about the range of qualifications and courses it offers.

TTC runs The Travel Training Programme, which is one of the largest Modern Apprenticeship training schemes in the country, and it is partially funded by local Technical & Enterprise Councils (TECs). Each year they accept about 2,000 school leavers onto this training programme which in the majority of cases leads to full-time employment in the industry. Although no minimum standard is stipulated for acceptance, many have three or four GCSEs, preferably in English, Maths, a foreign language and geography. Note that a few companies like Thomsons and American Express offer a training programme specifically for graduates, though this is unusual.

Occasionally, TTC also provides a range of one-day or evening courses for people currently employed in the industry. This depends on demand by students and is usually advertised through colleges and trade magazines. Day courses on effective sales techniques, techniques of public speaking, etc. cost around £100 plus VAT and are held in major cities throughout Britain.

One of the best known ABTA qualifications is for travel agents; the ABTAC which is granted after an exam. Ninety per cent of people taking ABTAC do so at college either by day release/evening classes or as part of a GNVQ. It is very flexible and can take between 6 months to a year to complete. The course is available at Primary and Advanced Levels and the distance course costs £126 (plus additional fees if studying at a college). TTC also offer information and leads for NVQs (see separate section below). Level 1 covers basic air travel, car carrying services, travel geography and package holiday services, while Level 2 covers advanced air travel, cruising and shipping, independent and overseas holidays, etc. The fees for each level are £150 plus college and exam fees. The highest stage is NVQ Level 4 covering staff management, agency layout and design, law and the travel agent, sales and marketing.

A current offering from TTC includes a Certificate in Tour Operation; the ABTOC, which is only available at a limited number of colleges, such as Greenwich College in London. TTC also offers an Air Fares and Ticketing course for an IATA approved qualification. A Resort Representatives course is also being established through partnership with companies like Thomson.

ABTA's American counterpart, ASTA (Association of American Travel Agents) also runs training courses for those working in the US and can offer information on qualifications. Call 703-739-2782 for details.

GNVQs

General National Vocational Qualifications (GNVQs) are intended primarily for students aged 16-18 as a kind of vocational A-level and an introduction to various industries. The 1737 colleges which offer the GNVQ in Leisure and Tourism offer up to three levels, Foundation, Intermediate and Advanced which can be completed in one or two years depending on the individual's background.

On successful completion of the course, participants receive a GNVQ awarded by the Royal Society of Arts, City & Guilds or BTEC EdExcel. The National Qualifications and Curriculum Authority (222 Euston Road, London NW1 2BZ; 0171-387 9898) describes GNVQs, rather vaguely, as 'a broad brush preparation for the world of work'. Yet many people in the tourist industry have complained that their usefulness is severely limited.

Bowing to pressure, these qualifications are being up-dated and the Leisure and Tourism GNVQ is being split into a Leisure stream and a Tourism stream, starting in 1999. If your local college offers GNVQs, ask if they include Travel Geography (the one unit the industry says is very useful) and if teachers have worked in the industry. Originally the Government required teachers on vocational qualification courses to have worked in the relevant industry. However, colleges often ignore this and excuse themselves by saying the GNVQ is only 'foundational'. Hence, leaders in the industry are not yet convinced that GNVQs for tourism are of much use. Additionally, because registration for these qualifications is earlier in the year than academic counterparts, the apparent drop-out rate is much higher. This has seriously damaged its reputation in the industry. Yet the Government has poured so much money into developing these vocational qualifications, that they are here to stay.

People should find out about local courses and ask questions about the practical content of the course and relevant experience of the tutors before deciding. It might be worth having a look at the Intermediate BTEC GNVQ Pitman textbook (ISBN 0 273 60976 9, £13.99) which serves as an introduction to the industry and may help young people to ask the right questions about courses.

NVQs

NVQs tend to be more practical and less academic than GNVQs. They too are open to students aged 16-18 but also appeal to mature students and career changers. The VQ in Travel Services will prepare candidates for a variety of tourist-related jobs such as tour managers, travel consultants, resort reps, etc.. However, as VQs have an element of assessment in the workplace, many employers are reluctant to allocate the amount of time required to fill in the paperwork.

There are no compulsory prerequisites. NVQs are available at Levels 1 to 4 in Travel Services (mainly for travel agency work), with options at Levels 2 and 3 in Field Operations (providing on-site services to tourists) and Guiding. NVQs are awarded at whatever level of achievement the candidate is assessed to have reached.

For example for the NVQ Level 2, students have to demonstrate that they can book package holidays, whereas for Level 3 they have to be able to design a package holiday. After gaining relevant experience, candidates become eligible for NVQ Level 4.

Under the EU's Mutual Recognition of Qualifications Directive, NVQs/SVQs levels 3 and 4 are recognised in other member states (as well as the RSA Coach Tour Guides Diploma and Certificate). However, countries can require you to make up any deficiencies they consider necessary in education and training. Variations in the EU still exist and to find out the position of each country, contact the National Academic Recognition Information Centre there. To obtain the address for the centre in a particular country, call 01242 260 010. Your best bet would seem to be to take a course with a qualification offered by a world-wide recognised examinations board; RSA, Trinity, City & Guilds, etc.

When the government first announced National Vocational Qualifications and. the Scottish equivalent (SVQs) in 1986, one of the most important criteria was that all students had to have some on-the-job training or, failing that, be taught by teachers and lecturers who had recognised and up-to-date industry experience. In some cases, that promise has been lost sight of in the drive to offer profitable courses, which means that vocational courses in the UK tend to be inferior to those offered in other European countries. The paperwork which NVQs can present has also discouraged many employers but the TTC is sorting out the maze and can offer sensible advice about suitable courses currently available.

In September 1995 the Government introduced the Modern Apprenticeship Scheme for school leavers with GNVQs or A-levels who do not wish to go to university but want to receive work-based training leading to an NVQ. The section about ABTA describes its coordination of the Modern Apprenticeship scheme in the tourism industry,

Award-Granting Bodies

The three principal skill-testing and award-making bodies in the UK are City & Guilds, BTEC Edexcel and RSA.

City & Guilds, 1 Giltspur St, London EC1A 9DD. Tel 0171-294 2468. Offers NVQs and non-NVQs such as: NVQ Sport and Recreation, NVQ in Travel Services, GNVQ in Leisure and Tourism, a Certificate in Business Travel, the City and Guilds Progression Award in Sport and Recreation, and the International Diploma in Tourism. They will send the relevant leaflet and a list of approved training centres on request.

Royal Society of Arts, Examinations Board, Westwood Way, Coventry CV4 8HS. Tel 01203 470033. The RSA offer a customer-specific Coach Tour Guide qualification which has to be taken at certain approved colleges, e.g. Hendon, Park Lane, Tourism Training Organisation, etc. (see *Directory of Training Centres* for addresses); ask the RSA for a complete list. Their diploma is suitable for reps, check-in and other people-handling jobs, as well as guiding. Anyone who intends to work abroad, especially in countries like Italy and Brazil which insist on paper qualifications, would be well advised to consider an RSA Certificate or Diploma because they are recognised worldwide. RSA courses are widely available on a part-time basis (though bear in mind that evening courses will rule out the possibility of practical tuition on coaches since it will be dark outside).

BTEC Edexcel Stewart House, 32 Russell Square, London WC1B 5DN. Tel 0171-393 4500. Fax 0171-393 4501. website edexcel.org.uk BTEC Edexcel offer National Certificates, and National Diplomas in Travel and Tourism, as well as

Higher Certificates and Diplomas. In England and Wales the normal entry requirement for the National Diploma is four GCSEs (Grade C or above), and for the Higher National Diploma (HND) one A level or equivalent. Travel & Tourism courses are run at more than 170 colleges. BTEC Edexcel also offer GNVQs at Foundation, Intermediate and Advanced levels in Leisure and Tourism, as well as NVQs and BTEC Awards in Travel Services. This includes Tour Guiding, Tour Operations, Overseas Resort Operations, Children's couriers and Worldwide Fares Training.

University Courses

The NLG (c/o David Airey, University of Surrey, Guildford, Surrey GU2 5XH) can send a copy of *The Profile of Tourism Studies and Degree Courses in the UK* to those who send £5.50. The following UK universities and colleges offer degree courses in tourism studies (the italicised names have entries in the Directory of Training Courses): Birmingham, *Birmingham College of Food, Tourism & Creative Studies, Bournemouth*, Brighton, *Cardiff Institute of Higher Education*, Central Lancashire, Cheltenham & Gloucester College of Higher Education, Christchurch College (Canterbury), *Glasgow Caledonian*, Humberside, Leeds Metropolitan, Luton, Manchester Metropolitan, Middlesex, Napier, Northumbria at Newcastle, Nottingham Trent, Oxford Brookes, Queen Margaret College, *Roehampton*, Schiller International, Staffordshire, *Strathclyde*, Surrey, Swansea Institute of Higher Education, Ulster, University of Wales (Cardiff), West of England (Bristol) and Wolverhampton.

The following British universities and colleges offer postgraduate courses in tourism: Birmingham, Bournemouth, Central Lancashire, Cheltenham & Gloucester, East London, Lancaster, Manchester Metropolitan, Northumbria (Newcastle), North London, Nottingham Trent, Roehampton, Sheffield Hallam, St Mark & St John (Plymouth), Strathclyde, Surrey, Thames Valley, Ulster at Jordanstown and Wales College of Cardiff.

Distance Learning

Sight and Sound Education Ltd. (c/o 54a Ifield Road, London SW10 9AD; 0171-351 4434) have distance learning courses for tour guides and reps. These are theory courses on tape with programme books, and they are useful as a grounding for this work.

USEFUL PREPARATORY COURSES

Languages

Although more than three-quarters of the world's tourism is handled in English, knowledge of a foreign language makes it much easier to advance along the path of a tourism career. German, Spanish, French, Italian, Japanese, Mandarin and Cantonese are probably the most important. Assuming you have not studied modern languages at school or college, evening language classes offered by local authorities usually follow the academic year and are aimed at hobby learners. Intensive courses offered privately are much more expensive. If you are really dedicated, consider using a self-study programme with books and tapes (which start at £30) or correspondence courses. One of the biggest publishers of self-study courses is Linguaphone (0171-589 2722) whose courses cost around £200. If you have any difficulty finding suitable courses, contact the National Business Language Information Service (0171-379 5131, telephone enquiries only), the CILT (Centre for Information on Language Teaching; 0171-379 5134) or the Institute of Linguists (0171-359 7445)

One of the best ways to learn a language is to go to the country and live with a family (for example as an au pair) or take a course. Numerous organisations offer in-country language courses, such as Euro-Academy (77a George Street, Croydon CRO 1LD). EF International Language Schools (5 Kensington Church St, London W8 4LD; 0171-878 3550) keep the cost down by arranging language exchanges between host families (mainly in Spain, Italy and France) and billeted English speakers. Euroyouth (301 Westborough Road, Westcliff, Southend-on-Sea, Essex SS0 9PT; 01702 341434) also arranges stays with families in different continental countries, with or without language courses, throughout the year. Opportunities also exist for au pairs through Euroyouth. US readers might like to contact the National Registration Center for Study Abroad (PO Box 1393, Milwaukee, WI 53201; e-mail study@nrcsa.com; website http://www.nrcsa.com) to receive information on language and culture institutes at over 120 schools in 25 countries. Many of the programmes also offer internships in marketing, education, communications and medical fields. .

Try to learn the 'purest' version of the language, usually the kind spoken in the capital city. Dialects are understood only locally, while 'classical' pronunciation is generally understood by everyone. Some regional dialects can be incomprehensible to other speakers of the language, for example Swiss German, Quebecois French or Neopolitan Italian. Castillian Spanish is totally different from Mallorquine.

For those whose mother tongue is not English, there are special courses in most countries designed for the tourist or hotel industry. The Trinity College Exam Board (16 Park Crescent, London W1N 4AH; 0171-323 2328) has developed a practical and efficient Oral Grade English Assessment, while the University of Oxford Delegacy of Local Examinations (Ewert Place, Summertown, Oxford OX2 7BZ; 01865 554291) also administers a test in English Proficiency which can be taken in the UK, Japan, Scandinavia, etc. The other major assessor is the London Chamber of Commerce (LCCI) whose qualification is EFTI (English for the Tourism Industry).

Computers

Information Technology (IT) training is invaluable for many jobs within tourism. Of course it is absolutely essential for travel agents or for reservation clerks in any travel company. Most tour operator executives have a computer on their desks. Conference companies will have computer programmes to run everything from the original enquiry through registration, badging and planning delegate kits, so if you can't use a computer, you are unlikely to find a job in a tourism office.

Health and Safety

Some tour operators are wary of allowing their reps or staff to attend to a medical emergency for fear of being sued later. That is why the NVQ for Reps does not include a requirement for Basic Emergency Aid. Other legal experts say that the rep who does nothing in a medical crisis might be accused of negligence. If something did go wrong, the rep should be covered by the company's public liability insurance. Whatever the legal niceties of the matter, any individual faced with a medical crisis would prefer to know the best action to take, so signing up for a first aid course is always a good idea.

A first aid certificate is valuable for many jobs in tourism. Find out about courses offered by the local St. John's Ambulance; their nine week course (one evening a week) costs £70 while their four-day First Aid at Work course costs £230. The London office is at 63 York St, London W1H 1PS (0171-258 3456). Alternatively, contact the Medical Indemnity Register Training Division, PO Box 838, London SW18 1PB (0181-874 0403). One-day courses cost £25 and 4-day courses cost £100. All courses are adapted to the needs of the industry. Similarly a basic food and hygiene certificate, offered by the Environmental Health Organisation, is a useful addition to your CV.

Safety Training Video has been produced by the Federation of Tour Operators for staff training in fire, swimming pool, hygiene and general safety. It clearly explains what you need to know and to check and costs £30 from 170 High St, Lewes, Sussex BN7 1YE (01273 477722).

SPECIALISED TRAINING

Many areas of the tourist industry require staff to have specialised training and experience, for example museum tour guides, chefs, safari leaders and ski or other sports instructors. Many of these are discussed in the previous chapter which describes the many kinds of employment available in tourism.

Tour Managers and Guides

Employers developed the RSA Tour Guides Diploma (this name may change to something similar to accomodate EU requirements), which is a basic qualification as a first step for tour managing and different types of guiding; walking, step-on, coach tour, site, museum, etc. This qualification is accepted worldwide.

Specialist guides are needed to look after visitors whose interests can range from engineering to embroidery. Contact the relevant association, museum or adult education centre for suitable courses leading to a qualification. Many tourist boards offer guide training courses and employ Registered Guides specifically for a region or city. In Britain these are known as 'Blue Badge' guides (due to their badge colour). Contact the English Tourist Board (0181-846 9000) for details of your local board.The IATM (International Association of Tour Managers) are working towards a certificate of tour managing.

Hotels & Catering Courses

The Hotel and Catering Training Company (International House, High St, Ealing, London W5 5DB; Hospitality Helpline 09068 443322) is the lead body and training provider for the industry in the UK. It can send a very useful *Careers Guide* free of charge which explains qualifications and lists recognised colleges and training centres. It promotes apprenticeships as well as college-based training and has recently produced a video aimed at 16 and 17 year olds to this end. For information about advanced qualifications contact the Hotel, Catering & International Management Association (HCIMA, 191 Trinity Road, London SW17 7HN; 0891 443322; http://hcima.org.uk).

The European Foundation for the Accreditation of Hotel School Programmes (EFAH, c/o HOTREC, 111 Boulevard Anspach, BP4, 1000 Brussels; 2-513 6323) can give details of training colleges in Europe.

Airlines

The Aviation Training Association in High Wycombe (01494 445262) overseas training in this field. Although it does not publish a list of members, it can give out individual addresses and may be able to offer advice to enquirers.

Airlines are looking for literacy, numeracy (for the arithmetic necessary to sell duty-frees) and geography. Each airline runs its own training course for cabin crew. Commercial courses do exist claiming to train airline cabin crew; however all new recruits to airlines have to complete the airline's own training setting out their specific safety procedures. However several companies do prepare candidates for the interview (see entry for *Airline Recruitment and Training Company* in the Training Directory). Although Rosemary was rather skeptical about the possible benefit of enrolling in one of these courses, she soon realised that it could be helpful:

> *Andrew (the instructor) went round the classroom asking trainees general knowledge questions, like the ones they might be asked in their airline interview, e.g. what are the capital cities of European countries, what is the currency in various countries, how do you spell Edinburgh (only three correct answers, two of whom were from non-Britons), what is the name of the Chairman or Managing Director of the airline to which you want to apply, and so on. Well over three-quarters got answers wrong, but we were told how to revise. Hints such as 'in your numeracy test you may be asked to give equivalents for £2 not £1' were much appreciated.*

The best preparation for becoming check-in or ground staff is a representatives' course. Further training will be provided by whichever airline hires you, though this may be rather perfunctory if there is a staff shortage at the height of the season.

Conference, Incentive and Corporate Hospitality Work

The forum for training and development in this sector is the Events Sector Industry Training Organisation (ESITO, Riverside House, High St, Huntingdon PE18 6SG; 01480 457595). This is the training wing of ACE (the Association for Conferences and Events) which is at the same address. In exchange for a large s.a.e. they will send a list of colleges and training centres, and can advise on whether the teachers and external verifier of an NVQ you are considering have industry experience.

For information outside the UK, it might be worth approaching the International Association of Professional Congress Organisers (IAPCO), 40 rue Washington, 1050 Brussels, Belgium (02-640 7105/www.iapco.org). Non-native English speakers might be interested in a certificate offered by Trinity College (16 Park Crescent, London W1N 4AP; 0171-323 2328) called the Certificate in Effective Communication for Conferences and Events. Contact ACE for details of approved colleges.

For those who wish to branch out into exhibition work, it is worth considering hiring the video *That's Show Business* about how to work at an exhibition, targetting objectives, knowing your visitors, presenting the product and closing the sale. It costs £175 to hire for two days from Video Arts, Dunbarton House, 68 Oxford St, London W1N 0LH (0171-637 7288).

Tour Operators

For Incoming Tour Operators, contact BITOA (British Incoming Tour Operators Association, Vigilant House, 120 Wilton Road, London SW1V 1JZ; 0171-931 0601) for information about relevant training.

Travel Agencies

ABTA's course for trainee travel agents is mentioned earlier in this section. The International Air Transport Association (IATA), in conjunction with UFTAA (Universal Federation of Travel Agents' Associations) offers its own qualifications for counter and ticketing staff. This training programme, administered by the IATA Learning Centre in Geneva offers Standard, Advanced and Marketing courses for travel agency staff, resulting in the award of diplomas which are recognised worldwide. The courses may be taken either at local colleges which are IATA approved, or by distance learning. Contact the IATA Agency Services Office (15 Kingsway, Imperial House, London WC2B 6UN; 0171-240 9036 Information booklets and rates are obtainable from this address).

British Airways runs its own ticketing course through its training partner Speedwing Training, 2nd Floor, East Wing, Heathrow House, Hounslow, Middlesex (0181-754 0011) or Grove Park, Waltham Road, White Waltham, Maidenhead, Berks. SL6 3LB (01628 826551), or at franchised colleges. This course covers ticket consolidation, which used to be the preserve of 'bucket shops'.

For information about training in business travel agency work, contact the Guild of Business Travel Agents for advice (0171-222 2744).

Bus & Coach Courses

To work as a host or hostess on express or shuttle coaches, you will need a food and hygiene certificate. National Express Coaches (0121-625 1122) run a training course for work on their Rapide (i.e. luxury) services which is open to those who are sent by their company.

The overseeing body for drivers is Bus & Coach Training (40 High St, Rickmansworth WD3 1ER; 01923 896607). They advise that those interested in training as a driver should approach the coach companies directly. Most offer in-house training courses on a one-to-one basis in a coach. Course duration and cost depend on how much previous driving experience the candidate has.

To work as a traffic manager in a coach company, you have to have a Certificate of Professional Competence (CPC). For details contact the Chartered Institute of Transport (80 Portland Place, London W1N 4DP; 0171-467 9423).

The Leisure Industry

Theme parks, visitor attractions, museums, leisure and sports centres, etc. represent an expanding market which employs staff at all levels. The Institute of Leisure and Amenity Management (Lower Basildon, Reading RG8 9NE; 01491 874222) can advise on qualifications and where to obtain them. They also produce the *Directory of UK Leisure Courses* for £25 (or £20 if a member). Student membership is £39 a year.

Childcare

With the trend for tour operators to cater to families, people with a background in childcare are finding it increasingly easy to find employment in this sector. The National Nursery Examination Board (NNEB) is the most widely recognised qualification and is taught as a two-year diploma course at 200 local authority colleges and several private ones throughout Britain. Write to the NNEB (8 Chequer St, St. Albans, Herts. AL1 3XZ) for a list of colleges. An alternative to the NNEB is the City & Guilds course on Family and Community Care (address above). Many colleges offer an NVQ Level 2 in Childcare; for example Lucie

Clayton Courses (4 Cornwall Gardens, London SW7 4AJ; 0171-581 0024) charges £1,428 (£1,100 with tax relief) for a 12-week course which includes two days a week at a nursery school.

Conservation

Conservation is now an integral part of many tourism jobs. The Association of Independent Tour Operators is doing a great deal of work to encourage clients to take ecologically-sensitive holidays. The Centre for Environmental Interpretation (Manchester Metropolitan University, St. Augustine's, Manchester M15 6BY) is supported by the Countryside Commission and runs an excellent series of short courses connected with planning, landscape, architecture, tourism, countryside management, etc. Grants are available to those working in the countryside.

For information about courses in museum conservation, send £4 to the UK Institute for Conservation (109 The Chancellry, 50 Westminster Bridge Road, London SE1 7QY; 0171-721 8721) for the publication *Training in Conservation*.

Qualifications and Training in Europe

For further information about whether certain qualifications will be recognised in the EU, request the booklet *Working in the European Union, Norway, Iceland and Lichtenstein* from the European Commission in London (Jean Monnet House, 8 Storey's Gate, London SW1P 3AT; 0171-973 1992). Recognition of experience and vocational training (as opposed to straight academic achievements) is especially important in tourist-related subjects and the EU Certificate of Experience has been designed for people in the travel, transport, food, drink and accommodation industries. Currently, there is no official document stating the comparability of vocational qualifications concerning the tourism industry. Previous attempts have been unable to regulate a system.

The Leonardo training programme was launched in 1995 for people seeking vocational training in the European Union. Training lasts between five and nine months, depending on the candidate's linguistic abilities. The programme is open to people under 25 or older people who have been unemployed for more than a year. Details are available from the Central Bureau for Educational Visits and Exchanges, 10 Spring Gardens, London SW1A 2BN.

A training organisation which may be of help is ProEuropa, 59 High St, Totnes, Devon TQ9 5PB (01803 864526) which organises training packages for suitable applicants. Because of their reliance on EU funding, programmes like the current Leonardo scheme change from year to year; details are normally available in the summer. One of their past programmes included one month's language tuition, return travel (from Totnes to the European destination), two months' work experience in the tourist field in Spain, Portugal or Italy and half-board accommodation throughout. The programme was open to people aged 18-27 with some relevant vocational training (but no university degree) or experience and a GCSE in the language.

Interspeak Ltd (The Pages, Whitchurch Road, Handley, Chester CH3 9DT) arrange *stages* or in-company work placements lasting between two and six months in France, Spain, Italy and Germany, in the field of hotels and tourism among others. The fee for British students starts at £150. For other organisations which offer hospitality training in European countries, see entries for *Horizon HPL* in the Directory of Training and *Eurotoques* in the Directory of Employers.

In Europe there are excellent guiding courses, though most will be in the predominant language rather than English. Qualification for entry to the tourism industry in France is the BTS Tourisme, a course which takes two years after completion of the Baccalaureate and covers languages, law, administration and history, and includes *stages* (work placements) lasting between one and seven months.

There are guide training schools in Vienna, Innsbruck, Graz and Salzburg and each Belgian province organises a two-year course each Saturday at a cost of approximately BF10,000. Countries like Italy are very selective about whom they train: guide courses are open only to Italian citizens. In Sweden guide training is organised through municipal adult education associations and involves a minimum of 150 hours of training leading to an authorisation test (in Swedish) by a board of examiners.

The European Foundation for the Accreditation of Hotel School Programmes (EFAH, c/o HOTREC, 111 Boulevard Anspach, B.P. 4, 1000 Brussels, Belgium; 02-513 6323/fax 02-502 4173) can give details of hotels and catering colleges in Europe. The organization Switzerland Tourism (Swiss Centre, Swiss Court, London W1V 8EE) can give details of restaurant and hotel training colleges in their country.

If you want to work in conferences, Trinity College Examing Body have developed a Certificate in Effective Communication for Conferences and Events. It is designed to encourage and evaluate oral communication skills in this sector. Colleges around the world will offer this qualification. Contact ACE or Trinity College (0171-323 2328).

American Courses

Vocational schools, community colleges and proprietary travel schools throughout the US offer courses in travel and tourism including seminars on tour escorting, hospitality and recreation. After meeting with the course organisers, it is worth finding out if the State Postsecondary Education Bureau or some other accreditation association has licensed the school. If in doubt, contact the State Department of Education. One of the best accredited schools for aspiring tour leaders is the *International Tour Management Institute*.

For information about which universities and colleges offer degree courses in travel and tourism, see *Peterson's Four Year Colleges* (published by Peterson's Guides Inc., 202 Carnegie Center, Princeton, NJ 08543-2123).

The American Society of Travel Agents (ASTA, 1101 King St, Alexandria, VA 22314; 703 739 2782) has over 20,000 members worldwide. Because of anti-trust legislation, ASTA cannot play the same role as ABTA's training board. However the Education Department does publish a 20 page list of ASTA-affiliated travel schools in the US and worldwide, and a page of advice headed *Choosing a Travel School*.

The Information Centre of the American Hotel and Motel Asociation will send a free list of colleges which offer hospitality degree programmes, as well as the addresses of useful organisations. Similarly, the Council on Hotel, Restaurant and Institutional Education (CHRIE) produces *The Guide to Hospitality and Tourism Education*, which is a comprehensive directory of education programmes for the industry. The guide includes valuable information on career prospects, salaries, scholarships and grants. For more information, contact CHRIE, 1200 17th St., NW, 1st Floor, Washington, DC 20036-3097; tel 202 331 5990/website http://chrie.org).

The National Tour Association, (NTF, 546 E. Main St.,Lexington, KY 40508; 606 226 4275) can provide information about grants and scholarships available for tourism studies.

The *Institute of Certified Travel Agents* offers distance learning courses for people who intend to make careers as travel agents.

CHOOSING A COURSE

In this popular field there is a plethora of choice. If you are going to invest some of your hard-earned cash in a training course, how do you choose the best course for your needs? One of the best ways to assess the value of a course is to talk to graduates and find out to what extent the course helped them in their job hunt. Another is to contact company recruitment departments directly and ask them what qualifications they prefer when hiring.

If you don't know anyone working in the industry, the telephone is one of the best introductory tools. Ask the relevant trade association which qualifications they recommend. Obtain a list of colleges or training centres (probably the ones near your residence) and phone for information, noting the following: the time it takes them to answer or to return your call if a message is left on an answering machine, whether or not you are put through to the right department or passed around the building because no one knows what anyone else is up to, and how promptly literature is sent. How your enquiry is handled can tell you something about a college or centre. After all, if their customer care is deficient, how can they teach it effectively? A request for a self-addressed envelope is probably a good sign, indicating that the course is popular and possibly oversubscribed.

Be prepared to ask questions about the course such as whether the qualification under consideration is recognised worldwide as well as in the UK. It is very important to ascertain whether the course tutors have extensive experience in the industry and, if so, how recent it is. Even if a college is on an approved list, the teacher who was teaching when the inspection was made may have moved on. These days colleges of further education and training institutes all have to make a profit, whereas in the past they could depend more on state funding. If one course is under-subscribed, teachers are regularly transferred from other departments. Tourism is such a popular subject that it is not unusual for colleges to have to scrounge for tutors. The course suffers if the teachers don't have first-hand experience of the industry.

When you visit the college or training centre, try to meet the lecturers. Some hold open days when you can inspect the place and ask questions. A good college will be very happy to tell you what industry experience the course tutors have. They may also be willing to put you in touch with past students or contacts in the industry who can comment on the quality and content of the courses. Naturally you will also be influenced by the general standard of the facilities. It is worth considering the health and safety standards. If you wouldn't want to use the loos, how can the college teach the fundamentals of the EU Directive on Package Travel?

As in most fields, there are some cowboy courses. These are set up by entrepreneurs who emphasise the glamour associated with the industry in order to attract students but do not offer much concrete training. There is of course more to working in tourism than talking about fun and sun, and some of the worst courses fold. But there are also some fairly useless courses which charge people to hear commonsense advice such as the importance of smiling, dressing neatly and not taking complaints personally.

One hopeful young courier answered an ad in her local Midlands newspaper to take a training course:

After paying to join the company's excursion to Paris, I was told to sit in the back of the coach and take notes. Arriving in Paris exhausted after an overnight journey, I was told that my bedroom wasn't ready so I should 'go around Paris looking for tourist places.' No one offered any suggestions about where I should go. That evening I worked as an unpaid courier marshalling

the group around on a night club tour. The next day we set off back to the UK.
On the return ferry I was given 'an exam' but no one told me who would mark
it or if I would be given the result. When we got home, it seemed as though they
couldn't wait to get rid of me.

No one had answered her questions, given any training in admin procedures, in
using a mike or anything else. And of course no one had helped her obtain a job.

Cost is no guarantee of quality. In the past, commercial courses available in
London have charged up to £4,000 and yet offered virtually no practical training on
a coach (which is both the most expensive and the most necessary part of any
guiding course) and could not offer a recognised qualification. So it is wise to carry
out thorough research before enrolling by asking senior industry employees familiar
with the course.

Overseas students who wish to study tourism in the UK should contact their
local office of the British Council for information on tourism courses. They can
then send two international reply coupons to the colleges which are of interest for
further details.

DIRECTORY OF TRAINING COURSES

The following colleges and private training centres offer various courses of possible
interest to people wishing to join the tourism industry. See the end of the section for
lists of other colleges to whom enquiries can be addressed.

UK Courses

ABTA - see Travel Training Company.

AIRLINE RECRUITMENT & TRAINING COMPANY
ARC House, Grove Park Court, Harrogate, HG1 4DP. Tel 01423 536 904.
Fax 01423 770597
Courses offered: one-day courses preparing candidates for interviews with airlines.
Course tries to assist numeracy skills (for duty-free sales) and geographical
knowledge.
Cost: £88.
Follow-up: candidates' job applications are evaluated and advice can be given with
which employers to approach.

BIRMINGHAM COLLEGE OF FOOD, TOURISM & CREATIVE STUDIES
Summer Row, Birmingham B3 1JB. Tel 0121-604 1000/0121-693 5959.
Fax 0121-604 1050.
Courses offered: Bsc (Hons) Tourism Management, BA (Hons) Tourism Business

Management, BA (Hons) Hospitality and Tourism Management, BA (Hons) Adventure Tourism, HND Leisure Management, HND Adventure Tourism, HND Business and Finance (Tourism), HND Leisure Management.
All courses include overseas cultural visits. Application is made through UCAS.

BLACKPOOL & THE FYLDE COLLEGE
Ashfield Road, Bispham, Blackpool, Lancs. FY2 0HB. Tel 01253 352352, ext. 2289.
Courses offered: courses at all levels in Hospitality Management and Tourism.

BOURNEMOUTH AND POOLE COLLEGE
The Lansdowne, Bournemouth BH1 3JJ. Tel 01202 205831. Fax 01202 205790.
Courses offered: GNVQ in Advanced Leisure & Tourism, BA fares and ticketing, ABTAC, ABTOC, Speedwing training programme, progression award in Sport and Leisure level 1 and 2, pre-university course for international students, in Leisure, Tourism and Hospitality management, certificate and Diploma in International Tourism - one year courses.

BOURNEMOUTH UNIVERSITY
School of Service Industries, Talbot Campus, Fern Barrow, Poole, Dorset BH12 5BB. Tel 01202 595146. Fax 01202 515707.
Courses offered: degree, diploma and post-graduate courses in tourism, leisure, hospitality management and catering.

CASTERBRIDGE TOURS
Casterbridge Hall, Bowden Road, Templecombe, Somerset BA8 0LB. Tel 01963 370753. Fax 01963 371220. E-mail tourops@casterbridge-tours.co.uk
Courses offered: introductory tour guide training courses, theory and practice. Suitable for people looking for a season of guiding on Continent and also for overseas visitors such as Australians who are making an extended stay in Europe.
Duration of courses: weekend (Friday-Sunday) courses held 5 times a year (1 in January, 2 in February, 1 in May, 1 in November).
Cost: £95 including accommodation at Casterbridge Hall.
Follow-up: work available for course graduates with Casterbridge Tours (see entry in Directory).

CORNWALL COLLEGE
Department of Leisure, Tourism and Sport, Trevenson Road, Camborne, Cornwall College TR15 3RD. Tel 01209 712911, ext 2030. Fax 01209 612387.
Courses offered: BTEC National Diploma in Travel & Tourism, BTEC Higher National Diplomas in Tourism Management, Leisure and Tourism Management. Heritage and Attraction Management, NVQ 2 and 3 in Travel Services, NVQ 3 Interpretation and Commentaries, NVQ Blue Badge Guide, Modern Apprenticeship, NVQ 2 and 3 Customer Care and Service. Specialist in tourism customer care programmes.

EAST ANTRIM INSTITUTE OF FURTHER & HIGHER EDUCATION
Newtownabbey Campus, 400 Shore Road, Newtownabbey, Co. Antrim, Northern Ireland BT37 9RS. Tel 01232 864331.
Larne Campus, 32-34 Pound St, Larne, Co. Antrim, Northern Ireland BT40 1SQ. Tel 01574 272268.
Courses offered: BTEC HND (Travel & Tourism Management), GNVQ Leisure & Tourism (Intermediate and Advanced), NVQ Travel Services (Levels 1 and 2), BTEC HNC Travel & Tourism Management, ABTAC, airline fares and ticketing, Galileo training courses.

EVENDINE COLLEGE
34-36 Oxford Street, London W1N 9FL. Tel 0171 636 5656.
Courses offered: Certificate in Travel and Tourism, Galileo and Air Fares and Ticketing.

GLASGOW CALEDONIAN UNIVERSITY
Department of Hospitality, Tourism & Leisure Management, 1 Park Drive, Glasgow G3 6LP. Tel 0141-337 4254. Fax 0141-337 4141.
Courses offered: degree courses in tourism management, international travel and information systems, hospitality management, leisure management.

HIGHBURY COLLEGE
Dovercourt Road, Cosham, Portsmouth, Hants. PO6 2SA. Tel 01705 283260. Fax 01705 325551.
Courses offered: overseas representatives, GNVQ Leisure & Tourism, NVQ Travel Services, HND Leisure Management, British Airways (fares and ticketing), Galileo training, etc.

HOLIDAY SOLUTIONS
41 Rose Valley Business Park, Brentwood, Essex, CM14 4HT. Tel 01277 231568. Fax 01277 260161. E-mail winningsol@aol.com.
Courses offered: introductory course for people wanting to work overseas as holiday reps. Provides realistic insight into what the job involves, what holiday companies are looking for and how candidates can best project themselves on application forms, CVs and interviews.
Duration of courses: one day. Held monthly in London, bi-monthly in Bristol, Birmingham, Manchester, Sheffield, Newcastle and Glasgow.
Cost: £99.
Follow-up: assistance given with applications and in some cases bypassing the preliminary interview stage with major tour operators.

LONDON TOURIST BOARD
Glen House, Stag Place, London SW1E 5LT.
Courses offered: part-time course for tour guides. Course covers core knowledge, evolution of English painting, communications, visits, etc.
Application procedure: pre-entry exam in June (which costs £20) and interview in July.
Duration of courses: September to March (18 months), with exam in April. 3 evenings a week plus Saturdays.
Cost: £2,000. Exam fee £300 plus VAT. Also run a one-day customer-service course called 'Welcome Host' which costs £55.

NATIONAL AIR TRAFFIC SERVICES LTD. – RECRUITMENT
Room T213, NATS, CAA House, 45-59 Kingsway, London WC2B 6TE. Tel 0171-832 5555.
Courses offered: in-house training for air traffic controllers. Applications procedure: all year round, contact the above number. Duration of course 72 weeks.

National Air Traffic Services Ltd

Air Traffic Controllers

There are few careers that offer more responsibility and rewards than Air Traffic Control. And before you say to yourself 'I can't do that,' chances are you probably can. Because even though this is an extraordinarily challenging and satisfying opportunity, we can train you to succeed if you:

- **Are aged between 18-26**
- **Have 5 GCSEs at Grade C or above, including English and Maths**
- **Have studied 2 A levels or equivalents**
- **Are interested in aviation**

An Equal Opportunities Employer

Applicants outside this age range with extensive, relevant aviation experience may also be considered.

Contact us now to find out more about a career that's different, interesting and enjoyable. We'll send you an application form and information pack which will tell you how you can become an Air Traffic Controller.

SALARY
c.£20k package

CONTACT TO APPLY
Recruitment Services
T1213
CAA House
45/59 Kingsway
London WC2B 6TE
0171 832 5413 or 5564
(24 hour voice mail) quoting
reference WT1.

LEADING THE BUSINESS OF AIR TRAFFIC CONTROL

OAKLANDS COLLEGE
The Campus, Welwyn Garden City, Herts. AL8 6AH. Tel 01727 737000. Fax 01707 377544.
Courses offered: Higher National Certificate and Higher National Diploma in Travel & Tourism Management. NVQs in Travel Services at Levels 2, 3 and Supervisory, GNVQ Leisure & Tourism at Foundation, Intermediate and Advanced Levels, KLM Level I and II Air, and Galileo Reservation Systems. OCN Certificate in Travel.
Duration of courses: full-time and part-time options.

OXFORD HOUSE COLLEGE
3 Oxford Street, London W1R 1RF. Tel 0171 734 3880. Fax 0171 287 1623. E-mail oxhc@easynet.co.uk/Website www.oxford-house-college.ac.uk
Courses offered: airline tour operations and travel agency training courses, including IATA fares and ticketing (levels 1 and 2), Galileo computer training.
Duration of courses: full-time and part-time options.
Cost: from £250.

PARK LANE COLLEGE
Park Lane, Leeds LS3 1AA. Tel 0113-216 2000. Fax 0113-16 2020.
Courses offered: GNVQ Foundation, Intermediate and Advance in Leisure and Tourism. At advanced level, major options in Travel and Tourism, Animateur (those wanting to work as overseas representatives, entertainment officers, event organisers, etc.), Sport and Outdoor Recreation. NVQ in Travel Services. A wide variety of full and part-time cousres up to HNC level.
Duration of courses: various.
Follow-up: opportunities for overseas placements as part of many courses. Work placements locally can lead to employment for some students. College is often approached by local employers in the tourist industry when they need to hire.

ROEHAMPTON INSTITUTE LONDON
Southlands College, 80 Roehampton Lane, London SW15 5LS. Tel 0181-3605. Fax 0181-392 3131.
Courses offered: MA/Graduate Diploma (awarded by University of Surrey) in Sociology and Anthropology of Travel and Tourism.

ST AUSTELL COLLEGE
Trevarthian Road, St. Austell, Cornwall PL25 4BU. Tel 01726 67911. Fax 01726 679 11
Courses offered: NVQ in Travel Services, BTEC EdExcel, GNVQ Leisure & Tourism, Hospitality & Catering, Tourist Information and Guiding.

SCOTTISH HOTEL SCHOOL
University of Strathclyde, Curran Building, 94 Cathedral St, Glasgow G4 0LG.
Courses offered: postgraduate coures in tourism, and hotel and hospitality courses (approved by HCIMA).

SIGHT AND SOUND EDUCATION LTD.
c/o 54 Ifield Road, London SW10 9AD. Tel 0171 351 4434
Courses Offered: distance learning course covers theory for tour guides, tour managers, representatives and coach host/esses.
Duration of courses: students choose the speed at which they want to work through 20 tapes, programme books, project book, working manual and link book which can be assessed as a record of achievement.

can be assessed as a record of achievement.
Cost: £70 - £200

SOUTH TRAFFORD COLLEGE
Manchester Road, West Timperley, Altrincham, Cheshire WA14 5PQ. Tel 0161-952 4699. Fax 0161-952 4672.
Courses offered: Travel Services, GNVQ Leisure and Tourism (Intermediate and Advanced), Airport Operations (recognised by Manchester Airport), cabin crew, BA fares and ticketing.
Duration of courses: part-time and full-time options.

STOKE ON TRENT COLLEGE
Cauldron Campus, Stoke Road, Shelton, Stoke on Trent, Staffs. ST4 2DG. Tel 01782 208208. Fax 01782 603728.
Courses offered: BTEC HND Travel and Tourism Management, BTEC HND Sports Science, GNVQ Leisure and Tourism (Foundation, Intermediate and Advanced), ABTAC for day release candidates and HND/HNC Sports Therapy.

STRATHCLYDE UNIVERSITY – see Scottish Hotel School.

THURROCK COLLEGE
Woodview, Grays, Essex RM16 2YR. Tel 01375 391199. Fax 01375 376703.
Courses offered: Gateway to a Career in Travel and Tourism (with the option of simultaneously learning English as a Foreign Language), Air Ticketing Courses levels I and II, HNC in Leisure and Tourism Management, Diploma in Travel and Tourism with languages, GNVQ Leisure and Tourism at Intermediate and Advanced.

TOURISM TRAINING ORGANISATION
54a Ifield Road, London SW10 9AD. Tel 0171-351 4434.
Courses offered: tour guides, site guides, trail guides and walking tour guides. Courses cover Tour Managing and Guilding, handling groups, transfers, check-ins, researching and delivering commentaries, basic emergency aid, selling excursions, and how to find jobs, etc. Recognised by British Council. One day seminars on Working for Airlines, Cruise Liners, Hotels, Conferences and Exhibitions.
Duration of courses: 10 days intensive course or one day a week for 10 weeks.
Cost: £500
Follow-up: course includes advice on how to find work.

TRAVEL TRAINING COMPANY
The Cornerstone, The Broadway, Woking, Surrey GU21 5AR. Tel 01483 727321. Fax 01483 756698. E-mail sales@tttc.co.uk Subsidiary of ABTA (Association of British Travel Agents).
Courses offered: wide range of qualifications for travel agents and others in the industry. The Travel Training Programme is a Modern Apprenticeship which offers an NVQ level 3 whilst gaining work experience. Also offer ABTAC, ABTOC and Lufthansa air fares and ticketing course.
Duration of courses: self-study courses are at student's discretion.

TRAVEL TRAINING SERVICES
Ty Gwyn, Catbrook, Chepstow, Gwent. Tel 01600 860341. Fax 01600 860341.

inbound and outbound tour operators, tourist boards, etc. Special skills and experience in developing countries.

Duration of courses: variable according to client requirements.

UWIC (UNIVERSITY OF WALES INSTITUTE)
School of Hospitality, Leisure and Tourism, Colchester Avenue Campus, Colchester Avenue, Cardiff CF3 7XR. Tel 01222 506315. Fax 01222 506930.

Courses offered: range of courses at MA, BA and HND/C levels. Specialities include hospitality, tourism, recreation and leisure management and an MBA in hospitality.

SCHOOL OF HOSPITALITY, LEISURE AND TOURISM

The School offers a range of courses designed for those interested in or currently pursuing a career in the Leisure and Tourism industry at MA, BA and HND/C levels. Specialisms include Tourism, Recreation and Leisure Management and Hospitality Management.

For further information contact:
School of Hospitality, Leisure and Tourism
Faculty of Business, Leisure and Food
University of Wales Institute, Cardiff
Colchester Avenue Centre
Cardiff CF3 7XR

UWIC

WEST LONDON COLLEGE
35 North Row, London W1R 2DB. Tel 0171-491 184. Fax 0171-499 5853.

Courses offered: Confederation of Tourism, Hotels and Catering Managing Advanced Diploma in Tour Operation (twice a year). This covers the ACE certificate for staff and the RSA Coach Tour Guides certificate. Recognised as efficient by the British Accreditation Council.

Courses Abroad

Europe (Countries in alphabetical order)

INTERNATIONAL ASSOCIATION OF PROFESSIONAL CONGRESS ORGANIZERS
40 rue Washington, B-1050 Brussels, Belgium. Tel 02-640 7105. Fax 02-640 4731.

Courses offered: professional course for conference organisers.

Duration of courses: one week.

Cost: approximately £2,000 (normally funded by employer).

INTERNATIONAL INSTITUTE OF TOURISM & MANAGEMENT
Krems an der Donau, Austria. Tel 2732 847636. Website www.krems.at/itm

Courses offered: Professional Hospitality Diploma Programme. Language of instruction is English.

Duration of courses: 2 years.

CLUB HABITAT
Kohlgrub 9, 6365 Kirchberg, Austria. Tel 5357-2505. Details available from Top Deck Travel, 131-135 Earls Court Road, London SW5 9RH.
Courses offered: an annual course in looking for a job in an Austrian ski resort. Course includes German lessons, lectures on job opportunities and red tape.
Duration of courses: three weeks in December.
Cost: about £400, including travel from London and half-board accommodation.

COLLEGE OF TOURISM & HOTEL MANAGEMENT
79 Aglangia Ave (POB 281), Nicosia, Cyprus. Tel 02-334271. Fax 02-336295. E-Mail cothm@spidernet.com.cy
Courses offered: travel and tourism administration; hotel administration. Diplomas awarded by IATA or the Educational Institute of the American Hotel & Motel Association. BA Hospitality Management.
Duration of courses: Travel and Tourism Administration: 2 years. Hotel Administration: 4 years. Courses start in September with an additional intake for hotel administration in March.
Cost: US$4,000 residential fees.
Follow-up: job placement assistance given.

ROSKILDE UNIVERSITY CENTER
Roskilde, Denmark. Tel 46 74 21 48. Fax 46 74 30 31.
Courses offered: guide course open to candidates who speak at least one foreign language fluently and have taken a preliminary multiple choice test on Danish culture and history.
Duration of course: 2 semesters with 400 hours on social, economic and political history of Denmark, art, culture and geography.
Cost: kr11,000.

HORIZON HPL
Signet House, 49-51 Farringdon Road, London, EC1M 3JP. Tel 0171 4049192. Fax 0171 4049194. Also 22-28 rue de Sergent Bauchat, 75012 Paris, France. Tel 1 40 01 07 07. Fax 1 40 01 07 28.
Courses offered: Anglo-French training organisation offers package combining language tuition and live-in hotel work placements as well as company placements all over France. Students are also prepared for a range of Chamber of Commerce (LCC) language exams including the Certificat de Français du Tourisme et de l'Hôtellerie and others which emphasise the language of the hospitality industry.
Duration of courses: 2-12 months.
Cost: from £240 fee though trainees earn a minimum of £50 a week plus free accomodation for hotel placements.

CERT
Amiens St, Dublin 1, Ireland. Tel 874 2555.
Government tourism training agency.
Courses offered: guide training and vocational tourism courses. Qualification is granted only after an assessor has observed a candidate in action after the course. Candidates must demonstrate ability to handle passengers and keep them interested.

LUXEMBOURG CITY TOURIST OFFICE
Place d'Armes, L-1136 Luxembourg. Tel 22 28 09.
Courses offered: for tour guides.

GUIDOR
Postbus 15272, 1001 MG Amsterdam. Tel 20 624 6072. Fax 20 428 4421.
Courses offered: guide training in Amsterdam (in Dutch) during the winter season.

THE NETHERLANDS INSTITUTE OF TOURISM AND TRANSPORT STUDIES
(National Hogeschool Voor Toerism en Verkeer)
Mgr. Hopmansstraat 1, 4817 JT BREDA, The Netherlands. Tel 76-5302203
Courses offered: higher professional management courses in three areas; transport, logistics and planning studies; tourism and leisure studies (with which there is an English option), and tourism and recreation studies (which offers a respected course in tour management).
Duration of courses: 2-4 years..
Tourism & Recreation Sector, Sibeliuslaan 13, 4837 Breda, Netherlands. Tel 076-65 26 50. Fax 076-60 04 60.
Courses offered: range of tourism courses including a new two-year course for tour managers which is respected worldwide.

NORGES GUIDEFORBUND
Myggveien 10, N-3218 Sanderfjord, Norway. Tel 33-45 07 54.
Can provide details of guiding courses in various regions of Norway.
Duration of courses: approximately 6 months.

ALLIANCE INTERNATIONAL HOTEL MANAGEMENT SCHOOL
MTF Management, Management AG,Thurgauersteraffe 54, Imperial-Gëaude, 8050 Zürich, Oerlikon, Switzerland. Info in UK from 0181-868 0385.
Courses offered: 2 year course in hotel administration, taught in English. Guarantees jobs in Swiss hotel as part of course with opportunity to earn money to defray fees. Has links with hotels abroad, such as the Hilton Group in Britain.

CENTRE INTERNATIONAL DE GLION
Hotel School, 1823 Glion sur Montreux, Switzerland. Tel 021-963 48 41. Fax 021-963 13 84.
Courses offered: prestigious training for hotel executive and management training. Bilingual French/English. Hospitality & Tourism Management and Hospitality Administration courses both cover food and beverage, kitchen and service, accommodation, marketing, financial management and human resources.
Cost: SFr 25,000 per semester (Bsc Programme comprises 4 paying semesters and 2 traineeships).
Follow-up: maintains contact with former students who have developed a networking system to help new graduates find good jobs.

ECOLE HOTELIERE DE LAUSANNE
Le Chalet-à-Gobet, 1000 Lausanne 25, Switzerland. Tel 021-785 11 11. Fax 021-784 14 07.
Courses offered: prestigious hotel administration and hospitality management courses leading to a bachelor degree. Entrance exams in February and August.

IMI HOTEL WALDSTAETTEN
CH-6353 Weggis, Switzerland. Tel 041-93 13 41. Fax 041-93 13 43.

Courses offered: Certificate in Food and Beverage Management (1 year), Diploma in Hotel Operational Management (1èyear), Higher Diploma in Hotel and Tourism Management (2è years), BA Degree in International Hotel and Tourism Management (3 years), Postgraduate Diploma in Hotel and Tourism Management (1 year).

HOSTA HOTEL & TOURISM SCHOOL
1854 Leysin, Switzerland. Tel 41 24 493 17171. Fax 41 24 493 1727.
Courses offered: hotel operations and management, tourism management, leading to executive positions within tourism or hotel industry.
Duration of courses: 1, 2 and 3 year diplomas and Bachelor of Science Degree. Courses begin in August and January. Students are required to complete on-the-job training which is found by Hosta. **Cost:** approximately SFr35,000 (£14,000) per year including tuition, board, lodging, books.
Follow-up: HOSTA is visited by companies such as Hyatt, Hilton, Intercontinental and Sheraton, who recruit students.

USA

CORNELL UNIVERSITY
School of Hotel Administration, G80 Statler Hall, Ithaca, NY 14853-6902, USA. Tel (607) 255-9393. Fax (607) 255-8749.
Internationally recognised hotel training centre.
Courses offered: BSc, MSc, PhD and other advanced courses in hospitality management.

EDUCATIONAL INSTITUTE OF THE AMERICAN HOTEL & MOTEL ASSOCIATION
PO Box 1240, East Lansing, MI 48826-1240, USA. Tel (517) 372 8800. Fax (517) 372 5141. E-Mail info@ei-ahma.org. Website http://www.ei-ahma.org
Non-profit educational foundation of the American Hotel & Motel Association. In operation since 1952
Courses offered: distance learning courses in hospitality management, food and beverage,club management, etc.
Certificates in Areas of Specialization (5 courses), Hospitality Operations Certificate (8 courses), and Hospitality Management Diploma (12 courses). EI also markets CD-ROMS, videos, books and course materials to hotel/motel employees for use in-house.
Duration of distance learning courses: up to 4 months per course.
Cost: $250 per course. $95 per challenge exam. Time payments available.

INSTITUTE OF CERTIFIED TRAVEL AGENTS
148 Linden St, PO Box 812059, Wellesley, MA 02181-0012, USA. Tel (617) 237-0280/(800) 634-3961. Fax (617) 237-3860. Non-profit educational institute founded in 1964.
Courses offered: Travel Career Development (TCD) Program provides basic foundation in the travel business. Self-study followed by test which leads to TCD Test certificate. Certified Travel Counselor (CTC) for career travel agents. Includes 5 courses on Communications, Selling, Management, etc. in the travel industry. ICTA can provide a list of institutes of education which offer the CTC programme. Further specialist programmes available including Education on Loction.

Duration of courses: TCD course at participant's own discretion, though suggested study period is 20 weeks. CTC requires more than 200 hours of study and testing over 18-36 months (in groups or independently) and at least 5 years travel industry experience.

Cost: $100 enrolment fee for CTC programme plus 5 courses costing $200 each.

INTERNATIONAL TOUR MANAGEMENT INSTITUTE
625 Market St, Suite 610, San Francisco, CA 94105, USA. Tel 800-442-4864 or (415) 957-9489. Only US school with specialist course in tour management. Accredited by California State Education Department.

Courses offered: group tour leading courses held in Los Angeles, San Francisco and Boston.

Duration of courses: intensive courses last 2 or 4 weeks; others last for one semester.

Cost: about $2,000 not including room and board for a semester.

Follow-up: ITMI offers help with résumés and job placement; many major tour companies interview graduates. ITMI produced an hour-long video in 1995 'An Introduction to Tour Management' which reviews full-time and part-time employment opportunities; cost $40.

Australasia

AUSTRALIAN FEDERATION OF TRAVEL AGENTS (AFTA)
Education & Training Division, GPO Box 1872, Adelaide, SA 5001, Australia. Tel 08-207 8450. Fax 08-207 8457. AFTA has four affiliated travel colleges in addition to the one at the above address: Level 1, 263 Clarence Street, Sydney, NSW 2000; Level 3 288 Edward St, Brisbane, Queensland 4000; William Angliss College, 55 La Trobe Street, Melbourne, VIC 3000; Edith Cowan University, Goldsworthy Road, Claremont, WA 6010.

Courses offered: Australian Travel Agents Qualifications (ATAQ) Certificate and Diploma courses by distance learning and full-time. Level II covers Australian ticketing, Level II covers Ausralian ticketing, Level III international ticketing. Further distance learning courses offered for managers and supervisors.

Duration of courses: full-time course lasts 6 months. National Assessments for the various courses are held in June and November of each year.

Cost: A$4,000 for full-time course and A$1,600 for distance learning.

PERTH HOSPITALITY PROFESSIONALS
67 Milligan St, Perth, WA 6000, Australia.

Courses offered: ATAQ Travel Career Development modules.

TOURISM EMPLOYMENT AND TRAINING CORP
15 Belvoir St, Surry Hills, Sydney, NSW 2010, Australia. Tel 02-93195033. Fax 02-93195128. E-mail tetc@ram.net.au.

Courses offered: Competencies aligned with the National Tourism and Hospitality Training Package. Categories include; traineeships and apprenticeships in commercial cookery; responsible service of alcohol; restaurant and catering licensees course; OHS; customised training programmes in all facets of hospitality and customer service. Also employment placements and recruitment organised.

Duration of courses: varied, depending on course.

TRADE WINGS INSTITUTE OF MANAGEMENT
Gouri Duh Mittal Vidyalaya, Behind Rupam Theatre, Sion (E), Bombay 22, India. Tel 2403776. Fax 2044334.
Courses offered: inflight services (air hostess/purser), travel, tourism and hotel management. Computer training and on-the-job training included.
Duration of courses: 5-13 months, starting throughout the year.
Cost: Rs3,500-9,300.
Follow-up: assistance given with job placement.

SKYLINE INSTITUTE
PO Box 5798, Safat, 13058 Kuwait. Tel 240 3776, ext 346. Fax 242 1312.
Courses offered: aviation training, ticketing, etc.

OTHER UK TRAINING CENTRES

The following colleges offer either National Vocational Qualifications (or the Scottish counterparts) approved by ABTA's Travel Training Company or BTEC Certificates and Diplomas in Travel & Tourism (or both). Note that a great many of these colleges also run catering and other relevant courses. (A complete list of catering colleges is printed in the Catering and Hotelkeepers, annual *Careers Guide* which is obtainable free of charge from the Hospitality Training Hotline 0891-443 322 (calls charged at 50p per minute).

Accrington & Rossendale College, Sandy Lane, Accrington, Lancs BB5 2AW (01254 389933).
Amersham & Wycombe College, Stanley Hill, Amersham, Bucks. HP7 9HN (01494 721121).
Arnold & Carlton College, Bath Street, Nottingham NG1 1DA (0115 9520562).
Aylesbury College, Department of Tourism & Hospitality Studies, Oxford Road, Aylesbury, Bucks. HP21 8PD (01296 434111).
Barnsley College, Old Mill Lane Site, Church St, Barnsley, South Yorkshire S70 2AX (01226 730191).
Barry College, Colcot Road, Barry Island, South Wales CF6 8YJ (01446 743519).
Belfast Institute of Further Education, Brunswick St, Belfast BT2 7GX (01232 265000).
Beneast Training Ltd, St. Annes, Lancs. (01253 720208).
Bexley College, Tower Road, Belvedere, Kent DA1 6JA (01322 442331).
Bilston Community College, Westfield Road Campus, Bilston, W. Midlands WV14 0DR (01902 821070).
Bolton Metropolitan College, Manchester Road, Bolton BL2 1ER (01204 31411).
Braintree College of Further Education, Church Lane, Braintree, Essex CM7 5SN (01376 321711).
Bridgend College, Cowbridge Road, Bridgend, South Wales (01656 766588).
Bridgwater College, Bath Road, Bridgwater, Somerset (01278 455464).
Brighton College of Technology, Pelham St, Brighton BN1 4FA (01273 667788).
Brooklands College, Heath Road, Weybridge, Surrey KT13 8TT (01932 797700).
Broxtowe College, High Road, Chilwell, Notts. NG9 4AH (0115 9175252).
Bury College, Market St, Bury, Lancs. BL9 0BG (0161 2808280).
Calderdale College, Francis Street, Halifax, West Yorkshire HX1 3UZ (01422 357357).
Cannock Group Training Ltd, Hollies Avenue, Cannock, Staffs. WS1 1DW (01543 462636).

Canterbury College, New Dover Road, Canterbury, Kent CT1 3AJ (01227 819000).

Carlisle College, Victoria Place, Carlisle, Cumbria CA1 1HS (01228 524464).

Carshalton College, Nightingale Road, Carshalton, Surrey SM5 2EJ (01817706800).

Castlereah College, Montomery Road, Belfast BT6 9JD (01232 797144).

Causeway Institute of Further and Higher Education, Coleraine, N. Ireland (01265 54717).

City of Westminster College, 25 Paddington Green, London W2 (0171 7238826.

Coleraine Technical College, Coleraine, Northern Ireland (01265 54717).

Craven College, The High Street, Skipton, N. Yorks BD23 1JY (01756 791411).

Croydon College, Fairfield, Croydon (0181 7706800).

Dearne Valley College, Manvers Park, Wath upon Dearne, Rotherham, South Yorkshire S63 7EW (01709 513333).

Derby Tertiary College, London Road, Derby DE4 8UG (01332 757570).

Discovery Training Company, 88 High Street, Weston-Super-Mare BS23 1HT (01934 620670).

Dundee College, 30 Constitution Road, Dundee DD3 6TB (01382 834834).

East Berkshire College, Station Road, Langley, Nr. Maidenhead, Berks. SL3 8BY (01753 793000).

Eastbourne College of Arts & Technology, Cross Level Way, Eastbourne, East Sussex BN21 2UF (01323 644711).

East Devon College, Bolham Road, Tiverton, Devon EX16 6SH (01884 235200).

Eastleigh College, Chestnut Avenue, Eastleigh, Hampshire. S05O 5HT (01703 326 326).

East Surrey College, Gatton Point South, College Crescent, Redhill, Surrey RH1 2FA (01737 772611).

Enfield College, 73 Hertford Road, Enfield, Middlesex EN3 5HA (0181 4433434).

Evesham College of Further Education, Cheltenham, Evesham, Worcs. WR11 6LP (01386 712600).

Farnborough College of Technology, Bourdan Road, Farnborough, Surrey GU14 6SB (01252 515511).

Fife College, St. Brycedale Avenue, Kirkcaldy, Fife KY1 1EX (01592 268591).

Glasgow College of Food Technology, 230 Cathedral St, Glasgow G1 2TG (0141 5523751).

Gloucestershire College of Arts & Technology, 73 The Park, Cheltenham, Glos. GL50 2RR (01242 532048).

Guildford College of Further and Higher Education, Stoke Park, Guildford, Surrey GU1 1EZ (01483 448500).

Harlow College, Velizy Avenue, Town Centre, Harlow, Essex CM20 3LH.

Harrogate College, Hornbeam Park, Hookstone Road, Harrogate, N. Yorks. HG2 8QT (01423 879466).

Hastings College of Arts & Technology, Archery Road, St Leonards-on-Sea, East Sussex TN38 0HX (01424 423847).

Headway Ltd, 14-16 Carlton Road South, Weymouth, Dorset D14 7PJ (01305 773751).

Henley College, Henley Road, Bell Green, Coventry, West Midlands CV2 1ED (01203 611021).

Herefordshire College of Technology, Department of Hospitality, Tourism & Leisure, Folly Lane, Hereford HR1 1LS (01432 352235).

Hertford Regional College, Department of Service Industries, Ware Centre, Scotts Road, Ware, Herts. SG12 9JF (01920 465441).

Highlands College, PO Box 1000, St. Saviour, Jersey, Channel Islands JE4 9QA (01534 608608).

High Peak College of Further Education, Harpur Hill, Buxton, Derbyshire SK17 9JZ (01298 71100).

Hopwood Hall College, Middleton Campus, Rochdale Road, Manchester M24 6XH (0161 6437560).

Huddersfield Technical College, New North Road, Huddersfield, W. Yorks. HD1 5NN (01484 536521).

Hull College, School of Business and Tourism, Queens Gardens, Hull HU1 3DG (01482 329943).

Isle of Man College of Further Education, Homefield Road, Douglas, Isle of Man IM2 6RB (01624 623113).

Josiah Mason College, Slade Road, Erdington, Birmingham B23 7JH (0121 3824757).

Kingston Adult Education and Training, Richmond Road, Kingston-upon-Thames, Surrey GU1 1EZ (0181 5476700).

Knowsley Community College, Roby Centre, Rupert Road, Roby, Mersyside L36 9TD (0151 4775700).

Liverpool Community College, Bankfield Centre, Liverpool L13 0BQ (0151 2591124).

Llandrillo College, Llandudno Road, Rhos-on-Sea, Colwyn Bay, Clwyd LL28 4HZ (01492 546666).

Lothian Training Ltd 21 Napier Square, Livingstone, West Lothian EH54 5DG (01506 430733).

Loughborough College, Radmoor Road, Loughborough, Leics. LE11 3BT (01509 215831).

Lowestoft College, St. Peter's St, Lowestoft, Suffolk NR32 2NB (01502 583521).

Macclesfield College, Park Lane, Macclesfield, Cheshire SK11 8LF (01625 427744).

Manchester College of Arts & Technology, Openshaw Campus, Whitworth St, Manchester M11 2WH (0161 9535995).

Middlesborough College, Kirby Campus, Roman Road, Middlesborough, Cleveland TS5 5PJ (01642 813706).

Mid-Kent College of Higher and Further Education, City Way, Rochester, Kent ME1 2AD (01634 830644).

Motherwell College, Dalzell Drive, Motherwell, Strathclyde, ML1 2DD (01698 232323).

Newbury College, Oxford Road, Newbury, Berks. RG14 1PQ (01635 37000).

Newcastle College, Sandyford Campus, Sandyford Road, Newcastle-upon-Tyne NE1 8QE (0191 2004000).

New College Durham, Framwellgate Moor, Durham DH1 5ES (0191 375 4000).

Northampton College, Booth Lane, Northampton NN3 3RF (01604 734251).

Northbrook College and Sussex, Littlehampton Road, Worthing, W Sussex BN12 6NU (01903 606060).

North Devon College, Sticklepath Hill, Barnstaple, North Devon EX31 2BQ (01271 345291).

North Down & Ards Institute, Castle Park Road, Bangor, Co. Down, Northern Ireland BT20 4TF (01247 271254).

North East Worcestershire College, Peakman St, Redditch, Worcs. B98 8DW (01527 570020).

North Lindsey College, Kingsway, Scunthorpe,North Lincs. DN17 1AJ (01724 281111).

North Nottinghamshire College, Carlton Road, Worksop, Notts. S81 7HP (01909 473561).

North Tyneside College, Embleton Avenue, Wallsend, Tyne & Wear NE28 9NJ (0191 2295000).

North West Kent College, Miskin Road, Dartford, Kent DA1 2LU (01322 225471/275517).

Norwich City College, Ipswich Road, Norwich, Norfolk NR2 2LJ (01603 660011).

Nova Training Ltd, 2nd Floor, Beechwood House, 22 New Road, Willenhall WV13 2BG (01902 366278).

Orpington College, Orpington, Kent (01689 899700).

Oxford College of Further Education, Oxpens Road, Oxford OX1 1SA (01865 245871).

Peterborough Regional College, Park Crescent, Peterborough PE1 4DZ (01733 767366).

Plymouth College of Further Education, Kings Road, Devonport, Plymouth PL1 5QG (01752 385888).

Preston College, St. Vincent Road, Fulwood, Preston, Lancs. PR2 4UR (01772 772200).

Protocol Group, 20a Wiggington Road, Tamworth, Staffs. (01827 62482).

Queen Elizabeth Training College for the Disabled, Leatherhead Court, Leatherhead, Surrey KT22 0BN (0137 2842204).

Redcar and Cleveland College of Further Education, Conservation Road, Redcar, Cleveland TS10 1ZE (01642 473132).

Ridge Danyers College, Hibbert Lane, Marple, Stockport, Manchester SK6 7PA (0161 4277733).

Rugby College, Lower Hillnorton Road, Rugby, Warwickshire CV21 3QS (01788 338800).

St Austell College, Trevarthian Road, St Austell PL25 4BU (01726 67911).

Salford College, Worsley Campus, Walkden Road, Worsley, Manchester M28 4QD (0161 7028272).

Salisbury College, Southampton Road, Salisbury, Wilts. SP1 2LW (01722 323711).

Sandwell College, West Bromwich Campus, High St, West Bromwich, Sandwell, West Midlands B70 8DW (0121 5566000).

Sheffield College, Loxley Centre, Myers Grove Lane, Stannington, Sheffield S6 5JL (0114 2602202).

Shrewsbury College of Arts & Technology, London Road, Shrewsbury, Shropshire SY2 6PR (01743 342342).

Solihull College of Technology, Blossomfield Road, Solihull, West Midlands B91 1SM (0121 6787000).

Somerset College of Arts & Technology, Wellington Road, Taunton, Somerset TA1 5AX (01823 366366).

Soundwell College, St Stephen's Road, Kingswood, Bristol BS16 4RL (0117-9675101).

South Cheshire College, Dane Bank Avenue, Crewe, Cheshire CW2 8AB (01270 654654).

South Devon College of Arts & Technology, Newton Road, Torquay, Devon TQ2 5BY (01803 291212).

South Downs College of Further Education, College Road, Havant, Hants. PO7 8AA (01705 797979).

South East Essex College, London Road, Southend-on-Sea, Essex SS2 6LS (01702 220400).

Southport College, Mornington Road, Southport, Merseyside PR9 0TT (01704 542411).

Stockport College of Further and Higher Education, Wellington Road South, Stockport, Manchester SK1 3UQ (0161 9583100).

Stoke-on-Trent College, Stoke Road, Shelton, Stoke-on-Trent, Staffs. ST4 2DG (01782 208208).

Stratford-upon-Avon College, The Willows North, Alcester Road, Stratford-upon-Avon CV37 9QR (01789 266245).

Swansea College, Tycoch Road, Sketty, Swansea SA2 9HEB (01792 284000).

Swindon College, North Star Avenue, Swindon, Wilts. SN2 1DY (01793 498266).

Tamworth College of Further Education, Croft St, Upper Gungate, Tamworth, Staffs. B79 8AE (01827 310202).

Thames Valley University, Ealing Campus, St. Mary's Road, Ealing, London W5 5RF (0181 5795000).

Thanet College, Ramsgate Road, Broadstairs, Kent CT10 1PN (01843 605040).

Thomas Danby College, Roundhay Road, Leeds LS7 3BG (0113 2846306).

Thurrock College, Woodview Grays, Essex RM16 2YN (01375 391199).

Travel Consult, 14 St Hildas Road, Harrogate, North Yorkshire HG2 8JY (01423 886230).

Tresham Institute, St Mary's Road, Kettering, Northants. NN15 7BS (01536 410252).

Trowbridge College, College Road, Trowbridge, Wilts. BA14 0ES (01225 766241).

Wakefield District College, Margaret St, Wakefield, West Yorkshire WF1 2DH (01924 370501).

Walsall College of Arts & Technology, St. Paul's Street, Walsall WS1 1XN (01922 720824).

West Anglia College, Tennyson Avenue, King's Lynn, Norfolk PE30 2QW (01553 761144).

West Cheshire College, Handbridge Centre, Handbridge, Chester CH4 7ER (01244 677677).

West Herts College, Cassio Campus, Langley Road, Watford, Herts WD1 3RH (01442 221500).

West Kent College, Brook St, Tonbridge, Kent TN9 2PW (01732 358101).

West Midlands Cooperative Society, PO Box 8, 10 hatherton Road, Walsall, W. Midlands WS1 1JH (01922 721255).

West Suffolk College, Out Risbygate, Bury St. Edmunds, Suffolk IP33 3RL (01284 701301).

West Thames College, London Road, Isleworth, Middlesex TW7 4HS (0181 5680244).

Wigan & Leigh College, Parsons Walk, Wigan, Lancs. WN1 1RS (01942 494911).

Wulfrun College, Paget Road, Wolverhampton WV6 0DU (01902 317700).

York College of Further and Higher Education, Tadcaster Road, York YO2 41UA (01904 770200).

GETTING A JOB

Jobs in tourism are either fixed up from home or sought on location. Sometimes this corresponds to working for a tour operator in your home country or working for a ground handler in the destination country. In fact most people pursuing a tourism career abroad work for companies based in their home country. Others who may be more interested in seasonal or casual jobs in tourism abroad wait until they are in their destination to look for work. Both of these kinds of job hunt are covered in this chapter.

The best time to apply to the major tour operators is September for work during the following summer season, and the main interviewing season is December/January, with only the occasional cancellation being filled after that.

Employment agencies such as *New Frontiers* register vacancies with tour operators at home and occasionally overseas. It may seem too obvious, but Jobcentres near airports, ferry ports and tourist resorts may have information about tourism vacancies (for instance see Directory entry for *Gatwick JobCentre*). The Overseas Placing Unit of the UK Employment Service (c/o Rockingham House, 123 West St, Sheffield S1 4ER; 0114-259 6051/2) coordinates overseas vacancies, which are distributed to Jobcentres via a computerised system called LMS.

ADVERTISEMENTS

The vast majority of jobs in tourism are never advertised. Thomson Tour Operations say that after receiving 50,000 job enquiries, they give up counting and most major tour operators receive scores of unsolicited applications for every vacancy they have. Still, it is possible that you will come across the one vaguely suitable ad by frequent scouring of daily papers like the *Daily Telegraph*, *The Times*, *Daily Mail* (Thursdays), *Daily Express* and London's *Evening Standard*, as well as major regional newspapers. Two mainstream travel journals (*Travel Weekly* and *Travel Trade Gazette*) carry advertisements only for travel agency jobs, mostly for entry level candidates. Both are expensive, so try to consult a copy in a library or at the office of a friendly local travel agent. Another possibility is the fortnightly newspaper *Overseas Jobs Express*, Premier House, Shoreham Airport, Sussex BN43 5FF; 01273 440220 (subscription charges are £19.95 for three months, £65 for 12 months).

One specialist publication is *Rolling Pin* which calls itself the 'international hotel and tourism newspaper'. Although some job ads are in English the majority are in German. Further information is obtainable from Postfach 8016, Graz, Austria (316-811 2770). It is mainly read by hotel professionals including ones looking for work on cruise ships.

Although the trade press does not carry many job advertisements, it does contain news items which can indirectly help you to find a job. To take one example, a past issue of *Travel GBI* contained the news that the Rank Organisation was to build a major holiday village near Penrith, that the former Irish Tourist Board director was about to launch a new car rental service, that Chester had been chosen to host the annual National Waterways Festival and that Stoke-on-Trent Tourist Office had launched a new visitor trail linked to the famous local author Arnold Bennett. New ventures like these might well be recruiting new administrators, receptionists or guides, and people with initiative will follow them up. *Travel GBI* costs £29 for an annual subscription from 3rd Floor, Foundation House, Perseverence Works, 38 Kingsland Road, London E2 8DD (0171-729 4337).

Interpreting Adverts

Beware of ads with no company name or address. 'Golden opportunity to travel' can mean the travel takes the place of a salary. 'Opportunity to meet people' might mean working as a time share tout. If in doubt a phone call to ABTA (7 Chertsey Road, Woking GU21 5AL; 0171-637 2444), AITO (133A St. Margaret's Road, Twickenham, Middlesex TW1 1RG; 0181-774 9280) or BITOA (British Incoming Tour Operators' Association, 120 Wilton Road, London SW1V 1JZ; 0171-931 0601) can be useful, often from what they don't say rather than what they can tell you legally. If a company has membership of one of these associations they have to abide by rules, and have responsibilities when employing staff. If the company is not a member, you need to find out why. It may be because it is highly specialised and doesn't fit into an Association's criteria. Or it could be a fly-by-night operation.

In the States, the best known national trade journals are the *Travel Trade* and *Travel Weekly* neither of which is of much use to the job-seeker.

RECRUITMENT AGENCIES

The Overseas Placing Unit of the Employment Service registers quite a few foreign vacancies in the tourist industry (particularly in Germany and Italy) with Jobcentres. The major hotel chains are represented at the regular Jobscene recruitment fairs held in the UK.

Specialist recruitment agencies for the travel and tourism industry tend to place people with relevant training or experience in jobs in the UK, though they may also be able to advise on training placements as well. Some specialise even further in placing candidates in, say, travel agencies, airlines, etc. *T&T Travel Recruitment and Resourcing* was established in 1983 and now employs 20 consultants working to place suitable candidates in travel-related employment.

The newer agency *New Frontiers* is a major consultancy for the travel industry. It registers temporary and permanent vacancies in the entire UK travel industry, including retail travel, business travel, tour operations, airlines and hotels. It also offers both careers guidance and ABTA/IATA approved training courses. The recruitment service is free and the careers training and advice is at a reasonable cost.

Mediating agencies are also involved to a small extent with job placement abroad in the hotels and catering industry. Specialist consultancies with client hotels and restaurants around the world undertake to place qualified chefs and other personnel, mostly in senior positions. In very few cases agencies and leisure groups can place people without any expertise in foreign hotels; however wages in these cases are normally negligible. Even more specialised agencies recruit personnel for cruise ships (see chapter) or for particular jobs such as disc jockeys and entertainers (see *Glamorous Jobs*).

In Britain the Federation of Recruitment and Employment Services (FRES, c/o Starfinder Ltd, PO Box 112, South Eastern L13 1HF; 0800 320588) publishes lists of its members according to specialisation; unfortunately the list of overseas placement agencies (which costs £3.75) contains only two or three firms involved in the tourism and hospitality industry.

The names and addresses of recruitment agencies are listed in the Directory at the back of this book.

SPECULATIVE APPLICATIONS

If you are trying to break into the tourism industry, you will have to resign yourself to doing a great deal of leg work or at least a lot of letting your fingers do the walking. The majority of companies are small owner-operated firms with occasional vacancies which are often filled through their network of contacts or with people who contact them on the off-chance of a job. That is why a good training course is worth its weight in gold. If the teachers know the industry they know where to find jobs, which companies are hiring locally, and will have their own list of companies worth applying to. Companies often contact good courses with job vacancies.

When you go it alone, try to improve your marketability as much as you can before actually approaching prospective employers (see chapter on Training). Without formal training, get as much exposure to the industry as possible, though tour operators are inundated with requests for work experience. Find out as much as possible about the business in general and the firms to which you might apply in particular. One possible source of advice is your local travel agent who may know which companies employ reps (but try to establish some rapport with the agent before asking such questions and choose a quiet time to make such enquiries).

As a preliminary to conducting a job search, it may be worth wandering round the lobbies of major tourist hotels looking for tour operators' notices, complete with their addresses. Try coach parks and ask the drivers if they know of any jobs going. Keep your eyes peeled at the charter arrivals section of airports and see which reps are meeting groups. Find out from porters which coffee bar the reps use when waiting for flights, and then offer to buy them a coffee and ask a few questions.

The earlier you decide to apply for seasonal hotel work the better are your chances. Hotels in a country such as Switzerland recruit months before the summer season, and it is advisable to write to as many hotel addresses as possible by March, preferably in their own language and enclosing international reply coupons. A knowledge of more than one language is an immense asset for work in a European hotel or restaurant. If you have an interest in working in a particular country, get a list of hotels from their tourist office in London and write to the largest ones (e.g. the ones with over 100 rooms). If you know someone going to your chosen country, ask them to bring back local newspapers and check adverts.

The *Travel Trade Gazette Directory*, which can be consulted in any library, lists thousands of tour companies in Britain. There is also a European edition (*Travel*

Trade Gazette Europa); an annual subscription costs £85, for more information phone 0181-309 7000. If you want to start by applying to companies based in your local area, try the coach companies listed in your local Thomson Directory or Yellow Pages. Many companies are so small with only occasional job vacancies that they prefer not to be swamped with photocopied letters or CVs. Often a quick telephone call will be tolerated more than an unsolicited letter of application, just to put the enquirer in the picture.

Many companies offer tours for special events (pop concerts, festivals, exhibitions, etc.) which they advertise as 'Readers' Holidays' in local papers. For work at exhibitions, consult the monthly *Exhibition Bulletin* which lists major exhibitions throughout the world, classified under venue and type (send £15to 272 Kirkdale, Sydenham, London SE26 4RZ). In the classified section they list conference and exhibition organisation and managements service companies, and demonstrators and stand attendant agencies, all of whom may be offering work.

The Directory at the back of this book provides a starting point for speculative applications to companies around the world. For more addresses of major American tour companies, you can also contact the National Tour Association (PO Box 3071, Lexington, KY 40596; 606-226 4245) for its list of members.

Tour Operators

Tour operators vary in size from the local coach company selling a dozen short tours a year, up to the giants such as the German company TUI and the Swiss company Kuoni which send millions of clients to all corners of the world. Many jobs exist in the Outgoing Tour market, e.g. a British tour operator sells tours to British people who fly off to holiday in Greece, Spain, Italy or a hundred other countries. For the general market they will employ staff selected in Britain principally because package tourists often prefer to be looked after by a compatriot and also the selection process is so long and involved that it is just not practicable to employ nationals of the destination countries. (There are exceptions, for example Poundstretchers normally employ local staff based in their resorts overseas.)

Most tour operators interview in their country (Britain, Germany, Netherlands, etc.) and send the selected staff out at the beginning of the season to stay in the resort for the duration of the season. Although this means that the majority of staff do not speak the language fluently, most tour operators do not consider this a priority. As one major operator says, perhaps a trifle optimistically, 'Anyone who speaks one foreign language will find it easy to learn another; and anyway most locals in a resort speak English'.

In many cases the recruiting departments of tour operators are open only during the recruitment period. Then when they have chosen the required number, the staff close the department down and go to work in the reservations department or wherever needed. Still, it is worth sending an s.a.e., requesting the tour operator's recruitment procedures. Large companies like *Thomson Tour Operations* and *Airtours* employ so many people to service their estimated three million customers that they publish a large-format brochure about their recruitment requirements, which can be requested from the Overseas Personnel Office. As is the case with most of the major companies, Airtours employs reps, children's reps, entertainers and ski resort staff. Their reps must have all the usual qualities (flexibility, diplomacy, etc.) and preferably knowledge of French, Spanish, Italian, Greek, Portuguese or German (in order of numbers needed). There may be an assumption that you have a commitment to make tourism a career, though this is not essential.

What Colour is the Sky in Your Part of the World?

Sun, sea, sand, blue skies and a career - what better reasons to join Airtours Holidays, part of the world's largest air inclusive tour operator?

Holiday Services Executives

You'll do everything you can to ensure our customers enjoy the most successful holiday ever! It's hard work, but very rewarding - so if you're the sort of person who enjoys helping people, are aged 21 or over and have had some experience in a customer focused role, we want to hear from you.

Children's Club Leaders

Sometimes customers can be quite demanding, particularly our youngest, so looking after them (aged between 3 - 15 years old) can be quite a challenge! If you have experience of working with children, are aged 20 or over and have boundless enthusiasm and energy, you're the person we are looking for.

Overseas Administration Executives

Office based in resort, you will support the team dealing with everything from flight lists and reservations to transfers. Aged 21 or over, you'll be well organised, with good PC skills and plenty of initiative.

Take the first step to the most exciting career move you'll ever make...

...call our recruitment line now on 01706 909027.

(Open 24 hours)

Airtours Holidays Ltd is committed to a policy of equal opportunities.

The Holiday Makers

A further advantage for the tour operator of employing expat staff is that if there is a crisis elsewhere in their empire, they can transfer a staff member at a moment's notice from Spain to Greece say, which is not possible if the employee is a local with local commitments. Nevertheless a few European operators do contract with a local ground handler who employs staff on location in the resort, but this is not common.

Because of price wars, the mass-market operators make little or no money on selling holidays. Instead their profits derive from selling excursions and, to a lesser extent, duty-free goods on their chartered aircraft (though this will have to change before June 1999 when duty-free shopping is scheduled to be phased out in Europe). If you don't feel comfortable with this emphasis on selling or know that you can't sell for toffee, you will have to try to find work with a more upmarket operator who does not rely on excursion sales.

Some tour operators advertise a training course for which you have to pay. This is more likely to be the case with companies like *Contiki* and *Topdeck* and also with overland expedition operators (see introductory section) which are well known 'fun' employers and therefore very popular. To ensure that applicants are serious about the work, these companies insist that they put their money where their mouths are. Before signing on, find out exactly what ratio of trainees are taken on from the course, and what your realistic chances are of numbering yourself among them. Normally this training fee will be refunded after you have worked for the company for a certain length of time.

Tour operators which provide summer tours of Europe for North American students employ a great many guides and tour leaders and pay well. Try companies like NECC, CHA, *EF Educational Tours* and *AIFS UK*.

Special Interest Tours

The vast majority of tour companies (particularly those offering 'the unspoiled Europe that only we know how to find') stick to the well trodden paths, herding their customers along the 'Milk Runs' whether that is around the Ring of Kerry in Ireland or to the castles along the Rhine. If you despair at the prospect of travelling in a coach along the same route taken by hundreds of others, it is worth considering trying to find work with a more specialised travel firm.

The variety and choice of what enterprising companies offer are increasing all the time. It seems that whatever hobbies people have, there is a tour company that specialises in providing holidays for this market, from battlefield tours to stamp collecting, and there is work for someone with a deep knowledge of just about any hobby. There are gourmet tours of Japan, garden tours of Italy, jungle bird tours of Peru, photo holidays to Lapland and so on. These tend to appeal to a more upmarket clientele, and the sharper focus of these tours often engage the interest of the rep or guide in charge to a much higher degree than ordinary tours. Judy Wilson was asked to take a group from America around East Anglia, searching for their families' roots:

> *That was fascinating, just like a living treasure hunt, and I got just as much satisfaction out of finding a grave or an item in a local library as they did.*

First check the free Directory of the 155 members of the Association of Independent Tour Operators (133A St Margaret's Road, Twickenham, Middlesex TW1 1RG) which contains several useful indexes of specialist holidays organised according to sport or theme. (Send a large s.a.e and two first-class stamps.) For example people with experience of hill-walking can find a range of companies looking for trek leaders, though there are plenty of others (like *Kumuka Expeditions*) which are not members of AITO. Anyone with an avid interest in a specific activity from orchid-hunting to wine-tasting should concentrate on the handful of firms which cover these specialities. In the US the *Specialty Travel Index* (303 San Anselmo Ave, Suite 313, San Anselmo, CA 94960) lists 600 companies twice a year; a single issue costs $6, both for $10 plus postage.

A great many orchestras and choirs tour other countries. Specialist firms like *Edwin Doran Music Travel* or *Specialised Travel Ltd* employ guides for the summer season, who need not be musical but they should speak languages and have experience of leading groups. Touring musical groups, particularly from the US, cause special problems. On arriving in Europe, the band or choir master suddenly feels that their reputation is at stake and will try to fit in extra rehearsals, which usually necessitate the use of the coach. While the company will not have costed in the extra kilometres and won't pay, your driver will baulk at the extra work. The solution is to point to the tachograph and explain that the driver's hours are very strictly controlled and, much as you would both like the driver to work extra hours, the law won't allow this.

If you have experience with horses, you might look in magazines like *Horse and Hound* especially in May to look for announcements of tours to Europe, or further afield to Australia and Argentina. Alternatively contact your local Polo Club and look in their programmes for companies that advertise. Tours go from Germany, the USA, Spain, etc. as well as from the UK.

Many attractions need guides with specialised knowledge. For example anyone with a background in marine biology has a good chance of being hired as a guide when they approach dive cruise firms from Queensland to Eilat.

INTERVIEWS

When tour companies come to choose their reps and guides, their priority is usually to find someone with the right kind of personality. Therefore the interview is even more crucial than it is in other fields of employment where experience and background may be of equal or more importance.

At one extreme is the 30-second interview for a job as a rep or guide in which the employer (usually an upmarket agency) is interested only in assessing a candidate's manner of dressing and speaking, claiming that the rest can be taught on-the-job. At the other extreme (and much more usual) is the gruelling day-long interview offered by the big tour operators like *Thomson* and *Olympic Holidays*.

Study the company's brochures thoroughly beforehand, especially the fine print of the Terms and Conditions. If you know a friendly travel agent, ask them informally to assess that company's strengths and what their target market is. Make a preliminary list of questions about the content of the job or the policies of the company.

Arrive well in advance of the starting time, bringing pen and paper and a copy of the brochure to demonstrate your keenness. Be friendly and polite to the receptionist. In smaller companies it is not unknown for the boss to slip out at the end of a tiring day, unable to differentiate one candidate from another, and ask the receptionist for her opinion.

It is very important to look presentable and immaculately groomed at any interview and especially for jobs in tourism which require a great deal of client contact. People in personnel departments (sometimes called Human Resources) say that first impressions are crucial, and often admit that they make up their minds in those first important seconds. Wear smart business-like clothes. Women may wear trousers if these are well tailored, but skirts are preferable. Bear in mind that most package tourists are conservative so wear what makes your mother happy, not your mates. Men should wear a tie and should refrain from wearing earrings. Women should avoid jangly jewellery, nose studs, heavily bleached hair, heavy make-up or too-short skirts and low-cut tops. Take spare tights and, if you wear nail polish, a carefully capped bottle for touch-ups. Dirty fingernails will certainly be noticed as will scuffed shoes and over-casual items of clothing like jeans or trainers, except possibly for sports jobs.

Although the various companies use different interview approaches, it may be helpful to give an example of how one might be structured. The day progresses from group interviews to individual ones, as people are weeded out. In the first place, all candidates are assembled in a room for a briefing on the company by a (charming) Senior Representative who tries to make everyone relax. But do not relax too much because you may later be quizzed on what you have been told. Basic working conditions should be set out. If this is the first time you have been told the proposed wage, try not to gasp at the lowness of the figure. It can normally be supplemented by the commissions you earn on the excursions, etc. that you sell.

You then have coffee and wait to be called for individual interviews in front of a panel. This is where you will be asked to demonstrate your suitability for the job; take along any relevant certificates you have earned. You then have lunch which is not normally laid on. Further in-depth interviews are held in the afternoon, individually or in small groups, when it will be appropriate to mention any relevant training or knowledge of languages (take your certificates). Sample tasks may be to sell an excursion so be prepared to design a poster, keeping your presentation simple but striking. You will have a chance to ask questions such as what are the prospects of work at the end of an initial season; what insurance the company offers; to which resort/s you would be most likely sent if selected; whether accommodation is shared, or a uniform provided, etc.

Even if the interview seems to be going well, do not allow your hopes to be raised too high. Applicants to Virgin Airlines have described how a certain number of candidates are asked near the end of their interview day to try on the company uniform. Some have even been given a complete make-up job. When you parade in front of the interview panel in uniform you think 'this is it'. It isn't, and many applicants are later upset to receive a letter saying no thanks.

Xuela Edwards was told that she was one of 30 applicants selected from a pool of 2,000 to be interviewed by a major tour operator, an experience she found intimidating. She didn't get through to a one-to-one interview:

> *Some other rejects and I went over the session afterwards and could find no common trait or logic at work, but then we didn't know who was successful. I have heard that other companies ask bizarre questions such as 'Which would you rather be – a bishop or a colonel?' Most companies require you to give a strictly timed presentation on your favourite holiday or hobby for which you are supposed to bring visual aids (I had 24 hours' notice). I can honestly say that I see no connection between the intimidating standards at interview and the general level of most reps. Although the operators all say they require a minimum of two languages, this is not necessary. Very few applicants bring genuine language skills to the job.*

Some companies use psychometric testing (to measure mental ability) at their interviews, which can be daunting and in some cases humiliating. Do not be downcast if you do not excel; the tests are normally bought in from outside consultancies and may be inexpertly administered and interpreted. One favourite test is to seat applicants in a circle and ask them who they would throw out from a sinking balloon. (Avoid choosing the interrogator unless you have decided you do not want the job after all.) A competent interviewer can find out what someone is like without having to demean him or her, so if the company does employ these tactics, you are probably better off not working for them. A good employer will explain what is expected of you in the interview, treat the candidates with dignity and inform the ones who have not been given jobs as discreetly as possible.

If, after the interview, you decide that you like the company, it is a good idea to write to thank the chief interviewer for a most interesting day, mentioning how much you enjoyed meeting everyone and, even if you are not suitable on this occasion, you would like to be considered for any future jobs.

Sometimes acceptance at this stage is still no guarantee of a job. It may be that you will now be invited to join an in-house training course, which gives the company more leisure to weed out weaker candidates. UK tour operators provide only local training, whereas some European tour companies send their successful candidates abroad, as Charlotte Jakobsen from Denmark describes:

After doing various jobs in the travel industry (air hostess, hotel work, etc.) I decided that becoming a tour rep would be great and therefore applied to one of Denmark's biggest companies, Tjaereborg. Thousands apply every year so I was lucky to be accepted for an interview and written personality tests. After the first meeting I was sent with 45 others on a three week training course in Costa del Sol (for an all-inclusive price of £400). After three brilliant but extremely hard weeks in which we learned a lot about doing guided tours, giving good service to clients, first aid, etc., only half of the group were offered jobs.

THE LAKE DISTRICT
Come and find your *Oasis*...

Set in stunningly beautiful Lake District Countryside, Oasis Lakeland Forest Village is one of the UK's premier leisure resorts. Our aim is to provide unforgettable breaks with the highest standards of service and friendliness in a superb setting.

We are looking for individuals who are smart, reliable, enthusiastic, motivated and have excellent references.

Catering Staff, Chef's, Lifeguards, Instructors and many other positions
Contact: HR, Oasis Lakeland Forest Village, Temple Sowerby, Cumbria, CA10 2DW

PREPARATION

The preceding chapters on how to find a job and on training set out ways in which you can make yourself more attractive to potential employers. One of the best ways in which to prepare for a stint of working in tourism abroad is to work with groups of people locally whether tourists or locals. Relevant experience for guides and reps can be gained by volunteering to lead groups around a museum, factory, nature reserve or whatever interests you. Even organising a day-trip advertised in your local library, school, church, club or community centre will stand you in good stead. It could have some charitable value, such as taking a group of senior citizens on an outing or disabled children to the zoo. Contact the Volunteers Organiser of the County Council for ideas. If you are more interested in the catering side, it should not be too difficult to get experience waiting on tables or assisting in a kitchen in a local establishment.

More prolonged exposure to the world of tourism can best be gained by getting a summer job in a resort or campsite in your home country. The skills of serving the needs of tourists are the same wherever you work and a summer spent organising activities at a language camp for European teenagers, operating a ride at a local theme park or chambermaiding in a 4-star resort hotel can be invaluable. This will not only provide a chance to find out whether you will enjoy the working world of tourism and enhance your CV, but it may put you in touch with people who are well-informed on other possibilities in the field.

WHILE YOU'RE WAITING

After you have secured a job, there may be enough time to organise the practicalities of moving abroad and to prepare yourself in other ways. If you are going to a country which requires immigration procedures, you can start the visa procedures. In addition to deciding what to take and how to get to your destination, you should think about your tax position and health insurance, plus find out as much as you can about the situation in which you will find yourself.

Red Tape

Since most tourism staff are employed by a company in their home country, they do not generally require a work permit. For example a resort rep working a summer season with a giant tour operator like Thomson does not need a permit to work in Turkey, whereas someone who works for a local employer does need to consider the legality of their situation. If you do need a permit, your employer should help you to obtain one. Try to ensure that the company which has employed you fulfils its legal obligations. For further information about the red tape necessary for EU nationals working in another member state, see the beginning of the chapter *Europe*.

Outside the EU, legislation varies from country to country. Most governments want to encourage tourism and therefore give more latitude to tour operators than in other industries. Normally RSA guides travelling with a group do not need work authorisation for the various countries they pass through. Some countries require tour operators to book and pay for a local guide who is a national of the country, but this does not mean that the accompanying tour manager cannot remain with the group.

If you are working in tourism and lose your passport, the Passport Office in Petty France London will make special arrangements for you to get a replacement speedily.

Research for going abroad

After you have studied all the relevant literature from the tourist office and in the library, the best way to prepare yourself is to buy reliable guidebooks, maps and phrase book or dictionary. Good English language books about the history and culture of a country are almost never for sale in souvenir shops, and good bookshops are seldom a feature of resorts.

Browsing in the travel section of any bookshop will introduce you to the range of travel guides. If in London, try to visit the famous map and travel book shop Stanford,s Ltd in Covent Garden (12-14 Long Acre, WC2E 9LP) which also sends maps by post. Swiss Hallweg maps (now published by Collins) are known as the 'tour guide's friend' as they are very helpful for tour planning.

There are dozens of travel specialists throughout North America, including the mail order company Travelers Bookstore (22 W 52nd St, New York, NY 10019; 800-755-8728). Blue Guides and Michelin green guides can seldom be faulted for historical accuracy and comprehensiveness. Some of the worst guide books are those spawned by a TV travel series. The celebrity presenter thinks he or she knows it all, even though they have been cosseted from reality by the local tourist board. One of the best examples of this kind of book was a guide to Turkey written by an American who had spent a total of 36 hours in the country. Guidebooks written for the independent backpacker are seldom much use to your average package tourist. Sometimes the dullest looking guidebooks are the best choice since they deliver the facts and you can supply the interesting gloss.

Local adult education institutes often run short courses on history, history of art, social history, archaeology, etc. which are worthwhile investments if you know which country you intend to work in. However no investment in learning is ever a waste. At the least you will learn how to do research quickly, and what to look for. Any course on European history can provide background information for talks from Moscow to Madrid and all places in between. The Hapsburgs went everywhere, as did the Medici, the Frescobaldi, the Hanseatic League – and the British. It can all be woven together into a fascinating pattern.

After you have done some homework, try to make contact with a previous employee of the tour operator which has hired you. Your employer should be willing to pass on a couple of addresses and may even pay for the calls. Past guides/reps will be in a position to pass on priceless minutiae like how to handle a prickly hotel owner on the route or recommending pubs, cafés, etc. which the punters seem to prefer. If you have an acquaintance who has visited or lived in the resort you are heading for, pump them for all the memories they can muster.

Tour managers will be given a list by their company of contacts along the route: managers of hotels, restaurants, sites of interest, etc. One useful preparatory exercise is to call these people even before the tour begins. Although confirmation should have been sought by the tour operator, a friendly call can only serve to improve relations with the service-providers and, on a first trip, help to lessen the feeling of casting yourself into the great unknown.

Study very carefully all the literature the company has sent you. Try to imagine problems which could arise which have not been covered in their training or briefings. What is your emergency fund and for what uses is it authorised? Find out if there is a budget for inessential extras, such as prizes for little competitions you might hold or stationery for making signs.

Don't forget to reread the brochure from the client's point of view, and be prepared to do your best to deliver whatever is promised. If it says 'all our staff have an in-depth knowledge of local amenities', this is what the clients have every right to expect, even if you have never been on that route or to that beach resort before.

Contracts

This is the point at which a formal contract or at least a memorandum of agreement should be drawn up. Any employer who is reluctant to provide something in writing is definitely suspect.

The following items should be covered in most contracts or at least given some consideration.:
– company name and address of employer
– details of the duties
– how much time off you will receive, provided there are no emergencies
– amount of pay and how it will be paid (i.e. into bank account in home country or as expense allowance in local currency). Is any held back against the return of the uniform or the completion of your contract?
– length of the contract and whether it is renewable
– type of accommodation. Will you have to share with another staff member? Are utilities included?
– tax liability
– provisions for health care and sick pay. What are you insured for under the company policy?
– payment of pension or national insurance contributions
– bonus and commission rates, if applicable
– details of the travel arrangements to and from your destination
– any probationary period and length of notice on either side
– penalties for breaking the contract and circumstances under which the penalties would be waived (e.g. extreme family illness, etc.)

Other issues have particular relevance to guides and reps. In addition to the routine points covered in most contracts, you can expect to see the following:
– emergency contact number/s. These are vitally important and you should try to insist on having them at the time the contract is signed. Any employer who does not provide an emergency contact will not be a good employer
– to whom are you expected to report
– return travel. Make sure you do not find yourself stranded at the end of the season (when airplanes are usually full) with no return ticket.
– commission rates (usually paid on a sliding scale, explained in the Reps section in the Introductory chapter).
– luggage allowance to/from resort (which is usually not a problem if you are flying on a company charter)
– float or advance payment for materials you will be told to buy
– conditions under which a company can move you from one resort or country to another
– the company insurance (may not cover individual items of high value).

Freelancers who lead a succession of tours quite often do not have a contract. It

is more usual to be sent a letter asking which dates and tours you would like to take, and this is often on a gentleman's agreement. But even if you are working only for a few days at a time, you should try to have in writing the routine points covered in most contracts (although freelance guides are usually expected to carry their own health insurance) plus the following:
- emergency contact number/s
- detailed itinerary including list of pick-up points and name of coach company (if applicable)
- positioning fee/wage (if you are expected to arrive at departure point the night before)
- return travel
- details of accommodation (it is important that both guide and driver have a private bath)
- what (if anything) you are insured for under the company policy
- float for expenses and what this covers

Health and Insurance

No matter what country you are heading for, you should obtain the Department of Health leaflet T6 *Health Advice for Travellers Anywhere in the World*. This leaflet should be available from any post office or you can request a free copy on the Health Literature Line 0800 555777.

If you are a national of the European Economic Area (most of Europe except Switzerland), and will be working in another EEA country, you will be covered by the European Community Social Security Regulations. Advice and the leaflet SA29 *Your Social Security Insurance, Benefits and Health Care Rights in the European Community and in Iceland, Liechtenstein and Norway* may be obtained free of charge from the Department of Social Security, International Services, Newcastle upon Tyne NE98 1YX.

The leaflet T6 contains an application form to obtain form E-111 (called the 'E-one-eleven') which is a certificate of entitlement to medical treatment within Europe. All EEA nationals going to another EEA country on holiday should apply for an E11 from the post office. If working abroad and your posting is 12 months or less, you need the E128 form, which is available from the DSS. They can also give advice if you will be working for a foreign employer.

But the E-111 covers only the basics and does not necessarily extend to non-emergency treatment, dental treatment, prescription drugs, etc. Furthermore it is not always treated as a sacred document by health officials. Resorts clinics in Greece and Spain often do not recognise it, and if they did, their fees would be considerably higher than what can be recouped on an E-111. It usually doesn't cover extras such as ambulance transport. One rep was very relieved he happened to be carrying his credit card when a stroppy Greek ambulance driver refused to convey an injured client until it was made clear how payment would be made.

Reputable employers will obtain health insurance for you. Read the fine print to find out whether you are covered both on and off the job. Most tourism professionals top up the company policy, making sure that they are covered for loss of personal effects, loss of earnings, public liability and repatriation insurance. Two brokers who have been recommended are:

Insurex-Expotel, Pantiles House, 2 Nevill St, Tunbridge Wells, Kent TN2 5TT (01892 511500).
Coaching Insurance Consultants, 11 Harvest Bank, Hyde Heath, Amersham, Bucks. HP6 5RD (01494 783595).

Specialist expatriate policies might be worth investigating. Americans could contact American Citizens Abroad (5B Liotard, Geneva 12, Switzerland) which offers various plans with reasonable rates for a one-year expat policy for Europe or worldwide excluding North America. Read the small print of your household insurance policy to see if you are covered if you are away for any length of time.

If your destination is tropical, consult an up-to-date book on health such as *Travellers' Health: How to Stay Healthy Abroad* by Richard Dawood (OUP, £8.99). Every year 10-12 Britons die from malaria after returning home (even some who have been swallowing their pills) so it is essential to be well-informed. British Airways has set up a network of 36 travel clinics which will give advice on specific destinations, administer jabs and prescribe the correct anti-malarials, etc.; ring 01276 685 040 for your nearest one. The Medical Advisory Service for Travellers Abroad (MASTA, Keppel St, London WC1E 7HT) publishes health briefs at varying prices depending on the depth of customised detail required. You can ring their interactive Travellers' Health Line on 0891 224100 with your destinations and they will send you a basic health brief by return of post, for the price of the telephone call (about £2-3). If a more personalised Health Brief is required, travellers should telephone 01705 553933 to find out the cost, which ranges from £10 to £32.50.

Some countries like Russia have introduced HIV antibody testing for long-stay foreigners and the certificate may be required to obtain a work or residence visa. If you are going to be spending a lot of time in countries where blood screening is not reliable, you should consider carrying a sterile medical kit including syringes, also sold by MASTA. If you are employed by a company at home, they should pay for your medical expenses.

Americans should obtain the booklet 'Health Information for International Travel' which is distributed free and includes information on vaccination requirements, malaria prophylactics, etc. The US Public Health Service updates it annually; to obtain a copy of this document (number 017 023 00 19 73), send $25.00 to the Superintendent of Documents, US Government Printing Office, Washington, DC 20402-9325. For general travel health advice, phone the Center for Disease Control & Prevention Hotline in Atlanta on 404-332-4559.

National Contributions and Social Security

If you fail to make National Insurance contributions while you are abroad, you will forfeit entitlement to benefits on your return. You can decide to pay voluntary contributions at regular intervals or in a lump sum in order to retain your rights to certain benefits. Unfortunately this entitles you only to a retirement/widow's pension, not to incapacity benefit or jobseekers allowance. Since tourism employees abroad are seldom in a pension scheme, it is usually worth maintaining your right to a state pension.

Tax

Some companies may tell you that your earnings are not high enough to be of interest to the Inland Revenue. Nonsense. Tax computers talk to each other all over the world and, sooner or later, any wages will have to be declared. Calculating your liability to tax when working outside your home country is notoriously complicated so, if possible, check your position with an accountant. Also consult the Inland Revenue information leaflets IR20 'Residents' and Non-Residents' Tax Liability' and IR58 'Going to Work Abroad'. Everything depends on whether you fall into the category of 'resident', 'ordinarily resident' or 'domiciled'. Most people working in tourism count as domiciled in the UK since it is assumed that they will ultimately return. If you are working abroad and are absent from the UK for a complete 365 days, you are classified as non-resident and should be eligible for a 'foreign earnings deduction' of 100%. There is a possibility of exemption also if you work abroad for at least 365 days, of which no more than 62 days (i.e. one-sixth of the year) are spent in the UK. Don't make the mistake of thinking that because no one looks at your passport Inland Revenue won't know if you have stayed longer than the permitted number of days in Britain. Declan had to return to England when his mother was taken ill and nearly made the mistake of disrupting his tax status. Instead he beat a hasty retreat across the Channel.

Note that people working offshore for cruise lines and even ferry companies may be eligible for claiming tax rebates. Keep detailed records of sailing times, and have these authenticated by the purser.

If you have been working for a foreign employer in a country which has a double taxation agreement with your own country, there should be no problem. See Inland Revenue leaflet IR6 'Double Taxation Relief'. But not all countries have such an agreement and it is not inconceivable that you will be taxed twice. Keep all receipts and financial documents in case you need to plead your case at a later date.

Don't forget that if you have a car, you can get a rebate on your Road Fund Licence for every calendar month it is off the road. Ask for Form V14 from the post office. However you must retax your car before taking it back on the road.

Travel

Anyone who is hired by a tour operator in their own country should have the travel to their place of work arranged and paid for by the company. But for those who are heading off to conduct a speculative job hunt, the following advice may be of use.

London is the cheap airfare capital of the world and the number of agencies offering discount flights to all corners of the world is seemingly endless. To narrow the choice you should find a travel agency which specialises in your destination. The Air Travel Advisory Bureau (0171-636 5000) will give you the phone numbers of a few discount travel agents appropriate to your needs. But because not all travel agencies are registered with them, this does not guarantee the best fare.

Consult specialist travel magazines such as TNT (which is free in London) plus *Time Out* and the Saturday editions of *The Times*, *Independent* and *Guardian*. By ringing a few of the agencies with advertisements you will soon discover which airlines offer the cheapest service. Student travel offices such as STA (40 Bernard Street, London WC1A 1LJ; 0171-361 6161 for Europe and 361 6262 worldwide) and Campus Travel (52 Grosvenor Gardens, London SW1W 0AG; Europe 0171-731 3402, N. America 0171-730 2101, Worldwide line 0171 730 8111; Website www.campustravel.co.uk/)are always worth consulting, though their popularity often means that there are queues both in their main London offices and on their telephones. Both have offices throughout the UK. Trailfinders Ltd. (42-50 Earls Court Road, London W8 6FT; 0171-937 5400/938 3366) are well-established and efficient and have other offices in Kensington, Bristol, Glasgow, Manchester and Birmingham.

In North America, the best newspapers to scour for cheap flights are the *New York Times* (the Sunday edition has a section devoted to travel with cut-price flights advertised), the *LA Times*, *San Francisco Chronicle-Examiner*, *Miami Herald*, *Dallas Morning News*, *Chicago Sun Times*, the *Boston Globe* and the Canadian *Globe & Mail*. Recommended agencies include Council Travel Services (part of the Council on International Educational Exchange) with branches in most major university towns, and STA Travel (1-800-925-4777). If your dates and even your destinations are flexible, contact *Whole Earth Travel* which operates a service called Airhitch (2641 Broadway, Third Floor, New York, NY 10025; 212 864 2000) which are repeatedly recommended as offering the best fares from New York. Airhitch also has offices in Paris, Bonn, Amsterdam and Prague. A similar company has been set up called Air-Tech (584 Broadway, Suite 1007, New York, NY 10012; 212-219-7000). Travel CUTS in Canada sell discount fares and have offices overseas.

Throughout North America, many churches run tours for their congregations to Europe, usually led by the pastor or priest. It might be worthwhile offering your services for free to help with the tour in return for an open air ticket to Europe. Robert from Vancouver contacted his local church to see if they needed anyone to assist the pastor in the church's annual tour of religious sites in Europe. They did, and in return for a promise to work as an unpaid tour leader assisting the thoroughly competent pastor, he received a free air ticket. Robert said he worked a very long day during the tour but valued the experience.

Airlines offer generous group discounts which can work out to one free ticket in every 20 sold, though it may not be as easy to benefit from this as it sounds, as Matt Tomlinson discovered:

> *We thought we had found an interesting angle on getting a free airfare. We were hoping to sell a cheapie flight of £690 to like-minded souls who wanted to join us in New Zealand for the ski season. It didn't really work. Airlines force you to commit really early and as well our marketing sucked. If anything had gone wrong, we would have been severely in the legal mire. However I can still recommend it if you have a solid group who want to go.*

WHAT TO TAKE

Consider taking a language course with you, since tapes and books (including a good dictionary) may not be available locally and your enthusiasm to learn may be rekindled once you are on location. Of course it is much easier to learn the language once you are on-site.

Take some money for your personal use to see you through the first few weeks. Having your own credit card can also be reassuring. Even those who know enough not to expect any expatriate perks are sometimes shocked by the expenses they incur living abroad, especially before they ascertain the cheapest places to shop.

The research you do on your destination will no doubt include its climate, which will help you choose an appropriate range of clothing to take. It is worthwhile taking warm clothing for the beginning and end of the season, including a raincoat. It is essential that the clothes that you take are simple to maintain, colour-coordinated and reasonably smart. Take comfortable shoes to go with your uniform (e.g. dark-coloured court shoes for women) plus another casual pair (e.g. espadrilles, deck shoes). You may be walking over cobblestones, across all sorts of uncomfortable surfaces and standing for hours. Shoes should be well broken into without looking broken down.

Looking neat, and in some cases smart, is important in most jobs so you must choose your clothing with this in mind. Blue jeans are rarely acceptable, apart from on wild and woolly overland trips. Several smart outfits are a great morale booster and also impress the local restaurateurs and other service providers whose hearts sink when confronted with a sea of T-shirts and flip flops. Bear in mind that resort reps do not really earn a high enough salary to go out and buy expensive new jackets or shoes after arrival, so it is necessary to take these with you. Be sure to take lightweight long-sleeved garments and a sun hat to guard against both sunburn and mosquitoes. If you are working in a Moslem country like Turkey or Tunisia, modest dress is essential. You also want to be able to set a good example to your clients who must be encouraged not to offend against local sensibilities.

To keep your clothes neat, it may be worth taking a travel iron (making sure you have any appropriate adaptors). On the other hand, many reps find that time is too short for this chore and prefer to use the 'courier's iron' (even if it does ride roughshod over considerations of conservation), i.e. by hanging clothes up in the bathroom, turning the shower to scalding, and shutting the door for ten minutes (making sure there is time for the clothes to dry). Skirts in particular get very creased so it is an idea to take a tip from models and ask for one size too large since it won't crease as easily.

Here is a list of items to consider packing which most often crop up in the recommendations of experienced workers in the tourism industry. Some may seem more relevant for certain areas of work but all are useful to consider taking. Keep receipts in case you are entitled to reimbursement from your company at a later date:

- passport photos for permits are essential.
- for reps, the employer will provide you with a reps' handbook and ancillary supplies (bag, clipboard, extra copies of the company brochure, possibly a uniform) which will have to be collected from the company offices.
- calculator
- portable typewriter (if you happen to have one already). Reps will normally have access to a typewriter or word processor in the resort office, but it can be much more convenient to do your paperwork in your own room. You keep your report in the machine and tap out the day's events on your return each evening, popping it in the post at the end of the week.
- travel alarm clock for those times when you have to meet a group at the airport at 5am
- emergency rations (e.g. muesli bars) in case you have to miss a meal sorting out a problem
- guide books, maps, dictionaries (see above)
- large notebook for jotting down tips for subsequent trips, noting client requests to which you will have to return and generally keeping track
- supply of greeting cards for when you find out that a client's birthday or anniversary is coming up
- ideas for games and quizzes to fill the hours you may have to spend on a coach, plus perhaps a few novelties to be given away as prizes
- one optional idea is a set of song sheets
- coloured pens and markers, cardboard, and assorted stationery like Blutack, stick-on labels, stapler, ruler, scissors and even Letraset if your handwriting is execrable. These should be covered by a float from the company
- basic medications like aspirin, sunscreen and lip salve for your personal use only and pre-moistened towels (like the ones given out by airlines) to refresh you when you're feeling hot and sticky

It is also not a bad idea to take any favourite toiletries to avoid having to pay inflated resort prices, though this is more worthwhile in some countries (like Portugal) than others (like Greece). If possible find out from recent company employees or anyone else what items, such as certain items of clothing or toiletries, are in short supply or very expensive, or perhaps if you would need a torch if lighting is unreliable.

If you can't live without marmite or a special brand of tea, take a supply, though it is more fun to explore the cuisine of your new country.

Staying in Touch

Consider taking out a subscription to the *Guardian Weekly* (164 Deansgate, Manchester M60 2RR) to guarantee access to world news, though you might prefer to wait until you arrive to see what newspapers are available. A one-year subscription costs £58 in Europe and N. America, £66 elsewhere. One resort rep (Sandie) offers a tip: make friends with the incoming flight crew who can save the passengers' newspapers, including the Sunday supplements.

Hotel radios never seem to pick up the stations you want to hear. Access to the World Service can be a godsend. You will need a good short-wave radio with several bands powerful enough to pick up the BBC. 'Dedicated' short-wave receivers which are about the size of a paperback start at £85. For advice on reception of BBC broadcasts in Europe, contact BBC Engineering Information, White City, 201 Wood Lane, London W12 7TS (0345-010313). Alternative English language broadcasting organisations are Voice of America (PO Box 23333, Washington, DC 20026; 202 619 4700), Radio Canada International (PO Box 6000, Montreal, Canada H3C 3A8; 514 597 7500) and Swiss Radio International (Jiacomette Stre. Bern 15, Switzerland; 31 35 09 222), all of which will send information about their services.

Bibliography

Career guides and travel books which may be of interest include the following:

The AA Truckers Atlas of Britain, (AA Publishing; 01256 491524). For all those minor roads where you do not know if bridges are high enough for a coach. ISBN 0749513071.

ABTA's Guide to Working in Travel, (£5.99). Call 01483 727321. ISBN 1900140497.

Airline Passenger's Guerrilla Handbook, by George Albert Brown (Blakes, UK, $14.95 or £8.95 in travellers' bookshops). Inside information about what goes on and how to get better treatment for groups. Also an amusing read.

Blue Guides (A & C Black). Available to most European countries (60 titles in all). All are written to a very high standard with accurate and helpful information, and heavily relied on by tour managers.

Careerscope Magazine, phone 01276 21188 and ask for their back numbers with tourism career information.

Careers in the Travel Industry, (Kogan Page, £8.99). Overview of the main career opportunities in hotels and catering, travel agencies, and as tour managers, guides, representatives or on board cruise liners. The same publisher also produces *Careers in Catering & Hotel Management*.

Coach Monthly Magazine,(01454 313128). Full of useful information for coach touring. Subscribers can also obtain specailised insurance;

Companion Series volumes are written by authors living in the country and give a good flavour of local life.

Dictionary for the Tourism Industry, (ISBN 0952750902; £9.99). Gives definitions of all those initials, jargon, industry-specific words, etc. Also has a very useful section on 'fillers' to make your talks more interesting.

English – Tourism English Dictionary, Has a collection of explanations of sayings and words used in the industry. Call 0171-244 7301/fax 0171-835 0761. ISBN 0952750902.

Hallweg, maps for Europe. Most guides will say these are probably the best and they are now under the UK umbrella company Bartholomew.

Intermediate Textbook for GNVQ Leisure and Tourism, (Addison Wesley Longman, £14.99). Helpful for anyone wanting a basic guide to the tourism industry and working at events. ISBN 058227841. .

Shell Guides (Penguin Group) have series of helpful guides for the public and professionals, clearly laid out with explanatory drawings and photos.

The Traveller's Handbook edited by Caroline Brandenburger (WEXAS; 0171 589 3315; £14.99 or £7.50 to WEXAS club members). 900 page reference book written by many expert contributors with useful appendices.

Travel & Hospitality Career Directory by Bradley Morgan, 1993 (Visible Ink Press, 835 Penobscot Building, Detroit, MI 48226-4094, USA). $17.95. Mostly for Americans who want to work in the US.

Working in Conservation, (UK Institute for Conservation; 0171 6203371/01274 391056). Free careers factsheet *Jobs for People Who Love Travel* by R & C Krannich, 1993 (Impact Publications, 9104-N Manassas Drive, Manassas Park, VA 22111, USA). $12.95. General introduction and now somewhat outdated.

Working in Tourism (Careers & Occupational Information Centre, Department of Employment; 0181 957 5030; £5.00). Also publish booklets in related fields such as *Working in Hotels and Catering* and *Working in Leisure*.

Worksaver Publications, a series of factual handbooks on working in the industry; conferences and events, reps, cruise ships, tour personnel, hotels and hospitality, airlines and airports. Each one costs £15 plus postage. Call 01670 789512 for details.

Work Your Way Around the World and *Directory of Summer Jobs Abroad*, (Vacation-Work Publications). Contact addresses and practical advice for people wanting holiday jobs or casual work in the tourist industry (among many others).

PROBLEMS

Travel advertising shows a glowing picture of attractive people walking on deserted moonlit beaches and sipping cocktails in a pavement café. But in the real world, delays, traffic jams, crowds and jet lag mar the happy picture. If travel was easy, no one would book a package holiday nor would tour companies employ a battalion of people to sort out problems.

As we saw in the introductory section about Rewards and Risks, the scope for disaster when trying to coordinate the requirements of groups of people on holiday and service providers wanting to make a profit is enormous. This chapter takes a closer look not just at the array of problems which can arise, but in concrete ways to avoid or solve them.

It may be unfair, but in many jobs you are the one who will have to solve problems, sometimes serious problems, on your own. The client who has been mauled by a wild animal on safari or who has had her passport stolen while wandering around Rome cannot wait for the rep to ask for instructions from head office. Action must be speedy and decisive. Remember that many problems have more than one solution. What is needed is someone in authority to start solving them in a confident manner. If people trust you, they will leave you to get on with the work, relieved that it is no longer their own responsibility.

Punters get robbed, get bitten by snakes, get sick, some even die.

Most reps are given a one-week induction in their resort before the season gets underway, in which the standard procedures for dealing with illness are covered, including a visit to the nearest clinic or hospital. You will always have telephone access to a helpline, for example the one operated by the insurance company Europ Assistance. Rob Williams worked for them as a controller and reports that some of his time was spent trying to calm down a badly shaken rep in charge of a sick or injured client by talking him or her through the necessary steps. In more than one case he had to remind the rep where the nearest hospital was.

PROBLEMS AT WORK

Make sure your company allows you adequate time off. Undoubtedly tour companies and hotels have a tendency to exploit staff, especially if they are deemed to be working illegally in a resort. Knowing that you have no rights and therefore can't complain about working long hours for slave wages, they will have you working a 16 hour day seven days a week and your health and spirits will suffer. Most people working in tourism spend so much time looking after customers that they tend to neglect themselves. Try to avoid this at all costs.

Accommodation is at a premium in resorts, and often staff are assigned to fairly undesirable rooms, often to be shared. Accommodation provided for staff on cruise liners probably hits an all-time low: cramped, noisy and airless. Anyone who thinks it is pedantic to worry about accommodation if the group are staying in hostels, etc. hasn't tried to find a telephone on a university campus in an emergency, or joined the early morning bathroom queue when in a hurry to supervise the loading of luggage. And your driver certainly can't do a good job if he has had to share a room with people who keep him awake.

Lost Luggage

Luggage is usually lost (or 'misrouted') by an airline and their ground staff will handle the PIR (Property Incident Report). It is the airline's responsibility to return the luggage to their passenger, and this almost always happens within 48 hours. In the meantime they may offer a necessities bag or compensation in cash. It is very rare for luggage to go missing for good.

On tour it is the tour manager's responsibility to ensure that all luggage is accounted for and loaded into the coach each day. Some lazy tour managers leave this to the driver, but if anything goes wrong it is up to you, as John Boon recounts. He had to represent his company in court when they were sued by one of their tour managers. One day a suitcase had been left behind and the tour manager had had to hire a taxi to pick up and deliver the luggage to the next stop many miles away. The company refused to pay, claiming that it was the tour manager's responsibility, and she took out a court summons claiming for the cost. After allowing both sides to put their cases, the judge concluded that tour managers are responsible for luggage throughout a tour and that this particular tour manager had not shown due care and attention, so the case was dismissed. The moral is to count, count and count luggage again and again.

There is always a chance that the tour manager's own luggage will go astray. It is a good idea to carry two small suitcases rather than one large one, so that you can have back-up clothes and toiletries in both. Smart suitcases are much more likely to be picked on by baggage handlers, especially in third world airports. Hard suitcases have the advantage that they cannot so easily be slit open but are of course heavier.

Delays

Aircraft delays are an every day occurence, especially in high season. Until passengers are checked in they are your company's (i.e. your) responsibility. After check-in it is up to the airline to pay for meals, overnight accommodation, etc. So pray when you arrive at the airport that the airline checks your group in before they realise there is going to be a problem. If your group is going to be late for a connecting flight or ferry, phone the carrier, explain the situation and they will tell you whether they will be able to hold the flight or ferry for you. It happens more often than you think. If you have to fly with your group, you are officially off-duty, so always ask for a seat away from the group.

Coaches cost up to a quarter of a million pounds new, and a coach operator must keep the wheels turning to make a profit. This means that they work to tight schedules, and any delay can have a domino effect. If the promised transfer coach has not turned up on time, encourage the clients to do their banking which will happily waste some time. If the driver is surly, he has probably been up since dawn, had to clean the coach before taking it out and may not have had breakfast. Like babies, most drivers work better after something to eat and drink. If a coach breaks down, it is the coach company's responsibility to provide a replacement, although you obviously do what you can to help the driver, which includes making phone calls if they don't speak the language. In alpine countries, snow can fall unexpectedly at any time of the year and if the NO COACHES sign is up, it means exactly what it says. Any driver who ignores the sign is subject to an automatic fine.

Problems with Clients

Everyone worries about the 'three losses': lost passport, lost luggage and lost passengers. If someone loses their passport you take them to their nearest consulate where a duplicate will be issued. Sometimes this is very easy and the whole process takes no more than an hour. Sometimes it can involve a journey from one end of a country to another. The rule is that you are as helpful as possible, but must remember that your first priority is to the majority of your group, even if it means you have to leave clients behind to sort things out for themselves.

The European Union was supposed to make travel simpler but in some ways it has become more complicated, for example with respect to visa requirements for non-EU nationals; check your passenger list and make the appropriate enquiries. Then when the passengers join, check their passport. If the necessary visa is missing, your company will probably refuse to accept them. Now that most internal borders in Europe have disappeared, it is rarely possible to buy a visa at the border.

Often someone in your care has an accident or gets sick; and even if they are not actually ill they think they are. One tip is to ban oranges on coaches since they commonly react badly with stomach acid and make some travellers sick. Drink cans are another problem. A coach driver was killed when a can rolled down the coach and stuck under the brake pedal. If people bring cans onto the coach, ask them to ensure that they put them into a rubbish bin. Clients often make the excuse of a gammy leg to lay claim to a front seat. They should be seated in the second row because, if the driver has to slam on the brakes, their gammy leg won't allow them to brace themselves and they will end up through the windscreen.

If you have any disabled clients, contact the police before arriving at each major stop and request permission to drop passengers off in the centre of town rather than the coach park.

Apart from health problems, the most common aggravation for tourists (and therefore reps, etc.) usually involve robbery. You must not only offer practical advice about what documents the victim will need to fill out, but you must offer constant reassurance that the loss of their camera or money is not the end of the world.

As noted in the section on Tour Personnel, certain kinds of punter can be a thorn in the sides of their manager, guide or even waiter. There is always a dizzy tour member who lingers too long in the souvenir shop or the rest stop toilet and cannot be found when the coach is ready to depart. Or perhaps they repeatedly leave their spectacles behind in the café and their passport under the pillow in their hotel room.

Persuading a large group to keep to the schedule may be problematic.

There is usually a compulsive whinger who complains about every little delay or deviation from the printed brochure. Fussy eaters are a real nuisance. Tom, who worked for Fourways, claims that Australians can be even more unadventurous eaters than Britons:

> *Italian cooking really seemed to set off the grumbles. I personally like Italian food so I got fed up with all the complaints about 'greasy' meals. Taking the mike one day, I proceeded to talk about how beautiful Italian women are, all because the olive oil in their diet gives them beautiful skin. As a result, all the women lapped up the food and told their husbands not to complain.*

What pleases one group will not work with another. Sandra Miller of Wholesale Tours tells the story of an American group in London who asked her why she didn't wear miniskirts. Promising to wear one on their last day, she went to the airport wearing boots, short skirt and lots of make-up, and was the focus of so many photos they almost missed the plane:

> *Then there was a tannoy announcement for me to phone my office. My boss asked me to bring a group back to London because their own tour manager was ill. The group leader's name was the Reverend Brown, and his religious group from the Bible Belt took one look at me in my gear and wanted to return home on the next plane. Giving my introduction on the way from Heathrow, the only time I captured their attention was passing Earls Court where I pointed out that this was where the Evangelist Billy Graham had recently preached. Dark mutterings along the line of 'Pity he didn't save her' were heard.*

There is usually a know-it-all who makes it his or her business to catch the tour guide out on minor mistakes. Trainee guides are always worried when they see a client arriving on the coach with their own guide book. Seeing someone flick though a guide book while you are delivering your speil can be nerve-wracking. One trick is to stroll over and say something like, 'I see you have guidebook X. They have some interesting ideas on dates, and I find most of their information is accurate'. After a chat about differences in guide book facts, you hope that they leave their book behind for the next excursion. Then there are the guide books that mention the delightful little hotels that are so much cheaper than the ones your group uses. Try to drive past some of the uglier examples, pointing them out in a friendly manner 'and that hotel is mentioned in X's guidebook' to stop comparisons.

Personality clashes are almost inevitable either between you and a client or among members of the group. When Mike Whitby was an Oxford undergraduate, he was taken on as a volunteer guide by a rather eccentric but charming classics professor who ran educational summer cruises around the Aegean on a somewhat downtrodden but adequate vessel. One of the paying clients (from Texas) was obviously not used to the prevailing standards of comfort and complained rudely and vociferously. With a temper inclined to the fiery and a zeal for defending his boss, our rugby-playing student picked up Sam the Texan and forcibly removed him from the boat. Professor Winspeare decided the only course was to leave both of them on the nearest island and the tour continued without either of them.

A high degree of tact, patience and charm is necessary when dealing with awkward customers who may be (wittingly or otherwise) offending against local customs or even breaking local laws. Drunkenness is a perennial problem. Lager louts can often be sensible when sober so that is the time to explain to him and his mates that although the local men drink copious amounts, they never become incapacitated with alcohol and they should try to follow local custom. Then just hope that the troublecauser's mates whisk him away before things get out of hand; it's worth a try.

Disagreeable and boring clients must be gently but effectively controlled so that there is no danger of their spoiling other clients' holidays. A windbag can be thanked for his contribution and told to share his anecdotes with his fellow passengers later at lunch. One way to win complainers over is by joining them and showing (feigning?) an interest in their experiences. On a long trip, there is no escape. The only chance of surviving all this is to hear the occasional compliment from a tour member who has had the time of their life just because of you. Experienced tour managers learn how to minimise negative behaviour, though very very occasionally the individual is so disruptive or even violent that the police have to become involved, which is very stressful.

But usually the situation does not deteriorate to such a level, and your anxiety may focus more on whether or not your jokes are getting a little stale on the umpteenth retelling.

Problems with Colleagues

Colleagues can be extremely helpful. The network of people doing the same job as you will pass on information, warn of changes, etc. Do not try to buck the system until you know what you are doing. There is a pecking order, and you will almost always benefit by asking advice from more experienced people in the field. Generally they will go out of their way to be helpful. Just remember this when it is your turn to help out a newcomer.

Occasionally you will come across someone who is unhelpful, probably because they are insecure in their job. There was a new tour manager on a tour of Ireland who thought she knew it all, so didn't need to ask advice. She proceeded to cause chaos by putting her people into the glass factory before they visited the coffee shop, and later when she arrived at the lunch stop at the same time as several other coaches. A driver kindly tried to tell her the form but she decided to ignore him. His revenge was sweet: he joined her group of Americans at lunch (something drivers almost never do) and casually mentioned how useful air-conditioning was in this spell of hot weather. He left an angry mob demanding to know from the troublesome tour manager why their coach lacked the up-to-date equipment the others had. The bumptious tour manager was never seen again.

Most drivers are stalwart rocks with broad shoulders, an ability to see the funny side of the worst problems and a colleague who supports you through thick and thin. Meals are eaten with the driver, not the group (to avoid jealousy). In the unlikely event of guides and drivers not getting on, never row in front of the passengers. Both end up with egg on their faces... and no tips.

Problems with Employers

With the EC Directive and increasing recognition of associations such as ABTA, the tourist industry is better regulated than it was, though standards of performance are still very uneven. There is nothing much in the way of employee associations or unions to protect workers' rights. So it is important to have a detailed contract, to protect yourself against exploitation.

Although a tour company should have ironed out any problems in the itinerary ahead of time, the arrangements do often go wrong (the longer the tour, the more scope for hiccoughs) and it is essential that the tour manager continually check and confirm reservations. Herding a group of holidaymakers into a roadside restaurant which is not expecting you or waiting for a coach which does not show up are unpleasantly commonplace experiences for many managers. You must have access to some alternatives in these cases, and make sure they don't happen the next time round.

Freelance guides should insist on being paid for one tour before starting another. Cowboy tour companies have been known to weasel out of giving their reps and guides an adequate float before they set off with their groups. When the tour operator Court Line collapsed, a team of reps and guides were told by the receiver that, although they had paid for some of the clients' expenses (luggage handling, etc.) out of their own pockets, they were not preferred creditors and would probably never get their money back. One rep had paid over £400 of her own money on behalf of the company.

Inadequate supervision or a muddled line of command are frequently cited. You must know ahead of time to whom you report and how often. It is not unknown for a rep to arrive in a resort and find that the ground handler's girlfriend has put herself in charge and you don't know where you stand.

Some countries require tour operators to book and pay for a local guide who is a national of the country. In some ways, this may make the job of the accompanying manager easier. But if the local person does not grasp what your group wants or expects, problems can occur. Officially you must defer to the local guide; unofficially you have to act as mediator.

Student Trips

Problems crop up when unofficial tour leaders, for example teachers accompanying a school trip, shift the burden of responsibility onto the tour manager. For example

Marie Bayliss was booked to work as a tour manager for a group of teenage students going to Belgium for an Easter holiday. After a day of hard work guiding the group around Bruges, Marie booked them into their hotel in Ostend and went to bed. At 3am she was awakened by one of the students who had a stomach ache and couldn't find a teacher. Nor could Marie. After calling the doctor and then making sure the girl was asleep, Marie waited up for the teacher-chaperones who came in at 5am from a disco crawl. She told them in no uncertain terms that they had been sent by the parents to look after their children and were getting a free trip on this understanding. It was her job to look after tour planning, theirs to be *in loco parentis* and around to attend to the children's needs.

Valerie, another experienced tour manager, had a different problem. She found her group of American students delightful but typically naïve. In Rome one night she was woken at midnight by a frantic teacher knocking at her door. Calming the teacher down, she discovered that three girls had decided to live it up by ordering a bottle of whisky from room service. When the room waiter arrived, the girls were dressed in short nighties and naturally the red-blooded Italian waiter thought all his fantasies had come true. As soon as he made his first overture, the girls panicked and screamed for their chaperone. Valerie deflected the teacher from her determination to see the waiter sacked, explaining that he may have been a tiny bit justified in making certain assumptions. She told the hotel manager to give the waiter time off to reflect until the girls had left the hotel. 'Phew. Did I earn my money that night. Being an agony aunt on one hand, telling the waiter not to be so stupid again and reassuring the manager that the girls were OK.' Sometimes the company manual is no use at all and you will have to rely on common sense.

Working in Hotels

If your only experience of hotels is as a guest, you may be in for a surprise when you go backstage. Even the most luxurious hotels have been known to have dirty, disorganised kitchens, inadequate laundering facilities and lousy (literally) staff quarters. It is quite possible that the waitress who smilingly emerges from the kitchen bearing your food has just been threatened and abused by the chef for not working quickly enough. It may have something to do with the heat generated by the ovens in large kitchens, the pride they take in their creations, or the pressures under which they work, but chefs have a terrible reputation for having volatile tempers. S. C. Firn describes the working atmosphere in a 'rather classy restaurant and bar' in Oberstdorf in Southern Germany near the Austrian border:

> I had to peel vegetables, wash dishes, prepare food, clean the kitchen and some-times serve food. Everything was done at a very fast pace, and was expected to be very professional. One German cook, aged 16, who didn't come up to stan-dard, was punched in the face three times by the owner. On another occasion the assistant chef had a container of hot carrots tipped over his head for having food sent back. During my three months there, all the other British workers left, apart from the chef, but were always replaced by more.

So if you consider yourself to be the sensitive fragile type, perhaps you should avoid hotel kitchens altogether.

On the other hand many people thrive on the animated atmosphere and on kitchen conviviality. Nick Langley, who also worked in a German kitchen loved the atmosphere. He maintains that once you're established you'll gain more respect by shouting back if unreasonable demands are made, but adds the proviso, 'but not at the powerful head cook, please!'. Heated tempers usually cool down after a couple of beers at the end of a shift.

The same complaints crop up again and again among people who have worked in hotels: long and unsociable hours (often 8am-10pm with a few hours off in the afternoon plus lots of weekend work), exploitative wages, inadequate accommodation and food, and unbearably hot working conditions exacerbated by having to wear a nylon uniform. A great deal depends on whether or not you are the type to rough it. The working atmosphere can vary a lot from hotel to hotel. If you are lucky enough to get a job in a small friendly family hotel, you will probably enjoy the work more than if you are just one in a large anonymous group of workers in a sterile and impersonal institution where you have little job security.

It can be very aggravating to be asked to do extra duties beyond the ones specified in your contract. It seems to be a common occurrence that hotel proprietors take for granted that you will do unpaid overtime, without time off in lieu at a later date. If a contract is being breached in this way, you should try your best to sort it out with the employer. If this fails don't hesitate to go to the appropriate employment authorities to lodge an official complaint. This has far more chance of success if you have a written contract to show the authorities.

Not all hotels are like this and many people emphasise the benefits which they have found in the experience of working in a hotel: excellent camaraderie and team spirit, the opportunity to learn a foreign language, and the ease with which wages can be saved, including the possibility of an end-of-season bonus. Although Kathryn Halliwell was forced to share a windowless room which had an intermittently working light and water streaming down the roof beams into constantly overflowing buckets, she still enjoyed her time working at a hotel in Corsica, simply because of the conviviality of her 'fellow sufferers'.

PROBLEMS OUTSIDE WORK

Culture Shock

Enjoying yourself won't be at all easy if you are suffering from culture shock. Shock implies something which happens suddenly, but cultural disorientation more often creeps up on you. Adrenalin usually sees you through the first few weeks as you find the novelty exhilarating and challenging. You will be amazed and charmed by the odd gestures the people use or the antiquated way that things work. As time goes on, practical irritations intrude and the constant misunderstanding caused by those charming gestures – such as a nod in Greece meaning 'no' or in Japan meaning 'yes, I understand, but don't agree' – and the inconvenience of those antiquated phone boxes and buses will begin to get on your nerves. Even if you are feeling depressed and disappointed, do not broadcast your feelings randomly, certainly not to the holidaymakers nor to the locals. Try to find a colleague or someone outside work – perhaps an understanding expat who has long passed through the phase of feeling hostility for the host country – with whom to let off steam.

The best way to avoid disappointment is to be well briefed beforehand. Gathering general information about the country and specific information about the job before arrival will obviate many of the negative feelings some tourism employees feel. If you are the type to build up high hopes and expectations of new situations, it is wise to try to dismantle these before leaving home. Have a realistic idea of the difficulties you might face and be open-minded about cultural differences. It may take time to settle into your surroundings but the local mannerisms which once caused frustration, might become charming and even make you feel at home.

Loneliness

When you are in resort miles away from home you can feel very lonely. Large tour operators try to place first-timers in major resorts where they will be working as part of a team. The job in the small resort on the other hand is given to someone who knows the country and will have enough friends to visit when they want to talk to someone other than a client. If you are really homesick, some companies have concessions for relatives to visit after a certain time, so take advantage of these. On tour you can be in the thick of a group, but alone. Here your coach driver is a friend, colleague, someone to joke and laugh with, who understands when you are tired and dispirited.

Creating a social life from scratch is difficult enough at any time, and so is even more difficult in an alien tongue and culture. However, you will probably find that many of your fellow reps and guides are lots of fun and able to offer practical help in your first few weeks (especially any who are bilingual). There may be a local support team most tourism workers never think of: the local English-speaking priest or vicar, the Consul, British Council (their library can be useful) and even English teachers. When you arrive in a resort make a point of searching them out and making friends before you need them. Bernadette Hayden from Holidayrama says she always makes a point of going to church on the first Sunday after she arrives to meet with the local community.

Whatever your hobby there will probably be one individual or even group locally who will welcome another enthusiast. Bridge breaks down barriers, bird watching, jazz or any number of sports can give you social contact and take you away from work when you feel like screaming. Often the local bookshop or post office can help. Or try the police who often know who does what locally.

Even if you don't have a hobby, an enquiry along the lines of 'I want to know about local stamps/flowers/history so I can tell my group' will find you instant friends longing to show off their knowledge. However much you feel frightened to leave the security of your working environment, make an effort to get out of your patch on your day off. Too much of the same place can make you very stale and this is a recipe for frustration and eventually disaster. It might even turn out that the idyllic village you discover on your day off has a rundown house which eventually you can convert to become a holiday villa. It happens.

Health and Hygiene

People in travel jobs which require frequent flying will develop their own ways to combat jet lag either by drinking gallons of water during the flight to avoid dehydration or using aromatherapy products (e.g. Danielle Ryman sells a special anti-jet lag combination in some duty-free outlets and in her store in the Park Lane Hotel, Piccadilly, London). Frequent flying and exposure to the sun is very hard on skin and many tourism personnel devote a great deal of time and money on skin protection. Some of the most often recommended products are Clarins' after-sun products (which contain an anti-mosquito preparation), moisturisers and fake tans. Hand cream is vital for men as well as women especially in the more rugged kinds of tour. Boots make a range of non-perfumed products though Kanebo and Christian Dior make much more expensive ones.

PART II

Country by Country Guide

WESTERN EUROPE

The European Union consists of some of the world's most beautiful tourist destinations: Britain, Ireland, the Netherlands, Belgium, Luxembourg, Denmark, Sweden, Finland, France, Germany, Austria, Greece, Italy, Portugal and Spain. The only outsiders in Western Europe are Norway and Iceland (which belong to the EEA or European Economic Area in which there is free movement of labour) and Switzerland. According to recent figures from Brussels, Europe is still the most popular tourist destination. With over 60 million arrivals, France is first, Spain second (45 million), Italy (29 million) followed by Hungary & the UK (20 million).

Yet, there are proposed future changes to the industry in the EU. For some time, EU member states have been living under the threat of withdrawal of 'duty free' privileges. When this happens, it will alter the league table of popular destinations, particularly as Europeans take more and longer holidays than most other nationalities (in Japan and the USA it is still normal to have only two weeks paid holiday; Europeans have at least three weeks, and often more). The European package tour market is heavily subsidised by duty free sales (approximately £56 per family) both on board the aircraft and from airport sales outlets which subsidise landing fees. In a price-sensitive market, tour operators will increasingly be looking to operate packages to countries outside the EU, so that passengers can still buy duty free goods. Destination winners will be Switzerland, Turkey, Tunisia, Gibraltar, Florida, etc. Losers will be Greece, Spain, Portugal and other EU countries.

European Commissioner Monti is deaf to the implications of abolition, repeating that he wants to harmonise all taxes across the EU. It is easier to abolish duty free, rather than tackle the different tax bands across Europe, even though the result would be that some airports will have fewer flights, meaning job losses. Some destinations such as the Greek islands are already suffering and will lose even more if they have to compete with Turkey.

RED TAPE

Legislation has existed for some years guaranteeing the rights of all nationals of the European Union to compete for jobs in any member country. According to Article 8a of the Maastricht Treaty, every citizen of the European Union has the right to travel, reside and work in any member state. The only reason for refusing entry is on grounds of public security and public health.

But this does not mean that all the red tape and attendant hassles have been done away with. Talk of the Single Europe should not lull Euro-jobseekers into thinking that the job hunt will be easy or that they need not worry about the formalities. Tourism jobs are often seen as the best jobs and perhaps the only jobs available to locals and many measures are in place to protect local employment. Nationalism still plays a large part in most employment situations. If you arrive to work as a rep and do not know how to do your job, the hotelier who thinks his sister could do the job better has the power to make your working life unbearable. EU rulings notwithstanding, barriers to the free movement of labour do remain which will fade only very gradually.

The EU Directive on Mutual Recognition of Qualifications requires tour managers and tour guides to provide proof of qualifications to work in many EU countries, Spot checks have taken staff off coaches and into police stations, sometimes resulting in a fine. Contracts or letters of appointment from your boss are not sufficient forms of proof.

The RSA Tour Guide's Diploma is accepted and IATM (International Association of Tour Managers) is currently looking into a mutually accepted qualification. If you work as a freelance, you can either ask your company to contact the DTI and obtain a certificate of recognition (approximate cost £100-150), or take the RSA assessment (easier but cost is approximately £200; call 0171-351 4434 for details).

Non-EU nationals who have the right to work in one EU country have the right to work in another. As the EU Directive starts to bite, all jobseekers will have to produce proof of their qualifications, so take a good training course leading to an internationally recognised qualification. It is important to work for a responsible employer. If they say they cannot get a work permit for you and expect you to work there illegally, you will face very stringent checks.

The standard situation among all EU countries is that nationals of any EU state have the right to work for up to three months. At the end of that period they should apply to the police or the local authority for a residence permit, showing their passport and job contract. The residence permit will be valid for the duration of the job if it is for less than one year or for five years if the job is permanent. The tourism job most commonly affected by this is seasonal rep, and the tour operator should be able to advise on the procedures.

But your employer cannot guarantee that these procedures will be easy. It has been known for EU nationals working in France to wait, say, eight months for their *carte de séjour* to come through or for a Greek residence permit to arrive on the last day of a seasonal contract. On his year out from university, Matt from Manchester worked in ski resorts in both France and Germany. In theory he should have had no problem regularising his status. In practice, he encountered many difficulties. The social security number for which he applied in France took 12 months to come through. In Germany he fared even worse, trapped in a vicious circle of 'no job – no papers – no accommodation'. Without papers he was turned away by the federal employment service, which all EU nationals are entitled to use. But resistance was useless.

The office of the European Commission in London (Jean Monnet House, 8 Storey's Gate, London SW1P 3AT; 0171-973 1992) issues a series of free *Citizens First* Brochures, including *Working in another European Country*. They also issue a booklet called *Social Security for workers posted in the European Union, Norway, Iceland and Liechtenstein*. The Information Office can provide details of in-service training schemes for people under 30 with a university degree. The European Commission also has offices in Cardiff, Edinburgh and Belfast. All enquiries of a legal nature are dealt with by an organisation called AIRE (Advice on Individuals' Rights in Europe, 74 Eurolink Business Centre, 39 Effra Road, London SW2 1BZ: 0171-924 0927).

Residents of Commonwealth countries may need visas for a short term of work; contact the relevant High Commission or Embassy for advice. Nationals of non-European countries who want to work longer than the three months standard for tourist visas in European countries normally find it virtually impossible to obtain work permits. Typically, they leave the country every three months, perhaps leaving with one group and returning with another, in order for their visitor status to be renewed on re-entry. In many cases the authorities know what is happening but turn a blind eye, since tourism is seen as such a big earner. Yet such a worker is in the unenviable position of having no employment protection.

Working in Europe for a UK Employer

A large proportion of Britons working in European resorts, ski resorts, campsites, holiday centres, etc. are working for British tour operators who do not have to conform to local employment regulations (minimum wage, protection from dismissal, etc.). That may change if a draft directive entitled *The Posting of Workers* which emerged from Brussels at the end of 1994 is accepted. This document stipulates that foreigners working temporarily in another EU state should abide by the host country's employment legislation, which would make it very difficult for UK companies to continue to pay their sports monitors, chalet girls, etc. little more than pocket money, typically £50 a week. According to a spokesman at ABTA, this would potentially triple the costs for British tour operators and therefore put smaller ones out of business, so the government is being lobbied to resist the proposal.

JOB-HUNTING IN THE EU

Every EU country possesses a network of employment offices similar to UK Jobcentres, details of which are given in the individual country chapters if relevant. Although EU legislation requires national employment services to treat applicants from other member states in exactly the same way as their own citizens, it is impossible to prevent a certain amount of bias from entering the system. For obvious reasons, an employer is allowed to turn down an applicant who does not speak enough of the language to perform his or her job adequately.

Average unemployment across Europe rose to 10.8% in 1997. No amount of positive legislation will force employment office officials to treat locals and foreigners equally. If there are two equally qualified job applicants of different nationalities, most employers will choose their fellow countryman/woman. In the words of Paul Winter from Cumbria who has worked several seasons in the German tourist industry:

> All this talk of one Europe and a Europe without borders doesn't mean that jobs are easy and simple to get abroad. It's not easy. Plan ahead, try to learn a language and take as much money as you can. That being said, the chances of working around Europe are still there to be enjoyed, just use a little common sense.

The UK Employment Service has a specialist office giving advice and guidance to jobseekers looking for work abroad. The Overseas Placing Unit (c/o Level 1, Rockingham House, 123 West St, Sheffield S1 4ER; tel 0114-259 6051/2/ fax: 0114-259 6040) coordinates all dealings with overseas/EU vacancies. These vacancies, distributed to Jobcentres via a computerised system called LMS, are usually for six months or longer, and for skilled, semi-skilled and (increasingly) managerial jobs. A random sample of job vacancies might include chefs for Germany and bar staff for Sicily.

All employment services in EU countries now have Euroadvisers, and it is worth addressing your employment queries abroad to them. The public employment services of EU countries cooperate with each other in the exchange of vacancies, usually for hard-to-fill posts or posts for which a knowledge of other EU languages is required. This computerised system is known as EURES (European

Employment Services) which in Britain is located at the Overseas Placing Unit. Under the EURES scheme, well-qualified multilingual applicants can complete an application form (ES13) in the appropriate language, to be sent to the relevant EU employment service for linking with suitable posts. These speculative applications are kept on file for six months.

The OPU also publishes a series of country-by-country factsheets called 'Working in...' which are free from Jobcentres or from the OPU. Although they do not contain much job-finding information which is not included in this book, they do provide some useful background information on taxation, health benefits, etc. for the job-seeker and are worth obtaining.

National Resource Centres, which are run by the European Commission and provide information about European careers, are set up in all EU and EEA member states. The UK office Careers Europe (Third Floor, Midland House, 14 Cheapside, Bradford BD1 4JA) produces a range of materials for those interested in studying, working, training or living abroad. For example, the Eurofacts and Globalfacts series of leaflets and the EXODUS database of International Careers Information. This information is available free of charge in careers libraries.

Regional offshoots of EURES exist in some cases. For example EURES Crossborder Kent (South Kent College, South Ashford Campus, Stanhope Road, Asford, TN23 5RN; 01233 655666/fax 01233655667) assists people looking for jobs in Belgium and Northern France. A new organisation, the International Careers Contacts Information and Training Service (TICCITS, Richard Huish College, South Road, Taunton, Somerset TA1 3DZ; 01823 251250/fax 01823 251255), matches young people over 18 and employers, for structured work experience in Europe and beyond, with special provision for the disabled. Details are also available on the internet site: http://www.ticcits.co.uk.

Suitable applicants may participate in EU-funded packages offered by ProEuropa, 59 High St, Totnes, Devon TQ9 5PB (01803 864526) or commercial work placements arranged by Interspeak Ltd, The Pages, Whitchurch Road, Handley, Chester CH3 9DT (01829 770101). See *Training in Europe* for more details.

US Students Work Exchange Programme

US Students can find assistance in looking for work through the Council on International Educational Exchanges (Council) in New York. It administers a Work Exchange Programme that enables US citizens who are students over 18 years of age to work legally in the UK, France, Germany, Ireland and Spain (see the relevant sections) as well as other countries. The cost of participating in this programme is affordable, and varies according to destination and includes travel, first night's accomodation, work documentation, a programme handbook, an orientation upon arrival in the country destination and a resource office which students can make use of during their stay. Applicants must be either full-time students (enrolled for at least 8 credits) or within one semester of study at an accredited colege or university and matriculated towards a degree. Applications must be made from inside the USA.For further details contact Council at 205 E.42nd Street, New York, NY 10017, USA (tel toll free 1-888-COUNCIL; e-mail INFO@ciee.org; website http://www.ciee.org)

United Kingdom

The World Travel and Tourism Council estimates that in 1997 the travel and tourism industry is providing jobs for more than three million people, despite the fact that the UK share of world tourism has fallen significantly (from 6.7% to 4.6% since 1980). Furthermore this figure will rise by a quarter over the next decade, as more visitors come to these shores and more British people take short breaks nearer home.

Traditional trips to the seaside and family holiday camps have been the staple diet of British tourists for more than a century. One of the pioneers of British tourism was Billy Butlin, who realised that visitors to his showgrounds would like to stay for a week. Hence, he started his popular holiday camps, of which famous institutions as disparate as the French Club Med and Dutch Center Parcs are perutations.

The British tourism scene has also widened its offerings with more glamorous locations discovered through television and film. The US blockbuster *Braveheart*, about one of Scotland's most celebrated heroes, helped lure 1.5 million tourists to Ben Nevis in Fort William in 1997. In the same year, Thirsk in North Yorkshire attracted 1.39 million tourists who wanted to see the location of the film and television series about the experiences of the famous vet, James Herriot.

The United Kingdom is split into the four national areas of England, Northern Ireland, Scotland and Wales, each with its own tourist board to promote their interests at home and abroad (addresses below). Under each National Tourist Board come Regional Tourist Boards. The Boards have to rely on government funding and members' fees so, in typically British fashion, they operate on a shoestring. That is why the response to requests for information is often disappointing; budgets do not allow for the printing and distribution of masses of free leaflets. And there is very little chance that the tourist board will be able to assist job-seekers.

The four principal tourist boards in the UK are:

English Tourist Board, Thames Tower, Black's Road, London W6 9EL (0181-846 9000).

Scottish Tourist Board, 23 Ravelston Terrace, Edinburgh EH4 3EU.

Wales Tourist Board, Brunel House, 2 Fitzalan Road, Cardiff CF2 1UY (01222-499909).

Northern Ireland Tourist Board, St. Anne's Court, 59 North St, Belfast BT1 1NB (01232 246 609)

FINDING A JOB

In the UK there is work as airport, rail and ship meet and greet staff, local guides and local reps. Attractions such as theme parks, nature reserves, national parks, etc. need local guides with specialised knowledge, as do stately homes and museums. The British Tourist Authority (Thames Tower, Black's Road, London W6 9EL) produces a series of information leaflets about careers, as well as publishing a booklet *Ground Handlers in the UK* (£5) with details of about 400 companies that might need guides and other staff throughout the country. Similarly, the British Incoming Tour Operators' Association publishes a list of their member companies for £35, ranging from companies which bring students into the UK to take English language courses to companies that operate tours around the UK; contact BITOA at 120 Wilton Road, London SW1V 1JZ (0171-931 0601). Anyone who speaks a language fluently should look through the BITOA list and approach those companies which handle visitors from the relevant country. For example Finlandia Travel (227 Regent St, London W1R 8PD) offer tours of the UK to Finns and other Scandinavians, Latin Travel (Thanet House, 19c Craven Road, London W2 3BS) for Spanish and Portuguese groups, Nippon Travel (161 Oxford St, London W1R 1TA) for Japanese tours, and so on.

You have to be prepared to work hard at finding a job, for example willing to make over a hundred phone calls to land a job. But first carry out some preliminary research. If you want to work locally, visit your local Tourist Information Centre (TIC) of which there are more than 800 in the country, and find out what types of visitor come to the area: backpacking students? families? older people with grown-up children who have more money to spend on leisure? If you are interested in working in the region, investigate the visitor attractions, stately homes, hotels, etc. If you want to work nationally and therefore away from home for extended periods, there are plenty of tours visiting every corner of the British Isles.

Although it is possible to find a job without any training, it is much more difficult. It is now incumbent on tour companies to abide by EU legislation which covers anyone on a package holiday or tour consisting of two of the three elements of accommodation, transport and services for an overnight trip or more. Every company in the tourism industry has become very conscious of customer care, and of their duty to look after visitors. Trained applicants will find it much easier to convince employers that they are conversant with the requirements and able to carry them out.

Even more than in other industries, many jobs are found by networking. Those that are advertised will have thousands of applicants. Most people find jobs from contacts met on their training course or by joining the appropriate industry association. To keep abreast of developments in the tourism industry of Britain and Northern Ireland, it is a good idea to read the industry newspaper *Travel GBI*; a subscription costs £29 per year (from 3rd Floor, Foundation House, Perseverance Works, 38 Kingsland Road, London E2 8DD; 0171-729 4337).

Guides

In the UK it is possible to become a Registered Guide by undertaking a rigorous training course monitored by one of the regional tourist boards. For general information contact the Association of Professional Tourist Guides (520 London Road, Mitcham, Surrey CR4 4YQ; 0171-717 4064) or the Guild of Guide Lecturers (52d Borough High St, London SE1 1XN; 0171-813 2800).

There are over 800 official guides in London offering tours in nearly 40 languages. They have taken the two-year part-time course run in conjunction with the London Tourist Board, and obtained the coveted blue badge. To work for a prestige organisation like English Heritage (23 Saville Row, London W1X 1AB; 0171-973 3000) or the National Trust (36 Queen Anne's Gate, london SW1H 9AS; 0171-222 9251), it will be necessary to be persistent in knocking on the doors of their human resources department. The National Trust runs in-house training for house guides, most of which are for volunteers though there are a few paid jobs.

Among other things, guiding courses will steer you towards the most dependable books and guides. One large British tour company used to hold a competition among its trainee guides to find the worst guidebook errors; the only London guide books that no one could fault were the *Blue Guide* and the *Penguin*

Guide. For touring round Britain one of the best resources is the AA's *Great Britain Road Atlas* (from AA Publishing, 01256 491524) for £20 which contains clear maps and useful information for tour planning. Another useful handbook is *The Architectural Heritage of Britain and Ireland* by Michael Jenner (Shell Guide Series) which clearly explains architectural terms. As mentioned elsewhere the free magazine *Group Leisure* (8 Vermont Place, Tongwell, Milton Keynes MK15 8JA) may provide some leads, as might *Travel GBI*.

Of course incoming groups always prefer to employ someone who speaks the group language fluently or is a national of the country from which the tour group comes. For example the huge incoming Scandinavian market will often employ locally (mostly London) based Scandinavian staff. The major Scandinavian tour operators can do this because they maintain offices in the UK and can therefore interview staff *in situ*. A few years ago this caused problems with the Home Office who asked these companies to employ British nationals. In response, the tour operators simply threatened to take their groups elsewhere and, as a result, were soon granted permits.

English language schools and centres often need guides to take their students out on sightseeing trips either as recreation or part of their studies of the British way of life. Other possibilities include universities and residential schools which run special courses during the holidays or let their accommodation to tour operators who may need local guides. One way of becoming known is to join the local Tourist Board as an individual member and offer to provide free guiding for familiarisation trips for tour operators coming into the area.

Guides in the London area should be aware that, officially, groups are not permitted in Westminster Abbey on Sundays, the Tower of London or Windsor Castle, but are admissible everywhere else. All guides in Britain must be prepared to cope with bad weather. Not only does a wet and rainy day make everyone feel gloomy but many sights and excursions will have to be hastily rearranged if it rains, for example the Changing of the Guard is cancelled when it's wet.

Tour Managers

There are over 3,000 touring coach companies in the UK, some of which are listed at the end of the *Directory of Travel Companies*. To contact local coach companies look in Yellow Pages. The weekly *Coach and Bus Magazine* (01733 467000) also publish *The Coach and Bus Guide* (£25) which lists all the major UK coach companies. Most of these companies will need tour managers to look after their tours as they travel around the UK (and continent). Many seasonal jobs are available with the companies which handle incoming groups. Some companies like *Anglo Travel* host groups of young people from the continent and require tour managers occasionally.

Eventually, when you have worked for two or three years as a tour manager, you can apply to become a member of the International Association of Tour Managers (397 Walworth Road, London SE17 2AW; 0171-703 9154). This association is very active on behalf of its members and represents them in the Brussels bureaucratic jungle. It also has a useful 'job bank'.

As a tour manager, bear in mind that student groups often arrive in Britain with a collection of tapes to play on the coach's sound system. Unless your coach has a blue PRS declaration that the company has paid a licence fee to the Performing Rights Society, you will be breaking the law, and fines can be stiff.

Freelance Work

Once you have gained experience working for an employer, you may want to explore the possibility of setting up your own business or filling some niche in the market (see introductory section 'Working for Yourself' in *Finding a Job*). In fact there is very little regulation and plenty of scope for entrepreneurs. Any guide with a convincing presentation can find it surprisingly easy to persuade companies to send foreign clients their way, especially during the busy conference season when business executives are looking for ways to keep their visiting contacts entertained. Become a member of ACE (Association for Conferences and Events) for job leads.

Administration Work

The National Trust (36 Queen Anne's Gate, London SW1H 9AS; 0171-222 9251) has career courses for gardeners and countryside managers training for horticulture and environmental conservation. English Heritage (23 Saville Row, London W1X 1AB; 0171-973 3000) which administer such sites as Stonehenge, often need stewards and wardens.

To make contacts and keep abreast of current developments in tourism, it is advisable to join the NLG (University of Surrey, Guildford, Surrey GU2 5XH) It has a varied membership, all working in tourism. They organise very useful evening and one day seminars about important changes in legislation, problems, etc. Joining the relevant Tourist Board is vital. Many have a special low fee for small businesses. They can give help in marketing your services, and often run one-day seminars dealing with everything from VAT to attracting business. The regional tourist boards are listed below.

If you are considering developing your own tours in the UK, bear in mind national preferences, as identified by the *Sunday Telegraph*: 'the Japanese are fond of woollen mills and clean restaurants, Arabs like halal picnics and casinos, Malaysians love gardens' and all nationalities seem to like tours which revolve around murder and ghosts. A Russian group recently complained that it had been shown banks and financial institutions but no factories and wanted to know where all the wealth comes from. Meanwhile a Korean group was thrilled to go round the British Museum taking notes to give to their children at home. One expanding section of the market is short breaks in southern England for Belgians and French coming through the Tunnel; apparently while Britons go to French ports to buy wine, French people cross the Channel to buy McVities biscuits and Mother's Pride bread.

Some of the following specialist organisations may be of interest:

Association of Independent Museums (AIM), London Transport Museum, 39 Wellington Street, London WC2E 7BB.They produce bulletins highlighting new museums, and may offer suggestions for special days out.

Association of Railway Preservation Societies (01707 643568) can advise on trips on steam railways.

British Arts festival Association (0171-247 4667) provides an information service for festivals.

British Horse Society, Stoneleigh Deer Park, Kenilworth, Warwickshire CV8 2XZ (01926 707700). Offer horse riding opportunities all over the UK at inspected and approved centres.

British Universities Accommodation Consortium or BUAC, Box 1639, University Park, Nottingham NG7 2RD (0115 950 4571/e-mail buac@ nottingham.ac.uk) can assist if you are looking for group accommodation in a university..

Racecourse Association (01344 625912) publish a list of major race days at all their

59 member racecourses in the UK.

Royal Collection Enterprises (0171-839 1377) handle enquiries for the opening of Buckingham Palace and also the special exhibitions in the Queen's Gallery, which are popular for day trips.

Society of London Theatre (0171-836 0971) represents 50 theatres in the West End of London and provides an information service.

Sports Council (0171-273 1500) can help you find out information about where sports championships are being held, addresses of clubs, events, etc.

In every corner of Britain there is scope for walking tours, whether to discover where famous people lived and died, or to see architectural oddities. This is a boom industry: who would have thought twenty years ago that we would want to visit old prisons, lead mines and pencil-making factories? After retiring from the Metropolitan Police, Allen Evershed took a guiding course and started a company called Diplomatic Guides which runs walking tours around the back streets of Southwark (where he had worked as a policeman). Although he doesn't talk about his police work, he can tell many interesting stories about the area which his clients seem to enjoy thoroughly.

Apart from the mainstream opportunities for freelance guides, there are other tourism-related openings for self-employed people. For example anyone who has some experience in the field of press and PR can set up on his or her own. Stately homes, visitor attractions and other tourism venues might want a short campaign to advertise an opening, a new feature, etc. Large companies don't want these one-off jobs, so turn to freelancers instead.

Farm Tourism and National Parks

As more and more visitors seek to escape the urban grind, the number of visits to working farms has increased at a much higher rate than other sectors of the tourist industry. Often these days farmers' wives make more money offering bed and breakfast than their husbands working on the farm. Even farms which do not offer accommodation often run open days and need reception staff to help out. Farms also turn their outbuildings into self-catering units, and need cleaners, carpenters and maintenance staff. Tourist Information Centres can tell you which farms are open to the public. The Farm Holiday Bureau (National Agriculture Centre, Stoneleigh Park, Warks CV8 2LZ. Tel 01203 696909) also produce a guide (£7.50) listing all farms open to the public.

National parks are having to balance conservation with visitor management, which means more people are needed to do the managing. Britain has 11 national parks which require wardens, trail guides, stewards, park attendants and shop staff as well as managers, legal advisors, planners and press staff. Obviously many of these people are distinguished by their love of the outdoor life and their commitment to interpreting the environment to the general public.

Further information may be obtainable from the Countryside Commission, John Dower House, Crescent Place, Cheltenham, Gloucestershire GL50 3RA.

Hotels & Catering

The best starting place for finding out about career prospects in the hotels and catering industry is the free *Careers Guide* from the Hotel & Catering Training Company, International House, High St, Ealing, London W5 5DB (Hospitality Hotline; 09068 443322). It may also be worth obtaining the list of 90 member recruitment agencies specialising in hotel and catering placements from the FRES (36-38 Mortimer St, London W1N 7RB) in exchange for a £2 postal order.

Thousands of vacancies at all levels have to be filled in hotels and restaurants every week. But be warned that the recession was not yet over at the time of writing and reports still crop up in the media of 1,500 people queuing for 80 job vacancies in a new hotel. Seaside hotels normally provide staff accommodation and food, though the standard will be considerably lower than that enjoyed by the paying guests at the hotel. There is also plenty of hotel work in London from the international hotels on Park Lane to the budget hotels of Earls Court, though it is the norm in London for the staff to live out.

Wages in the hotel trade are notoriously low, and exploitation is common, but this is set to change when the new minimum wage becomes gradually introduced from April 1999 onwards (at the time of going to press this is £3.70 per hour for those over 20). Until then, hotel staff with silver service or other specialist experience can expect a wage at the higher end of the earnings spectrum in a three or four star hotel, as can restaurant staff in London. Waiting staff can supplement their wages with tips, however chamber and bar staff will generally have to be content with their hourly wage.

People who are available for the whole season, say April to October will find it much easier to land a job than those available only for the peak months of July and August. Most hotels prefer to receive a formal written application in the early part of the year, complete with photos and references; however it can never hurt to telephone (especially later in the spring) to find out what the situation is. You can work systematically through a hotel guide such as those published by the Automobile Association, the Royal Automobile Club or the Tourist Boards. The more bedrooms listed in the hotel's entry, the better the chances of a vacancy.

It is worth contacting large hotel chains for up-to-date vacancy information only if you are going for senior positions like chef or manager. For example Hilton National & Associate Hotels (Maple Court, Reeds Crescent, Watford WD1 1HZ; 01923 434 000) can give advice on which of their 33 UK hotels have current vacancies, although these should be applied to individually for employment. Similarly Choice Hotels Europe can give advice on the opportunities they have available in over 60 hotels in the UK. For information on the current vacancies and how to apply, contact the Human Resources Department, 112-114 Station Road, Edgeware, Middlesex HA8 7BJ; 0181 233 2001. However, they will only consider applicants with hotel and catering experience The Sheraton Hotel chain is often looking for staff as well. Smaller chains might be worth trying too like Hatton Hotels Group Services Ltd. (Hatton Court, Upton Hill, Upton St. Leonards, Gloucester GL4 8DE) which hire staff for hotels in the Cotswolds.

Fast food restaurants generate an enormous and constantly fluctuating number of vacancies. If you are prepared to work overtime, you should be able to earn a living from McDonalds, Pizza Hut, etc. working as a 'crew member', though usually you have to be content with part-time work (at about £3.75 an hour) until you prove yourself reliable. Full-time wages are normally about £4 or slightly more. Having a reference from one of these chains can be useful if you want to move to another branch.

Many London employment agencies specialise in catering work and once you are on their books, you can earn reasonably good money. An employment agency which deals with hotels throughout Britain is Montpelier Employment, 34 Montpelier Road, Brighton, Sussex BN1 2LQ (01273 778686). Anyone who can acquaint themselves with EU hygiene regulations before an interview would have the edge.

Pubs

Live-in pub work is not hard to come by. You usually have to work throughout pub opening hours six days a week, but you should be rewarded with approximately £115-150 a week cash-in-hand in London, about £20 less elsewhere. A part-time barmaid or barman makes between £12 and £15 for an evening session 6-11pm. Women with bar experience normally find it easier to find a job than barmen, and can often negotiate a better package. Waiting for an ad to appear is usually less productive than going pub to pub. Americans may need to be reminded that you do not get tips in a British pub though you may be bought a drink now and then.

Regional Tourist Boards

For a job in most national and regional Tourist Board offices, a minimum of two languages is a requirement. Experience in marketing, PR, administration, media, publications or advertising are also useful. The regional tourist boards are:

Cumbria Tourist Board, Ashleigh, Holly Road, Windermere, Cumbria LA23 2AQ (015394 44444).

East of England Tourist Board, Toppesfield Hall, Hadleigh, Suffolk IP7 5DN (01473 822922).

Heart of England Tourist Board, Woodside, Larkhill Road, Worcester WR5 2EZ (01905 763436).

London Tourist Board, Glen House, Stag Place, London SW1E 5LT (0171-932 2000).

North West Tourist Board, Swan House, Swan Meadow Road, Wigan Pier, Wigan Lancs. WN3 5BB (01942 821222).

Northumbria Tourist Board, Aykley Heads, Durham DH1 5UX (0191-375 3000).

South East England Tourist Board, The Old Brew House, Warwick Park, Tunbridge Wells, Kent TN2 5TU (01892 540766).

Southern Tourist Board, 40 Chamberlayne Road, Eastleigh, Hants. SO5 O5JH (01703 620006).

West Country Tourist Board, 60 St. David's Hill, Exeter EX4 4SY (01392 425 426).

Yorkshire Tourist Board, 312 Tadcaster Road, York YO24 1GS (01904 707961).

There are over 800 Tourist Information Centres in the UK, some open on a seasonal basis, others open year round. A knowledge of Japanese is especially useful in this job. Whereas most of the time is spent replenishing stocks of leaflets and answering questions about the location of toilets, there is plenty of variety in the questions which tourists ask (e.g. why didn't the Queen choose a quieter location to build Windsor Castle instead of under the flight path for Heathrow?) Winter is obviously quieter but weekend break holidaymakers still fill up the TIC.

Holiday Camps and Activity Centres

Anyone with a qualification in canoeing, yachting, riding, climbing, etc. should be able to find summer work as a children's leader or instructor. If you don't know what the governing body initials stand for, you should seek further qualifications before trying for a job in which the safety of others will be in your hands: horse riding (BHS), sailing/windsurfing (RYA), canoeing and kayaking (BCU), rowing (ARA Instructor), swimming (ASA), lifesaving (RLSS), fencing (AFA Club Leader), judo (brown belt), cricket (NCA leader), climbing (MLTB Single Pitch Sup. Award), orienteering (BOF Level 1 Instructor), and archery (GNAS Leader). See the introductory section *Sports & Activity Instructors*.

There are also plenty of jobs as general assistants for sports-minded young people, especially at children's multi activity centres. In these jobs, character and personality are more important than qualifications. The trouble is that the pay is not usually very much for this kind of work, perhaps about £40-45 per week in addition to all food and accommodation costs, though this will be supplemented by an end-of-season bonus at some centres. Quite often foreign applicants will be asked to provide police clearance forms for any job working with children. Seasonal staff who work for language holiday operators tend to be better paid; try for example *Academic Travel, EF Language Travel*, Embassy Tours (44 Cromwell Road, Hove, Sussex, BN3 3ER; 01273 207481) and International Language Centres (International House, White Rock, Hastings, TN34 1JY; 01424 720100).

One of the largest employers is *PGL Travel*, with a staggering 3,000 vacancies during the season March to October. The Youth Hostels Association Adventure Holidays programme (Trevelyan House, 8 St. Stephen's Hill, St. Albans, Herts.; 01727 840211), which employs a large number of sports leaders, offers only free board and lodging, rail fares and sometimes pocket money.

Once you have the appropriate qualifications, try the travel ads in the quality papers, ask Regional Tourist Boards which companies are in membership and send a s.a.e. to the British Activity Holiday Association Ltd (BAHA, Orchard Cottage, 22 Green Lane, Hersham, Walton on Thames, Surrey KT12 5HD) for a list of more than 30 member companies.

Here are some of the most important ones which may require domestic as well as leadership staff:

Ardmore Language School, Berkshire College, Burchetts Green, Maidenhead SL6 6QR (01628 826699). Multi activity and English language camps mainly in London and region.

Barracuda Summer Activity Camps, Graphic House, Ferrars Road, Huntingdon, Cambs. PE18 6EE (01480 435090). Various day camps in southern England.

Camp Beaumont, Linton House, 164-180 Union Street, Waterloo, London SE1 0LH (0171 9221234).Bridge House, Orchard Lane, Huntingdon, Cambs. PE18 6QT (01480 456123). 4 residential centres in Britain, plus one in France.

EF Language Travel, EF House 1-3 Farman St, Hove, Sussex BN3 1AL (01273 723651). Residential courses for European students throughout Britain.

Prime Leisure, 4a Chorley Lane, Cumnor Hill, Oxford OX2 9PX (01865 750775). 5 centres in the Home Counties.

Superchoice Adventure Ltd., Operations Dept. Osmington, Weymouth, Dorset, DT3 6EG (01305 835 966 - 24hrs).

Family holiday centres proliferate around the British Isles and employ a large range of people to do catering, entertainment and managerial work. As well as the usual skivvying jobs, they may also require entertainers for both children and adults, lifeguards, DJs, shop assistants, etc. The main disadvantage is that accommodation is generally unavailable. Try the following:

HF Holidays, Recruitment & Training Department, Redhills, Penrith, Cumbria CA11 0DT (01768) 899988. Operate 20 country house hotels throughout the UK for people on walking and special interest holidays.

Holiday Club Pontin's, Chorley, Lancashire PR7 5PH. Hiring takes place at eight individual centres. Among the most sought-after job is that of 'Blue Coat' or entertainer-cum-host. They are paid £120 for a 90-hour week, including food and accommodation, yet there are often as many as 2,500 applicants for 120 vacancies.

Theme Parks and Leisure Centres

American-style amusement parks, which are fast gaining popularity in Britain, have large seasonal staff requirements. Alton Towers in Staffordshire is the most popular attraction (charging admission) in the UK with more than 3 million visitors. Major theme parks (including Alton Towers) run their own training programmes; apply to their Personnel Officers for information.

Jobcentres often have details of seasonal jobs at visitor attractions and theme parks. Among the largest are:

Alton Towers, Alton, North Staffordshire ST10 4DB (01538 703344). Approximately 1,000 vacancies between March and November.

Bourne Leisure Group, Normandy Court, 1 Wolsey Road, Hemel Hempstead, Herts. HP2 4TU (01442 241658). 500 team members needed at 20 holiday parks throughout Britain.

Chessington World of Adventures, Leatherhead Road, Chessington, Surrey KT9 2NE (01372 729560). Employs between 500 and 1,000 people each year, between March and November.

Frontierland Western Theme Park, The Promenade, Morecambe, Lancs. LA4 4DG (01524 410024). 100+ ride operators and other assistants. Accommodation available for £25 per week.

Harbour Park Ltd., Seafront, Littlehampton, West Sussex BN17 5LL (01930 721200).

Pleasurewood Hills Theme Park, Leisureway, Corton, Lowestoft, Suffolk NR32 5DZ (01520 508200).

Thorpe Park, Staines Road, Chertsey, Surrey KT16 8PN (01932 577120). Approximately 500 vacancies from March to November.

Leisure centres are an expanding market, both individual sites and those developed in conjunction with hotels. Often they require their staff to maintain meticulous standards of hygiene. For example it may be necessary to check the water in a swimming pool three times a day to satisfy Health & Safety requirements. Swimming pool staff will need first aid and a lifesaving qualification. Jobs are often advertised in *Leisure Management Magazine* (Portmill House, Portmill Lane, Hitchin, Herts. SG5 1DJ; 01462 431385); a student subscription costs £25 per year.

Youth Hostels

From February to October, the YHA recruits over 500 Seasonal Assistant Wardens to work in Youth Hostels throughout England and Wales. Duties include general domestic work, cooking, manning the hostel shop and the reception desk. They provide food and accomodation and the salary depends on experience. You must be over 18 years old, have experience of dealing with the general public, an appreciation of good customer service and a pleasant personality. A proven ability to cater for numbers and perform clerical tasks would be an advantage. For further information, send a SAE to The National Recruitment Department (WIT), YHA (England and Wales) Ltd., PO Box 11, Matlock, Derbyshire DE4 2XA. The YHA encourages employees to undertake nationally recognised occupational qualifications while working in a hostel.

Special Events

Conferences, seminars, exhibitions, outdoor events and pop concerts all need freelance staff as well as full-time organisers known as Professional Conference

Organisers or PCOs. Established members of ACE (Association for Conferences and Events, Riverside House, High St, Huntingdon PE18 6SG; 01480 45759) receive lists of upcoming events and attend ACE functions at which they put out the word that they are looking for work, and jobs are fixed up accordingly.

Events such as the Henley Regatta in June, Test Matches at Headingley in Leeds, the Edinburgh Festival in August/September and a host of golf tournaments and county shows need temporary staff to work as score board operators, stewards, car park attendants, ticket sellers, caterers, etc. Ask the local tourist office for a list of forthcoming events and contact the organisers. Colin Rothwell from South Africa recommends looking for work at fairs, horse races and rock concerts, and enjoyed the perk of hearing Joe Cocker, Status Quo and Rod Stewart in Newcastle while working on a food stall.

Scotland

Although unemployment is high in Scotland (and Wales as well), there are still plenty of tourist-related jobs available. Charlotte Jakobsen from Denmark (who 'fell in love with this country, its people and lifestyle' on arrival) travelled to Edinburgh for interviews with the Hilton and Sheraton Hotels, among others, and was soon working evenings in a hotel bar. Her employer did not provide accommodation but she was able to stay longterm at the Frances Kinnaird Christian Hostel for women (14 Coates Crescent) for less than £50 a week, and concluded that although it is next to impossible to find a bar or hotel job with a decent wage, it is a very enjoyable way to pass a few months.

Many foreign job-seekers in Britain tire of the London scene or are attracted to the peace and quiet of Scotland as Isak Maseide from Norway was:

> *We were originally going to Edinburgh to work at the Festival, but we preferred somewhere quieter, so went to the resort of Oban on the west coast of Scotland. Even though we arrived in the middle of the season (which lasts from mid-May to the end of September) we soon found work. Apparently McTavish's Kitchens in George Street is the place to go first since it is the biggest employer and has live-in facilities, pays well and employs a large number of seasonal staff.*

Paul Binfield from Kent travelled further north in Scotland and was rewarded with a healthy choice of casual work in the Orkney Islands:

> *Unemployment here is about 5% and from March to September there is an absolute abundance of summer jobs. We worked in one of the several youth hostels on the islands, have done voluntary work for the Orkney Seal Rescue and I am currently earning a very nice wage working at the historical site Skara Brae on a three-month contract. There is loads of seasonal work available in hotels and bars, gardening, etc.*

Consider also trying the ferry and cruise companies such as Caledonian MacBrayne Ltd., The Ferry Terminal, Gourock, Renfrewshire PA19 1QP.

Seasonal winter work (Christmas week apart) is not common in Britain, with one important exception. Aviemore Mountain Resort Ltd. (Aviemore, Inverness-shire PH22 1PF) in the Cairngorms of Scotland absorbs a large number of non-local people, preferably on a permanent basis. Fourteen-day work packages are arranged for the Christmas/New Year period which combine festivities with work. Some jobs are registered with the Inverness Jobcentre though it is probably more efficient to apply to the Personnel Office at the Centre (01479 810624). The Centre provides staff accommodation.

As has been well covered in the media, Glasgow has been enjoying a renaissance as a tourist destination since it hosted the Garden Festival in 1988 and was the City of Culture in 1990. All the same, local unemployment remains at such a high level, that it is not a job-seeker's paradise.

Channel Islands

The flourishing tourist industry of the Channel Islands is sustained by a large number of seasonal workers who work in the hotels and other businesses that service tourists from April to October, since the small permanent populations of these islands can never provide enough employees for the huge tourist industry. Among the many hotels in St Peter Port (the capital of Guernsey) which need chamber and waiting staff for the season are Braye Lodge Hotel (Ruette Braye; 01481 723787) and Fermain Hotel (Fort Road; 01481 37763).

Eric Mackness is one of dozens of people from throughout Britain who worked the summer season of 1995 in this part of the world:

> *I applied to Stocks Hotel after seeing it listed in* The Directory of Summer Jobs in Britain *and was given the job by post, though most people who were hired attended an interview. A foreign language is not necessary, despite the proximity to France, though it would be a bonus. My job consists of the usual kitchen porter duties, working 60 hours a week, split shifts. Compared to northern Cyprus where I was working earlier in the year for pocket money, I am relatively rich here, plus there is no tax or national insurance (though there is in Jersey and Guernsey). It did take me a little time to adjust to the unique environment on Sark. It is a very small place in every sense of the word – a great place to get away from it all (whatever your own particular 'all' is).*

Despite the untrained horses, they loved driving the horse-drawn carriages on Sark

One unusual seasonal opportunity on Sark is driving the horse-drawn carriages, a job which Lyn and Dave Howard saw advertised in the *Horse and Hound*. Despite working very long hours with untrained horses for £40 a week, they loved the job and the island.

For a list of the 200 hotels on Guernsey, write to the States Tourist Office, White Rock, St. Peter Port, Guernsey. Towngate Personnel (65 Seamoor Road, Westbourne, Bournemouth BH4 9AE; 01202 752955) specialise in filling permanent live-in vacancies in the tourist industry of the Channel Islands.

RED TAPE

Nationals of the European Union (plus Norway and Iceland) are not subject to immigration control and are therefore entitled to enter Britain to look for work. Many find the job hunt easier than the natives do, simply because they can speak more than one language fluently. For non-EU/EEA citizens, most of whom enter on six-month tourist visas (which can normally be renewed on reentering the country after an absence), it is exceedingly difficult to obtain official permission to work, unless one of the special schemes listed below are applicable. In general the Department of Employment does not issue work permits to unskilled and semi-skilled workers (though unofficial catering work is still abundantly available). However if you can offer a sought-after skill such as a knowledge of Japanese and are applying for a high-level permanent position, an employer may be prepared to go through the rigamarole of applying for a work permit on your behalf.

There are some special schemes which allow qualifying non-EU nationals to work legally in Britain, for example the Training & Work Experience Scheme (TWES) which allows foreign university graduates to work in their field for up to a year. Further details are available from the Overseas Labour Service of the Employment Department (W5, Moorfoot, Sheffield S1 4PQ) and their advice line can be dialled on 0114-259 4074.

The British Hospitality Association (Queen's House, 55-56 Lincoln Inn Fields, London WC2A 3BH; 0171 404 7744) which is the trade association of the hotel and catering industry in the UK can act as an agent or legal representative on behalf of member hotels and restaurants in helping to obtain permits for overseas students who have arranged work experience placements in UK companies (normally through an overseas training college).

Nationals from outside the European Union who are registered as students in the UK are allowed to work up to 20 hours a week. Such students wishing to take a part-time or vacational job while studying in Britain will need to visit their local Jobcentre for a form OSS1. This is an application for an overseas student work permit and contains sections to be completed by the student's educational establishment and potential employer.

Non-EU nationals who want to extend their visas or have queries about work permits and other immigration matters should contact the Immigration and Nationality Department of the Home Office at Lunar House, Wellesley Road, Croydon, Surrey CR9 2BY (0181-686 0688); be prepared to wait in a queue both on the telephone and in person.

Special Exchange Schemes

Students and others from EU and non-EU countries may be able to participate in work exchange programmes, many of which charge a substantial placement fee. Careers advisers in universities and colleges should be the best source of information. A company based in Chester called Interspeak Ltd. undertakes to find traineeships (*stages*) in the UK for European students mainly in the fields of commerce and hotel work. The fees start from £150 and are payable for placements which last from two to six months. Details are available from The Pages, Whitchurch Road, Handley, Chester, CH3 9DT; 01829 770101.

American students wishing to work in Britain can apply to the Work in Britain Program, which allows about 3,700 full-time college students over the age of 18 to look for work after arriving in Britain or participate in pre-arranged employment. They must obtain a blue card for a fee of $225, which is recognised by the British Home Office as a valid substitute for a work permit. They may arrive at any time of the year and work for up to six months. Candidates must be US citizens residing in the USA and studying at a US institution at the time of application and able to prove that they have at least $700. For further information contact BUNAC USA (PO Box 49, South Britan, CT 06487; 202-264-0251 or 1-800-GO-BUNAC/Website www.BUNAC.ORG). The Work in Britain programme is the counterpart of BUNAC's Work America Programme for British students (see chapter *United States*). US citizens who have been offered a full-time position may apply for a work permit through the Association for International Practical Training (Career Development Exchanges, Suite 250, 10400 Patuxent Pkwy, Columbia, MD 21044-3510). The AIPT runs an International Hospitality Tourism Programme in the UK and many other countries (see *Introduction*).

According to statistics compiled on the Work in Britain programme, about 15% of participants arrange their jobs before leaving the States, and almost all of these are in career-related jobs, often fixed up through campus contacts. The remaining students (about 3,000) wait until they arrive in Britain, and spend an average of four to five days job-hunting before finding work. The majority work in hotels, restaurants, pubs, shops and offices. The BUNAC offices in London (16 Bowling Green Lane, EC1R 0BD) and Edinburgh have files of possible employers around the UK.

The cultural exchange organisation Alliances Abroad can place American full-time students in temporary jobs in British hotels and restaurants for between one to six months; details available from Alliances Abroad, 2830 Alamameda, San Fransisco, CA 94103; fax 415-621-1609. Fees range from $285 for one month to $710 for six months.

Australians, New Zealanders and Canadians may obtain 'Working holiday-maker' status if they are between the ages of 17 and 27 inclusive (with no dependants over the age of five). It is estimated that about 25,000 do so each year. The permit entitles the holder to work in Britain with the primary intention of funding a holiday, for up to two years. It is now essential to apply in the country of origin, rather than at the point of entry. Immigration officials will want to be reassured that the employment they will be seeking is incidental to their travels and that it is their firm intention to leave the UK after no more than a total of two years which must be continuous from the date of entry to Britain. They now have stronger powers to stamp the working holiday visa with the type of work permitted, preferably casual and low-paid work. You may also be asked to prove that you have enough money to support yourself and fund a return airfare; around £2,000.

Canadian students who want the security of a package arrangement may participate in the Student Work Abroad Programme (SWAP) which is comparable to the Work in Britain programme. It is administered by the Canadian Universities Travel Service (Travel CUTS) which has 30 offices across Canada. After paying the registration fee and showing that they have support funds, eligible students aged 18-27 are entitled to work in Britain for up to six months at any time of the year. As on the American Work in Britain programme, the facilities of BUNAC in London are available to SWAPPERs. The equivalent for Australians is the SWAP scheme administered by STA Travel (PO Box 399, Carlton South, VIC 3053) which is open to Australians aged 17-27 for up to two years.

A reciprocal Swiss/UK trainee exchange agreement began in 1989. This arrangement allows up to 400 Swiss trainees to gain work experience in the UK for up to 18 months. Those wishing to participate will require a Training and Work Experience Scheme (TWES) permit. Applications for permits can only be made by UK based employers on behalf of the trainee they wish to employ. Further advice can be obtained from the Department for Education and Employment, W5, Moorfoot, Sheffield S1 4PQ.

The organisation Trident Transnational (Saffron Court, 14b St Cross St, London EC1N 8XA; 0171-242 1515) offers work experience placements to young foreigners aged 17^{1}/$_{2}$ to 27 in various fields including travel and tourism and hotels and catering. Some expenses are paid, but on the whole these placements lasting between three weeks and six months are voluntary. The placement fee starts at £140.

Tax and National Insurance

Most new employees are put onto the emergency tax code (denoted by 'X' at the end of your tax code) and immediately begin to forfeit roughly a quarter of their wages. UK and Commonwealth nationals are entitled to the single person's personal allowance (currently £4,195 per year). Foreign nationals can claim personal allowances if they have been in the UK for at least 183 days in any tax year (which starts on April 6th). Eligible candidates who have earned less than the personal allowance, such as those who have done a seasonal job, may be entitled to apply for a rebate of the overpaid tax. When they finish work, they should send both parts of the P45 given to them by the employer to their employer's tax office. When they are ready to leave Britain, they must complete and submit form P85, a leaving certificate which asks your intentions with respect to returning to the UK to work. Inland Revenue operates a telephone information service for the public on 0171-667 4015.

Many companies, such as those who hire freelance guides, pay cash. Do not think that this will enable you to avoid paying income tax. Every company has an accounting department which will insist that all money paid out be accounted for, so your name and address will figure in the accounts sent to Inland Revenue at the end of the year. Inland Revenue has tried to make tour operators deduct tax at source (PAYE/Pay as you Earn) but without success in most cases. If you are paid gross, you can claim against tax for training courses, taxis, books, even some clothes expenses in some circumstances.

In addition to income tax, you must also pay National Insurance Contributions. If you earn over £64 you must pay 2% on the first £64 and 10% on earnings above this. Companies may tell you that you don't have to pay National Insurance contributions but unless you keep up voluntary payments, you may land yourself in trouble in years to come. You can make things easier for yourself by having an accountant. All freelance workers or people employed on seasonal contracts must make their own arrangements for pensions and (sometimes) insurance.

UK TOUR COMPANIES

The following operate tours or provide travel services in the UK:

Albatross, 31 Rochester Road, Ayelsford, Kent ME20 7TT (01622 690279). Guides who can speak German, Dutch, Scandinavian languages or Italian needed.

American Express, 19-20 Berners Street, London W1P 4AE (0171-838 5555). Meet and greet staff to work in London.

Anglo American Travel, 35 Spencer Road, London SW20 0QN (0181-947 3416).

APA Travel Services, 138 Eversholt St, London NW1 1BL (0171-388 1732). Incoming operator for groups from Spain, Italy and Portugal.

Axistours, 15 King's Terrace, London NW1 0JP (0171-388 3838).

Barton Hill, 30 Parkstone Road, Poole BH15 2PG (01202 665500). UK tours, conference work.

Big Bus Company - 0181-944 7810. Train guides for their round-London sightseeing tours.

British Airways Customer Services Staff - 0181-564 1003. Good linguists and staff with customer service experience sometimes required, to welcome visitors arriving at Heathrow.

Creative Tours, 5 Hanover Square, London W1R 0DH (0171-408 1606). Mainly Japanese clients.

Daysaway, 118 Cromwell Road, London SW7 4ET (0171-370 0655).

Destination Scotland, West Renfrew House 26 Brougham St, Greenock PA16 8AD (01475 785220). Upmarket tours.

Ecuador Travel, Palladium House, 1-4 1st Floor, Argylen Street, London W13 2CE (0171-434 0070). UK tours for Spanish-speaking clients.

English Wanderer, 13 Wellington Court, Spencers Wood, Reading RG7 1BN (0118-988-2515). Walking tours.

Eurocare, Harrods Luxury Tours, Harrods Ltd, Knightsbridge, London SW1X 7XL (0171-581 3603). Harrods sightseeing bus may need hostesses to serve tea and coffee.

Eurowales, Princes Square Montgomery, Powys SY15 6PZ (01686 668030). Tours of the UK.

Finlandia Travel, 227 Regent St, London W1R 8PD (0171-409 7333). UK tours for Finns and other Scandinavians.

Guide Friday - 01789 294466. Guides for open-top bus tours in Windsor, Canterbury, Windermere, Salisbury, Bath, Oxford, Cambridge, Edinburgh, Stratford-upon-Avon, York and Portsmouth. Training given.

Holland International - 071-734 0922. Dutch company with large incoming programme into Britain.

IGS, 1 Argyll St, London W1V 1AD (0171-434 0070).

Interopa, 21-23 Chilworth St, London W2 3HA (0171-258 0009). UK tours for Italian speaking clients.

Japan Travel Bureau, 95 Cromwell Road, London SW7 4JT (0171-663 6000). Handles Japanese groups into Britain (and Europe).

Latin Travel, Thanet House, 19c Craven Road, London W2 3BS (0171-447 2750). Spanish and Portuguese-speaking clients.

London Airways - 0171-403 2228. Meet and greet service at airport. Need friendly, cheerful people able to work early hours.

London Coaches - 0181-877 1722. London sightseeing trips on double deckers.

London Handling, 12 Kendrick Mews, London SW7 3HG (0171-589 2212).

Manpower, 18 High Street, Uxbridge, Middlesex, UB8 1BX (0181-897 0330). Agency which supplies summer staff at Heathrow Airport.

Miki Travel, 18-20 Cannon Street, London EC4M 6XD (0171-398 5040). UK tours for Japanese people.

Pino's Welcome, 2 Lower Grosvenor Place, London SW1W 0EJ (0171-828 9231). Guides need to speak European language or Turkish.

P & O, 25 Camperdown St, London E1 8DQ (0171-805 3800). Meet and greet staff for Heathrow and Gatwick.

Principality Travel, St. Bride's Hill, Saundersfoot, Dyfed SA69 9NH (01834 812304). Tours in Wales and England.

Queensberry Travel, 311 Fulham Palace Road, London SW6 6TQ (0171-736 6211). May need guides and drivers for incoming UK tours.

Reliance Tours, 12-13 Little Newport Street, London WC2H 7JJ (0171-439 2651). Incoming Chinese groups to UK (and Europe).

St. Paul's Cathedral - 0171-236 4128. Need cathedral guides and information staff to work on daily basis.

Scandinavian Seaways, Scandinavia House, Parkeston Quay. Harwich, Essex CO12 4QG (0990 333111). Shuttle work for good linguists between London and Harwich to meet incoming groups of Germans, Dutch and Scandinavians.

Sovereign Tours, 6 Weighhouse St, London W1Y 1YL (0171-491 2323). European, American and Asian clients, including religious groups.

Tourwise of London, 177-179 Hammersmith Road, London W6 8BS (0181-741 8666) Meet and greet staff for Americans arriving at Heathrow. Uniform provided.

Trina Tours, 74 New Oxford Street, London WC1A 1EU (0171-436 4488).

Visit Britain, 68 Lower Road, London SE16 2TP (0171-232 2659). Special interest tours in UK, for example on a theme like agriculture, financial institutions, etc.

Wedgewood Travel, Broadway Chambers, Hammersmith Broadway, London W6 7AI (0181-748 1199).

Wembley, Wembley Stadium, Wembley, Middlesex HA9 0DW(0181-902 8833). Behind-the-scenes tours of Wembley Stadium given in various languages.

Austria

Although Austria is only about the size of Scotland or the state of Maine, it is one of the most important tourist destinations in the world. It is becoming the case that more money is being spent by tourists in Austria than in the UK. With more Alps than Switzerland, a multitude of both winter and summer resorts, cultural, historical and sporting attractions and well-developed conference venues, Austria offers tremendous employment opportunities.

Even before Roman times, Austria attracted travellers who used the Brenner Pass to cross between northern and southern Europe. When the Romans arrived they built the Via Salaria (traces of which remain) to convey the precious salt from the mines near Salzburg to Rome to be used as payment for their soldiers (hence the English word salary). In later centuries, the great Austro-Hungarian Empire exerted its influence from Paris (Napoleon married a member of the Habsburg family) to Mexico (where the haloes on images of saints are still composed of stars in the Austrian style).

But during the 19th century the Habsburg empire began to crumble and when the heir to the throne was assassinated at Sarajevo, Europe went to war. The empire collapsed entirely at the end of World War I, taking with it Austria's industrial might. No sooner had the country started to rebuild than it was invaded again. In the aftermath of the Second World War, the Austrian government realised that snow and mountains were its principal resources, and so helped towns, villages and hamlets to build the infrastructure needed for winter tourism. Later it gave grants to hotels and pensions, which would be otherwise empty in the summer, to build swimming pools, etc., so that today the country has a year-round tourist industry.

Prospects for Work

In winter there is employment for resort managers, ski reps, children's reps and chalet staff in addition to all the usual jobs. Austria is popular among ramblers, birdwatchers, opera and music lovers, etc. and a number of mostly upmarket tour operators offer Danube cruises. Many British coach companies run ten-day holidays to the lakes and mountains.

With Austria's admittance to the European Union, employment opportunities have increased and the red tape is simpler but thousands of economic migrants who have poured into Austria from former Eastern bloc countries already provide a pool of labour for unskilled jobs. So the main demand is for trained staff, especially those who can communicate in German, not just because that is the language of Austria but because the majority of tourists come from neighbouring Germany.

Vienna is a favourite destination for British incentive conferences, though there are also conference centres in Graz, Innsbruck, Salzburg, Villach, etc. Speakers of German and English (and preferably one other language) who want to enquire about temporary work as stewards, etc. should contact the centres (see below) for a list of local conference organisers.

FINDING A JOB

There is no shortage of hotels to which you can apply either for the summer or the winter season. Get a list from the local tourist office. The state-run regional employment offices (*Arbeitmarktservice*) set up special departments for seasonal work in the hospitality industry (*Sonderteil: Saisonstellen im Hotel und Gastewerbe*) and publish lists of winter vacancies in September. There are no private employment agencies in Austria.

Outside the cities, the largest concentration of hotels is in the Tirol though there are also many in the Vorarlberg region in western Austria. One possibility for the summer season is *Travelbound* which hires a large number of people to work in hotels in Austria; no qualifications are required.

Winter Resorts

The majority of British ski holidays are based in the resorts of the Tirol. The main winter resorts are St Anton, Kitzbühel, Mayrhofen, Brand, Klösterle, St. Johann-im-Pongau, St. Johann in Tirol, Lech, Söll and Zell-am-See. The Innsbruck region normally offers more reliable snow conditions from early December until the end of April due to the proximity of the Stubai Glacier.

British tour operators which are active in Austria include *Crystal Holidays* and *Ski Total*. Another operator which specialises in Austria is *Ski Partners* for whom Camilla Lambert worked near Innsbruck as a high-season ski rep because the only requirement was that applicants be fluent in German.

Club Habitat, Kohlgrub 9, 6365 Kirchberg (05357 2505) employ about 15 alpine staff in winter and eight in summer. If you want to improve your chances of finding work in a ski resort, you could consider joining the annual December trip to Club Habitat in Kirchberg (see Training section).

Summer Camps

Village Camps (see entry in Directory)) needs monitors and EFL teachers for its summer camp at Zell-am-See. Room and board, insurance and a weekly allowance of approximately £75 and £200 respectively are offered.

Tour Operators

UK companies often arrange sightseeing and cultural tours (some with a musical bias or for other special interests), such as Martin Randall Travel (10 Barley Mow Passage, London W4 4PH. Also see the directory for; *The British Museum Traveller, Casterbridge Tours, Inghams Travel, Insight, Kuoni, Prospect, Specialised Travel* and *Swan Hellenic*.

Those who look after music or opera groups are always given free tickets to concerts and may get the chance to meet international performers. If working for a budget operator, make sure that your accommodation has heating in the winter and access to bath or shower. 'Getting away from it all' is popular in the Alps, which can sometimes mean getting away from what are normally considered basic necessities.

If working on a campsite or for activity holiday operators, make sure you are vaccinated against Tick Encephalitis; the vaccine is made in yearly batches at the beginning of the season, so get in early before it runs out.

Conferences

For details and addresses of conference centres, contact the Austrian Convention Bureau (c/o Congress Centre Hofburg, Heldenplatz, 1014 Vienna; 1-587 3666). The major hotels which offer conference facilities are worth contacting to ask if their organising clients need staff. Most belong to Round Table Konferenzhotels (Seigasse 18, 1040 Vienna; 1-505-5349). The major conference centres in Austria are the Austria Centre Vienna (1-23 690), Bregenz Congress House (5574-4130), Grazer Congress (316-80-490), Congress Innsbruck (512-59-360) and Salzberg Congress (662-889-870).

Incentive Tours

Some British-based companies which organise incentive tours to Austria if asked by clients are: Motivation Travel Planners (0181-390 8312) Travel Organisation (01908 214700) and World Meetings (01422 360846).

Ground Handlers

Fluent speakers of German or tourism professionals may find it worthwhile approaching one of the following ground handlers: Dregener Reisen, Intropa, Lüftner, Resebüro Mondial, Okista Reisen, Raffeisen Resebüro, Sato and Tyroltour.

CASUAL WORK

Competition for unskilled jobs is intense, particularly from the thousands of East Europeans who have flooded into Austria in the past five years. According to a report in *The Times* of London:

Hard-working immigrants from former Yugoslavia are taking over chalet jobs and freezing out the ski bums. This season in St Anton in the Austrian Tirol the large immigrant population, particularly of Slovenians and Croatians, has taken up the skiing jobs. Hotels and bars have found a pool of ideal employees who work hard to maintain their relatives back home.

Ian McArthur encountered the same thing in Vienna where he worked as a cleaner in a bar:

I worked 25 hours a week and was paid £4 an hour cash-in-hand. I had the opportunity, had I stayed longer, to work as a bartender which required a basic knowledge of German. I was paid every day, which permitted me a care-free disregard for financial prudence. This is common practice among illegal workers in Vienna, many of whom are Czechs and Yugoslavs (who are notoriously badly paid).

Yet at the height of the winter season there are opportunities for those who persevere. Once you are in a resort like St Anton or Brand which accommodates and services thousands of holidaymakers from December to April, it should be possible to find an opening. Try putting an ad in the *Tiroler Tageszeitung* newspaper. Camilla Lambert found a live-in job this way with a family whose father coaches the Austrian ski team. Several years before this, she prearranged a job in a hotel in Brand after talking to a woman from York who had worked there, but says that there are plenty of on-the-spot opportunities:

It is easy to find out about jobs in hotels, shops, as an au pair, in specialist areas like the 'skiverleih' (ski hire) as a technician or just working on the drag-lifts. If you arrived without a job, it would probably be best to target one or two villages where there are a lot of guesthouses and hotels. Ask in the Tourist Information first, but I found the bus driver who whizzed up and down the valley every day a good source of info, as were most of the bar staff in the various cafés and the 'British' pub. I was offered several positions for the coming winter.

There is a department in the Kitzbühel employment office whose sole function is to cater for foreigners seeking work. Arbeitsamt Kitzbühel (Wagnerstrasse 17, 6370 Kitzbühel) publishes a comprehensive list of local vacancies which is updated daily. A personal visit to this office is much more likely to achieve a result than a written enquiry.

Pubs, clubs and discos should not be overlooked since many of them regularly hire foreigners. Karin Huber, a native of Zell am See, reckons there are plenty of openings for foreigners, especially in the winter, since she found herself the only Austrian working in a club. The best time to arrive is late November.

Asking door to door is the most effective way though it is by no means guaranteed to succeed as Carolyn Edwards discovered in January:

We arrived in Söll on a Sunday and things looked very quiet. They were. It took me only two days to try everywhere in Söll with no luck. So I started on day trips to other resorts with no luck. The reps told me that the tour companies had brought very few people because of the bad snow conditions.

Ordinary wages in hotels and restaurants are low compared to Switzerland, starting at AS4,500 a month plus free room and board. A good wage before deductions is about AS11,000. Yet the cost of living is about a quarter higher than in Britain. So many foreigners work on a casual basis that exploitation is rife in this sector and there are many stories of people being treated shabbily, for example being fired after an injury.

REGULATIONS

Since Austria joined the European Union in January 1995, citizens of the EU plus Scandinavia have been able to work in Austria with minimal formalities. Many employers who in the past have been desperately short of labour during the tourist seasons will be delighted that the restrictive immigration policies have been abolished, as will European job-seekers. However, various factors still complicate the job-search. The arrival of refugees and others from Eastern Europe has increased competition in the job hunt in Austria. In addition, workers are officially supposed to obtain a work permit before departing from their home country which, as usual, is virtually impossible for casual and seasonal work.

According to a handout from the Austrian Embassy in London, EU nationals have six months rather than the usual three to look for an employer willing to support their application for a residence permit.

People working officially for an Austrian employer can expect to have up to 16% of their gross wage deducted for contributions to the compulsory Health and Social Security Scheme.

DIRECTORY REFERENCES

For companies which operate in Austria, see the following entries in the Directory section: Astons Holidays, Canvas, Crystal Holidays, Edwin Doran Music Travel, Equity Ltd., Eurocamp, Eurosites, Inghams, Keycamp, Neilson, Ramblers Holidays, Skibound, Leisure, Ski Miquel, Ski Total, Tall Stories, Travelbound, Village Camps.

Belgium

Among the first of the numerous invading armies that have trampled over Belgium were the Romans, who left behind a massive problem that is still around today. When Rome withdrew from the region, many legionnaires stayed on and settled in the south of the country, eventually merging with the neighbouring French to form the nucleus of the French-speaking Walloons. Meanwhile the north was swept by invading Germanic tribes who spoke a language which eventually became Flemish, a dialect of Dutch. The country is still divided linguistically: French is spoken in Wallonia (south and east) while Flemish is spoken in Flanders (north and west) which is now much more prosperous and bitterly resented by the Walloons. In 1971 Brussels was declared bilingual, although a large majority are French-speaking.

Prospects for Work

UK coach companies looking to expand their weekend breaks programmes are keen on Belgium. The excellent rates being offered by the ferry companies (thanks to competition from EuroTunnel) together with relatively inexpensive hotels and superb food makes Belgium a highly attractive destination for short breaks. Small coach companies have plenty of work, particularly during September (for the Belgian Beer Festival at Wieze) and October to May for weekend breaks. Ostend has a mini-season in February/March during its annual Carnival.

Because of its ease of access, Belgium attracts a large number of British school groups and musical tours. Many American universities have student tour programmes which are handled out of Brussels and Luxembourg. The number of Belgian coach companies which run tours of scenic and historic Belgium far exceeds what one might expect for such a small country (population ten million). The majority are based in Flanders and may have vacancies for English-speaking personnel prepared to work hard. Coach drivers, tour guides and shuttle staff are taken on in March/April for the season which lasts until September. Openings may also be available on barges.

Although such Belgian seaside resorts as Knokke-Heist, Blankenberge and De Panne, and other holidays centres like Bouillon in the Ardennes are hardly household names, there is a sizeable tourist industry in Belgium where seasonal work is available. The more mainstream tourist centre of Bruges is very busy in the summer, and will become even busier now that incentive tours have begun to send clients there via the Eurostar service to Lille in northern France. At the other end of the tourist spectrum, work may be available in one of the five unofficial hostels. According to Brett Archer, who worked several seasons at the Bauhaus International Youth Hostel at Langestraat 135, there are never enough people around to work in restaurants and bars during the summer. Expect to earn at least BF200 an hour.

FINDING A JOB

The best way of finding short term work, apart from contacting possible employers directly, is to visit a branch of the Belgian employment service in any town. A special division called T-Service in French-speaking areas and T-Interim in Dutch-speaking areas specialises in placing people in temporary jobs. As the headquarters of the European Union, Brussels hosts many international conferences for which bilingual reception and other staff are needed.

Private employment agencies in Belgium are licensed either to make temporary or permanent placements but not both. One of the most important is Randstad Interim which operates an English-speaking personnel department at its office in central Brussels (Hoofdkantoor, Muntplein, Prinsenstraat 8-10; 02-209 12 11) and has 35 branches throughout the country. Randstad is particularly strong on placing catering personnel. For many years the agency has organised specialised training for waiters and 'hygiene in the kitchen' courses for personnel in the catering and food industries. In cooperation with a number of companies in the industry, Randstad has written a manual for temporary personnel in this sector. Another Belgian employment agency which specialises in hotel and catering work is *Sobeir*.

Car drivers are in demand in Brussels because of the high density of official and company cars. Anyone with a good driving record and preferably a qualification such as the Advanced Motorists diploma might find work in one of the car pools used by EU departments, Embassies, NATO, multinational companies, etc.

Some companies advertise in the *Herald Tribune* and receive thousands of applications. It might be better to approach companies directly. One way to make contact with Belgian coach companies is to follow Sam's example. Sam had grown up speaking basic Flemish (because his father had worked for an American company in Antwerp) and decided that he wanted to work in tourism. One Saturday he went to London and walked down the row of coaches parked in Park Lane.

Several had Flemish names and, when he approached the drivers, was willingly given names and telephone numbers of the company offices. Armed with these, he went off to stay with friends in Antwerp and landed a job as a shuttle host from the second company he contacted. Belgians love a joke, and Sam came in for some teasing over his accent, but he didn't mind, especially when he found out what generous tippers Belgians can be.

If military history is your forte, there are many UK-based companies like Holts' Battlefield Tours (The Golden Key Building, 15 Market St, Sandwich, Kent CT13 9DA) which offer tours to the battlefields of the First World War, Mons, Waterloo, etc. Just as the local French-speaking Walloons did little to help the Duke of Wellington to victory at Waterloo, so today most of the souvenirs sold at the site of the battlefield are devoted to the famous loser.

LUXEMBOURG

Luxembourg is an independent country, though bound by historical and financial union into the Benelux federation. With an unemployment rate of less than 2% and a thriving tourist industry of its own, Luxembourg is worth considering. The national employment service (*Administration de l'Emploi*) at 10 rue Bender, L-1229 Luxembourg (478 53 00) operate a *Service Vacances* for students looking for summer jobs in restaurants, etc. To find out about possibilities, you must visit this office in person, although EU nationals looking for long-term jobs may receive some assistance by post. Other branches of the employment service are located in Esch-Alzette, Diekirch and Wiltz, but the headquarters is the only one to have a *Service Vacances* section. Paul Newcombe found the service very helpful and was delighted to be given details of a job vacancy at an American bar in the capital. While cycling through the country, Mary Hall was struck by the number of foreign young people working on campsites and in restaurants in Luxembourg City.

With a population of just 395,200, job opportunities are understandably limited, but they do exist in the tourist industry. Even the Embassy in London at 27 Wilton Crescent, London SW1X 8SD (0171-235 6961) maintains that 'seasonal jobs are often to be found in the hotels of the Grand Duchy of Luxembourg' and will send a list of the 250+ hotels in exchange for an A4 envelope with a 60p stamp. Wages are fairly good in this sector, often about £500 per month after room and board. (The franc is identical to the Belgian franc.)

Work exists with the large Luxembourg-based coach companies, working as a tour guide for groups of Americans and Australasians, and as shuttle staff for Benelux nationals going to Spain. Ask the Luxembourg Tourist Office (same address in London as the Embassy) for an up-to-date list of companies.

Cyprus

Cyprus is a divided island. The southern part is the Republic of Cyprus, a member of the British Commonwealth. The north, occupied by Turkey since the intervention of 1974, is called the Turkish Republic of Northern Cyprus (Kibris). It is not recognised by any country except Turkey.

Job opportunities exist in both the Greek and the Turkish parts, though mass tourism is much more established in the Greek-dominated south. For the present, Turkish Cyprus must be entered via a Turkish airport as there are no direct flights from the UK, which is a serious impediment to expanding the tourist industry. (Turkish Cyprus is considered separately at the end of this section).

Prospects for Work

As in many other countries, the Cypriot tourist industry was hit hard by the European recession causing local unemployment to escalate and a further crackdown on foreigners working on the island. Most big tour operators consider placement in Cyprus as a perk to be offered to staff who have worked well for the company elsewhere, especially if they have worked in Greece and picked up some of the language. Cyprus has the advantage of offering work during the winter as well as the summer, though it has special short seasonal attractions when it is especially busy, such as for the spring flowers.

Self-catering is a major part of most tour operators' work, so villa reps are hired by some of the main companies like Golden Sun Holidays (158 Kentish Town Road, London NW3 28O; 0171-485 9555), Manos Holidays (168/172 Old St, London EC1V 9BP; 0171-216 8070), Sunvil Holidays Cyprus (Sunvil House, Upper Square, Old Isleworth, Middlesex TW7 7BJ; 0181-568 4499) and Travel Club of Upminster (54 Station Road, Upminster, Essex RM14 2TT; 01708 225000). The British and Germans in particular like to see well-kept gardens surrounding their rented villas, so there is work for gardeners.

Special Interest Tours

Botanical tours are organised by specialist companies like Andrew Brock Travel Ltd (54 High St East, Uppingham, Rutland LE15 9PZ; 01572 821330). The Crusaders made their mark in the Middle Ages, and companies such as Holts' Battlefield Tours (The Golden Key Building, 15 Market St, Sandwich, Kent CT13 9DA; 01304 612248) bring in tours to follow in the Crusaders' footsteps. Walking holidays in the beautiful Troodos mountains are organised by, Explore Worldwide and Naturetrek (The Cadcam Centre, Bighton, Nr. Alresford, Hants. SO24 9RB; 01962 733051). The Mediterranean waters which surround the island of Cyprus are perfectly suited to cruising, and both the international liners and local companies berth in the harbour at Limassol, etc. One indigenous cruising company is Jolly Roger Pirate Cruises, Aranthi Court, 2nd Floor, 50 Ayias Zonis St (PO Box 4174) Limassol (05-379199) which hires mostly Cypriot crew but does hire foreign entertainers through ads in UK papers, British agents or the entertainers' agent in Cyprus, Andreas Agapiou, 231 Ledra St, 4th Floor Office, No 41 (PO Box 2074), Nicosia (02-476202).

The long-established diving holiday operator Cydive (Myra Court, Poseidon Court, Kato Paphos, Cyprus; 06-234271) may be worth approaching if you have the relevant background.

CASUAL WORK

As in Greece, women are at a great advantage when looking for work in cafés, bars and restaurants, but they should exercise caution according to Karen Holman:

> *In my two years there I heard stories about Cypriot employers expecting more of their barmaids than just bar work. I worked in two pubs and I would say that both bosses employed me with an ulterior motive. I was lucky – both of them were shy. By the time they realised I wasn't going to be their girlfriend, they had found me to be a good worker and were used to me being around. Many*

employers will sack the girls, or threaten to report them for stealing. If you're
legal, your work permit is valid for that job only, so if you leave the job, you
have to leave the country.

" They introduced themselves to
a man in a supermarket
whose trolley was so full of
bottles they reckoned he must
run a restaurant "

Just such a serious case of exploitation and harassment was reported in the
British press. A 23 year old trainee lawyer who had met her employer on a previous
holiday found herself working 15 hours a day without a day off in temperatures of
over 100° The final straw came when the manager made advances which she
declined which prompted her employer to hit her. She instantly quit and was paid
C£40 for 15 days work. She had no recourse because she had no work permit.

Rhona Stannage was much luckier: her boss (whom she met in a novel way)
was gay. In the supermarket in Protaras she and her husband Stuart introduced
themselves to a man whose trolley was so full of bottles, they reckoned he must run
a restaurant. He practically offered Rhona a job on the spot as waitress and cleaner,
and offered Stuart a cooking job two days later.

Tom Parker arrived in Limassol in April and started the search along the
seafront, with little success:

The same evening we headed for the tourist area and were soon told that we
would stand a better chance if we bought a drink for the manager before asking
about jobs. The only concrete result was that we got very drunk. No job oppor-

tunities (they told us we were too early). The next day we concentrated on the small cafés in the back streets of the old town. Here my two companions (both girls) were offered jobs in separate cafés. The kitchen job paid £13 a day and the waiting job £16, both plus tips. They both also worked in a bar in the evening, sitting round talking to the mainly local customers and being bought drinks for which the customer was charged £6.50 whether it was water or vodka and they earned a commission of £1 per drink, in addition to the evening fee of £13.

REGULATIONS

Cyprus hopes to become a member of the EU by the year 2000, but until that time the regulations stipulate that for both paid and unpaid work, a work permit must be obtained by the employer in advance from the Department of Aliens and Immigration, Ministry of the Interior, D. Severis Avenue, Nicosia (02-300 3138/fax 449221). This is very difficult. Yet some foreigners do manage it. Karen Holman from Nottingham has been working legally as a barmaid for two years. Work permits must be applied for by your employer while you are out of the country, and will be granted for an initial three months only for jobs which a Cypriot national won't or can't do (and very few Cypriot women are prepared to work behind a bar). Other documents which will be required are a police clearance certificate and HIV test.

Employers who want to hire English-speaking staff are likely to maintain that work permits are not needed for temporary work and many foreigners accept work on this basis. However it should be stressed that the penalties are strict; you risk a fine of up to £500 and a five or ten-year ban from the country. Until recently the risk to employers was negligible. However proposed legislation is set to increase the penalties on employers who hire foreigners without papers, which may reduce the numbers prepared to take the risk.

Cyprus is one country where the regulations are enforced. The Immigration Police have very sharp eyes and ears and frequently visit cafés and bars likely to employ foreigners. Two of Tom Parker's friends working at back street bars in the old town of Limassol had to impersonate a customer whenever the police visited. A Briton called Dave who was helping to renovate a yacht in Larnaca boatyard was discovered by immigration after three days and was forced to leave town. Yet the same man went on to work a season as a drinks waiter in Protaras (he had had the foresight to bring a pair of black trousers and white shirt) and was not troubled by immigration once. It seems that the authorities concentrate their efforts in May (which is when the resort of Ayia Napa was recently 'purged') and are less inclined to bother you once the season gets busy.

Tourist visas expire after three months but may be renewed if you can show enough money to support yourself. It might be easier to cross the border (to Greece or Israel) and return to Cyprus when your tourist visa will be renewed. You cannot cross between Greek and Turkish Cyprus for longer than one day.

TURKISH CYPRUS

Although the scope for employment is much smaller in Kibris than in Greek Cyprus, many people do find work in the country's tourist industry, mainly in bars, restaurants and hotels. Most of the tour operations are managed by local companies, though some British tour operators do employ some staff in the UK, such as *Tapestry Holidays*. Other jobs may be found in holiday villages and on cruise boats.

There is a sizeable English-speaking community with British churches and a British Residents Society (behind the Post Office). A number of restaurants and bars are owned by expats, many of which advertise in the English-language paper *Cyprus Today* (owned by Asil Nadir) and many employ at least one foreigner to communicate with the tourists. The larger restaurants belong to a local association whose members cooperate over job vacancies.

Northern Cyprus is not a cheap package holiday destination and tends to attract a more discerning clientele, who are interested in visiting the sites as well as enjoying the marvellous climate. It is a popular destination for Germans, so an ability to speak some German would improve your marketability. After making friends with several residents, Theresa Thomas (a trained teacher) accepted a job with a local tour operator. Typically, the interview took place in a café:

> *My job was to take out daily coach tours (the clients were mostly profession-als from the UK) six days a week, explain the history of the island and commu-nicate with bus drivers, restaurateurs, etc. (in Turkish). The good features were that I was able to see so much of this beautiful island and mix with interesting people. The bad features were poor pay for long working hours sometimes in extreme heat, having no workers' rights and always having to deal with sexual harassment.*

With a population of just 170,000, job vacancies become known as soon as they exist. Most opportunities lie in the catering trade and are open to men and women. The wages are poor by British standards, say £30-40 per week which may or may not include food and accommodation, but which can usually be supplemented with tips. But the cost of living is low and life is relaxed, like Greece was 20 or 25 years ago. Eric Mackness spent more than two years working in a village near the capital Kyrenia (Girne in Turkish) and is filled with praise for the country:

> *I can't praise Northern Cyprus enough, for its wonderful scenery, excellent climate and friendly people. There are mountains, fairytale castles, Roman ruins, all virtually tourist-free. I'm sorry if I sound like a holiday brochure but it's all true and at the moment 99% unspoilt. My village, Lapta, has just begun tarmacing the village roads. Prior to this we drove on gravel. The Turkish army is here, but they are very low profile and separate from the community.*

Eric arranged the job (at a restaurant called Rita-on-the-Rocks) before he left Coventry by writing directly after seeing it mentioned briefly on a BBC travel programme.

Red Tape

To date, the authorities have seemed unconcerned about the red tape, whatever your nationality, though there have been indications that the authorities were becoming a little more efficient in checking paperwork. It is possible to obtain a work permit after you have been offered a job, which involves a trip to the Hospital in Nicosia for medical tests which cost £100. Because of the expense, some seasonal workers prefer to renew their tourist status every three months by leaving the country; this entails a two-hour catamaran trip to mainland Turkey at a cost of about £20 return. Long-stay travellers may be able to persuade an employers to obtain a work permit on their behalf, costing from £37 to £135 depending on the length of the stay. Note that a stamp from TRNC (the Turkish Republic of Northern Cyprus) could make future visits to Greece difficult. At entry you can request that the stamp be put on a separate form.

DIRECTORY REFERENCES

Airtours, Sunvil, Sunworld, Tapestry.

France

Ideally placed between the two great travelling nations of Germany and Britain, France is the most popular country for tourists in the world, welcoming over 60 million a year. These tourists (including seven million Britons) head for four main areas: Paris (including Disneyland), the Côte d'Azur, the Alps and the vineyards and cultural highlights of the interior. The French kings built mediaeval visitor attractions which today bring visitors to see the chateaux and palaces of the Loire Valley and environs of Paris.

Britain helped develop the Riviera in the last century, when the Côte d'Azur was a favourite winter destination for the British leisured class. When the lemon crop of Menton failed one year, the British set up a fund to pay for unemployed farm workers to construct the Promenade des Anglais in Nice. Today the Riviera is packed in summer, mostly with people staying in the campsites behind the hills. The quieter times of spring and autumn are when the high-spending conference delegates take over the casinos and shops.

Prospects for Work

In an industry which employs 1.4 million people and accounts for more than 11% of the country's GNP, employment prospects are good in all the areas mentioned above. With impeccable French and an immaculate presentation, there is work at the elite end of the market in conference, cruise and incentive travel. Opportunities are less exclusive with ordinary tour operators. A great many UK companies which run activity holiday centres, campsite or ski tour operations, etc. in France employ Britons. However this is becoming problematic under new French legislation, which says that foreign companies must abide by the same employment regulations as French employers, e.g. pay the minimum wage (called *le SMIC*) and make social security contributions. Obviously the wage of a typical British seasonal worker, i.e. £50 (in addition to free travel, board and lodging, insurance, etc.) for working a 50 hour week does not come close to *le SMIC* (about F36 an hour). At the moment British tour operators have been exempted, at least unofficially, from many French regulations on the grounds that the jobs they offer are domestic (i.e. live-in) positions. But pressure continues for the government to change that, especially in areas where Britons are seen to be taking jobs away from locals, as in the case of ski chalets.

Hotels throughout France absorb many foreign workers, both at the skilled and unskilled level. Children's activity centres, canal holidays, escorted cycling tours and every imaginable themed holiday operate in France, all of whom are potential employers of your skills.

Coach holidays leave from most parts of the UK throughout the season. The best way to find the jobs is to look in the local UK press for companies advertising

'Bargain Breaks' or 'Fun Weekends in Paris.' If the company wants shuttle staff, often for overnight trips to the Riviera or on to Barcelona, they don't usually ask for languages; the ability to work for 36 hours with only cat-naps on the front seat of the coach is more important. On the other hand coach tour guides accompanying trips to Paris which operate year-round should be able to speak French fluently (though many don't). The better your French the better the jobs. Freelance reps in Paris can do very well on commissions, especially on a 'Paris by Night' tour; for example competition among cabarets is so fierce that they have been known to pay a commission of F120 per head.

Campsites are the big success story of French tourism. (See the introductory section *Campsite Reps* for further information.) This end of the market is still expanding, and large numbers of reps, children's reps, maintenance officers and activity instructors are needed each season. Theoretically the companies want you to speak French but many say that they were hired without being tested.

Paris is the most popular destination for short breaks from the UK. The Channel Tunnel *Eurostar* train has hundreds of job opportunities (see entry in the Directory). As the service expands with destinations further than Brussels and Paris, and with trains connecting at Lille with the TGV network (the fast French trains), even more jobs will be coming on stream. Many continental tours start from Paris, as this is one of the major European gateway airports. For example, the many tours that fly in to Charles de Gaulle airport from Quebec need tour managers who speak French (or, better, Canadian French).

Outside Paris there is scope for people with a background in architecture or history of art. Many special interest tour operators combine the chateaux of the Loire with vineyard tours, cycling, walking or even hot air balloons.

Anyone who is looking to invest in a tourism project will find plenty of opportunity in France, particularly in the field of upmarket B & B (called Chateau Acceuil). Hosts that can offer 'English spoken here' have an added advantage. One recommended area for purchasing affordable alpine chalets is in the Savoie, where farmers who once practised transhumance (moving herds to high pastures in the summer) owned several large huts at different altitudes. British families who have bought these abandoned buildings are normally welcomed into the valleys. Once these properties have been converted they can be rented out as *gites* or run as B & Bs.

FINDING A JOB

Skilled personnel should find out if there are any relevant vacancies registered with EURES, the European Employment service which can be accessed through Jobcentres. One regional office in south-eastern England is of specific interest to people looking for work in northern France. EURES Crossborder Kent (South Kent College, South Ashford Campus, Stanhope Road, Ashford, Kent TN23 5RN; 01233 655 666/fax 01233 655 667) can offer information and advice to job-seekers, though it does not hold current vacancy specifications.

The French Employment Service

The *Agence National pour l'Emploi* or ANPE is the national employment service of France, with dozens of offices in Paris and hundreds throughout the country. The headquarters are at 4 rue Galilée, 93198 Noisy-le-Grand (1-49 31 74 00). Although EU nationals are supposed to have equal access to the employment facilities in other member states, this seldom seems to be the case in France especially if the job seeker cannot speak flawless French. But there are exceptions. For example last summer the ANPE in Paulliac managed to place two Britons in silver-service waiting jobs in a Bordeaux hotel, even though at least one of the pair had no relevant experience and could not speak French.

Seasonal offices are set up in key regions to deal with seasonal demands like the *Antennes Saisonnieres* set up in ski resorts. These may be more likely to assist working travellers than the permanent offices which deal primarily in full-time jobs for French citizens. The addresses of ANPE offices recommended as offering seasonal work are listed in the relevant sections later in this chapter.

Anyone with access to a private telephone should be aware of the widely used French Telecom subscriber service *Minitel* similar to Ceefax. With it, ordinary people can access a variety of databases including one for job vacancies or even to advertise their own availability for work. The general Minitel number for *Offres d'Emploi* is 3615 CIJPA. There are also a few specialist numbers such as 3614 Alpes for vacancies in winter resorts. Dustie Hickey used the system to make contact with hostels in Avignon where she wanted to fix up work for the festival.

CIJ

There are 32 *Centres d'Information Jeunesse* or CIJ in France which may be of use to the job-seeker. The main Paris branch is CIDJ (*Centre d'Information et de Documentation Jeunesse*, 101 Quai Branly, 75740 Paris Cedex 15; 1-44 49 12 00) whose foyer notice board is a useful starting place for the job-hunter in Paris. Employers notify centres of their temporary vacancies; some offices just display the details on notice boards, while others operate a more formal system in co-operation with the local ANPE. You will find *Centres d'Information Jeunesse* in the following towns: Amiens, Angers, Bastia (Corsica), Besancon, Bordeaux, Caen, Cergy Pontoise, Claremont-Ferrand, Dijon, Evry, Grenoble, Lille, Limoges, Lyon, Marseille, Melun, Montpellier, Nancy, Nantes, Nice, Orleans, Poitiers, Reims, Rennes, Rouen, Strasbourg, Toulouse and Versailles. The CIJ in Marseille at 96 rue de Canaber (4-91 24 33 50) mainly holds details of jobs at holiday centres, especially as *animateurs*. Needless to say it is necessary to visit the Centre in order to find out about these.

Hotels and Restaurants

People with enough time to make long term plans can write directly to the hotels in the region which interests them, listed in any tourist hotel guide. Remember that the vast majority of restaurants are staffed by waiters rather than waitresses.

Hotels often employ non-French staff provided they speak the language. It is regarded as *très chic* to have foreign reception staff. Since the French (like the British) are not noted linguists, there is less competition for such jobs than there would be in Holland or Germany. If you want to make a career in the hotel industry, a stint in a French hotel is obligatory. Superb country hotels are listed in the Relais et Chateau brochure, many of which attract incentive groups from Britain and the US. People with professional training in hotels and catering may well find suitable adverts to which they can reply in the weekly publication *L'Hôtellerie* (5 rue Antoine Bourdelle, 75737 Paris Cedex 15). Newspapers in holiday towns (e.g. *Nice Matin*) also carry adverts. Two related hotel companies that employ a large staff are Forte, 23 Place Vendome, 75001 Paris and Sogerba Forte, 90-92 rue Baudin (BP 316), 92305 Levallois Perret, Paris.

Horizon HPL is a French-British training organisation which offers a package combining language tuition and a live-in hotel job in Paris or beyond. The fee is £240 and the wages are on a trainee scale of £40 per week though accommodation is provided.

Barges

Holiday barges which ply the rivers and canals of France hire cooks, assistants (i.e. stewards/hostesses), deckhands and even captains. In addition to crew for the hotel barges, boatyard assistants are needed at bases in Burgundy and the south of France. The best time to apply to the companies is in the new year; addresses may be found in the travel advertisement sections of English Sunday papers. Try for example the relevant companies listed in the Directory, *European Waterways Ltd*, and *Fluviale Auxerroise*(33 Quai National, 21170 Saint-Jean-de-Losne; Tel 03 80 39 24 09).

After being hired over the phone in Ireland by European Waterways, Pauline Power was flown to Amsterdam to meet her vessel (**Stella Maris**) and spent April to October as a hostess (even though she had previous seagoing experience as a deckhand) earning £100-120 a week plus tips of up to a further £100 a week.

Campsites

A number of British-based travel companies offer holidaymakers a complete package providing pre-assembled tents and a campsite courier to look after any problems which arise. Since this kind of holiday appeals to families, people who can organise children's activities are especially in demand. In addition to the Europe-wide companies like *Eurocamp* and *Canvas*, the following companies listed in the Directory all take on site reps and other seasonal staff: *Carisma Holidays, French Life Holidays, Haven Europe, Keycamp Holidays, Ian Mearns Holidays, Matthews Holidays, Sandpiper Holidays* and *Select France*.

The best time to start looking for summer season jobs with UK operators is between November and January/February. In most cases candidates are expected to have at least 'A' level standard French, though some companies claim that a knowledge of French is merely 'preferred'. It is amazing how far a good dictionary can get you.

There are 7,000 campsites in France, some of them small family-run operations which need one or two assistants, others on an industrial scale. You can write directly to the individual campsite addresses listed in any guide to French campsites (e.g. the Michelin *Camping and Caravanning Guide*), or you can simply show up (see *Casual Work* below). *NSS Riviera Holidays* wants mature couples to maintain a mobile home holiday village near St. Tropez.

Activity Holidays

Outdoor activity centres are another major employer of summer staff, both general domestic staff and sports instructors. Try the companies listed in the Directory which cater for children such as *Acorn Ventures* and *PGL*, or the ones for adults like *Mark Warner, Headwater Holidays* and *Discover Ltd*. You might also be able to find work with a French firm like one of the numerous canoe hire centres in the Ardèche. Keen cyclists could try to get a job with a cycling holiday company active in France such as *Belle France* or *Susi Madron's Cycling for Softies*.

Well over 20,000 *centres de vacances* employ an army of *animateurs/ animatrices* (counsellors and instructors) to look after the mostly French children who spend part of their school holidays there. People who look after children at

French holiday centres need to acquire the *Brevet d'Aptitude aux fonctions d'animateur* (BAFA) certificate. The training consists of a week in the classroom, 50 hours spent on a special acitivity and a week spent on-the-job. The cost of this course is roughly equivalent to the monthly wage paid to monitors, i.e. F4,000. The following organisations all based in Paris arrange the BAFA training and also refer trainees to prospective employers:

Organisme Protestant de Formation, 47 rue de Clichy, 75311 Paris Cedex (1-42 80 06 99).

Centre d'Entrainement aux Méthodes d'Education Active, 76 boulevard de la Villette, 75019 Paris (1-42 024 315).

Union Franaise des Centres de Vacances, 10 quai des la Charente, 75019 Paris (1-44 721 414).

A law was passed in 1994 (aimed primarily at unregistered ski instructors) prohibiting the teaching or supervision 'in any sport, whether as a principal, secondary, seasonal or occasional occupation' without a recognised diploma. If this were to be enforced, it would have a devastating effect on some British-run holiday companies.

The reps have to know their Baguettes from their Boules

Christine Pennington describes the way she was hired by Headwater:

After studying the brochure to make sure I'd like living in 'rural, unspoilt France', I filled out the lengthy application form and sent it off from France where I was working in a ski resort. I was then contacted by telephone by the owner herself, inviting me for an interview in Cheshire. All was well until I thought we were subject to a crossed line. After three 'excuse mes,' it occurred to me that she had suddenly switched to French to test my knowledge of the

*language. In shock and with a low muffled voice, I told her (in French) what
my ski resort was like and that yes I do enjoy cycling and walking. To this day
I don't know if that is what she had asked me. I must have done something right,
because I was eventually given the job of senior rep, though I was expecting
to go as an ordinary rep.*

At Headwater's informal training weekend in England, the new reps learned
some bicycle mechanics and practised reversing minibuses with canoe trailers
around corners. One of the major parts of the job was doing the 'bag runs' which
involved transferring clients' baggage (and in some cases, the clients themselves)
from place to place. At the height of the season with 50 bicycles, 20 canoes, and
lots of clients and their luggage to keep track of, bag-moving becomes a
complicated business and requires keeping to a tight schedule. Many of
Headwater's clients come year after year so the reps have to know their baguettes
from their boules.

Disneyland Paris

'Cast members' (Disneyspeak for workers) are needed to staff the scores of hotels,
restaurants, shops and attractions. The majority of jobs are in food and beverage,
housekeeping and custodial departments, though one of the best jobs is as a
character like Micky Mouse. Contracts are from 3 to 8 months between March and
October. Further details are available from Service du Recruitement-Casting, Euro
Disney SCA, BP 110, 77777 Marne-la-Vallée Cedex 4, France.

Vicky Nakis describes the way in which she landed her job as a receptionist
which lasted for seven months though in retrospect she wishes she had stayed for
three or four months:

*I was in Paris and noticed in the papers that Euro Disney was hiring. So I
turned up at the Casting Center at Noisy-le-Grand at Mont d'Est which is on
the RER A Line about five stops before Euro Disney. (Follow signs to Place
Vendôme then follow signs to the Casting Center.) I filled in an application form
(in French) and waited for four hours for an interview. The interview was
conducted with three candidates at a time to test team spirit. Because I spoke
four languages I was given the job of receptionist, but your French doesn't
have to be perfect since I met other receptionists whose French wasn't at all
good.*

For all jobs a professional look is required, and of course they are looking for
the usual friendly, cheerful and outgoing personalities. The monthly gross wage is
F6,798 from which deductions would be made for social security (about F1,000).
Assistance with accommodation in the Disney residences is provided by the
company's housing department for around F1500 per month. Although Vicky Nakis
was allocated accommodation in the staff quarters, Euro Disney cannot house all its
staff. Whether you will be impressed by the fringe benefits is a matter of individual
taste; they consist of discounts on merchandise and in the hotels, free entrance to
the theme park itself and the occasional chance to 'meet' the superstars. Because
Vicky didn't work inside the park, she missed seeing Michael Jackson and
Madonna. The only brush with fame she had was when a famous French singer
came to reception and she asked him his name.

A secondary theme park is Park Asterix, also within easy range of Paris, which
operates its own training programme. There are also aqua parks in France which
need lifeguards.

Ski Resorts

Recently there have been numerous stories in the British press about tour operator staff who were working as ski guides, being flung into jail. Ever keen to save money, the British will spend hundreds on the latest skiing gear but baulk at paying for safety. The top companies are happy to pay for official ski guides to take their clients around. Some companies however, who claim to offer 'guiding', say that their chalet staff 'will show you around', and then excuse themselves by saying this is only pointing out where to find the lifts, the bars, etc.

Official ski guides in any alpine country have to take a stringent training course which includes very important lessons on reading and understanding local weather conditions. Although British staff can take a BASI course, this will not include this valuable training. When the avalanche season comes it is important that a ski guide can read weather signs to help steer clients away from danger.

At La Rosiere, high in the Savoie Alps, they welcome trainee British ski guides who go through the ESF (Ecole du Ski France) training course. Your French must be good and you must be dedicated, in exchange for excellent training. In Britain, BASI offer training and are trying to get their courses accepted in the Alps.

In resorts, ski guides, local weather forecasters and avalanche specialists work closely together. Despite all safety precautions, dog handlers can still sometimes be called out to rescue skiers who have been avalanche victims. The rescue services warn that it is essential to be properly trained if you are going to be responsible for people's lives.

Between 20 and 30 British tour companies are present in Méribel alone, so there are plenty of jobs in French resorts with UK ski holiday operators. Resorts like Méribel are flooded with British workers and British skiers, many of them on school trips. Among the many UK ski tour operators, the ones which go to France listed in the Directory are: *Crystal Holidays, Equity, Esprit Holidays, Lotus Supertravel, Silver Ski Holidays, Simply Travel, Ski Chamois, Ski Miquel, Ski Olympic, Ski Scott Dunn, Ski Total* and *Skiworld.*

The ANPE mounts a concerted campaign every winter called A3 (ANPE Alpes Action) to attract qualified resort staff. Temporary job centres are set up in most resorts and are coordinated by the permanent ANPE offices. For example the ANPE in Albertville (12 rue Claude-Genoux, BP 133, 73208 Albertville Cedex; 79 37 87 80) has a centralised placement service for vacancies in a wide range of resorts including Chamonix, Megève, Les Arcs, Tignes, Val d'Isère and Méribel. Some other relevant offices open year-round include:

Aix-les-Bains ANPE, 12 rue Isaline (4 79 88 48 49).
Annecy ANPE, 1 Av de Genève (4 50 27 99 82).
Cluses & Flaine ANPE, 10 rue Charles Poncet (4 50 98 92 88).
St Jean-d-Maurienne ANPE, 7 rue de l'Orme (4 79 64 17 88).
Sallaches ANPE, 704 Av de St Martin (4 50 58 37 12).
Thonon ANPE, 6 Av St Francois de Sales (4 50 71 31 73).

There are one or two agencies which arrange for young people to work in ski resorts. *Alpotels* carry out aptitude tests on behalf of Nouvelles Frontières and other hotels to recruit workers for various French resorts. The net monthly salary is approximately £640.

Another agency is UK Overseas Handling (*UKOH*) which recruits for both large and small British ski companies operating in the Trois Vallées, Tignes/Val d'Isère, La Plagne and Les Arcs, as well as for a French company called Eurogroup which owns and operates hotels, restaurants and nightclubs in Méribel and Courchevel. Both agencies are looking for people with excellent French, though in the latter case fluent French is not a requirement for skilled chalet girls/boys.

Corsica

The tourist industry of Corsica is concentrated in a small number of towns: Ajaccio the capital, Bastia, Bonifacio, Calvi, Ile Rousse and Propriano. Fortunately these have not been targeted by separatists' bombs in recent years. Anyone with a knowledge of German would be at an advantage since the level of German tourism in Corsica is very high. Kathryn Halliwell found her job in the hotel Grand Sofitel at Portticio, a resort about 12km down the coast from Ajaccio, by the time-honoured method of asking from door to door. She worked as a chambermaid on a hotel staff of 150, and mentioned that the worst problem faced by the female members of staff was the level of unwelcome attention from local men.

Alison Cooper found the heat to be a more serious impediment to her enjoyment of the summer as a Eurocamp courier in Corsica, but managed to have a great season:

> *I enjoyed this job immensely even if it did get unbearably hot when it's 40°C and you're trying to clean a tent in direct sunlight and with a hangover. We had one and a half days off a week on average with a fantastic beach to go and chill out on, or a quick dip in the campsite pool after cleaning. On the whole it was a good summer.*

The British tour company *VFB Holidays* need a small number of resort reps in Corsica (as well as for French alpine resorts). The pay is low but the living is free, including flights between London and Corsica and subsidised watersports.

Special Events

Many famous events in the French calendar may employ people as guides and interpreters as well as general dogsbodies. The Monte Carlo Rally is in late January while the Monaco Grand Prix is in late May and *Les 24 Heures du Mans* is in mid-June. Although the latter race is 24 hours long, the event stretches over a week; for information about the race and possible job opportunities for French-speakers, contact Automobile de l'Ouest, 7200 Le Mans (243 40 24 20).

Four-wheel drive exhibitions like the major one held each August in Val d'Isère are increasingly popular in the French Alps. They generate plenty of casual work, so ask the tourist office for dates and venues.

One of the biggest summer festivals is in Avignon in August, though there are jazz festivals in Antibes, Nice and Nimes as well.

CASUAL WORK

Those without any training or experience in the tourist industry will probably end up in a low-expectation job like that of *plongeur*. At least such jobs will allow you to improve your standard of spoken French and give you a glimpse into French working practices. Most people succeed in finding casual work by turning up at a resort and asking door to door. In the opinion of veteran British traveller Jason Davies, 'door-to-door' should be just that:

> *Before I was down to my last F100 I had been choosy about which establish-ments to ask at. 'That doesn't look very nice' or 'that's too posh' or 'that's probably closed' were all thoughts which ensured that I walked past at least three in five. But in Nice I discovered that the only way to do it is to pick a main street (like the pedestrianised area in Nice with its high density of restaurants) and ask at EVERY SINGLE place. I visited 30-40 one morning and I would say*

*that at least 20 of those needed more employees. But only one was satisfied with
my standard of French, and I got the job of commis waiter.*

Speaking French to a reasonable standard greatly improves chances of finding a
job, though fluency is by no means a requirement. Kimberly Ladone from the
American east coast spent a summer working as a receptionist/chambermaid, also
in Nice, though her job hunt did not require the same dogged determination as
Jason Davies' did:

> *I found the job in April, at the first hotel I approached, and promised to return
> at the start of the season in June. While there, I met many English-speaking
> working travellers employed in various hotels. My advice to anyone seeking
> a job on the French Riviera would be to go as early in the season as possible
> and ask at hotels featured in English guidebooks such as* Let's Go: France*,
> since these tend to need English-speaking staff. My boss hired me primarily
> because I could handle the summer influx of clueless tourists who need help
> with everything from making a phone call to reading a train schedule.*

If in Avignon, the Koala Bar (run by Australians, naturally) has been recommended
for having a notice board useful to job-seekers.

Côte d'Azur

Beach restaurants are another hopeful possibility. Julian Peachey put on his one
white shirt and pair of smart trousers and began visiting the restaurants along the
beach by Avenue Montredon in the eastern part of Marseille. After the third request
for work he was handed a tea towel, and proceeded to work 14-16 hours a day,
seven days a week. Only the thought of the money kept him sane. The wage was
severely cut on days when it rained or the mistral blew and no one came to the
beach.

Campsite jobs proliferate along the Mediterranean coast, especially in August
when almost everyone in France takes their annual holiday. There is a point in the
summer at which workers who have been there since the beginning of the season
are getting bored and restless, which creates a demand for emergency substitution
to cover the last two months of the season. Jobs include cleaning the loos, manning
the bar or snack bar, doing some maintenance, etc. Some will be especially
interested in people with musical ability; all will want you to speak French and also
German if possible.

In the opinion of Andrew Giles the best time to look for work on the Côte
d'Azur is the end of February when campsites well known to job-seekers, such as
Prairies de la Mer and La Plage at Port Grimaud near St Tropez host representatives
from camping holiday companies trying to get organised in time for Easter. If you
can't be there that early, try the middle of May at the beginning of the peak season.
Bars recommended by Andrew where you can meet local workers and residents
include Marilyns (Prairies de la Mer), Mulligans (Holiday Marina), Finnigans (Port
Grimaud) and L'Utopée (Marines Cogolin). Also, try to listen to the English station
Radio Riviera based in Nice which at 9.30am and 4.30pm broadcasts job vacancies
along the coast and will also announce your request for a job free of charge. When
Peter Goldman couldn't find work on boats as he had hoped (because of rainy
September weather) he tuned in to Radio Riviera and got a job stripping wallpaper
from luxury apartments in Monte Carlo for F400 a day.

One of the most well known summer jobs in the south of France consists of
selling refreshments on beaches. You can find foreigners doing this on beaches in
and around Port Grimaud, San Tropez, Fréjus, Pampelonne and indeed all along the

Mediterranean coast. Buy one of them a drink and he or she will direct you to the boss. Sellers are paid on commission and earnings differ enormously.

Yachts

Bill Garfield headed for the south of France with the intention of finding work on a private yacht. He went round the yacht harbour at Antibes asking anybody who seemed to be in a position of authority on a boat if they had any work. After a week of failure, Bill began asking at every single boat including the ones which were already swarming with workers and also all the boats big and small in the 'graveyard' (refitting area). Two weeks after leaving Solihull this tactic paid off and he was hired for a nine-week period to help refit a yacht in preparation for the summer charter season.

Antibes is one of the best destinations, especially since there are several crewing agencies based in La Galerie du Port on boulevard d'Aguillon. Also frequent the yachties' bars and listen to Radio Riviera. Smaller places like St Tropez tend not to be so promising, though people have recommended Beaulieu-sur-Mer, Villeneuve-Loubet-Plage and Cros-de-Cagnes. It is essential to start early, preferably the beginning of March, since by late April most of the jobs have been filled. Bill Garfield describes the process in Antibes:

> *Boats frequently take on people as day workers first and then employ them as crew for the charter season if they like them. I had no previous experience of this work, which turned out to be to my advantage because the captain wished the work to be done his way. I lived on board with plenty of food provided and the pay was quite good, though some boats were paying much more.*

Look tidy and neat, be polite and when you get a job work hard. The first job is the hardest to get, but once you get in with this integrated community, captains will help you find other jobs after the refitting is finished. Of course many continue through the summer as deckhands on charter yachts and are paid £100 a week plus tips (which sometimes match the wage). The charter season ends in late September when many yachts begin organising their crew for the trip to the Caribbean.

Casual Work in Ski Resorts

For several reasons France ought to be the best of all countries in Europe for British and Irish people to find casual jobs in ski resorts. France is the number one country for British skiers most years, and Eurostar connections make the region even more attractive. 200,000 British skiers going there annually, and most of the resorts are high, with snow conditions reliable throughout the season. The main problem is the shortage of worker accommodation; unless you find a live-in job you will have to pay nearly holiday prices. Since many top French resorts are purpose-built, a high proportion of the holiday accommodation is in self-catering flats or designed for chalet parties. This means that not only is there a shortage of rental accommodation, but there are fewer jobs as waiters, bar and chamber staff for those who arrive in the resorts to look for work. There is an increasing number of English and Irish style pubs which are good places to find out about work.

Méribel is one of the best resorts in which to conduct a job hunt, as is Chamonix, where Sean Macnamara obtained a series of manual jobs as a dishwasher and handyman through the local ANPE. It may even be worth calling into the tourist office in these resorts to ask about seasonal employment at a local hotel, etc.

Success is far from guaranteed in any ski resort job hunt, and competition is increasing for the jobs available. Val d'Isère attracts as many as 500 ski bums every November/December, many of whom hang around Dick's Bar or the ANPE for days in the vain hope that work will come their way. With such an inexhaustible supply of ski bums, some employers are ready to hire people for Christmas, work them non-stop over the high season, pay them far less than the *SMIC* and fire them if they complain.

Paris

This city is the most popular destination on the continent for British short breaks. Each year there are thousands of coaches crossing over by ferry and there is plenty of work in looking after these groups, even in winter. However the French authorities will stop coaches and demand to see a tour guide's 'equivalence', ie. a certificate of qualification under the EC 75/368 Directive on Mutual Recognition of Qualifications. To get one, take a course for the RSA Coach Tour Guides Certificate. Then, to make doubly sure, carry a photocopy of the certificate translated into French, so that any agent de police can see that you possess the appropriate qualification.

For casual work, pubs are a good place to pick up job tips. There is a chain of three Guinness-serving bars with the same kind of clientele: Au Gobelot d'Argent in the rue du Cygne (*métro* Les Halles), Au Caveau de Montpensier (The Cav), 15 rue de Montpensier (*métro* Palais Royal) and Molly Malone's (21 rue Godot-du-Mouroy in the 9th). Yet the job hunt in Paris doesn't get any easier, as Mark Davies describes:

> *Although it has taken me five and a half weeks to find paid employment (as a* plongeur *in a creperie) I console myself with the fact that there is high unemployment here at the moment. To give you an example, I turned up as stated on the job notice at 5pm for a dishwashing job, and there were eight other people doing the same, and they were by no means all poor-looking immigrants. The pay for the job I'm doing now is lousy but it pays the rent while I look for something better. But as long as I'm in the Jardin du Luxembourg and the sun is shining I can't complain.*

Stephen Psallidas went around all the Greek restaurants in the Quartier Huchette in the Latin Quarter and found a job in half an hour (though the pay was appalling). Sarit Moas from Israel doggedly enquired at all the restaurants and street food stalls until she got a job selling crepes and taffy in the Tuilleries amusement parks.

One of the easiest places to find work is at fast food establishments; Americana is very trendy in France at present and English-speaking staff fit well with the image. There are many American-style fast food restaurants in Paris which employ a majority of non-French staff. Among the best known employers are the Quick chain (3 avenue de Général Galliéni, 93100 Montreuil) and the Chicago Pizza Pie Factory with two locations: 5 rue de Berri, 75008 Paris (*métro* George V; 1-45 62 50 23), 1 rue de Coquillere in the *third arrondisement* (1-4028 22 33). If you write in advance, the most that will happen is that they will write to assure you that you will be offered an interview after arrival in Paris. If you show up, you will be asked to fill out an application form before seeing the manager on duty. If there is a vacancy (as there often is) you could be offered a 45-hour-a-week job at SMIC rates plus tips and one meal a day.

Hostels

Hostels are always worth trying. The Fédération Unie des Auberges de Jeunesse (27 rue Pajol, 75018 Paris; 1-44 89 87 27; www.fuaj.org) employ cooks, kitchen helpers, receptionists and sports leaders at a number of their hostels throughout France; applications from French speakers should be sent to the individual hostels.

REGULATIONS

As in all other member states, EU nationals are permitted to stay in France for up to three months without obtaining a residence permit (*carte de séjour*). Once you have a job with a French employer and know you are going to stay longer than three months, you should apply for a *carte de séjour* at the local police station (*préfecture*) or town hall (*mairie*). Take your passport, four photos, some proof of your local address (e.g. rental contract, receipt for rent) and a job contract. The *carte* can take some time to come through – eight months to be precise in Stephen Psallidas's case – but in the meantime a *récépissé* for a *carte de séjour* should satisfy most employers. Having a residence permit improves your chances of being hired; for example Vicky Nakis is fairly sure that she missed out on a short-term job at Disneyland Paris the first time round because she lacked one.

Confusingly, some employers and job centres have insisted that prospective employees obtain a *fiche d'état civil* from the *mairie* (town hall). For this you will need the same documents as for the *carte de séjour* apart from the job contract.

When you start work, you or your employer should apply for a social security number (usually referred to as a *sécu*) from the relevant local office who should issue you with an emergency number straightaway. Social security deductions amount to approximately 18% of your wages, and these can be counted towards National Insurance in Britain, if you subsequently need to claim benefit.

Non-EU Formalities

Non-EU nationals must obtain work documents before they leave their home country in order to work legally. These must be applied for by the employer through the Office des Migrations Internationales (44 rue Bargue, 75732 Paris). Special exemptions exist for certain categories such as students.

There is a special scheme by which **American students** with a working knowledge of French (normally a minimum of two years' study at university) are allowed to look for a job in tourism or any other field and work for up to three months with an *authorisation provisoire de travail*. This scheme is organised by CIEE, at 205 East 42nd St, New York, NY10017 (212-661-1414 ext 1130). Eligible Americans already in France may apply to the CIEE office in Paris (1 Place de l'Odéon, Paris 75006; 1-44 41 74 74). There is also a possibility of extending the permit in France.

DIRECTORY REFERENCES

The following companies which employ staff in France are listed in the Directory: Acorn Venture, Alpine Tracks, Alpotels, Alternative Travel Group, Canvas, Carisma, Club Cantabrica, Crystal Holidays, Discover, Equity, Esprit Holidays, Eurocamp, Eurosites, Fluviale Auxerroise, French Life Holidays, Haven Europe, Headwater Holiday, Ian Mearns Holidays, Lotus Supertravel, Matthews Holidays, NSS Riviera, NST, PGL, Sandpiper, Select France, Silver Ski Holidays, Simply

Travel, Skibound Leisure, Ski Activity, Ski Chamois, Ski Miquel, Ski Olympic, Ski Scott Dunn, Ski Total, Skiworld, Susi Madrons Cycling, Tall Stories, UKOH, Venue Holidays, VFB Holidays.

Germany

The most important tourist magnets in Germany for foreign tourists are the River Rhine and Bavaria. The most popular coach tour to Germany from the UK is the three or four day tour of the Rhine Valley including Rudesheim where many thousands of day-trippers crowd into the Drosselgasse and similarly overcrowded streets.

According to the most recent figures, Germany has over one and a half million jobs in tourism, more in fact than both Spain or France. The best job opportunities in cities like Bremen, Hamburg, Hannover and Stuttgart are at conferences and exhibitions, and in hotels, as all major (west) German cities have excellent venues for international events. Berlin, which replaces Bonn as the capital of the united Germany in 1999, is enjoying a huge resurgence in popularity among tourists. Famous towns like Heidelberg (the oldest university in Germany) and the spa town of Baden Baden, now visited mainly for its casinos, attract other groups. Extensive tourist developments elsewhere, such as along the Baltic coast and inland lakes near Munich, attract mainly German tourists, and the Bavarian Alps (along the border with Austria), the shores of Lake Constance, the Bohmer Wald (along the Czech border) and the Black Forest (in south-west Germany) all have flourishing tourist seasons. Employment opportunities in the old east Germany are few unless you can find a UK operator which is too small to tap into the East German workforce, or which wants the same person to look after their group from departure from the UK.

Prospects for Work

It is difficult for foreigners to obtain skilled work in the indigenous tourist industry, though work is sometimes available with German ground handling and conference organising companies. Competition to work in a tour operator's office in Germany is fierce, unless you are fluent in German and are already employed by a major British or American tour operator who is able to transfer you to work for their German ground handler.

With the fall of the Berlin Wall, many thousands of Germans from the eastern *Lander*, some of whom were trained bilingual guides, flooded into western Germany. At the unskilled level, the German tourist industry depends heavily on immigrants and students during the busy summer months. In the past couple of years the country has been inundated with economic migrants from eastern Europe and in particular the former Yugoslavia, who are often willing to work for exploitative wages. But since 1993, the authorities have insisted that hotel and catering staff have the appropriate documents, so EU nationals have a clear advantage.

Prospects exist for German-speakers to become tour managers taking UK groups to Germany and for tour managers working for American companies using Frankfurt as their European gateway city. People looking for rep work should apply to the big camping tour operators like *Eurosites* and *Keycamp Holidays* (see their entries in the Directory).

In summer the deluxe German coach operators often hire English-speaking drivers with a PCV licence and valid First Aid certificate for American groups. (German coach drivers take a compulsory first aid course before they can obtain a licence.) An endorsement for driving double deckers such as Neoplans is useful, and also an ability to translate the sign *Umleitung* (which is not a place on a map but the German word for 'Diversion'). Coach driver/guides are obliged to point out the emergency exits to passengers. The police can board a coach and ask a randomly chosen passenger to point out their nearest exit; if they can't, the guide is fined.

Interest in 'green' tourism is very strong in Germany, so rambling and cycling holidays offer possibilities. The old hearty hiking holidays are giving way to tours that include cultural visits as well. These are often run by enthusiasts who organise and lead the tours themselves; anyone who has the ability, training and a good prospective client list may be tempted to do likewise.

FINDING A JOB

The best chance for finding work in Germany is with a UK company which sends clients to Germany. Otherwise, it may be worth consulting a German Jobcentre or *Arbeitsamt*.

The Employment Service

The Federal Employment Institute (*Bundesanstalt für Arbeit*, Regensburgerstr. 104, 90237 Nürnberg) has a network of 181 principal *Arbeitsamter* and a further 646 branch offices. *Arbeitsamter* normally refuse to help anyone who lacks residence papers. However they can be exceedingly helpful to anyone who can speak German and who has sorted out the red tape. Usually there is a special department for restaurant and hotel work, with counsellors to handle enquiries, tell you what's on offer and arrange interviews. There is also a microfiche reader listing hundreds of vacancies in the area. Unlike Jobcentres in the UK, *Arbeitsamter* do not have facilities for drop-in job-seekers.

It is possible to use the Federal Employment Service from outside Germany. The Zentralstelle für Arbeitsvermittlung (Central Placement Office, Feuerbachstrasse 42, 60325 Frankfurt) has a specialist department with the acronym ZIHOGA for hotel and catering staff. It publishes an explanatory leaflet in English and French which indicates that it is concerned with the placement of skilled and managerial staff from the EU in first-class restaurants and hotels, as well as with the promotion of German workers in the industry. There are placement officers who specialise in the placement of temporary hotel and catering workers from the EU in German establishments (069-71111 Ext 225).

The Zentralstelle also has a special department which finds summer jobs for students of any nationality, because this is felt to be mutually beneficial to employers and employees alike. Students who wish to participate in this scheme should contact the Zentralstelle before March. Students must be at least 18 years old, have a good command of German and be available to work for at least two months. Work is available in hotels and restaurants, as chamber staff and kitchen helpers, etc. Jobs are assigned centrally according to employers' demands and the level of the candidate's spoken German. For example those with fluent German may be found service jobs while those without will be given jobs such as chambermaiding and dishwashing. If you decline the first job offered by the Zentralstelle, you may not be offered another.

The Bundesanstalt also operates mobile temporary employment offices, called

Service-Vermittlung in addition to permanent *Arbeitsamter*. These are set up as an emergency measure where employers need extra workers immediately for short periods of time. It is worth looking for them at any of the trade exhibitions and wine or beer festivals in which the Germans take such delight.

Rhine Cruises

For general touring inside Germany, the average tourist thinks exclusively of the Rhine and its valleys. At a minimum, they take the obligatory hour-long trip from Cologne (Köln) past the Loreley Rock and stay overnight in Heidelberg. If you are guiding a group which is going to take a short trip down the Rhine or perhaps spend some days in one of the boats of the Köln-Dusseldorf Line (221 20880), founded in 1826, they will probably embark in or near Köln. (Passengers should be warned that the ships stop just long enough to allow disembarkation and then move across to the other side of the river.)

Specialist cruise operators such as the KDL Köln-Dusseldorf Line sometimes hire English-speaking waiters, chambermaids, etc. to staff their vessels, as Lyn Bayley relates:

> *After answering a newspaper advert in England and having a short interview, I was employed as a cabin girl on a Rhine cruiser. The boat trip began in Amsterdam, but the rest of the season was spent in Germany. We travelled the same section of the Rhine every week, which I enjoyed because I came to know each place really well. We five cabin girls seemed to have the best deal, mostly working 8.30am-5pm, compared to the catering staff whose hours extended from 7.30am to 10.30pm. I stayed on the boat for four months and made lots of great friends. I also managed to save £300 which subsidised further travels.*

Lyn was paid a modest monthly wage in addition to free food, accommodation and travel to and from Britain.

Bavaria

Bavarians like to think that they inhabit a separate country. Throughout the country you see the blue and white chequered flag of the Wittelsbachs (a royal family installed in the 12th century) and people wearing the traditional costume of lederhosen and dirndl.

Both Amersee and Starnbergersee can be reached by S-Bahn from Munich. These two lakes are ringed by towns and villages which all have hotels and restaurants, popular mainly with German tourists. Paul Winter has worked several seasons on the lakes near Munich:

> *I found that it is best to apply around April/May in person if possible. What they usually do is to tell you to come back at the beginning of June and work for a couple of days to see how you get on. As long as you are not a complete idiot they will keep you on until September. Even as late as July I knew of places looking for extra staff but as a rule most places are full by the end of May. I worked for the summer as a barman/waiter earning DM1,600 per month, net. With the tips I got, I generally managed to double this. The guy who worked in the kitchens pulled in DM1,200 after his room and board were taken off.*

Apparently the recession of the mid-90s hit this region hard and it looks as though it will be more difficult to find work here in the next year or two, especially given the competition from students from the east.

Winter Resorts

Not many UK tour companies operate skiing holidays in Germany, and yet people do find work in the resorts. Alpotels (a branch of the agency *Jobs in the Alps*) helps in the recruitment of 25 British workers for the winter season in Germany. If you are interested, send an s.a.e. to Alpotels, 17 High Street, Gretton, Northants NN17 3DE. Three resorts to consider are Garmisch-Partenkirchen (which also has hotels and services for the American Army) on the Austrian border 80km southeast of Munich, the spa resort of Oberstdorf in the mountains south of Kempten and Berchtesgaden in a portion of Germany which juts into Austria, south of Salzburg.

At one time the US Forces Recreation Camp in Garmisch generated a lot of employment. However the strict labour laws which protect German employees (and by extension EU nationals) mean that the base has stopped hiring local nationals and only hires Americans since they are not subject to the same regulations and are therefore much cheaper to employ. Check adverts in the US army newspaper *The Stars and Stripes*. So there is plenty of work for Americans but others will have to try for jobs in German-owned establishments. For example the Ramada Sporthotel (Am Riess 5, 82467 Garmisch-Partenkirchen; 088 21-75 80) has seasonal vacancies in the kitchen or housekeeping departments where the net pay is around DM1,000 after deductions for tax, social insurance and accommodation.

Special Interest Tours

Opera tours are a possible avenue to explore, with companies like Brompton Travel (0181-549 3334) who organise trips to opera festivals, Prospect Music & Art Tours (0181-995 2151) and Travel for the Arts (0171-483 4466). If you need to learn more about the legends and myths which inspired Wagner's *Parsifal*, *Lohengrin*, etc. before approaching music tour operators, go to the children's section of the public library.

Tourism professionals may wish to approach tour operators specialising in Germany, such as Moswin Tours Ltd (Moswin House, 21 Church St, Oadby, Leicester LE2 5DB; 0116 2714982) who run a large range of tours from basic escorted tours of the Moselle region to wine, painting, walking and language study tours. Another company with a Germany-only brochure is Taber Holidays (126 Sunbridge Road, Bradford. West Yorks. BD1 2SX; 01274 393480).

Predictably, the major language tour operators for students such as Euro Academy (0181-686 2363) have extensive programmes in Germany. Reps on these tours may well have less-than-luxurious working conditions and (as in other areas of employment) may be paid substantially less than a German counterpart. Theresa worked for an American company offering holidays with language tuition:

I was booked for the whole summer, and they expected me to work from my bedroom which had no telephone. Trying to contact the company from a public phone meant I would lose out on lunch and any other free time. It's not good for discipline if you have impressed on your students that they must always be on time for excursions, and then you are late because you are in a queue to wash in the morning.

"I was booked for the whole Summer, and they expected me to work from my bedroom which had no telephone"

A few 'failed' attempts to return urgent phone calls from her company soon convinced them that if they needed to contact her they would have to provide her with a room in the local hotel with a telephone and an en-suite bathroom as well.

Hotels & Catering

As usual, international hotel groups may allow staff to move between countries. If you want to work in Germany, try to get a part-time job at a hotel which is a member of one of the marketing chains focused on the German market (e.g. Steigenberger and Romantik Hotels).

Alpotels, mentioned above, carries out aptitude tests on behalf of German hoteliers looking for English-speaking staff for the summer or winter seasons. If interested in this scheme, send them an s.a.e.

An organisation which finds jobs for German-speaking foreign young people in German hotels is the *Bloomsbury Bureau* (see entry) It began primarily as an au pair agency but in 1995 started a programme of placing up to 50 young people in Bavarian hotels during the summer season. The wages for chamber and kitchen staff start at DM1,100 a month, plus accomodation. The maximum working schedule a week is 48 hours and a knowledge of German is needed. They also have some vacancies throughout the year in other parts of Germany

Specialist journals which accept advertisements include *Allgemeine Hotel und Gaststättenzeitung* (available from H Hugo Matthaes, Verlag, Olgaste 87, 70180 Stuttgart) and *Gastgewerbe aktuell* (Zülpicher Str. 10, D - 4059 Düsseldorf). The former is the official publication of the German hotel and hospitality industry (DEHOGA) and costs DM5.20 per issue.

Be prepared for hard work. In hotels, it is not unusual to work 10 or 12 hours a day and to have only a day or two off a month. The punitive hygiene laws do not help matters. Once you realise that restaurants and hotels are frequently visited by the health department you will appreciate why it is that the head cook insists that the floors be scrubbed, the fat filters cleaned regularly, etc. But the high wages make it worthwhile.

Exhibitions and Special Events

Some of the largest fairs and exhibitions in the world are held in Germany. For example Berlin's ITB is attended by three times as many visitors as London's World Travel Market. British companies exhibiting at German fairs, especially the Hannover Fair, often need interpreters. (Contact the British Chamber of Commerce, Heumarkt 14, W-50667 Köln for further information.)

The following companies handle conferences and may need bilingual staff for incoming groups. A Convention Bureau (CB) or Convention Centre (CC) should be able to provide addresses of companies handling events:
Incoming Incentive Congress Organisation (Frankfurt) – 69-75-75 3000
Deutscher Reisebüro-Verband – 69-27 39 07 0
Dresden CB – 351-48 66 22 1
Berlin Conference & Touring – 30-30 69 57 0
ICC Berlin – 30-30 38 30 49
Hartmann Service (Rhine) – 211-56 920/Tourist Office Köln 221-22 13 345
Düsseldorf Messe – 211-45 60 84 07
Köln Congress Management – 221-821 21 21
Reisebüro Rominger Stuttgart – 711-20 86 300/Tourist Office Stuttgart 711-23 85 80
Stuttgart Liederhalle – 711-2589-0
Welcome Touristic, Mauerkircherstrasse 4, 81678 München/Tourist Office Munich 89-23 30 30-0
München CC – 89-51 07 246/89-51 07 244
Bielefeld Stadhalle – 521-96 60/Tourist Office 521-17 88 99
Braunschweig Stadhalle – 531-70 770/Tourist Office 531-470-3145
Karlsruhe CC – 721-37 200
Osnabrück Stadhalle – 541-3490

Accommodation is always a problem at Fair times, and company offers should be carefully checked. One interpreter found herself in a B&B 60 miles from Hannover, which meant four hours of commuting a day and 'whenever I wanted a bath, the landlady's tights were dripping down my neck'. If you are doing some freelance work, from translating to stall dismantling, it is better if you can arrange accommodation independently, preferably with local friends.

Oktoberfest starts each year on the last Saturday in September and lasts a fortnight. They begin to erect the giant tents for the festival about three months ahead so you can begin your enquiries any time in the summer. Some of the hiring is done directly by the breweries, so it is worth contacting the Hofbräuhaus and Löwenbräu for work, as well as pubs, restaurants and hotels. There is also work after it finishes as Brad Allemand from Australia discovered:

"Whenever I wanted a bath, the landlady's tights were dripping down my neck"

On the Monday after Oktoberfest finished I went around to all of the Beer Halls which were being taken down asking for some work. The first one I went to was Spatenbräu and the boss obliged. Even though my German was almost non-existent, I managed to understand what was needed of me. Many other foreigners were also on the site – English, Australian, Yugoslav, etc.

Brad enjoyed the work, which lasted about six weeks. He worked 7am-5pm five days a week for an hourly rate of DM12.

In Hamburg they hold a fair (*Dom*) three times a year, for a month after Christmas, Easter and late summer. 'Worker Wanted' signs are often posted on the stalls. Here are some other special events which need large numbers of people to set up stands and deal with the maintenance, catering, etc. Some of the major ones are listed below:

March	Frankfurt Trade Fair
April	Hannover Trade Fair
August	International Frankfurt Trade Fair
August	Mainz Wine Festival
August	Wiesbaden Wine Week
August	Rüdesheim Wine Festival
late Sept/early Oct	German Wine Harvest Festival (Neustadt)

late Sept/early Oct	Wiesbaden-Rheingau Wine Festival
late Sept/early Oct	Cannstadt Folk and Beer Festival (Stuttgart)
late Sept/early Oct	October Beer Festival (Munich)
early October	Frankfurt Book Fair

The Frankfurt Book Fair has an employment office at the City entrance hall 1 (Ludwig-Erhard-Anlage 1, 60327 Frankfurt; 069-75 23 39).

Incentive Tours

UK incentive tour companies often organise programmes to Germany, since the standard of deluxe hotels is excellent. These companies normally take German-speaking freelance staff from the UK, but sometimes there is work from their ground handlers. American and Canadian companies often organise incentives to Germany, especially from Texas and other states with large German communities. Contacting firms such as Maritz in Chicago (10 South Riverside Plaza, Suite 1470, Chicago, IL 60606; 312-466 2700) can produce job offers if you speak German.

Ground Handlers

Fluent speakers of German or tourism professionals may find it worthwhile approaching one of the following companies:
Brühler ICS, Königswinter – 22-23 23 061
Compass, Düsseldorf – 211-40 70 21
Columbus Tours, Hamburg – 40-37 05 385
CPO Hanser Service Berlin – 30-30 53 131; Dresden – 351-32 169; Hamburg – 40-67 06 051
Hartmann, Düsseldorf – 211-56 920
Icontas, München – 89-64 30 11; Adelaide, Australia – 08-294 6377; Reading, UK – 01734-699288; Chicago, USA – (312) 644-4679
Interplan, München – 89-59 44 92
Travel Incentive Agency (Hannover) – 511-36 49 40
TUI (Hannover) – 511-5670

German Coach Companies

This is a selective list of German companies which run coach tours:
Bayern Express, Berlin – 30-86 00 96 43/4
Binder-Reisen (Stuttgart) – 711-13 96 50
Domberger (Augsburg) – 821-50 22 50
F.E.C. Travel (Düsseldorf) – 211-49 21 428
Hanseat Residebüro (Hamburg) – 40-30 90 31 22
Haru Reisen (Berlin) – 30-24 24 362
Merican Reisen – 66-41 30 38
Schielein Reisen (Nuremburg) – 911-64 20 636
Taeter (Aachen) – 241-18 20 00
Touring International (Frankfurt) – 69-79 030

CASUAL WORK

If your German isn't up to scratch, taking a job at a basic level is the best way of learning quickly. But beware, it is no use taking a job if all your fellow workers are non-German speaking.

Many jobs in catering require a *Gesundheitszeugnis* (health certificate) and it can help if you have taken a course in basic kitchen hygiene. Ask the Environmental Health Office at your local town hall, or contact the EHO of Kensington and Chelsea (0171-937 5464) who run regular courses.

Seasonal jobs for summer or winter can be fixed up by sending off speculative applications. This worked for Dean Fisher, an unemployed engineering apprentice, who went to wash dishes in Berchtesgaden on the Austrian border:

> *I spent 2¹/₂ months working in a very orderly and efficient kitchen on the top of a mountain in the Kehlsteinhaus (Eagle's Nest) with the most amazing view I've ever seen. I actually enjoyed the work even though it was hard going. I met loads of good people and learned a lot of German.*

Look for adverts in the local press, especially *Abendzeitung* in Munich. Key words to look for on notices and in adverts are *Notkoch und Küchelhilfe gesucht* (relief and kitchen assistant required), *Spüler* (dishwasher), *Kellner, Bedienigung* (waiters/waitresses), *Schenkekellner* (pub type barman); *Büffetier* (barman in a restaurant), *Büffetkräfte* (fast food server), or simply *Services*.

If your German is shaky and you are finding that a door-to-door search is not producing results, take Emma Forster's advice and concentrate on fast food outlets, as she did in Hamburg:

> *Go in person to any McDonalds or Burger King. We had no trouble getting job offers on the spot, without speaking a word of German. The wages by British standards are high. I get over £5 an hour and 20% extra if I do the night shift. We reckon we can save DM2,000 after two months work.*

So if you want to save money quickly, selling hamburgers in Hamburg would seem to be the answer.

Munich is estimated to have 2,000 pubs and restaurants (concentrated in the fashionable suburb of Schwabing) and Berlin is similarly well endowed with eateries (try the Kurfürstendamm area). The Munich beer gardens, especially the massive Chinese Tower Biergarten, pay glass collectors and washers-up (most of whom would have lined their jobs up at the beginning of the season) DM100 a day tax free at the height of the season, when people work 14-hour days.

REGULATIONS

EU nationals who are employed by a German employer should benefit from the good working conditions and high wages standard throughout regulated industries in Germany but will have to contend with the labyrinthine bureaucracy. Procedures are supposed to be standard throughout the country, but they can still be confusing. Assuming your UK employer (if you have one) has not registered you, the first step is to register with the local authority (*Einwohnermeldeamt*) at the town hall (*Ortsamt* or *Rathaus*). After the form (*Anmeldung*) has been signed by your landlord and employer, it should be taken back to the *Ortsamt* in order to pick up a tax card (*Lohnsteuerkarte*), after which you will be fully legal. Legal workers can expect to lose between 33% and 40% of their gross wages in tax and social security contributions, including a church tax (*Kirchensteuer*) which accounts for 8-9% of income tax, unless you claim an exemption due to atheism (and thereby forego the possibility of ever being married or buried in a German church).

For jobs which involve food service, you must acquire a *Gesundheitszeugnis* (health certificate) from the local *Gesundheitsamt* (health department). Restaurants will be heavily fined if they are caught employing anyone without it. When you go for the examination, you have to show either your *Anmeldung* or a job offer, pay a fee of about DM100 and wait about a fortnight for the certificate.

Some companies do not bother with the paperwork, which means they do not bother to provide legislated benefits either. EU nationals are unlikely to get in serious trouble this way, though they may have problems if they require medical attention.

Non-EU nationals must obtain a residence permit (*Aufenthaltserlaubnis*) if they intend to stay longer than three months. The minimum requirements for this are a certificate of good conduct notarised by your embassy or consulate (the US Embassy charges $10 for this), a *Gesundheitszeugnis* (as above), proof of health insurance, a stable address and means of support. If you intend to work and to apply for a work permit (*Arbeitserlaubnis*) from the *Arbeitsamt*, your *Aufenthaltserlaubnis* must bear the appropriate stamp.

The authorities have begun to enforce the immigration rules more enthusiastically. Raids on hotels and restaurants are frequent in some places, to clamp down on people working black (*Schwartzarbeiter*), including illegal workers from Eastern Europe and elsewhere. American students who are seeking a short-term exposure to the tourist industry of Germany should contact the Council on International Educational Exchange in New York (205 E 42nd St, New York, NY 10017) which can arrange for American students who have studied some German at college to work for up to three months between May and mid-October. Details are available by phoning 212-822-2600. A similar scheme is open to Australians from Student Services Australia (PO Box 399, Carlton South, VIC 3053; 399-257 269).

DIRECTORY REFERENCES

For companies which operate in Germany, see the following entries in the Directory section: Alpotels, Bloomsbury Bureau,, Canvas, Edwin Doran Music Travel, Equity, Eurocamp, Eurotoques, Keycamp, Panita.

Greece

Since the days of the Grand Tour when privileged young Englishmen (and a handful of women) braved the journey to Greece to explore the ruins of ancient civilisation, Greece has attracted culture vultures. But it also hosts a huge number of sun-seekers as well. The range of resorts and tourist destinations varies enormously from glamorous yacht marinas frequented by wealthy Athenians (such as Aegina) to young people's 'party islands' like Ios.

After the last war, Greece was in turmoil, and tourism was seen as a saviour for the poor economy, until eventually so many visitors poured over the land frontiers that the Greeks had to rethink their tourism strategy. Since joining the EU the country benefited from EU funding to improve its infrastructure, becoming one of the most popular tourist destination countries in the Mediterranean. However, tourism has suffered in recent years purely because of the low standards of bathroom facilities in many Greek hotels. This has led to the withdrawal of some tour operators who now prefer to focus more attention on areas like Turkey.

Obviously there are still many employment opportunities at both ends of the spectrum, both casual and professional, in a country whose tourist industry employs a third of a million people. Yet there will always be competition for jobs in a country which is one of the poorest in Europe. Unemployment is expected to hover around 10% throughout the 1990s. The huge influx of economic migrants from Albania and the Balkans has reduced the pool of available jobs further, though they tend to take labouring and agricultural jobs more than jobs in tourism.

Prospects for Work

Recently the emphasis on tourism promotion by the Greek National Tourist Office has changed to encourage families who rent villas or stay in hotels and conference delegates. At this end of the market, the main areas for employment are as villa company reps and, to a lesser extent, tour managers and conference staff. Athens is the main venue for conferences, particularly connected wtih shipping and the oil industry.

Many tourist establishments around Greece are family businesses where the concept of 'marketing' is alien and the cooking is done by a female relative, not by someone who has been to catering college. This is all part of the charm. Yet there is also a growing demand for a more professional and sophisticated brand of tourism, and an acknowledged shortage of people with experience and qualifications to work in these.

Corfu, Crete, Rhodes, Ios and Paros seem to offer the most job openings in tourism, though Naxos, Santorini and Mykonos, and to a lesser extent Aegina and Spetsai, have been recommended. The vast majority of reps working in Greece are hired by the large tour operators in their home country. However anyone who takes a holiday in Greece or has an extended stay and falls in love with the country can sometimes fix up a repping job, by meeting and making a good impression on the reps and their supervisor.

Apart from conference work, there is almost no work to be had in the winter. Once the autumn storms come, the villages and resorts fade into ghost towns. However many operators run programmes to Cyprus during the winter, and may employ those staff who have worked well for them in the summer (especially if they speak some Greek).

FINDING A JOB

The hundreds of tour operators that feature Greece want reps, kiddies' reps, resort office staff and transfer staff, most of whom are hired in the tour operator's country of origin. Opportunities for advancement from junior rep to manager in charge of reps on one or more islands are good. People who are on self-catering holidays in villas or apartments are looked after by company reps who will be in charge of several locally-owned villas/apartments. Companies which employ reps in the UK include:

Kosmar Villa Holidays – 0181-368 6833.

Manos Holidays, 168/172 Old St, London EC1V 9BP (0171-216 8070/fax 0171-216 8099).

The season is usually a long one, from Easter until October. Most major tour companies do not seriously expect applicants to speak Greek, though a smattering certainly helps when wanting to explain to a Greek villa owner that the plumbing needs repairing. You can also avoid the mistake Rhiannon Bryant made in a Cretan resort, of greeting everyone 'psari' which means fish during the first week of her job. At the least, job-seekers should familiarise themselves with the Greek alphabet.

Many members of the Association of Independent Tour Operators specialise in

Greece. Various indexes indicate to which islands each company sends clients, from Crete to 'very small remote islands'. However these companies may need to take only a couple of seasonal staff, and so can afford to be choosy and in some cases (like *Simply Travel*) insist on a knowledge of Greek. One interesting possibility is to work as a volunteer wildlife guide for *Friends of the Ionian*, an organisation sponsored by British tour operators worried about the impact of tourism on the Ionian islands of Levkas, Zakinthos, Kefallinia, etc.

Other companies that feature Greece are:

Golden Sun, 15 Kentish Town Road, London NW1 8NH (0171-267 2657). British only aged 19-24, with knowledge of Greek if possible. Lively personality and ability to work on own.

Sunvil Holidays (Greece), Sunvil House, Upper Square, Old Isleworth, Middlesex TW7 7BJ (0181-568 4499/fax 0181-568 8330).

Sunworld, 29 Elmfield Road, Bromley, Kent BR1 1LT (0181-290 1111).

Unijet, Sandrocks, Rocky Lane, Haywards Heath, Sussex RH16 4RH (01444 459100).

Up-market tour operators often look for guides with a good classical education. Although these tours will pick up excellent local Greek guides for visits to classical sites, the tour manager will be expected to discuss everything from Homer's *Iliad* to Byron's poetry (since Byron went to Greece to fight the Turks) to the ethics of Lord Elgin removing the marbles to the British Museum. Many American student and college tours visit Greece, though the level of sophistication may not be so high on these, as one guide points out:

> *All I needed to know was where to find ice cold coca cola especially as our tour was a cheapie and the coach didn't have air-conditioning.*

High-season transfer reps are recruited locally in resorts where the number of arrivals is too high for full-time reps to accompany each coachful. Most transfer reps meet night flights. At the beginning of the season, companies are quite selective but as the drop-out rate is high, they sometimes become desperate, perhaps desperate enough to offer a free end-of-season flight. Initially, you must present yourself as somone who is well-groomed, sober and reliable. The pay is usually equivalent to £15-20 per night, and you might get two or three per week. According to Nicky Brown who did this for a UK tour operator on Rhodes:

> *In theory the job of seeing a coachload of passengers into their accommodation sounded easy. But sometimes it was a nightmare if the self-catering apartments had been wrongly numbered, double booked, occupied by passing drunks, locked and the key lost, not cleaned, trashed, unlit, not what the customer expected or any combination of the above. The driver will certainly not have had enough sleep and may be a danger on the road, rude, uncooperative, lecherous, violent, stupid or any combination of the above. (Your customers may be likewise.) I tried without success to find out whether I was insured to be driven at high speed without a seat belt in clapped-out coaches full of beer monsters driven by bug-eyed xenophobic misogynists around narrow mountain roads in the middle of the night. I suspect the answer was no.*

Greek Employers

Because of the downturn of tourism in Greece, there are less employment opportunities for the wandering traveller. In addition, working for a Greek company can be a hazardous enterprise because the contract you sign before the job starts may be worth very little once you arrive at the site. Cases have been reported of reps travelling all the way to Athens, only to be disappointed with the hours and wages they were expected to accept. With this in mind, if you are still insistent upon working for a local company, make sure the contract is legitimate and, if possible, try to talk to previous employees for reassurance.

Work is often advertised in the English language papers, the *Athens News* and the *Greek News*. Travel agencies in Athens may well be willing to take on an assistant even if they do not know Greek. Ana Güemes from Mexico always carries her diploma from the tourism course she had completed at home and on the strength of that was offered a summer job in the travel agency attached to the Athens hostel in which she was staying (Hostel Lozanni, 54 Kapodistriu Str., Vathis Square). Without tourism training, Rhiannon Bryant spent the season working in a Cretan resort travel agency, on the strength of having spent several previous seasons there doing less elevated jobs (see section on Casual Work below).

Largely because of his ability to speak some Greek, Jerry Graham was hired several years ago by a Greek tour operator as an excursion guide in Aghia Galini (southern Crete). In a typical week he did three excursions, one of which was an overnight trip to the Samaria Gorge) and one or two days in the office. Although he didn't receive commissions (which was what kept guides working for British tour operators solvent), he did earn generous tips. The experience did not leave him with a very favourable impression of Greek tour operator bosses:

> *Without wanting to get into racist stereotypes it is important to be flexible, since your average Greek tour operator runs on an emotional rollercoaster which, depending on the state of business, means you can be treated anywhere from the best thing since sliced bread to something you would scrape off the underside of a shoe.*

Jerry went on to say that his boss asked him not to point out defects (apart from life-threatening ones) in cars that were being hired, hotels or restaurants on excursion routes, etc., all of which has been made illegal under EU-wide regulations. The money was generally poor, though Jerry did receive lots of perks including free food and drink, reduced car hire on days off and free Greek lessons.

Jobs at Sea

Flotilla sailing companies like *Sunsail* cater for Germans, Swiss, Austrians, and Scandinavians as well as Britons, so European languages are an advantage. Hostesses, cooks and other crew are sometimes taken on by skippering brokers and yacht agencies around Piraeus. English companies such as Camper & Nicholson (0171 4912950) prefer to hire English speakers, as do many local firms. This can also be fixed up in any island marina after meeting the right people.

The numerous cruise ships which play the Aegean Sea are occasionally looking for personnel to replace people who have left their jobs. Phone numbers of the relevant companies can be obtained from travel agents or in the Yellow Pages under *Krouazieres*. A number of cruise lines have shipping offices on the same street, Akti Miaouli in Piraeus, i.e. Epirotiki at number 87, Royal Cruise Lines at 81, Square Ltd at 65 and Dolphin Hellas at 71.

Freelance Work

Foreigners (especially women) may also be hired on-the-spot in tourist resorts to deliver cars for car rental firms or to act as transfer couriers. Xuela Edwards and her companion Nicky Brown went to the package resort of Lindos on Rhodes in April and were offered several jobs on the first day. They worked as tour guides on day-trips from the village and also did airport transfers for British tour companies. They found this work by asking around at those local travel agencies which acted as the headquarters for overseas reps. According to Xuela this work requires that you be 'presentable, reliable, able to work all night and get up very early in the morning'.

Bear in mind that guides who take responsibility for a group must have the correct insurance cover.

CASUAL WORK

Casual work is readily available (mainly for women) in bars and tavernas all over Greece. Word of mouth and the direct approach are the only effective ways to find work in Greece. Anyone who looks for work at the beginning of the season (from early May) should be able to find an opening somewhere. A good time to look is just before the Orthodox Easter when the locals are beginning to gear up for the season. If you do fix up a job that early, you will have to be prepared to support yourself until the job starts. There is very little work outside the May to September period although, in a few cases, a bar or restaurant may keep you on on a commission-only basis.

Most foreigners are employed in American/European style cocktail bars and other places frequented by a tourist clientele, though jobs in cafés patronised by locals are not an impossibility as Rhiannon Bryant discovered in Crete:

I was the only bar girl in Paleohóra who enjoyed working at the Jam Bar; all the others had left within a month. The only customers were Greek men, no English-speaking modern types, just local 'cowboys'. Late each night, the cowboy saloon doors would swing open and in they'd step, always in a group with synchronised movements. The right foot, a twiddle of their moustaches, then the left foot, followed by a flick of their worry beads, their pockets bulging with pistols and bullets. I was fascinated. The Cretan music would drive them to a frenzy, smashing bottles, glasses and on one occasion, a guy was so excited he shot the toilet. The atmosphere was explosive. If I wasn't dodging bullets and glass, I'd stare mesmerised. Actually one of them is now my boyfriend. Beneath their macho exteriors they are very kind-hearted, gentle guys.

Women travellers will find it much easier than men to land a casual job in a bar or restaurant. As one disgruntled male traveller wrote to us:

In general I would say that if you're a girl you have a 50% better chance of finding work in the tourist industry abroad. In Greece I would say women have a 500% better chance. Every pub I went into on Corfu seemed to have an English barmaid.

If men are finding it difficult to find a service job, they may find taverna-owners willing to hire them as washers-up or roof menders. Some men are needed to build, paint or clean villas and hotels. In populous resorts, men are hired to unload trucks of supplies (crates of soft drinks, Retsina, etc.) for the cafés.

"Late each night the saloon doors would swing open and the local cowboys would step in, twirling their moustaches and shooting up the toilet"

Employment Agencies

Athens agencies which place young people in tourism jobs do not generally enjoy a good reputation. Jane McNally visited the agencies in search of work recently and offers the following warnings:

> *I've come across some very dodgy agencies which ask for applicants' passports and hold them as security while they go off on a wild goose chase for a job. They have also been known to promise the same job on an island to more than one person. Never pay an agency fee before you leave for the job. If they are unwilling to negotiate taking the money out of your first month's salary, do a vanishing act. Instead of leaving your passport, leave some less important document like an old student card. Women should never accept a job outside Athens unless they have enough money to flee if they have to. Agencies sometimes send girls to seemingly safe waitressing jobs which turn out to be as 'company girls' in sleazy bars.*

Hostels

The competition for business among hostels and cheap pensions is so intense that many hostel owners employ travellers to persuade new arrivals to stay at their hostel. In exchange for meeting the relevant boat, train or bus, 'runners' receive a bed, a basic sum (normally only DR1,500-2000) and a small commission for every 'catch.' The work is tough, but it can be surprisingly lucrative if you benefit from end-of-season bonuses, including international air tickets. Well established hostel runners also earn kickbacks for giving tourists advice, i.e. recommending certain bars, nightclubs and restaurants. Apparently some employers reward good runners with island-hopping passes or even free plane tickets when the season finishes.

A great many hostels offer a free bed, pocket money (e.g. DR4,000 a week) and in some cases meals to people who will spend a few hours a day cleaning. Many enjoy the hostel atmosphere and the camaraderie among hostel workers, and they regard the job as a useful stop-gap while travel plans are formulated, often based on the advice of fellow travellers. Anyone who sticks at it for any length of time may find themselves 'promoted' to reception; in this business a fortnight might qualify you for the honour of being a long-term employee. This work is easy-come, easy-go, and is seldom secure even when you want it to be.

WORKING CONDITIONS

Anyone working in the Greek tourist industry will soon come across problems in the infrastructure, especially on the islands. In some cases airport services are woefully inadequate and leave weary tourists who have arrived in the middle of the night waiting hours for a run-down baggage system to deliver their luggage, only to be faced with a coach and ferry journey of five hours or more to their resort. Representatives often have to work very long shifts on changeover day due to the long transfer times and airport problems. Michelle, who worked for Manos, claims that it was not unusual to start work at 8am, finish at 6pm in time to shower, change and pick up last week's guests for an airport transfer. All being well, she was back in her resort by 4am the next morning, but sometimes not until nearer 9.30am when it was time to attend a welcome meeting.

The Greek infrastructure is not always sufficiently robust in other respects to deal with the pressures put on it by the mass invasion of tourists. Camilla Lambert enjoyed her job as a bar manageress with Sunsail in Levkas except when the fridge, freezer and ice machine all packed up in a heatwave and she had to take the brunt of the guests' fury while trying to rouse someone to come and repair the faulty machinery.

As a rep 'your' villas and apartments are often located in different villages; the normal mode of transport is a bicycle or moped. (Make sure you have a crash helmet. With some tour operators it is a dismissable offence not to wear one, even if the locals scoff.) One advantage of working for a large tour operator is that you are unlikely to be posted to a small island where you will be very isolated (unless you speak fluent Greek). The disadvantage is that you will be expected to sell, sell, sell excursions. The commission is often pooled, so if you don't make the target you may incur the censure of your colleagues. Something else reps dread is the client assessment forms distributed by certain tour operators.

People working on a casual basis in the Greek tourist industry tend to earn between dr3,000 and dr5,000 for an evening shift, occasionally dr6,000, enough to cover accommodation (from dr50,000 a month for an apartment), food and a social life.

Alison Cooper describes the transience she experienced working in the tourist industry:

> I spent the summer on the island of Ios doing the typical touristy work: wait-ressing, touting, dishwashing, etc. It was very common to have worked at four different places in a week due to being sacked for not flirting with your boss, but I had a great time partying all night and sunbathing all day long.

As soon as the guests start to dwindle, your job will disappear.

Some women find the legendary attention paid by prowling male Greeks intolerable; others have said this unwanted admiration is not unduly difficult to handle. Once you have established your reputation (one way or the other) you will be treated accordingly, at least by the regulars. But still, you might not want to undertake the sort of job Sharon Inge found in Khania's bars sitting around outside to attract tourists and American soldiers inside. When Nicola Sarjeant's bar at Perissa Beach on Santorini was quiet, she was expected to liven things up by dancing, to which she said 'No thanks'.

Always insist on getting paid at the end of each day's work, so no misunderstandings can arise. Laura O'Connor describes the difficulty she had with her employer on Mykonos:

> *I would not recommend this job to a fellow traveller. We worked in the laundry room from 11am-7pm, and had all our meals (which were hearty) and accommodation provided. The only problem was in getting our money. It's like blood out of a stone. We were told dr4,000 per day but when you go for your money there's no one around, or you wait ages then they say 'tomorrow, tomorrow'. Well, we finally got our money but only dr3,000. You haven't a leg to stand on. They'll pay if you stand up to them, especially if you are a woman since they are so shocked.*

Stephen Psallidas agrees. He describes his life as a waiter on Mykonos as idyllic but did not relish the constant attempts to rip him off. His advice is to stand up for yourself from the beginning since any weakness will be exploited. He was not prepared to act in the unprofessional way his boss expected, i.e. to present 'fiddled' bills to customers and he would not stand for his tips being pinched. He recommends threatening to leave and, if necessary, carrying out the threat, as much for the sake of working travellers who come along next.

But not everyone expresses such dissatisfaction with their Greek bosses. Safra Wightman was delighted at how easily she found work on Naxos by strolling the *paralia* and stopping at a café which caught her eye. She decided that the direct approach was the best approach and asked the man standing in the door whether he had a job for her. He simply said yes and she started work that evening. She concluded that 'Greeks are kind, welcoming, generous people.'

Working in heavily touristed areas can leave you feeling jaded. Scott Corcoran describes Kavos in the south of Corfu as a 'nightmare resort town full of northerners drinking Newcastle brown ale and eating chip butties' but since it has 200 bars and restaurants there is plenty of employment. (Scott got work as a 'PR' persuading tourists into 'his' restaurant which paid dr2,000 a day and which he found a 'real doss'.) Jill Weseman describes the 700-bedded Pink Palace on Corfu as a cross between a Club Med for backpackers and an American summer camp. It employs an army of foreign workers as bartenders, cooks, receptionists, etc. but the pay and conditions are reputed to be below average. On Paros, there are jobs in the main town of Parikia and also in the quieter town of Naoussa where the season is shorter, accommodation less expensive and wages higher.

REGULATIONS

When EU nationals stay in any member country longer than three months, they are supposed to apply for a residence permit at least three weeks before that period expires. To get a residence permit in Greece, take your passport, a letter from your employer and a medical certificate issued by a state hospital to the local police station. The bureaucratic procedures are still fairly sluggish and frustrating and some working travellers continue to find it easier to pop over a border and re-enter on another three-month tourist visa.

Non-EU nationals who find employment are supposed to have a 'letter of hire' sent to them in their home countries. In its desire to conform to EU policies, the Greek government has increased the fines for illegal workers to dr200,000 while guilty employers are liable to jail sentences. Yet so much of the work undertaken in Greece (including by Greeks) is done 'black', many casual workers encounter no problems, in many cases with the full knowledge of the local police.

DIRECTORY REFERENCES

Most of the major tour operators have large contingents of reps in Greece. See the following entries in the Directory: Airtours, CV Travel, Greek Islands Club, Olympic Holidays, Manos Holidays, Mark Warner, Simply Travel, Skyros Holiday Centre, Sunsail, Sunvil and Sunworld.

Ireland

Southern Ireland has always managed to maintain a very high tourism profile, particularly in North America, and tourism has been a mainstay of its economy. A new departure is the increased attractiveness of Northern Ireland in the current political climate. It has been estimated that 10,000 new jobs in both Northern and Southern Ireland will be created if the peace is permanent. Recently there have been moves to market the island jointly, which can only result in an overall increase of the number of arrivals. As confidence in the peace process gathers momentum, bookings will undoubtedly increase. To service this increase, a lot of investment will be needed, especially in providing accommodation in Belfast and throughout Northern Ireland.

Prospects for Work

Ireland is most famed for its unspoiled scenery and lack of urban bustle and development. Consequently many companies organise holidays which take advantage of Ireland's rural charms, perhaps with a bird-watching or botanical theme, or for people who fish, ride, cycle or golf. Self-catering holidays are very popular and are readily available from companies like Shamrock Cottages (50 High St, Wellington, Somserset TA21 8RD). Unfortunately such holidays do not create much employment.

The beautiful scenery is undoubtedly a great attraction, but what Ireland is most appreciated for by many visitors is the friendliness of the Irish people whom they meet. Anyone who comes from outside to work will find that they have a hard act to follow. Furthermore the very high rate of unemployment (nearly 17%) means that opportunities with Irish-based companies are few, apart from some seasonal work at the lower end. But a great many UK companies take accompanied tours to Ireland and anyone with some tour managing experience can try to get taken on as a tour director by a company like *Insight International Tours* or *Trafalgar Tours*. The standard brochure from the Irish Tourist Board contains a list of British tour operators offering tours of Ireland. In addition to the mainstream coach tour operators like Page & Moy, Shearings, Travelsphere and Saga, the following offer the best chance of employment:

Appleby Coaches, Lincolnshire (01507 358781)
Bakers Dolphin Coaches, Avon (01934 635666)
Cresta Holidays, Cheshire (0161 9277000)
DA Study Tours, Williamton House, Low Causeway, Culross, Fife KY12 8HL (01383 882200).

Excelsior Holidays, Bournemouth (01202 309555)
Grand UK Holidays, 6 Exchange Street, Norwich, Norfolk NR2 1AT (01603 628828)
Headwater Holidays, Cheshire (01606 486999)
Whytes Coach Tours, Aberdeen (01651 862211)
Yorks Tours & Holidays, Town Centre House, 8 Mercers Row, Northampton NN1 2QC (01604 621014)

American tours, especially student groups, employ a large number of UK-hired guides who meet the group at Heathrow, accompany them round Britain on the milk-run, cross from Fishguard to Ireland, tour Ireland, then leave on one of the northern ferry routes to Scotland. French, German, Belgian and Dutch groups are also a possible source of guiding opportunities. The ferry companies, especially Stena Sealink, have been doing a massive marketing exercise to encourage continental tour operators to bring their coaches to Ireland by ferry. The giant German crane-manufacturing company Liebherr has built and converted hotels in southern Ireland suitable for such tour groups. Note that the ferry operators and airlines also act as tour operators offering coach and special interest tours, including:

Aer Lingus Holidays/Drive Ireland, 223 Regent St, London W1 (0181-569 4001).
Irish Ferries, Ground Floor, Reliance House, Water St, Liverpool L2 8TP (0990 171717).
Ryanair Holidays, Dublin Airport, Co. Dublin, Ireland (1-844 4400).
Stena Holidays, Charter House, Park Street, Ashford, Kent TN24 8EX (01233 647033).

Ireland is a popular country for conferences. With the new Waterfront Conference Centre opened in Belfast there are even more opportunities.

US students seeking work should contact Council in New York (1-888-COUNCIL). They administer a work exchange scheme which allows US citizens to work in Ireland for up to 4 months at any time of year.

Special Interest Tours

The superb lakes and rivers found throughout Ireland including Lough Neagh in Northern Ireland, the largest lake in Britain, are meccas for fishermen and boat enthusiasts (and their families). The following companies organise specialist angling holidays in southern Ireland:

Anglers Abroad, 6 Park St, Wombwell, Barnsley, S. Yorks. S73 0DJ (01226 751704).
Angler's World Holidays, 46 Knifesmithgate, Chesterfield, Derbyshire S40 1RQ (01246 221717).
Cliff Smarts Holidays, The Coach House, 90g High Street, Burton Latimer, Northants. NN15 5LA (01536 724226).
Kings Angling Holidays, 27 Minster Way, Hornchurch, Essex RM11 3TH (01708 453043).
Leisure Angling Breaks, 33 Dovedale Road, Liverpool L18 5EP (0151-734 2344).

There are supposed to be more golf courses per head of population in Ireland than anywhere else in the world, so there are jobs to be found on these, especially at the times of the big tournaments. Golf holiday specialists are worth approaching by people who are involved in the sport, such as 3D's Golf Promotions (01292 263331), who are based in Scotland.

Every time there is a famous horse race in Ireland, hordes of Britons fly over to attend. Some of these go in incentive travel groups, others are organised by pubs, social clubs and local coach companies who often need tour guides; watch your local press.

Activity Holidays

Experienced trek leaders and instructors may be needed by riding stables and watersports centres throughout Ireland. Monitors and instructors are needed for children's activity centres, for example the holidays run by *PGL*. The Errislannan Manor Connemara Pony Stud (Clifden, Co. Galway) need pony trek leaders for three months in the summer.

Working Conditions

Although visitors may find the *manana* attitude to which many Irish people subscribe quaint and charming, it is not so appealing when you are working and trying to keep customers happy. Mig Urquhart from Glasgow has variously worked in an Irish hostel, bed and breakfast and now for the new boat taxi on the River Liffey which will be patronised by tourists, school groups and commuters. According to her, 'Irish time' is a wonderful concept when one is doing the work, but when one is waiting for something to be finished it can be frustrating. Nevertheless she hopes that it will never disappear because it beats the uptight stressed out life in other countries where she has worked like the United States. She goes on to point out one important exception: 'pubs have some of the best trained and fastest barmen in the world, who take great pride in their profession'.

A longstanding problem for tour guides is the resentment they encounter from coach drivers. Before Ireland joined the European Community, Irish coach drivers were used to being the courier and guide as well: the roads were nearly empty and the passengers invariably fell in love with the wit and charm of their drivers. As has been mentioned elsewhere, driver-guiding is now officially banned in the EU and is gradually being phased out even in Ireland, so there should be more jobs for trained guides in coming years and less open hostility between driver and tour guide. Note that the Irish government tourism training agency CERT (Amiens St, Dublin 1; 1-874 2555) offers excellent vocational courses in guiding, etc.

There is such a high concentration of tour coaches at peak times following the same narrow roads to the same destinations (especially the Ring of Kerry) that it is essential to liaise with coach drivers working for other companies when planning the day's itinerary. Normally the level of cooperation is high with drivers agreeing times among themselves so that their groups can see castles, shop and have meals in comfort rather than have to queue because another coach has arrived at the same time.

CASUAL WORK

Outside Dublin, the largest demand for seasonal workers is in the southwestern counties of Cork and Kerry, especially the towns of Killarney (with 107 pubs) and Tralee. Write to the addresses in any guide to hotels in Ireland. One hotel which hires chefs, and may need porters and waiting/bar staff for the summer season is The Olde Railway Hotel (The Mall, Westprot, Co. Mayo; 353 98 25166). When applying, you should mention any musical talent you have, since pubs and hotels may be glad to have a barman who can occasionally entertain at the piano. Directly approaching cafés, campsites, amusement arcades and travelling circuses is usually more effective than writing.

In Dublin, try the trendy spots in Templebar in the city centre, such as the Elephant & Castle (18 Templebar; 679 3121). This is an eating spot which hires mostly foreign workers and where the tips can be good. Also try the Tex/Mex restaurant in Nassau Street called Judge Roy Beans, downstairs from the nightclub Lillie's Bordello (where workers can earn excellent tips). The owner is said to be well informed about other Dublin restaurants and clubs so a visit to JRB can be worthwhile. There are always jobs in fast food franchises. Try the Irish-owned chain Supermacs which pays more than the average (from IR£3 an hour). The advantage of these jobs is that you get fed and usually have the chance to work so many hours that you can save.

An Oige, the Irish Youth Hostels Association (61 Mountjoy St, Dublin 7; 1-830 4555) has 44 hostels throughout the country and relies to a large extent on casual assistance, mostly on a voluntary basis. Private hostels may also hire assistants; try Morehampton House , 78 Morehampton Road, Donnybrook, Dublin 4; tel 1-6602 106.

There are innumerable festivals throughout Ireland, mostly during the summer. Big-name bands often perform at concerts near Dublin. A small fortune can be made by amateur entrepreneurs (with or without a permit) who find a niche in the market. Heather McCulloch had two friends who sold filled rolls and sandwiches at a major concert and made a clear profit of over £1,000 in just a few hours.

'The Rose of Tralee', a large regional festival held in Tralee, Co. Kerry in the first week of September, provides various kinds of employment for enterprising workers, as Tracie Sheehan reports:

> As 50,000 people attend this festival each year, guest houses, hotels, restaurants and cafés all take on extra staff. Buskers make great money, as do mime artists, jugglers and artists. Pubs do a roaring business, so singing or performing in a pub can be very profitable.

DIRECTORY REFERENCES

See the following entries for companies which operate in Ireland; Bike Riders Tours, European Waterways, Expo Garden Tours, Guide Friday and Trafalgar Tours.

Italy

Italy is the favourite country of many people working in tourism. It has good food and wine, fantastic scenery and culture and the Italians go out of their way to welcome visitors. The country is a collection of states which have been unified for a scant hundred years, of Romans, Venetians, Florentines and so on. The regional and cultural differences add to the interest and excitement of working in Italy.

Italy's tourist industry employs between 6% and 7% of the Italian workforce and on the whole is rather protectionist. There are difficulties working for a UK tour company due to legal restrictions on the hiring of non-Italian staff. Most foreign tourists head for the major cities – Florence, Rome, Venice, Pisa and so on – where there is a ready supply of well-trained, impeccably dressed and trilingual guides to look after the tourists. Some foreign companies do employ foreign staff by finding a loophole in the rules, e.g. calling themselves 'art and cultural associations.'

Tour managers taking groups to Italy must have a recognised qualification such as a diploma from BREDA or the RSA Tour Guides Certificate and carry a copy of their certificate translated into Italian and certified by the local Italian consulate. Recently, tour managers who had no certificate were hauled off coaches and faced fines as high as 2 million lire.

Prospects for Work

There are tourism jobs to suit everyone, from meet and greet staff working at the major airports and ports, tour guides for coach tours of culture vultures, ski reps for school groups, reps looking after young groups holidaying on the Adriatic and older groups taking in the Italian lakes and cities, incentive tour managers at glamorous resorts like the Costa Smeralda in Sardinia and so on.

British coach operators need tour guides to take groups around Italy, either by coach from Britain or flying to an airport in Switzerland or Italy, picking up their coach and then touring. The UK is the main marketplace for obtaining jobs with coach companies touring Italy. American students come over in large numbers each year to visit Italy, and most of the companies handling their travel have their European offices in London. British coach companies offer every kind of tour to Italy, from the cheap and cheerful based on one or two centres, to upmarket tours around the cultural high spots.

Most of the potential work opportunities are found in the northern half of the country, between the alpine borders and Rome. The south is poorer with high unemployment and not as easy to visit as the north with its excellent communications with the rest of Europe. The relatively low unemployment in the Veneto region (which includes Venice, Padua and Verona) makes it a better bet than some of the other tourist regions of Italy such as the Adriatic coastal resorts of Rimini and Pescara and the Italian Riviera (Portofino, San Remo, etc.), though it may be worth trying resorts on Lake Maggiore like Stresa and Cannero. Michael Cullen worked in three hotels around Como and Bellagio and found 'a nice friendly and warm atmosphere, despite the heat and long hours'. High unemployment together with a huge population of migrant workers from poor countries in the south of Italy means that it is probably not worth trying the resorts south of Naples, viz. Capri, Sorrento and Amalfi. Even in flourishing resorts like Rimini, there seems to be nearly enough locals and Italian students to fill most of the jobs. As Stephen Venner observed, 'Although prospects appeared to be good in Rimini, café and hotel owners were unwilling to take on foreigners because of the paperwork.'

Although less well known than the seaside resorts of other Mediterranean countries, there may be seaside possibilities for foreign job-seekers, especially in the resorts near Venice, as a local resident Lara Giavi confirms. She is familiar with two holiday regions: the Lake Garda resorts like Desenzano, Malcesine, Sirmione and Riva del Garda; and the seaside resorts near Venice like Lido di Jesolo (which she says is a great resort for young people), Bibione, Lignano, Caorle and Chioggiaa, all of which are more popular with German and Austrian tourists than Britons so a knowledge of German would be a good selling point. Lara thinks that there are opportunities for foreigners in catering, bars and hotels in Italy, though she admits that a knowledge of Italian is necessary in most cases, apart from the job of *donna ai piani* (chambermaid).

FINDING A JOB

Most major British tour operators have programmes to Italy, and if you want to work in the winter they offer summer staff first pick of winter sports jobs. Italian-owned tour operator *Citalia* accepts Italian-speaking staff in the UK, as do the following operators, in addition to the ones included in the Directory (listed at the end of this chapter):

ICT, Studios 20-21 Colmans Wharf, 45 Morris Road, London E14 6PA (0171-538 4627).

Italiatour, 9 Whyteleaf Business Village, Whyteleaf Hill, Whytleaf, Surrey CR3 080 (01883 621 900). In-house tour operator of Alitalia.

Magic of Italy, 227 Shepherds Bush Road, London W6 7AS (0181-748 7575/fax 0181-748 6381).

Page & Moy, 136-140 London Road, Leicester LE2 1EN (0116-250 7000).

Sunvil Holidays, Upper Square, Old Isleworth, Middlesex TW7 7BJ (0181-568 4499/fax 0181-568 8330).

Trina Tours, 74 New Oxford Street, London WC1A 1EU (0171-436 4488).

If you can stand the pace, are young, footloose and fancy-free, there are jobs as shuttle hosts and hostesses taking groups by coach to Italy. Try *Cosmos* or any of the major coach companies. If you are less young, a more sedate pace might be preferable, working on Inghams and Saga mountains and lakes tours where the temperatures are cooler.

Contiki's coach tours for an 18-35 clientele spend some time in Italy, and staff are needed for their stopovers (e.g. Florence, Venice, Rome). Without knowing much about the company or the job she was applying for, Carolyn Edwards was interviewed by Contiki and in her first season was employed as a general assistant at their Florence stopover site (a haunted villa). The job involved everything from cleaning toilets to delivering the welcome spiel.

The major camping tour operators (see Introduction) employ courier/reps and children's reps on their Italian sites, for which an ability to speak some Italian is a basic requirement. Many of these sites are on the Adriatic coast between Catolica and Rimini, Job-seekers who turn up at the gates on the off-chance of work might find some employment though at local casual rates without commission and perhaps without accommodation. Catherine Dawes enjoyed working for a UK camping tour operator near Albenga on the Italian Riviera – 'a fairly uninspiring part of Italy' – even more than she did her previous summer's work on a French campsite. She reports that the Italians seemed to be more relaxed than the French, especially under high season pressure, and would always go out of their way to help her when she was trying to translate tourists' problems to the mechanic or the doctor.

EU nationals can try using official channels to find work at the beginning of the season (mid-May), i.e. the *Ufficio di Collocamento* and the local *Associazione Albergatori* (hotels association) which should know of vacancies among its members.

Any EU national aged 18-27 with a vocational qualification in Leisure and Tourism (but not a university degree) should investigate the EU-funded schemes administered by ProEuropa (Europa House, Sharpham Drive, Totnes, Devon TQ9 5HE; 01803 864526). In the recent past they have been able to offer attractive summer packages of one month's language tuition in Florence followed by three months' work experience in the Italian tourist industry for a mere £100.

Special Interest Tours

Anyone with a degree in history, history of art, archaeology or any subject related to Italian culture may be able to find work with upmarket firms like *Alternative Travel* who run exclusive walking tours through the Tuscan hills. Groups often go to Rome and the Vatican on pilgrimages; your local church may have some leads. Two companies which specialise in pilgrimages to Rome (and elsewhere) are Tangney Tours (Pilgrim House, 3 Station Court, Borough Green, Kent TN15 8AF; 01732 886666) and Mancunia Travel (Peter House, 2-14 Oxford St, Manchester M1 5AW; 0161-228 2842).

Operators who sometimes require tour leaders with specialist knowledge and tour guides to look after their groups include:

Alternative Travel (see entry). Wild flowers, mushroom hunting, walking and cycling.

Arblaster & Clarke, Clarke House, Farnham Road, West Liss, Hants. GU33 6JQ (01730 893344). Wine tours of Tuscany, Umbria, Piedmont and Veneto.

Cox & Kings, 4th Floor, Gordon House, 10 Greencoat Place, London SW1P 1PH (0171-873 5006). Gourmet tours

Prospect Tours, 454 Chiswick High Road, London W4 5TT (0181-995 2151). Art tours.

Voyages Jules Verne, 21 Dorset Square, London NW1 6QG (0171-616 1000). Art tours.

On the Spot

Once you get a toehold in an Italian community you will find that a friendly network of contacts and possible employers will develop. Without contacts, it is virtually impossible to find work. Arriving in Diano Marina on the Ligurian coast to look for work, Bernie Lynes went to church on her first Sunday. The local grapevine decided she was a 'nice' girl, and she was soon offered a job with Holidayrama whose rep had fallen sick.

Local sightseeing companies may need meet and greet staff; their leaflets are often displayed at tourist offices, hotels and airports. This often requires 6am pickups from hotels for a long day tour such as the Capri tour from Rome, or to meet early flights. Anyone who knows Japanese might be hired to meet the very early arrivals from Japan since local staff prefer to start work at a more civilised hour. Meet and greet staff hired locally are generally paid around £20 per transfer.

Charter yachts may need experienced sailors as crew. Harbour masters along the Adriatic coast, Italian Riviera and in Sardinia can tell you if there are yachts looking for crew.

Winter Resorts

Opportunities exist on-the-spot in the winter resorts of the Alps, Dolomites and Apennines. Many of the jobs are part-time and not very well paid, but provide time for skiing and in many cases a free pass to the ski-lifts for the season. Sauze d'Oulx and Courmayeur seem to be the best resorts for job hunting. Although Cortina is probably the most famous, it has a high percentage of year-round workers, and is too sophisticated and expensive. Sauze d'Oulx is particularly recommended because it hosts so many British holidaymakers that every bar and shop in the resort likes to hire an English speaker. Remember that places like this will be dead before the season. If you are job-hunting in November, choose a weekend rather than a weekday to catch some businesses open. It doesn't always work of course. Susanna Macmillan gave up her job hunt in the Italian Alps after two weeks when she had to admit that her non-existent Italian and just passable French were not getting her anywhere.

PGL Ski Holidays offer reps' jobs and instructor positions to BASI-qualified skiers, whose fare to the resort is provided and whose salary is between £100 and £150 per week. As in other alpine resorts there are also jobs for chalet staff, though not as many as in neighbouring countries due to the very strict regulations which govern chalets in Italy.

Dog sledding is the fastest growing team sport in the Alps, with good facilities in the Trentino regio. Resorts such as Madonna Di Camiglio and Passo Di Tonale have excellent dog kennels and facilities, with several teams in each resort. One of the top sledders with large kennels is Armen Khatchikian, who always has two or three assistants for the season. These kennels are very small and cannot handle many enquiries from jobseekers, so if you are serious about working with the dogs, contact the local tourist board for addresses and approach them in person.

CASUAL WORK

The large hotels usually recruit their staff in southern Italy and then move them en masse from the sea to the mountains in the autumn. Relatively few students and others find work serving pizzas or cleaning hotel rooms in Italy compared to other European countries, but there are cheering exceptions to the rule. Dominic Fitzgibbon from Australia spent six weeks unsuccessfully looking for a job which used up a large proportion of his travel fund. But the landlady of the flat he was renting off the magnificent Piazza Navona took a shine to him, and arranged for him to work as a night porter for one of her friends who owned a 3-star hotel off Piazza Barberina, although he had 'no work permit and practically no Italian':

> *When I told my landlady that perhaps I would head off to Greece, she said I was far too nice to look for dishwashing work and told me about a friend who needed help running his seasonal hotel. Within 20 minutes I was behind the counter having the telephone system explained to me and was told I would be paid L1,100,000 a month for six nights a week as a night porter. After praying the telephone wouldn't ring for the first few weeks (since I spoke virtually no Italian), everything settled down. It's quiet, a little boring, but allows me to read and study Italian, more than the few key words related to the hotel trade I knew before. My boss is even going to lend me a TV to help me improve my Italian. I now know how lucky I was to find my place and this job.*

Another success was reported by Carolyn Edwards who had the advantage of having spent the summer season in Florence with Contiki. At the end of the season in October she got a job in an American-style bar in Florence called the Red Garter. She worked here for four months with barely enough Italian to get by. Unlike many people in jobs like this she was legal, at least for three days of the week, when she netted the equivalent of £30 for five hours work. If she worked any extra evenings, she was paid L50,000 cash.

As throughout the world, backpackers' haunts often employ travellers for short periods. Jill Weseman recommends trying the Pension Il Nido (a.k.a. Fawlty Towers) at Via Magenta 39 (5th floor) near the Termini Station in Rome where she noticed several Antipodeans working in reception, maintenance and cleaning. Beaches are a possible source of employment, needing refuse collectors, umbrella and bed dispensers, and drinks servers.

For hotel jobs, try the major chains such as Jolly and CIGA. If you don't get a job in a hotel, you might get work servicing holiday flats or gardening. You can also try Italian-run campsites which have a large staff to man the on-site restaurants, bars and souvenir shops. Stephen Venner noticed that the two main campsites in Rome (the Tiber and the Flamignio) take on English help before the season begins (i.e. March). There is work for Japanese speakers in the luxury boutiques in Rome's Via Condotti and Milan's Galleria.

CONDITIONS OF WORK

Tourism staff are generally treated extremely well. Hotels and restaurants usually provide tour guides and managers with the best rooms and anything they want to eat and (within reason) drink. Groups are welcomed at shops with gifts and treated very well. For example coaches arriving in Venice are met by a team of public relations staff from the major glass factories. Once you tell them which one your clients will be visiting, the company takes care of luggage and boat transport, confirms the guide and takes you for a drink.

Pay and commission for experienced tour guides is very good. Most British coach and tour companies offer between £25 and £40 a day as a starting salary, which may increase to £100 in the second season. Generally perks like free coffee and drinks, taxis if you work early or late and a chance to see the best operas, etc. flow freely, which makes up for the long hours.

Things may not be so rosy for casual workers. The seaside resorts are full of Italians (and others) working black and not being paid the going wage, overtime or holiday pay, but earning plenty of tips. A legally employed waiter should clear between L1,100,000 and L1,300,000 per month plus an end-of-season bonus of about L400,000, with a monthly deduction of just L50,000 for board and lodging. But most people working in bars, restaurants and hotels earn far less than that, something that travellers looking for a working holiday may not mind too much.

Tour guides should try to work for a company that has air-conditioned coaches. The heat can easily reach more than 100°F in high summer and sightseeing trips are often scheduled for the middle of the day.

Women don't normally have too many problems with the legendary Italian male. Once employed, you are looked upon as an honorary cousin which can mean the locals keep a watchful eye on you.

REGULATIONS

Unfortunately there are more red tape hassles in Italy than there are in other EU countries. Many job-seekers have found Italians reluctant to consider hiring them because of the bureaucratic hurdles which must be jumped. Even if working for an established tour operator who knows the ropes, it will take about four months to get the paperwork in order. Matters have been made worse by legislation intended to prevent an influx of refugees from eastern Europe. Be prepared to be given the run-around and for delays in the processing.

If you arrive with the intention of working, you must first apply to the police (*questura*) for a *Ricevuta di Segnalazione di Soggiorno* which allows you to stay for up to three months looking for work. Upon production of this document and a letter from an employer, you must go back to the police to obtain a residence permit – *Permesso di Soggiorno*. Then in some cases you will be asked to apply for a *Libretto di Lavoro* (work registration card) from the town hall or *Municipio*, although this should not be necessary for EU nationals. Roberta Wedge recalls the red tape:

> *I had to visit three different government offices about eight times in total. Not exactly the free movement of labour! My health card arrived six months after the wheels were set in motion.*

People working in the food and beverage departments of hotels will have to obtain a *Libretto sanitario* after having a free medical check-up at the local *Unita sanitaria locale* or USL. As mentioned above, Italy is very strict about qualifications in the tourist industry. Local guides have to take a stringent course and do not welcome unqualified people taking their work. It is not unknown for a policeman to stop a foreign touring coach and order the non-Italian tour manager out of their seat if they are found giving a commentary on the mike. Italy may be part of the EU but try explaining that to the policeman who thinks you are taking work away from his cousin the guide. Make sure your company has booked a local official guide for city sightseeing, who are excellent and very helpful if there are problems in the height of the season. In general it is advisable for reps to pay a courtesy call on the local police station.

Work permits for non-EU nationals will be issued only to people outside Italy and only for jobs where the Provincial Office of the Ministry of Labour is satisfied that no Italian can do the job. The *Autorizzazione al Lavoro* must then be presented at the Italian Embassy in the applicant's home country. In other words, they are virtually impossible to obtain except for elite jobs.

Remember that medical expenses can be crippling if you're not covered by the Italian Medical Health Scheme (USL). If your employer is not paying contributions, you might want to take out your own insurance at an office of SAI, one of the major Italian insurance companies.

DIRECTORY REFERENCES

Acorn Venture, Alternative Travel Group, Bike Riders Tours, Canvas, Casterbridge Tours, Ciclismo Classico, Citalia, Club Cantabrica, Contiki, Cosmos, Crystal Holidays, Equity, Eurocamp, European Waterways, Eurosites, Expo Garden Tours, Haven Europe, Headwater, Inghams, Magic of Italy, Mark Warner, Neilson Ski, Ramblers Holidays, Shearings, Simply Travel, Skibound, Ski Total, Skiworld, Topdeck, Venue Holidays.

Malta

Although small in area (30km by 15km), Malta has a flourishing year-round tourist industry. With its sister islands of Gozo and Comino, Malta hosts package tours in summer from throughout Europe (especially Britain, Scandinavia and Italy). In winter many elderly North Europeans go for an extended stay and in spring and autumn the conference season brings in high-spending visitors. Some go to Gozo which tends to be more exclusive than the main island. Malta is not such a popular destination for families (because the beaches are rocky or sparse) so children's reps are not much in demand. Also, very few North American groups find their way to Malta.

It is a surprise to many visitors that these islands have some of the oldest archaeological sites in the world. But most people visit the islands for the climate.

From the time St Paul was shipwrecked here about 60AD, the Maltese have welcomed visitors, despite having suffered incredible hardships from invaders throughout their history. The Ministry of Tourism is encouraging Maltese hotels to upgrade, and trying to encourage the more mature tourist who visits Malta for its history rather than the sun.

Working conditions are generally good for tour operator reps working in Malta. Everyone speaks English as well as their native Maltese (a language with Arabic/Semitic origins). Among the general population, the quality of education is high, and the standard of hotel and tour administration is correspondingly good (arguably better than the standard of driving; most buses have a little shrine over the driver's compartment).

Although Malta has successfully been sold as a winter sun destination, the weather does not always live up to the promises in the brochures. So any reps working the winter season should be sure to have a warm coat and wellies (for when the roads are flooded by heavy rains) and also plenty of sunny smiles to cheer up disgruntled clients.

FINDING A JOB

Most major tour operators go to Malta, especially those catering for the older market. The Maltese government is helping hotels to upgrade and modernise, which will mean better facilities for conferences. Many incentive companies send clients to Malta, so there is work with British, Scandinavian and German companies for freelancers who go out with clients.

Professional hotel staff may find work in the Forte, Hilton or Holiday Inn groups. Locally owned Ta'Cenc in Gozo and the Corinthia group are among the best and occasionally need staff. The student and youth travel organisation NSTS (220 St Paul St, Valletta; 356-244983/246628/e-mail nststrav@kemmunet.net.mt) might be able to place registered catering students in hotels or restaurants so it is worth contacting them. NSTS also run week-long activity holidays in the summer for which they may need experienced instructors for windsurfing and other sports, as well as general catering staff.

Of the relatively few special interest holiday companies which go to Malta, ones offering scuba diving and other water sports are the most popular. Multitours Malta/Gozo (7 Denbigh St, London SW1V 2HF; 0171-821 7000) offer tennis and diving holidays. Other specialist tour operators to Malta include:

Meon Villas, Meon House, College St, Petersfield, Hants. GU32 3JN (01730 268411).

Sunspot Tours Ltd, The Hill, Cranborook, Kent TN17 3ST (01580 715333).

For young people who wish to subsidise an extended stay, the *Malta Youth Hostels Association* (see entry) provides free accommodation in various member hostels to people who work for 21 hours a week, for up to a maximum of three months. Work includes administration, decorating, building and office work. Work permits must be obtained before beginning the job and this can take up to three months. Applicants must be aged 16-30. If you are interested, send 3 International reply coupons to Malta Youth Hostels Association, 17 Triq Tal-Borg, Pawla PLA O6, Malta.

On-the-Spot

There is not much work to be found in Malta, due to a high rate of unemployment, the impossibility of obtaining a work permit, the good standard of English spoken by most Maltese and the insular nature of the islanders. Still, there are so many cafés, bars, souvenir shops, etc. in the popular resorts of Sliema, Bugibba, etc. that the occasional opportunity may crop up.

DIRECTORY REFERENCES

For companies which employ people in Malta, see entries for Airtours, First Choice, Malta Youth Hostels Association, Panorama, Thomson and Unijet.

The Netherlands

The word Netherlands means low lands. The two most famous provinces are North and South Holland; when sailors from the ports of Amsterdam and Rotterdam were asked where they came from, they would give the name of their province, hence the rest of the world refers to the country as Holland.

The Netherlands is a major intercontinental gateway into Europe, particularly for groups of Americans, South Africans and people from the old Dutch colonies. For such a small country, it has a high profile in tourism terms. Several mega coach companies operate huge fleets of air-conditioned coaches servicing the incoming visitors to Europe, so this is a country that is a jumping-off place for tours and for finding tour management work. More immediately, the bulb fields between Leiden and Haarlem attract an enormous number of coach tours in April and May when the flowers are in bloom, and this is a standby of any tour guide's annual calendar. (See list of UK coach companies at the end of the Directory.)

The tourism infrastructure is very sophisticated. The Dutch government recognises that tourism is an important industry and ensures that there is good access to sights, good signposting and a high standard of cleanliness and efficiency in hotels, hostels and restaurants. World class exhibition and conference venues draw in business visitors, and museums and galleries provide the framework for cultural tours. Large family theme parks, notably Efteling run their own training programme for new employees.

Any prospective employees from outside the country have to compete with people who speak more languages per head of population than any other (with the possible exception of the Swiss). Asking a Dutch person whether or not they speak English is almost tantamount to hinting that they lack a good education. German is widely spoken, although there is still some resistance with memories of the last war.

Prospects for Work

Although groups arriving in Amsterdam on intercontinental flights pick up their coaches at Schiphol (pronounced Skipple) Airport for their round-Europe tour, many of the companies that organise these tours are based in London, so London-based tour managers are competing on an equal footing with Dutch staff. There is a need for speakers of Japanese, Chinese and other Asiatic languages, with no requirement to speak Dutch.

Most job opportunities will be found in the twin commercial capitals of Amsterdam and Rotterdam, rather than the capital Den Haag (The Hague). In Amsterdam the giant RAI exhibition and conference hall complex hosts many of the world's major international exhibitions and conferences, with consequent demand for suitable staff and a knock-on effect for tours, etc. Hotels such as the Marriott, Hilton, Grand Hotel Krasnapolsky, etc. have facilities for over 500 delegates, with similar venues in Rotterdam. However if you want to work in the hotels and catering industry, it is imperative to speak several languages or have professional training, unless you are prepared to take the lowliest jobs (see section on Casual Work below).

Cycling is the classic way to see the country, because of the Netherlands' famous network of cycle tracks and its undaunting terrain. Many Dutch companies offer bike tours for example Cycletours (20-627 4098)and Yellow Bike (20-620 6940).

Although the hotel boats that ply the Rhine are mostly German-registered, many start in Rotterdam or Amsterdam where they are sometimes looking to recruit cabin crew and entertainers. English is the major language, but it helps if you speak German.

FINDING A JOB

Because of its proximity to Britain, many school orchestras and other musical tours head for Holland each year. Try Gower Tours (2 High St, Studley, Warwickshire B80 7HJ; 01527 851410) or *Edwin Doran Music Travel* for example.

If you are in the Netherlands it is worthwhile visiting the state employment service, Directoraat Generaal de Arbeidsvoorziening at Volmerlaan 1, Rijswijk ZH or any local Arbeidsbureau. To find the local address, look up *Gewestelijk Arbeids Bureau* in the local telephone directory. There is a special division of the employment service for university graduates, the Bureau Arbeidsvoorziening Academici, Visseringlaan 26, Postbus 5814, 2280 HV Rijswijk.

There is not much point looking out for ads in newspapers such as *De Telegraaf, De Volkskrant* or *Algemeen Dagblad* unless you are a Dutch speaker. Guide training takes place in the major towns of Amsterdam, Rotterdam, Utrecht, etc. For details contact Guidor, PO Box 404, 2260AK Leischendam (70-419 55 44/fax 70 419 5519).

Conferences and Exhibitions

For details and addresses of organisers of forthcoming conferences and conventions, contact the Amsterdam Congress Bureau, Postbus 3901, 1001 AS Amsterdam (20-551 2570/fax 20-5512575), Rotterdam de Doelen (10-2171700), Rotterdam Congress Bureau (10-405 4464)or Utrecht Fair (30-2955466).

Two major conference organisers are: Congrex, AJ Ernstraat 595K, 1082 LD Amsterdam(20-5040200/fax 20-5040225) and Eurocongres, Koningslaan 52, 1075 AE Amsterdam (20-679 3411/fax 20-673 7306).

For details of exhibitions and the companies which are organising them, contact Amsterdam RAI, Europlein 8, Amsterdam (20-549 1212/fax 20-646 4469).

Some Dutch incentive conference organisers and tour operators include:
Arke Reisen, Damrak 90, 1012 LP Amsterdam (20-625 6520).
Arttra, Staalstraat 28, Amsterdam 1011 JM (20-625 9303) specialises in art tours.
Beuk, World Trade Centre, Tower A, 9th Floor, Strawinskylaan 915, Amsterdam 1077 XX (20-662 6277).
Dutch Travel Trade, Willemsparkweg 34, Amsterdam 1071 HG (20-673 5959).
Erasmus – 10-408 2606.
Evenements Reizen – 20-5869499.
Holland Arrival Travel – 20-622 6911.
Holland Organisation Centre – Parkstraat 29, 2514 JD Den Haag (70-3657850).

Holland Incoming – 20-614 8101.
Holland Travel Promotions, Boompjes 594, 3011 XZ Rotterdam (10-4135463).
ITB, Jan Luykenstraat 6, Amsterdam 1071 CM (20-675 7876).
Key Tours, Dam 19, Amsterdam 1012 JS (20-6235051).
Lindberg, Damrak 26, Amsterdam 1012 LJ (20-622 2766).
Mars Travel, Weteringschans 130, Amsterdam 1017 XV (20-622 8378).
Molino, Nic. Witsenkade 12h, Amsterdam 1017 ZR (20-6391063).
NBBS, Postbus 360, 2300 AJ Leiden (71-5688747).
Pool Travel – 20-626 5856.
Travel Team, Postbus 157, 2280 AD Rijswijk(70-3076307).

CASUAL WORK

Dutch hotels and other tourist establishments employ a large number of foreign workers both full time and temporarily during the tourist season. Most are from southern Europe, but a certain number are from Britain and Ireland. According to Simon Whitehead, foreigners are the last to be hired and the first to be fired, so do not expect job security in a hotel job. Although you may be lucky enough to obtain a hotel job through an *uitzendbureau*, your chances will normally be better if you visit hotels and ask if any work is available, or keep your ears open in pubs patronised by long-stay foreigners.

Private Employment Agencies

The majority of employers turn to private employment agencies (*uitzendbureaux* – pronounced 'outzend') for temporary workers, partly to avoid the complicated paperwork of hiring a foreigner directly. Therefore they can be a very useful source of temporary work in Holland. They proliferate in large towns, for example there are over 125 in Amsterdam alone. Look up *Uitzendbureau* in the telephone directory or the *Gouden Gids* (Yellow Pages) and register with as many as you can in your area. Not all will accept non-Dutch-speaking applicants. Most of the work on their books will be unskilled work such as washing dishes in canteens, cleaning, hotel work, etc. Schiphol Airport's catering division often hires casual workers mainly through Amsterdam *uitzendbureaux*. Among the largest *uitzendbureaux* are Randstad (with about 300 branches), Unique, Manpower, BBB and ASB.

REGULATIONS

All job-seeking EU nationals must first acquire a stamp in their passport which grants permission to work for up to three months. This is available over-the-counter in most cases from the local aliens police (*Vreemdelingenpolitie*) or Town Hall. The stamped passport should then be taken to the local tax office to apply for a *sofinummer* (social/fiscal number). It is also possible to apply for a *sofi* from outside the Netherlands, though this will take at least six weeks; send a copy of your passport details to Belastingdienst Particulieren/ Onderneminenbuitenland, Postbus 2865, 6401 DJ Heerlen. The registration office for foreigners in Amsterdam (*Register Amsterdam*) is at Stadhouderskade 85, 1073 AT Amsterdam, while the tax office (*Belastingdienst*) is at Kingsfordweg 1, 1043 GN Amsterdam.

DIRECTORY REFERENCES

For travel companies which operate in the Netherlands, see entries for the following: Amsterdam Travel Service, Edwin Doran Music Travel, Eurocamp, Eurosites, Expo Garden Tours, Travelsphere, Village Camps; plus the list of coach tour operators.

Portugal

Britain's oldest ally is a beautiful and relatively unspoilt country. Because of is situation on the furthest side of the Iberian peninsula where the sea water is colder than the Mediterranean, it has not been mobbed to the same extent as Spain, apart from the Algarve coast between Faro and Lagos which is lined with tower blocks. Other areas of Portugal such as Lisbon, Oporto and the north attract a more upmarket clientele. Hotels tend to be luxurious and self-catering villas have their own swimming pools and maids. None of the major UK camping tour operators include Portuguese sites, partly because of the great distance for motorists.

Prospects for Work

Many visitors return year after year to their own villas or a resort they know well, which means that it is not easy to find jobs as these people know the country and don't need anyone to look after them. Furthermore many of the local people speak excellent English, so there are limited jobs available.

As in Italy, the Portuguese are protective of their tourist industry and this has been formalised in law. For example foreign tour managers in charge of a coach must ensure that they pick up an official Portugese guide at major tourist venues.

FINDING A JOB

The mass-market beach resort operators (*Thomson, Airtours, First Choice*) employ a certain number of reps in Portugal. *Style Holidays* (see entry in the Directory) looks for 5-10 resort reps every year for seasonal work between April and October. They also offer part season short term contracts. *Unijet* also places reps in Portugal. First Choice have about 100 staff in place who speak another language (not necessarily Portuguese). Apart from these and some of the Europe-wide tour operators like Page & Moy (136-140 London Road, Leicester LE2 1EN; 0116-2507000), many of the tour operators which feature Portugal are specialists. The founders of the well known Travel Club of Upminster (Station Road, Upminster, Essex RM14 2TT; 01708 225000) virtually started tourism to Portugal from the UK when they fell in love with the country after the war. Occasionally the Travel Club and other specialist tour operators like Mundi Color 'Discover Spain & Portugal' (276 Vauxhall Bridge Road, London SW1V 1BE: 0171-828 6021), Caravela (0171-630 9223) and First Choice Portugal (0161-745 7000) need staff, but only if they can speak Portuguese.

A number of upmarket villa companies employ English staff to oversee the properties. Anyone applying for such a job would have to have a driving licence since the properties are often scattered. Note that these are plum jobs so there is little turnover:

Bonaventure Holidays, 2 The Mews, 6 Putney Common, London SW15 1HL (0181-780 1311).

Casas Cantabricas, 31 Arbury Road, Cambridge CB4 2JB (01223 328721).

CV Travel's Mediterranean World, 43 Cadogan St, London SW3 2PR (0171-591 2800).

Individual Travellers (Spain & Portugal), Manor Courtyard, Bignor, Pulborough, West Sussex RH20 1QD (01798 869485).

Most tours from Brazil use Lisbon as their gateway to Europe, and people who can speak the language and know about European culture may be hired by one of these. One of the biggest is the Portuguese-owned company Abreu (109 Westbourne Grove, London W2 4UW; 0171-229 9905) which handles incoming groups from Brazil.

Any EU national aged 18-27 with a vocational qualification in Leisure and Tourism or Marketing (but not a university degree) should find out whether the scheme is being repeated whereby candidates studied Portuguese for one month in Devon before taking up a three month work placement in the Portuguese tourist industry in the autumn. Contact ProEuropa (59 High St, Totnes, Devon TQ9 5PB; 01803 864526) for current details.

Wine Tours

For over 600 years the British have drunk the wines of Portugal, and many companies offer specialist wine tours of the Oporto region. Many of the families that work in this industry are of British ancestry. Henry is lucky enough to be related to one of these families and was delighted to be given a summer job as a guide showing visitors around the wine cellars. Henry soon got used to dealing with visitors who were more interested in the free tastings (even at 10am) than in the history of wine-making. He found it harder to accommodate himself to the fact that he spent most of the day underground instead of in the sunshine. Others who are not cousins of port-makers have found similar jobs. For example one guide fixed up his job when he was working for a well-known wine merchant in Britain and happened to meet a rep from one of the large port companies in the shop. The rep told him that their company often took on keen interested young students. Ask your local wine merchant for the addresses of major wine importing companies for leads.

The Douro River, lined by port wineries, is a hive of activity during the annual September barge event, when the *caravelles* glide down the river. To work on these you would need to know both the language and the wine trade. There is also a hotel barge that operates on the river and occasionally needs staff.

Other Special Interest Tours

The lush countryside makes for some wonderful golfing facilities. Anyone who has worked at a golf club in the UK or US might try to work for a specialist operator in this field. Two companies to consider are Longshot Golf Holidays (Meon House, College St, Petersfield, Hants. GU32 3JN; 01730 268621) and Lotus Supertravel Golf (Sandpiper House, 37-39 Queen Elizabeth Street, London SE1 2BT.

Portugal is a highly religious country and many religious pilgrimages are made, especially to the site of Our Lady at Fatima. The enormous piazza in front of the Basilica is said to hold a million people on the two main religious festivals (May 12/13 and October 12/13, the dates of the first and last apparitions of the Virgin). Catholic church newspapers carry adverts for companies organising tours. Contact them if you speak Portuguese and want to work as a tour guide.

"*Visitors to the cellars were more interested in the free tastings than in the history of Viniculture*"

Walking and nature holiday operators take groups to the National Park of Peneda-Geres in the remote northern Serra da Peneda.

On the Spot

There is an estimated population of 12,000 expat Britons in Portugal, a great many of whom run bars, restaurants, bookshops, etc. catering mainly for an Anglophone clientele and therefore staffed by English speakers. The majority of expatriate businesses are small (and therefore have only occasional job vacancies) and located in the Algarve or on the Lisbon coast from Setúbal to Cascais. Entertainers and watersports instructors may find on-the-spot openings. Ask expatriates for help and advice in your search for a job in tourism.

Scan the advertisements in the weekly *Anglo-Portuguese News* (Apartado 113, 2765 Estoril; 466 1471) or place your own advert in this paper, though the rates are fairly expensive. Also check *The News* (PO Box 13, 8400 Lagoa; fax 82-341201) which covers the Algarve and is published fortnightly. It has a large English language classified section in which you can place a 12-word advert free of charge.

Portuguese speakers can approach travel companies about the possibility of work, e.g. Sociedade Comercial Blandy Brothers Lda (Rua Vitor Cordon 31-1°, 1200 Lisbon; 1-3466551 or Av de Zarco 2, 9000 Funchal, Madeira), Agencia de Turismo Garland Laidley (Trav do Corpo Santo 10-2°, 1200 Lisbon; 1-3640953) and James Rawles & Ca. Lda (Rua Bernadino Costa 47, 1200 Lisbon; 1-3470231).

REGULATIONS

Portugal has always had comparatively liberal immigration policies, possibly because it has never been rich enough to attract a lot of foreign job-seekers. Like other EU countries, it stipulates that foreign workers from EU countries should obtain a residence permit if they are staying more than three months. But the regulations say that seasonal workers who will be working for less than eight months do not require a residence permit, which simplifies the red tape for anyone working a season in the tourist industry. To apply for a residence permit, you need among other things a letter of confirmation and duration of employment from your employer.

The Consular Section of the British Embassy in Portugal (Rua Sáo Bernardo 33, 1200 Lison; 1-392 4000/4160;fax 1-392 4188) distributes information on employment and on taking up residence in Portugal (updated August 1997) which goes into more detail than the information from the Consulate-General in London.

Non-EU nationals must provide the usual battery of documents before they can be granted a residence visa, from a document showing that the Ministry of Labour (*Ministerio do Trabhalho*) has approved the job to a medical certificate in Portuguese. After arrival the non-EU applicant must take the contract of employment to the *Serviço de Estrangeiros e Fronteiras* (Aliens Office) in Lisbon at Avenida António Augusto Aguiar 20 (1-314 3112) or in Oporto, Coimbra, Faro, Madeira and the Azores. The final stage is to take a letter of good conduct provided by the applicant's own embassy to the police for the work and residence permit. There are stories of non-Europeans arranging a residence permit after finding a job on arrival, but this is difficult.

DIRECTORY REFERENCES

For companies which employ staff in Portugal, see Airtours, First Choice, Magic of Portugal, Style Holidays, Thomson, Travelsphere and Unijet.

Scandinavia

Scandinavia comprises the countries of Finland, Norway, Sweden, Iceland and Denmark (which includes Greenland). In many areas there is a two-season year for tourists: winter sports from December to March/April and the relatively short summer season June to August. UK coach companies send many tours to Scandinavia, particularly to Norway, since the 1994 Winter Olympics raised the country's profile. Sweden too has been doing well and recorded a steady increase in the number of visitors over recent years, most of them independent tourists and families on self-catering holidays. Although tourism is an important industry in Iceland, few foreigners are employed in it. Scandinavia is popular with student groups, and companies like *EF* and *AICS UK* need tour guides (who can cope with constant moans about the high price of drinks).

The standard of living throughout Scandinavia is very high and so are prices, e.g. £4 for a soft drink in a modest café and up to £20 for a simple meal out. A tour guide's standard European wage will not go far in Scandinavia, where it is not the custom as it is elsewhere for restaurants to offer a free meal or complimentary drink. Reputable companies will pay a supplement to take account of the higher cost of living. Commission sales in the rest of Europe usually bump up a guide's salary, but prices are so high in Scandinavia that tour groups tend to choose the tours which include all excursions so there is no chance of making extras. Also clients usually have less money at the end of their holiday for tips than they would in southern Europe.

Prospects for Work

A few UK camping tour operators, notably *Eurocamp*, send clients (and therefore reps) to Denmark, Norway and Sweden. Self-catering and farm holidays are extremely popular in the region, with visitors escaping to the simple life in a log cabin in the forests or by a lake – idyllic, perhaps, but affording few work opportunities. The relevant country's tourist office can provide a list of campsites which may employ some foreign staff. It helps if you can write to such addresses in the relevant language, but don't worry if you can't find someone to translate for you; the majority of Scandinavians working in the tourist industry speak excellent English.

Winter sports companies in the UK occasionally need reps, though there are still very few British ski tour operators active in Scandinavia. Originally best known for cross-country skiing (sometimes called Nordic or *langlauf*), Norway has developed its downhill facilities and resorts like Lillehammer, Oppdal, Geilo and Voss are excellent. Elsewhere in Scandinavia, the skiing is mostly cross-country. Other winter sports are available, including dog sledding. Many incentive companies offer their more adventurous clients the opportunity to take part in a short dog sledding expedition, so anyone who has worked with dogs in Alaska or the Alps should ask the local tourist board for addresses of operators featuring these holidays.

Scandinavian cities offer superb conference venues and facilities and anyone who speaks a Scandinavian language might find administrative work. Addresses can be obtained from *The Buyer's Guide* from ACE (see Working for Yourself/Freelance section).

FINDING A JOB

One of the best opportunities for work is on the giant ferries that criss-cross the North Sea between the UK and Scandinavia. To attract passengers on the long crossings, many of these monster ships offer the same facilities as a cruise ship, so there are jobs in the pursers' department, catering, cabin stewards or croupiers. Some companies to try are Color Line which sails from Newcastle to Bergen or Stavanger (0191-296 1313) and Smyril Line (315 900) who are based in the Faroes, and operate a service from the Shetlands to Bergen.

Tour operators that feature Scandinavia include:

Arctic Experience, 29 Nork Way, Banstead, Surrey SM7 1PB (01737 218800).

Canterbury Travel, 42 High St, Northwood, Middlesex HA6 1BL (0181-206 0411).
   Very smart staff needed for day-trips to Lapland, incentives, etc.

DA Tours, Williamton House, Low Causeway, Culross, Fife KY12 8HL (01383 882200). Coach touring holidays in Scandinavia and Europe.

Inntravel, Park Street, Hovingham, York YO62 4JZ (01653 628811). Walking, riding, cycling and skiing holidays in Norway.

Scandinavian Travel Service, 2 Berghem Mews, Blythe Road, London W14 OHN (0171-371 4011).

Scantours, 47 Whitcombe Street, Leicester Square, London WC2H 7DH (0171-839 2927).

Taber Holidays, 126 Sunbridge Road, Bradford BD1 2SX (01274 393480). Long-time specialist programme to Norway.

Travel Trade Gazette Europa, published fortnightly, carries regular information on Scandinavia (£85 a year from TTG; 0181-309 7000).

Denmark

Every year thousands of families head off to the theme park at Legoland near Copenhagen to see fantastic models made out of the famous children's building bricks. A number of large campsites within range service the park and employ the usual range of seasonal staff.

As the centre of the Danish tourist industry as well as the commercial and industrial centre of the country, Copenhagen is as good a place as any to look for work. The Jobcenter in Copenhagen is at Kultorvet 17 (33 55 17 14) and may be able to assist EU nationals to find temporary work, especially those with a sought-after skill and a knowledge of Danish. It is also worth looking for jobs door to door in hotels and restaurants. Many of the large hotels have personnel offices at the rear of the hotel which should be visited frequently until a vacancy comes up. Some job-seekers may have to call only once, as in the case of the Dutch traveller Mirjam Koppelaars:

> *My Norwegian friend Elise and I rather liked Copenhagen but realised that money was going quick again and decided to try to find some work. After filling in an application form and having a very brief interview at the Shera-ton, we both got offered jobs as chambermaids starting the next day. The next five weeks I cleaned 16 rooms and 16 bathrooms a day in a very funny uniform. Although I had to pay over half in tax, I was able to save for more travels.*

Fast food restaurants, such as Burger King and McDonalds, which have a considerable turnover of unskilled foreign staff are also recommended.

The attractive Danish countryside also absorbs tourists and people to look after them. Sam and Petra set off to spend the summer in Denmark and found work in the farmhouses that cater for visitors. The barman on the ferry going over told them that his aunt and uncle's farm took in paying guests and recommended they make contact on arrival. When they mentioned the nephew's name, they were greeted like long-lost friends and the aunt phoned all her friends in the farmers' network until they found one who needed two assistants.

Finland

Finland has had a long and uneasy association with Russia, one which at last is bringing some benefits to Finland as many tours are now combining Helsinki and St Petersburg, thereby boosting Finland's tourist industry. The Finnish Tourist Boards are actively promoting their country for holidays, especially in the high revenue sectors of conferences and incentive conferences.

Finland encourages trainees to come to Finland for short-term paid work. The International Trainee Exchange programme in Finland is administered by CIMO, the Centre for International Mobility (PO Box 343, 00531 Helsinki, Finland; 9-7747 7877/fax 9-7747 7064). British tourism students and graduates who want on-the-job training in their field (e.g. tourist offices, travel agencies, hotels, restaurants) should request an application form from the CIMO. To qualify to become a trainee, you must have studied for at least one year, preferably with a year's related experience as well. Despite the designation 'trainee', wages are on a par with local Finnish wages for the same work.

Traineeships last one month or longer: the norm is a few months between May and August. Applications for summer positions must be in to CIMO by the end of February. This programme is also open to people from outside Europe, for whom the red tape is relatively straightforward. Readers in other countries should write to CIMO for their list of cooperating organisations in 13 countries. Work and residence permits are granted for an initial three months but may be extended in Finland for the whole training period.

Norway

For both winter and summer seasons, you can try to get something fixed up ahead of time by writing to hotels listed in the accommodation brochure available from the Norwegian Tourist Office (send a 50p stamp), in which hundreds of hotels are listed. There is a greater density of hotels in the south of Norway including beach resorts along the south coast around Kristiansand, and inland from the fjords north of Bergen (Geilo, Gol, Vaga, Lillehammer, and in the Hardanger region generally). Remember that even in the height of summer, the mountainous areas can be very chilly. As mentioned, winter resorts like Lillehammer, Nordseter, Susjoen, Gausdal and Voss employ a certain number of foreign workers.

Officially the starting net monthly wage of an unskilled hotel worker is kr7,500-8,000 with a deduction of between kr500 and kr1,000 for board and lodging. However it is not uncommon for foreign seasonal workers to be paid considerably less. For example John worked at the Neverfjell Turisthotel in Lillehammer where he was given full board and accommodation in return for keeping the carpark clear of snow and other maintenance chores. Lucy made friends with one of the waitresses at a hotel in Nordseter who put her name forward for a job, a ploy which worked. She did not mind the low wage she was paid because she earned quite a bit in tips and had two full days off a week to ski.

Norwegian youth hostels have a steady demand for unskilled domestic staff who are willing to accept little more than a living wage. The Norwegian Hiking Association takes on some people to be caretakers at their network of mountain huts, though the only foreigner we have heard of who did this job was studying at the University of Oslo and therefore was on the spot.

If you choose to go job-hunting on spec in Norway, be prepared to pay high prices for food and accommodation while you're looking for work. First do the rounds of the hotels in a resort like Lillehammer where there are about a dozen hotels in the centre of town. Neil Tallantyre, who spent several winter seasons in Lillehammer, found that there is quite a demand for British workers. He has been amazed at the resourcefulness of travellers who have extended their time in ski resorts (primarily to ski), by doing odd jobs like snow clearing and car-cleaning, waitressing and DJing (especially common since the British are thought to know their way around the music scene).

One intriguing avenue to pursue is to work on one of the eleven working ships which cruise the fjords of Norway to the Arctic Circle, known as the *Hurtigruten*. A brochure for Norwegian Coastal Voyages can be requested from the Scandinavian Travel Service (address above, 0171-371 4011). Woden Teachout from Vermont describes how she came close to finding work on this route:

Because the trip under the midnight sun is so luxurious, a lot of staff are needed to pander to the passengers. I called the offices and asked if they needed help; they said to meet the boat in Bergen at the docks and ask the captain. I did this on three successive days and none of the captains wanted help. But they didn't laugh at me (as I'd expected) and in fact were quite encouraging, saying that chances were I'd get something within the week. I imagine the trick is to catch them quite early in the season. I don't know what the wages were but the trip is supposed to be so spectacular that it would be worth doing one 14-day run for nothing. Ask as early in the season as possible.

Sweden

A few UK ski tour operators like *Crystal Holidays* are beginning to feature Sweden in their brochures but as yet the programmes are relatively small. The principal ski area is Arefjällen in northern Sweden.

It may be worth trying to find work in hotels, usually in the kitchen. The best bets are the large hotels in Stockholm and Göteborg. Elsewhere you might try areas where tourism is well established. Try the Sunshine Coast of western Sweden including the seaside resorts between Malmö and Göteborg, especially Hölsingborg, Varberg and Falkenberg. Other popular holiday centres with a large number of hotels include Orebro, Västeras, Are, Ostersund, Jönköping and Linköping. The chances of fixing up a hotel job in advance are remote. After writing to dozens of Scandinavian hotels, Dennis Bricault's conclusion was 'Forget Sweden!'.

Coach drivers working a season in Sweden occasionally find work delivering Volvos to their home country at the end of the season. Ask the Personnel Department of Volvo at Göthenburg.

REGULATIONS

Sweden, Finland and Denmark are fully-fledged members of the EU. The Norwegian people voted against joining in a referendum; however Norway and Iceland are members of the European Economic Area (EEA) which permits the free movement of goods, services and people among the 15 members of the European Union and the two Scandinavian members of the EEA. This means that EEA/EU citizens are now entitled to enter any Scandinavian country for up to three months to look for work. When they find a job and get a 'Confirmation of Employment' from their employer, they can then apply to the police for a residence permit.

In order to work legally, North Americans and others will have to obtain work permits before leaving home, which is very difficult. However, the American-Scandinavian Foundation (Exchange Division, 725 Park Avenue, New York, NY 10021; tel 212 879 9779; website www.amscan.org) can assist 'self-placed trainees' to fix up a work permit, i.e. those who have fixed up their own job or traineeship in a Scandinavian country. They charge a fee of $50 which also includes a 12-month student membership in the Foundation.

DIRECTORY REFERENCES

The travel companies listed in the Directory which have operations in Scandinavia include: Crystal, Eurocamp, Headwater Ski Holidays, Scantours, Top Deck.

Spain

Spain hosts a staggering 40 million visitors a year and is by far the most popular destination for British tourists. Over ten percent of the country's gross national product is due to tourism. Of the top ten package holiday destinations for Britons last year, five are Spanish: Majorca, Tenerife, Ibiza, Menorca and the Costa Blanca.

99.9% of visitors go to Spain for the sun, sand, sea, etc. and not for the history or culture. After World War II Spain was ideally placed to offer cheap holidays to the rest of Europe devastated by bombing, and the government support for their tourist industry meant boom times for farmers and fishermen lucky enough to own a few acres of land on one of the Costas. Concrete buildings grew up where once there had been scrubland, and Spain became the playground of Europe. Although not quite so booming as in the late 1980s, the coastal resorts continue to draw hordes of tourists, especially Lloret de Mar, Calella (Costa Brava), Benidorm (Costa Blanca), Torremolinos, Benalmadena, Fuengirola (Costa del Sol), Mojacar (Costa de Almeria) and Ibiza and Palma (Majorca).

First-time reps working for major tour operators, whether British, German or Scandinavian, have a 60% chance of being sent to a Spanish resort. Once, it was easy to find this work, but today competition is tough and you will need to be able to offer a qualification even to get your first job. At the interview, you will not be asked questions about history, culture or language. Instead you will be asked to sell an excursion, e.g. a Sangria Evening, Flamenco Evening or Boat Trip.

But even if some of these excursions make you cringe, you have to bear in mind that each year millions of satisfied holidaymakers have a wonderful time in Spain and book to return to the same resort and hotel as soon as they arrive home. They know that the product is excellent value for money. You haven't lived until you have seen 2,000 Britons swaying to Viva Espana, drinking sangria and having the time of their lives.

The Spanish infrastructure is generally well organised which makes your work much easier. The hotels are of an acceptable standard, the coaches are modern, the excursions good value and cater well for the various nationalities. If you do well in your first posting on the Costa Brava, you may be moved mid-season to another country where there are more problems.

An example of the care that tour operators take in maintaining standards was provided by Kim who was given no choice of resort and was sent to Benidorm by a UK tour operator. She flew out a week before the season started and was immediately handed a long list of local contacts to get to know: chemist, police, doctor, clinic, hotels, car hire, windsurf and cycle hire, photo developer, ground handlers, etc. Once she had done that she had to go round the hotels checking everything from swimming pool depth to fire exits, door widths for wheelchairs to height of balconies. By the time the first clients arrived, Kim was already well known in Benidorm.

FINDING A JOB

Most of the British camping tour companies such as *Canvas Holidays*, *Club Cantabrica*, *Keycamp Holidays* and *Eurocamp* have sites in Spain. *Haven Europe* needs Spanish-speaking couriers and children's staff to work at mobile home and tent parks from early May to the end of September. *Panorama Ibiza*, *Majorca* and an extensive children's programme which employ British nannies and animators. Holiday villages like the *Lanzarote Beach Club* often employ English-speakers to serve their clientele. In some cases, a knowledge of German is more useful than Spanish as in the case of Club Punta Arabi (Apartado 73, Es Cana, 07840 Santa Eulalia del Rio, Ibiza).

Of course there are other companies which send tours to Spain for different reasons, perhaps to the interior to stay in *paradores* (a series of 86 government-owned inns, usually in old stately homes or palaces) or village hotels. The usual range of special interest tours and upmarket villa holidays is available in Spain. Companies like the following are looking for staff who speak good Spanish and know the country:

Individual Travellers Spain & Portugal, Manor Courtyard, Bignor, Pulborough, West Sussex RH20 1QD (01798 869485).

Magic of Spain, 227 Shepherds Bush Road, London W6 7AS (0181-748 7575).

Mundi Color 'Discover Spain & Portugal', 276 Vauxhall Bridge Road, London SW1V 1BE (0171-828 6021).

Spanish Harbour Holidays Ltd, 12a High St, Keynsham, Bristol BS18 1DS (0117 986 9777).

Style Holidays, (see entry in Directory).

Sunworld, 29 Elmfield Road, Bromley, Kent BR1 1LT. Part of Iberotravel Spain. Employ property reps (minimum age 21) and kiddies' reps (over 18).

Other companies operate upmarket walking tours, wine appreciation tours or trips for pilgrims to Compostella. English-speaking guides for horseback expeditions in Spain may be needed by Horse Riding Holidays (Inntravel, Park Street, Hovingham, York YO6 4JZ; 01653 628811) who take riding tours into the Sierra di Guarda and Andalucia.

After arrival in Spain, it is worth checking the English language press for the sits vac column. Many English language magazines and newspapers thrive on tourism and resident expatriates, for example, the *Costa Blanca News* (Apartado 95, 03500 Benidorm, Alicante; 965 85 5286), *Lookout* (Puebla Lucia, Fuengirola, 07012 Malaga; 52-46 09 50), the *Majorca Daily Bulletin* (Calle San Felio 17, Apartado 304, Palma; 71-21 61 10) and the monthly *Canary Island Gazette* in Tenerife (22-33 51 62). Also the free English paper in Benalmadena (the *Sur*) occasionally carries adverts for chefs, bar staff, etc. It is usually not very expensive to place your own advert.

People have successfully found (or created) jobs in highly imaginative ways. One of the most striking examples is a 19-year-old Finnish student who wrote to the address on a Spanish wine label and was astonished to be invited to act as a guide around their winery for the summer. Tommy Karske returned home 'knowing a lot about wine and believing that anything is possible'.

There is a vague rumour that a Spanish Euro Disney is being considered for the redundant site of EXPO 92 in Seville which, as in France, would provide an enormous amount of temporary employment. In the meantime the theme park Port Aventura, 70 miles southwest of Barcelona, has boosted the nearby resort of Salou which has to accommodate many of the visitors.

Activity Holidays

Acorn Venture need qualified windsurfing, sailing, kayak and climbing instructors for their activity centre on the coast north of Barcelona, for the summer season.

A number of indigenous organisations, including language schools, run summer language and sports camps for children and teenagers which require monitors, animators and instructors. *Vigvatten Klub* runs three of these camps in rural Spain. They recruit monitors, maintenance staff and cooks who are required to work for a minimum of two weeks. Monitors are responsible for the children 24 hours a day, helping them with their English and organising activities. Wages are between £150-250 depending on the positon and the camp.

Also try the following:

Relaciones Culturales Internacionales (RCI), Calle Ferraz 82, 28008 Madrid (915 417 103). A youth exchange organisation.

Technical College, C/ Maria Lostal No. 22, 50008 Zaragoza (976-227909). Runs summer courses in the Pyrenees for which it hires sports monitors and EFL teachers.

Sailors from around the world congregate in the hundreds of marinas along the Spanish coast and create some opportunities for employment on yachts. One UK operator in this field is Minorca Sailing Holidays (58 Kew Road, Richmond, Surrey TW9 2PQ; 0181-948 2106).

Ski Resorts

Although Spain is not the first country to come to mind when thinking of skiing, there is a flourishing industry and a few British tour operators like *Thomson* take skiers to Spanish resorts such as Cerler, La Molina or Formigal in the Pyrenees. One UK company which has ski chalets in Spain is *Ski Miquel*. See below for some information about working in ski resorts in Andorra.

Canary Islands

Almost every large tour operator features the Canaries. Demand for staff is so high that a knowledge of Spanish is not always needed, while those who know Spanish have an excellent chance of finding a company to hire them. Some specialists include: Bonaventure (0181-780 1311), Lanzarote Leisure (0181-449 7441); Meon Villas (01730 268411) and Villanza (01245 262496).

Although they belong to Spain, the Canaries are situated close to the coast of Africa and therefore have a warm climate year round. They are extremely popular with European tourists, especially Germans, Scandinavians and the British, and offer probably the best employment prospects for anyone starting in the tourism industry.

There are seven main islands which are remarkably different from each other and attract a different clientele. Tenerife is the Benidorm of the Canaries and most major British operators offer inexpensive holidays, either self-catering or in hotels, to this island. Gran Canaria is much greener than the other islands and attracts more upmarket tourists and 'golden oldies' to its many hotels and self-catering apartments. It is also a popular stop for cruise ships.

Lanzarote has grown at a tremendous rate yet, thanks to the council, its development is reasonably attractive with only one high-rise hotel. Lanzarote Villas are one of the main specialist companies employing UK staff as reps. Most major tour operators offer holidays in the many self-catering complexes, especially the huge development in the south built by the British company Wimpey and the huge hotel resort centre of La Santa developed for sports-loving holidaymakers.

La Palma has the world's steepest ascent from sea level to mountain top, so the temperature drops sharply within a few minutes. There are a few self-catering complexes and some specialist tour operators feature the island because of its remoteness, but the majority of visitors come ashore on day-trips from cruise ships such as those of the Fred Olsen line. Connie is Dutch, speaks English and German, and is kept busy looking after arriving cruise groups. From her balcony she can see when a ship arrives, whereupon she strolls down to the quayside to welcome the clients and take them on walking tours of the charming town.

With a mainly German clientele, Fuerteventura offers job openings for German-speaking staff. Gomera has no airport so is probably the least spoilt of the islands. Traditionally Christopher Columbus's last stop before his discovery of the New World, it has an old-fashioned atmosphere and is quieter than the others. Finally, El Heirros is a small barren island with not much more than a *paradore* (national hotel).

The busy islands have attracted many entrepreneurs from abroad who wish to cash in on the Canaries' popularity. Like so many others, Peter and Roseanne Grubb were attracted to the climate and decided to settle on Lanzarote. As Peter had worked for one of the major Champagne houses and was an expert on food and wine, everyone expected him to open an upmarket restaurant. But his market research revealed that holidaymakers wanted something less grand. So he opened a fast food outlet on the beach at Puerto Carmen, decorated it with sporting memorabilia he had collected over the years and called it the Sports Bar. Every night the bar is full of young Britons who can't live without their daily fix of fast food and almost-British beer.

CASUAL WORK

It is possible to pick up work in the Canaries during the season (November to March), with Lanzarote and Tenerife providing the best chances. Along the beachfront at Puerto del Carmen in Lanzarote and Playa de las Americas in Tenerife, almost every building is a pizzeria, *hamburgeria*, etc. Just walk along the front until you come to a place whose client language you speak, and go in and ask. If you want to camp while looking for work, you will generally have to use a recognised campsite, as land is scarce and there are not many public places which allow camping.

If you can arrange to visit the Spanish coast in March before most of the budget travellers arrive, you should have a good chance of fixing up a job for the season. The resorts then go dead until late May when the season gets properly underway and there may be jobs available. Bear in mind that while working in these environments you will barely get a glimpse of genuine Spanish culture.

Year-round resorts like Tenerife, Gran Canaria and Lanzarote afford a range of casual work. Nick Crivich, who worked a season as a rep in Tenerife for a subsidiary of Thomson, observed that there were ample opportunities for bar staff, DJs, beach party ticket sellers, timeshare salesmen, etc. in these places and on the islands. Many young people make ends meet by working for a disco or bar as a 'PR' or 'prop', i.e. someone who stands outside trying to entice tourists to come in. Magaluf on Majorca is another busy resort full of English bars like Prince Williams where you can enquire about local jobs. At one time there were many jobs in the tourist industry of Ibiza but recent reports indicate that the only thing available is for young women dancing in clubs.

Although Euro-legislation introduced in the 1990s has limited the kinds of selling techniques used, time share developments (or 'holiday ownership' companies which is the new euphemism) continue to market their properties, and the job of OPC ('Offsite Personal Contact') is still around. For this job you have to be aggressive and also prepared to face a lot of rejection.

REGULATIONS

The procedures for regularising your status are similar to those in other EU countries. Those who intend to stay more than three months must apply for a residence card (*Tarjeta de Residencia*) within 30 days of arrival. If working for a UK tour operator they will appy on your behalf. Otherwise application should be made to a regional police headquarters (*Comisaría de Policia*) or a Foreigners' Registration Office (*Oficina de Extranjería)* which in Madrid is at Comisaría de Tetuan, Pasaje Maestros Ladrilleros s/n, (Metro Valdeacederas); 914 028 100. The documents necessary for the *residencia* are a contract of employment, three photos and a passport. This information is confirmed both in the hand-outs from the Labour Counsellor's Office of the Spanish Embassy (20 Peel St, London W8 7PD) and in 'Settling in Spain' (revised February 1998) from the British Consulate-General in Spain (c/o Marqués de la Ensenada 16-2°, 28004 Madrid; 913 190 200).

The red tape for which Spain is famous does not stop at residence cards. One young Briton who was working for an expat British bar owner on the Costa del Sol was suddenly paid a visit by a Social Security inspector who pointed out that he had not yet applied for his *residencia* as he should have and the landlord hadn't done 'this and that'.

The rules for non-EU citizens have not changed and those who find a legitimate job working for a tour company, etc. will have to go through a complex rigamarole (unless the Council scheme mentioned below applies). They must obtain a *visado especial* from the Spanish Embassy in their country of residence after submitting a copy of their contract, medical certificate in duplicate and authenticated copies of qualifications. In some cases a further document is needed, an *antecedente penal* (police certificate). Invariably the Spanish authorities take months to process this and when the visa (normally Type A which is for one specific job) is finally issued, it must be collected in the home country.

Council in New York (toll-free: 1-888-COUNCIL) administer a scheme which enables US students to work in Spain for any 3 months between May 1 and October 31. Otherwise, the strict rules make it difficult for people from outside Western Europe to pick up casual work as Ana Güemes from Mexico found:

> *Although we Latin Americans speak Spanish, I insist in saying that Spain is one of the hardest countries to find a job in. Everywhere you go they ask to see your identity card because of the problems they have with Moroccans.*

Americans, Canadians, Australians, etc. do sometimes find paid work as monitors in children's camps or touts for bars and discos. When their tourist visas are about to expire, they usually follow the example of others who simply cross into France or Portugal to extend their tourist visa for a further three months on their return to Spain.

The official minimum wage is just over pta 50,000 per month. The Spanish employment service (*Oficinas de Empleo*) has a monopoly on job-finding, so private employment agencies are banned.

ANDORRA

There are limited opportunities for finding employment in Andorra, chiefly because of its small size. Andorra is not a member of the European Union, this means that all foreigners need work permits before they can take up employment, which are obtained by the employer.

The main source of possibilities is the ski industry. There are seven or eight skiing areas in the tiny country, though the two best known are Soldeu and Arinsal. These attract a steady flow of British skiers and many English-speaking people fill the usual range of ski resort jobs. For ski tour operators which go to Andorra, try *Top Deck Ski*, *Skiworld*, *Crystal Holidays* and *Panorama Ski*.

GIBRALTAR

Gibraltar used to be a mecca for working travellers who, in the past, have found seemingly endless possibilities to work in bars and cafés. But recently the situation has changed. The Gibraltar Government has withdrawn the automatic right of Britons to live and work on the Rock, in response to a rising unemployment rate. They must now obtain a work permit from the Employment & Training Board (Duke of Kent House, Line Wall Road; 42995) before they can legally take up a job. To get a work permit, the prospective employer must prove that no Gibraltarian or other resident is available to fill the vacancy, undertake to repatriate the worker if necessary and show that suitable accommodation has been found. Needless to say, not many employers are willing to jump through these hoops for the sake of legally employing a temporary worker. Furthermore, the winding down of the defence presence in Gibraltar has meant a significant decrease in the amount of work around and is partly responsible for the climbing unemployment rate.

Gibraltar opted out of the EU's tax legislation which removes duty free advantages from the rest of Europe. Duty free shopping in Gibraltar has a turnover of over £200 million a year, which is not bad for a country of less than 30,000 inhabitants. Currently the Spanish government is making things difficult for tourism by imposing petty restrictions upon entrance to Gibraltar but when hoteliers on the Costa del Sol see their clients disappearing off to Turkey, Tunisia and other non-EU countries, they may be prepared to allow more flights into the country. This would create employment for meet and greet staff, reps and tour managers.

The Ocean Terminal is being enlarged to cope with this increase of visitors and there may be work for cruise personnel and specialised guides for excursions to Jerez, Seville, etc. See *Working on Cruise Ships* (£9.99), from Vacation Work Publications, for more detail.

Currently, most jobs in duty free shops such as the Seruya chain and international hotels like the Rock Hotel (00350 73000) and the Eden are filled by locals. However, the general managers of both hotels are British and there is work for those with the right qualifications and experience, especially in duty free retail.

Despite the regulation problems, there are still 365 bars and restaurants in Gibraltar (one for every day of the year, or so it is said) and occasional unfilled vacancies are made available to temporarily resident foreigners.

DIRECTORY REFERENCES

For travel companies which employ staff in Spain, see entries for: Acorn Venture, Airtours, Alternative Travel Group, Club 18-30, Club Cantabrica, Crystal, Eurocamp, Eurosites, First Choice, Haven Europe, Keycamp, Magic of Spain, Panorama Holiday Group, PGL, Ski Miquel, Style Holidays, Tall Stories, Thomson, Unijet, Venue Holidays, Vigvatten Klubb and Village Camps.

Switzerland

For centuries travellers used Switzerland's valleys as routes across the continent to France, Germany, Italy and Austria. Many of its famous buildings are monasteries built to offer shelter to pilgrims on their way to Rome. One of the most enduring of alpine legends is of the dogs from St Bernard rescuing travellers in snowdrifts. This happened, but the brandy keg around the neck is reputed to be folklore.

The Alps take up more than 60% of the territory, and provided protection from invaders. Left to themselves, the Swiss developed a fiercely nationalistic mentality which persists (so that even now the Swiss immigration policies are very restrictive; see the section on Regulations below). During the time of the Grand Tour many young gentlemen travelled through Switzerland to reach Italy, although it must have been a frightening experience. To cross the mountain passes, your coach had to be dismantled and carried by mule, with you trudging along behind and, according to one diary, running to keep up with the mules as they tumbled down the other side.

The Victorians loved alpine grandeur. After Queen Victoria took a holiday in Switzerland, the country became the fashionable place to go. Victorian gentlemen followed the fashion and came to climb the mountains, while the locals looked on in amazement. Thomas Cook brought his tours here. When skiing became popular, pioneers like Sir Arnold Lunn (who was famous for winter sports before travel agencies) made Switzerland their second home. In 1922 the world's first skiing races were held under Lunn's direction at Murren. The British started the idea of international ski competitions, and then had to stand aside and watch the rest of the world win all the races.

Most educated Swiss speak all of their country's three official languages, German, French and Italian, plus many also speak the unofficial language of English. The fourth language, Romansch, which derives from Latin, is spoken in and around St. Moritz and the Engadine Valley. During the Reformation, Switzerland produced the stern Calvin and Zwingli, and it is a paradox that the light-hearted French-speaking part of Switzerland today is mostly Protestant, whereas the German-speaking valleys overflow with exuberant Baroque and Rococo Catholic churches.

FINDING A JOB

Quite a few British travel companies and camping holiday operators are active in Switzerland, and most ski tour operators mount big operations in Switzerland. As Switzerland is not in the EU, passengers will still be able to buy duty free goods. This could persuade coach tour operators to start their tours in Switzerland, rather than in other EU countries. The *Jobs in the Alps* Agency places waiters, waitresses, chamber staff, kitchen assistants and porters in Swiss hotels, cafés and restaurants in Swiss resorts, 200 in winter, 150 in summer.

For summer work, most coach tour companies have tours that go through Switzerland but not many (apart from Lakes and Mountains specialists) have Switzerland-only tours. There are two very large Swiss tour operators, Kuoni and Globus. Upmarket Kuoni deals with the business end of travel and employs some of the best tour directors in the business. They also have very glossy long haul holidays. If you want to work for them you have to speak several languages and

Gateway and *Cosmos Coach Tours* (Via alla Roggia, PO Box 6919 Grancia; 9-985 7111) which operate tours from the UK to Spain, Turkey, etc. If offered work, make sure you have all details before you leave.

Summer language and sports camps abound in Switzerland. The Swiss organisation *Village Camps S.A.* (CH-1260 Nyon; 22 990 9405) advertises widely its desire to recruit people over 21 as general counsellors, EFL teachers, sports instructors and nurses on its summer and winter camps in Leysin, Saas Fee, Saas Grund, Fiesch, Les Collons and Morgins. In exchange for working fairly long hours, counsellors and domestic staff receive free room and board, insurance and an 'expense allowance' of SFr275 for 10 days and SFr325 for 14 days.

Susanna Macmillan arrived in Crans Montana in the autumn and within three days had arranged a job as a *monitrice* at the International School there. The job, which was to teach sports and English, came with room and board plus pocket money. Adventure holiday operators often need qualified instructors, but your qualifications must be good.

Hotels & Catering

Swiss hotels and tourism courses are still the training ground and model for hoteliers worldwide (see Directory of Training Courses). For the hotels and catering industry, a rapid short-term injection of labour is an economic necessity both for the summer and winter season – June/July to September and December to April.

Provided you have a reasonable CV and a knowledge of languages (preferably German), a speculative job hunt in advance is worthwhile. For example Katherine Jenkins wrote to several Swiss hotels in August/September and was gratified to have a choice of three definite contracts for the winter season. Eighteen-year old Kate Billington also wrote (in the relevant language) to about 20 hotels taken from a hotel directory and was offered a contract for the period mid-April to early July by the Hotel Beau Rivage in Thun. Three hotel groups worth trying are Fassbind Hotels, Via Basilea 28, 6903 Lugano (91 966 1112); Park Hotels Waldhaus, 7018 Flims-Waldhaus (81 928 4848); and Residence & Bernerhof Hotels, 3823 Wengen.

The Swiss Hotel Association has a department called Hotel Job SHV which runs a placement scheme (in German-speaking Switzerland only) for registered EU students from the age of 18 who are willing to spend three to four months doing an unskilled job in a Swiss hotel or restaurant between June and September. Excellent knowledge of the German language is essential to apply for a job. Member hotels issue a standard contract on which salary and deductions are carefully itemised. From the gross salary of SFr2,500 for a standard 42-hour week, the basic deduction for board and lodging (for any job) is SFr810 and a further 12-15% is taken off for taxes and insurance, with slight cantonal variations. Tips for waiting staff can bring net earnings back up to the gross. Application forms are available from the Swiss Hoteliers' Association, Monbijoustrasse 130, 3001 Bern; 31-370 43 33. The deadline for applications is 20th April and there is an upfront registration fee of SFr50.

On-the-Spot

Although the Swiss rate of unemployment is incredibly low by world standards, it is rising and all employers will hire a Swiss in preference to a foreigner. The difficulty of obtaining permits and the very high cost of living while job-hunting mean that going to Switzerland to find work can be fraught with difficulty. Yet many people do fix up their jobs in person, especially if they are able to visit resorts several months before the season begins (i.e. September for the winter season and March/April for the summer). Try Les Portes de Soleil at Champery, Les Crosets as well as the major resorts of Leysin, Verbier, Thyon and Crans Montana. This valley is a major road and rail route and is ideal for concentrated job hunting.

Surprisingly, tourist offices may be of use. Susanna Macmillan reported that the tourist office in Crans Montana issued photocopied lists of 'Jobs Available' and were advertising for summer staff in March. Always check notice boards and adverts in local papers like *L'Est Vaudois* for the Montreux region or *Le Nouvelliste* in the Rhone Valley.

Like most people, Andrew Winwood found the job hunt tough going:

> *All in all I asked in over 200 places for ski-season work, but eventually could have counted 10-12 possibilities. Going on that rate, it would be possible to get work after asking at 50 or 60 places, but of course the 'Grand Law of Sod' would prevail. As far as I can see, it's a simple case of ask, ask, ask and ask again until you get work. It was costing me about £80 a week to live in Switzerland, so I couldn't let up until I definitely had a way of getting the money back.*

Ski Resorts

See the introductory section on working in ski resorts. Apart from applying to all the ski tour operators for the following winter season, try *The Lady Magazine* (published Tuesdays) for classified ads for jobs as chalet maids, cooks, etc.

November is a bad time to arrive since most of the hotels are closed and the owners away on holiday. When David Loveless arrived in Verbier in mid-November, he declined an invitation to add his name to the bottom of eight sheets of people waiting for jobs. After moving on to Crans Montana, David soon found work at the Hotel de l'Etrier as a *chasseur* (messenger/odd jobs man).

Rob Jefferson had no luck whatsoever and describes his discouraging experiences job-hunting in Swiss resorts:

> *We arrived in Grindelwald in mid-December, and stayed in the youth hostel (along with 11 others all looking for work). After ten days, only one of the hostellers had found work, and so we left for Saas Fee with half-promises of work from seven hotels of the many we'd phoned. We were flatly refused by six but the seventh promised Sonja my girlfriend a job as a waitress if the pre-contracted waiter did not show up the next day. Sonja is very attractive, speaks near perfect English and good German. We had been around about 70 hotels in all and it took a late non-arrival for her to get a job. If this was the case for her, what about me? No chance.*

One recommended meeting place, is Balmer's Gasthaus in Interlaken (Hauptstrasse 23-25, 3800 Interlaken; 36-22 19 61). With a staff from all over the world, Balmer's prides itself on cleanliness and service. The most important requirement for its employees is the ability to work well with others. They offer the arrangement of free room and board to those who do a few hours of work a day. Summer season hiring is done in April and early May.

In spring and summer, ski resorts take on a new guise as more and more companies look for staff to take walking tours, rambles, flora and fauna tours, birdwatching, etc. Attractive areas such as Zermatt and Saas Fee often have walking tours, so it is worth trying your luck there.

WORKING CONDITIONS

In Switzerland, it is a case of last in first out. As soon as the season ends or bookings drop, the foreign workers will be let go before the locals. Otherwise, working conditions are favourable, with better live-in accommodation than in most other countries. Hotels are very helpful to tour guides, and large shops such as Bucherer and Gubelin in Luzern have dedicated departments to service tour groups. Everything is clean, clean, clean which puts tour groups in a good frame of mind. But the high cost of living means that tours do not spend long in the country. Representatives are well looked after both winter and summer. Ski reps get free ski lift passes, free or reduced hire of equipment, free drinks in the places frequented by your group and free transport passes in many places.

Steve Rout sums up the joys of working in a Swiss resort:

> *In my opinion Switzerland can't be recommended too highly, especially in the winter. If you are lucky, you will get fit and healthy, learn a new language, earn plenty of money, and make some great friends, all in one of the most beautiful areas of the world.*

Hotels

Swiss hotels are very efficient and tend to be impersonal, since you will be one in an endless stream of seasonal workers from many countries. The very intense attitude to work among the Swiss means that hours are long; a typical working week would consist of at least five nine-hour days working split shifts.

Whether humble or palatial, the Swiss hotel or restaurant in which you find a job will probably insist on very high standards of cleanliness and productivity. After working at an independent hostel and then a 3-star restaurant in Interlaken, Kathy Russell from Australia concluded that 'the Swiss are very picky to work for, so a good temperament is needed'.

On the other hand, the majority are *korrekt*, i.e. scrupulous about keeping track of your overtime and pay you handsomely at the end of your contract. Alison May summarised her summer at the Novotel-Zürich-Airport: 'On balance, the wages were good but we really had to earn them'. The main disadvantage of being hired outside Switzerland is that the wages will be on a British scale rather than on the more lucrative Swiss one; however perks often compensate.

REGULATIONS

If working for an overseas tour operator, you are unlikely to need to worry about work permits, or your company will apply for these on your behalf. Although the Swiss tourist industry depends in large measure on foreign workers, the authorities do not make it easy for Swiss employers to hire foreigners. Although Switzerland is not a member of the EU or the EEA, it has now joined the European Free Trade Agreement and will allow the free exchange of labour. A free booklet *Living and Working in Switzerland* can be obtained from the Swiss Embassy, but do not expect too many concrete facts and tips.

In Switzerland, there is no separate document for working. A residence permit (*Aufenthaltsbewilligung/autorisation de séjour*) covers both the right of abode and employment. Employers are entitled to a certain number of *Permis A/Saisonbewilligung*, permits which are valid for up to nine months in one year. Rules and quotas vary from canton to canton. Official regulations require that the permit be posted to an address outside the country, though it is sometimes possible to obtain one on-the-spot. One significant advantage of the Swiss system is that there is no requirement for the work permit to be applied for or picked up in your home country. There are about 100,000 *saisonniers* or *Permis* A holders at present. *Permis* B and C are for more permanent work and very difficult to get. One way of acquiring a *Permis* B without being subject to the strict quotas is to become a cross-border commuter (*frontalier/Grenzganger*) which refers to people who work in Switzerland but live in France or Germany within 10km of the Swiss border.

Although the official literature does not mention it, readers have written to say that they have obtained four-month permits. These do not seem to be so strictly limited, though the fee which the employer must pay is much higher. According to Mary Hall who worked as a nanny at a hotel in Wengen, everyone in Wengen had a permit. Her employer had no trouble obtaining the four-month permit for her (though he never did pay for it as he promised). After picking it up from the hotel, she nipped across the border into Italy so that she could have the compulsory chest X-ray on crossing the border back into Switzerland.

Unfortunately Australians and New Zealanders are not eligible for permits, a regulation enforced in some resorts by up to five policemen, who are there simply to check visas. There are frequent purges, especially at the beginning of the summer and winter seasons, and possible fines of SFr3,000 for an employer caught employing people illegally.

With a residence permit you become eligible for the state insurance scheme, for the minimum wage (approximately £800 a month) and the excellent legal tribunal for foreign workers which arbitrates in disputes over working conditions, pay and dismissals. Accident insurance is compulsory for all foreign workers and the employer pays the bulk of the premium, though foreign workers should take out their own health insurance. One advantage of having a residence permit is that in certain resort areas it entitles the holder to a *Carte d'Indigène* or 'red card' available from the *Controle de l'Habitant/Fremdenpolizei* (Aliens Police). The card may allow you to travel on public tranpsort at a subsidised local rate, and also to buy a cheap seasonal ski pass.

A reciprocal Swiss/UK trainee exchange agreement began in 1989 which allows for a special annual quota of 400 British trainees to gain work experience in Switzerland for 18 months. British trainees can obtain advice on how to obtain permits for temporary trainee placements (*stagiares*) from BIGA, Emmigration and Stagiaire, Monbijoustrasse 43, 3003 Bern. When writing, it would be advantageous to mention the UK/Swiss Agreement and the term Stagiare Agreement.

Laws and rules in Switzerland are normally obeyed by the locals. Cross the road against the lights (even if the road is empty) and a Swiss will come running to point out in a helpful tone that you must wait for the lights to change. Arriving at the pretty mountain resort of Engleberg, Lucien and his driver were annoyed to see 'No Parking' signs by the cable car where they usually parked. Carefully removing the signs, the driver parked the coach and left it. While sitting on a café balcony on their return a couple of hours later, they watched in horror as their coach sank into a hole. The coach had been parked on top of a chasm which had been dug to install cables. Because the Swiss are so law-abiding, they had not thought it necessary to put up any explanatory notices. Lucien spent the rest of the afternoon watching while the Swiss Army made an efficient (and expensive) job of lifting the coach out of its hole.

LIECHTENSTEIN

This independent principality is represented by Switzerland abroad and is a member of the European Economic Area. Ruled by an hereditary Prince from his castle perched high overlooking the country, the economy exists on tourist shops and manufacturing false teeth. Tour guides love this country. Their groups can add another one to their list, it takes less than an hour to drive through, the food is excellent, there is easy parking outside the two rival tourist supermarkets which sell everything from maps and guide books (a good place to stock up) to souvenirs the group might have forgotten to buy in Switzerland. A few foreigners are employed in the shops, provided they are good linguists. There is skiing in winter, but not much work.

"The Liechtenstein economy exists mainly on tourist shops and manufacturing false teeth"

DIRECTORY REFERENCES

The following companies listed in the Directory employ staff in Switzerland: Astons Ski Holidays, Crystal Holidays, Esprit Holidays Ltd., Eurocamp, Jobs in the Alps, Keycamp, Lotus Supertravel, Neilson Ski, Silver Ski Holidays, Shearings, Ski Scott Dunn, Ski la Vie, Ski Miquel, Ski Total, Skiworld, Swiss Travel Service, Top Deck, Venture Abroad, Village Camps.

Turkey

During the 1980s Turkey became the flavour of the decade and tourist development was permitted to run riot. When Spanish hotels began to increase their prices, European tour operators looked elsewhere for a cheaper alternative and Turkey was ripe for the picking. The operators offered huge contracts to a country which had previously concentrated on an upmarket and cruise market. The Turkish government offered help to build tourist facilities as quickly as possible. Hotels were thrown up without much planning, and the government was not able to develop services (sewerage, electricity, communications, etc.) fast enough to keep up. The southwest coast which takes the brunt of the tourist invasion is sometimes referred to as the 'Costa del Kebab'. These tourists are paying as little as £170 for 14 days including flight, accommodation and meals; it doesn't take a mathematician to work out that there wasn't much profit, particularly for the poor hotelier.

Despite recent bad publicity and earlier incidents in 1994, when bombing by the Kurdistan Workers Party was responsible for the deaths of four holidaymakers and again in 1995 when three holidaymakers with the company Inspirations were killed in a coach accident, Turkey continues to increase its share of the package holiday market. Some people feel that the Mediterranean coast of Turkey has been completely spoiled. Development has been concentrated in the main Aegean resorts of Marmaris, Kusadasi and Bodrum, where many English-speaking people in the tourist industry end up working. Today the Turkish government is keeping a much stricter eye on tourism development. The country is lucky that it still has one unspoilt coastline, the Black Sea, where development is proceeding very cautiously and keeping the ecology of the region in view. On the south coast local construction companies had their fingers burnt when a giant German hotel corporation tried to build a complex right on top of a loggerhead turtle breeding ground. This so inflamed the European green lobby that the resulting protest is still reverberating around the coast.

Yet the trappings of modern tourist development with all its problems has done little to diminish the extraordinary charm and hospitality of the people. Turkey remains a superb country, a cultural crossroads of immense riches. From the dawn of Biblical times, Asia Minor has been at the centre of the known world. It comes as a surprise to many holidaymakers how many famous places from the Bible and history are located in Turkey, from Tarsus (where St Paul was born) to Mount Ararat (where Noah's Ark came to rest).

Prospects for Work

Most British tour operators feature Turkey for the summer. Also, the upmarket tourists have not been completely driven away. There are still plenty of cruises which come into the harbours, and companies run tours to see the spring flowers, explore Hittite ruins and so on in the Anatolian interior. Those with an appropriate history or religion degree may find a company which needs tour leaders and specialist lecturers. (Get a list of companies that feature historical or architectural tours from the Turkish Tourist Office.)

Anyone who knows the country and the language well may eventually be employed to take tours into the heart of the old Ottoman Empire. Now that the border has been opened with Armenia and the southern Russian states, it is possible to follow the Silk Route, which so fascinated Marco Polo, and people are beginning to take tours to follow it to China.

FINDING A JOB

Turkey is set to become a more popular destination, as it is a non-EU country, and therefore benefits from the heavy subsidies of duty free sales. It may be that tour operators will look to increase capacity here at the expense of Greece and Spain. In addition to the standard range of tour operators, *Mark Warner* employs a large range of staff for its beach club hotels in Turkey from bar staff to nannies, night watchmen to watersports instructors. Reserve staff are employed throughout the summer season as vacancies arise. Flotilla holiday companies take advantage of the many beautiful moorings along the Turkish coast. *Sunsail* has many openings for skippers, hostesses, mechanics/bosuns and dinghy sailors, as well as cooks, bar staff and nannies to work in their watersports centres at Yedi Buku near Bodrum, Perili near Datca and an additional club at Marmaris. Other companies like *Simply Turkey* and Discovery (address just below) offer holidays on *gulets*, traditional wooden schooners, which employ crew and cooks.

Operators which feature Turkey include:

Cresta – 0161 9290000.

Discovery, 41 North End Road, West Kensington, London W14 8SZ (0171-602 7444). Large range of Mediterranean and Aegean resorts.

Manos Holidays, 168-172 Old St, London EC1V 9RA (0171-216 8000).

Simply Turkey (address in entry for Simply Travel). Range of holiday accommodation and special interest holidays.

Sovereign – 01293 588000

Tapestry Holidays, 24 Chiswick High Road, London W4 1TE (0181-742 0055).

Travelscene, 11/15 St Ann's Road, Harrow, Middlesex HA1 1AS (0181-427 4445).

Well-presented people have a good chance of being given jobs as reps once they have arrived in one of the big resorts. As usual, these reps who are locally hired will be paid lower wages than the UK tour company employees (and will of course be paid in Turkish lire which loses value at an alarming rate, since Turkey suffers from an horrific rate of inflation of 60-75%). Furthermore they are not insured and may be sacked without pay if there is a downturn in bookings (e.g. after a Kurdish terrorist attack).

The youth exchange organisation *Genctur* in Istanbul organises summer camps in Turkey at which English-speaking young people work as volunteers. Participants help with social activities, drama, music, sports, crafts and English teaching.

CASUAL WORK

'Help Wanted' signs can sometimes be seen in the windows of bars, carpet shops, etc. As elsewhere, proprietors aim to use native English speakers to attract more customers to buy their souvenirs or stay at their hotels. In the majority of cases, this sort of work finds you once you make known your willingness to undertake such jobs.

Major Turkish yachting resorts are excellent places to look for work, not just related to boats but in hotels, bars, shops and excursions. A good time to check harbourside notice boards and to ask captains if they need anyone to clean or repair their boats is in the lead-up to the summer season and the Marmaris Boat Show in May. Laura O'Connor describes what she found in Marmaris:

There's a large British community living there, retired and fed-up Brits who have sold their houses, bought a boat and are whooping it up. There's plenty of work opportunities in the Marina, especially for boat painting and varnishing in April. Also girls can do hostessing on the boats. I was cleaning boats with a friend for enough money to cover my accommodation and evenings in the pub. Just walk around the Marina and ask.

Laura recommends asking for advice at two English-style establishments: the Scorpion Bar and The English Pub. She eventually found a waitressing job at the Planet Disco in the Marmaris Palace Hotel in the neighbouring beach of Ichmeler, popular with German tourists.

Xuela Edwards is another recent traveller who found many opportunities in Marmaris but points out the down side:

Affordable accommodation is hard to find and wages are appalling. The Turkish work ethic can be difficult to handle too. Most Turkish businesses stay open from 10am to midnight, and much later for bars and clubs. You might not actually be doing anything but those are the hours. Turks have said to us that the English are strange because they always want to leave as soon as their hours are up and they want a day off. This is alien to the Turkish mentality which regards the office or shop as an extension of the home. Many other travellers we met also found the hanging around element frustrating.

Paying and accepting commissions is the traditional way of doing business and not regarded as ripping off the tourist because these commissions are built into the basic price of everything. Therefore it is possible for talented salesmen/women (preferably multilingual) to make good money in Turkey.

Ian McArthur decided it would be an advantage while travelling in Turkey to be musical:

There is a great demand for musicians, particularly guitarists, in places where the 'Marlboro, Levis and Coca Cola generation' predominates. I have travelled around with my friend Vanessa and she has found work playing in bars in Istanbul, Marmaris, Olu Deniz and Patara (near Kas). Marmaris was the goldmine – £30 a night. The problem was that we both hated Marmaris – too many bloody tourists! In Patara she got a job in a bar called the Lazy Frog and played for a place to stay and food.

See chapter on *Cyprus* for information about Northern Cyprus.

WORKING CONDITIONS

Problems are par for the course for reps working in Turkey. Even companies like *Tapestry Holidays* with an upmarket image and presentation do sell packaged holidays at budget prices to people who invariably complain that Turkish facilities and nightlife are not equal to those they have enjoyed in Spain.

Long transfer times of up to five hours one way are commonplace from Dalaman Airport. Often the staff accommodation is sub-standard. Mike was put in an airless windowless room until he complained. He was calm yet firm and got it changed. One of the features of the job he particularly disliked was having to explain the loo arrangements to clients, i.e. that the plumbing system cannot cope with toilet paper which must therefore be deposited in a bin. He soon became adept at the Turkish phrases for dealing with plumbers, since many clients ignored the warnings and caused blockages.

One of Mike's biggest problems was excursions. A large part of his income came from commission, but his company sold their excursions at double the rate the local operators charged. Eventually Mike solved this by inviting his clients to take a local excursion but suggested that they ask to see insurance certificates before booking. While showing them the company certificate, he told stories (all true) of what had happened to previous clients who had not been insured. They soon came back to book his tours.

Many clients suffer from gippy tummy at some point, so reps should get to know the local chemist and try to find a suitable remedy, preferably homeopathic. Sunburn is another problem. Few clients seem to believe the rep's warnings at the Welcome Meeting (especially when the rep has red hair and pale skin as Mike does) and soon come back lobster red.

Although Turkey is a secular state (due to the reforms introduced by the influential leader Ataturk in the first part of this century), the people are Muslim and their religion should be respected. Topless sunbathing is illegal in most places and limbs and women's heads should be covered when visiting mosques. Islamic fundamentalism is gaining ground which has resulted in the enforced segregation of males and females in some municipalities. So people working in Turkey should be attentive to such things.

Although the social distortions found in stricter Islamic countries are absent in Turkey, women will not escape overtures from local men, though these normally take the form of unwanted gallantry rather than sexual harassment. The army plays an important part in Turkish life and all males aged 20 must do military service for 18 months. Soldiers are in evidence everywhere and they often carry out police duties. They are invariably friendly, but never forget that their rifles are their proudest possessions.

REGULATIONS

Without paper qualifications and a dedicated local employer, it will be very difficult to obtain a work permit and therefore a residence permit. Those who enter Turkey on a tourist visa (which costs £10 in cash at the border) and then find work must leave the country every three months (normally to a Greek island like Rhodes or to Northern Cyprus). If you do this too many times, the border officials may become suspicious.

At the time of writing Turkey was under the threat of terrorist activity. The Foreign Office Travel Advice unit (0171-238 4503) was warning intending travellers to try to avoid visiting eastern and south-eastern Turkey.

DIRECTORY REFERENCES

For companies which operate in Turkey, see entries for the following: Airtours, First Choice, Club 18-30, Genctur, Mark Warner, Regent Holidays, Simply Travel, Sunsail, Tapestry Holidays, Thomson.

EASTERN EUROPE

The new democracies of Eastern Europe are all targeting tourism as a means of aiding their economies and are encouraging foreign tour operators to develop resorts, etc. which in time may have large staff requirements. Once the Iron Curtain fell, tourism chiefs in former Eastern Bloc countries expected that their end of Europe would be opened up to visitors, eager to see the wonderful scenery and beautiful buildings. To some extent this has been true, with cities like Prague and Budapest almost overrun by tourists. But outside the capitals, the inadequacies of the infrastructure have deterred high-spending tourists, and it will take many years before these countries can offer facilities equivalent to the west. For example the warm sandy beaches of the Black Sea coast are often next to factories belching out fumes and polluting the water. Instability in the Balkans hasn't helped with many tourists too afraid to visit places like Slovenia, a country which has a sophisticated tourist industry and is unaffected by the Bosnian conflict.

Today many of the visitors to Eastern Europe are attracted by the cheap holiday prices, and end up spending very little in the host country. Others come on weekend breaks to the capital cities, staying in hotels owned by international chains which take the profits out of the country. Staff to look after these visitors are mostly local. The pool of labour in these countries (where there is massive unemployment) is on the whole well educated and multilingual. A further source of competition for any work in tourism comes from all the emigrés who have returned from Europe and North America to homelands which they had fled. Having made good elsewhere and knowing the difficult languages of the east, they are ideally placed to develop tours and participate in other aspects of the expanding tourist industry. Anyone who fits this category can obtain a list of tour companies from the national tourist offices.

A few coach companies run summer tours from the UK, France and Belgium for which they hire tour guides, preferably with a knowledge of the countries and the language. Bookings are more volatile in this market than in others and tours are liable to be cancelled at short notice. The long-time specialists in tours to the former Soviet Union and Eastern Europe normally employ only established experts:

New Millenium Holidays, 20 High St, Solihull, West Midlands B91 3TB (0121-711 2232). Offers inexpensive coach holidays to Poland, Hungary, Czech Republic and Romania.

Progressive Tours Ltd, 12 Porchester Place, Marble Arch London W2 2BS (0171-262 1676/e-mail 10533.513@compuserve.com).

Regent Holidays – see entry.

Major management consultancies such as Coopers and Lybrand and the hotel consultants Howarth have carried out surveys of the tourism potential in the old communist countries. Specialist companies such as *FM Recruitment* and Carl Bro International (Hoff & Overgaard, Granskoven 8, DK-2600 Glostrup, Denmark; 4363 2622) employ professional personnel and senior advisors for contracts in the Russian republics and elsewhere in Eastern Europe.

There is tremendous scope for anyone with money to invest, who is in a position to offer a specialised tourism product, service or tour. For example the beautifully kept trains of Romania have the potential to provide 'Orient Express' type holidays, but need enthusiasts to market them to specialist tour operators. Those with money and/or time and/or expertise can make a worthwhile contribution to a local community and make a good living at the same time. A favourite target for investment by individuals is small hotels. The concrete monstrosities which accommodated the endless stream of Russian groups in the old days need to be brought up to European standards with fire escapes (to help avoid a repetition of the terrible fire in 1988 which killed a British rep at a hotel in Borovets, Bulgaria), better security, safer swimming pools, etc.

The main hotel chains are opening up in Romania, Bulgaria, Hungary and the Czech Republic in particular. Hilton has taken over the old Athenee Palace in Bucharest which re-opened in 1977. All these hotels need accounts staff, head housekeepers, admin staff, etc. with experience from the West. Luxury boats ply the Danube and need casino staff, pursers and admin staff.

Special Interest Tours

There is a wealth of cultural sites in these countries, and fantastic objets d,art, from the Faberge in the Hermitage, to Queen Marie of Romania's, Golden Furniture. As hotels improve, so more and more tour managers with specialist knowledge will be needed.The beautiful and unspoilt provinces of these countries invite special interest nature tours such as those offered by Naturetrek (Chautara, Bighton, Nr. Alresford, Hants. SO24 9RB; 01962 733051).

Hunting was a very popular pastime for party officials in the days of Communism. That activity has fallen out of international favour, which has caused problems in some areas; the increase in the bear population with insufficient food for them to forage means that they have become a menace. Less squeamish than the British, Germans have started to organise hunting parties in most of the eastern bloc countries, which will necessitate the refurbishment of lodges and country villas.

Hungary, Romania and Slovenia offer a lot of potential for setting up riding holidays especially by people who have contacts with UK riding schools. At Lipica in Slovenia there is a stud which is probably the oldest in the world, set up 400 years ago to breed horses for the Habsburg armies and the Spanish Riding School in Vienna. There are tremendous possibilities for anyone who wants to offer package tours to horse lovers and riders, who can have lessons in dressage and carriage driving. There is easy access from Trieste in northern Italy.

Trans-Siberian Express

As one of the most famous rail journeys in the world, the trans-Siberian from Moscow to China continues to attract thousands of people on packaged trips as well as independent travellers. Corinna had worked as a tour manager in Europe and Britain and was offered the chance to look after a group going through Russia to Hong Kong. Although she realised there would be potential problems, mainly relieving the tedium of the journey for her clients, she wanted to add the experience to her CV in order to help her achieve her ultimate goal, to work in Asia:

> *By the third day of looking out across the deserted landscape, peope were at each other's throats. I was kept busy by all the problems I had to sort out, from lack of food because the train hadn't made the scheduled supply stop to trying to answer the frequent question 'where are we?' when I didn't have a clue. Thank goodness I had grabbed some of my nephew's puzzle books before . I left. I tore these up, handed them out and organised a competition between carriages, and thereby managed to divert all the aggression.*

Having survived this experience, Corinna is now a seasoned tour director and has visited over 60 countries in her working life.

Winter Sports

Romania and Bulgaria in particular have fine terrain for downhill skiing and langlauf and are anxious to capture a larger share of the European ski touring market. The best known resorts are Borovets and Pamporovo in Bulgaria, Sinaia and Poiana Brasov in Romania and Bled and Kranjska Gora in northern Slovenia near the Austrian border. Prices for skiing packages here are generally lower than elsewhere, but there are drawbacks: the hire equipment tends to be decrepit, the après ski facilities limited and hotels of a poor standard. Tour operators admit that their reps do not want to be sent to these countries as conditions are difficult, the nightlife is limited and the pay is lower than in the Alps.

The only work opportunities are as reps for foreign ski tour operators like Thomson, Inghams, Neilson and the specialist Balkan Tours Ltd (61 Ann St, Belfast, Northern Ireland BT1 4EE; 01232 246795). Given the unpredictable nature of East European bureaucracies, these jobs tend to go only to seasoned reps or those fluent in the local language. One company which actively recruits reps, chalet staff and ski guides for holidays in Bulgaria and Romania is *Crystal Holidays*.

An initial explosion of interest by British tour operators in East European ski resorts has now waned due to the number of unhappy clients. Michelle has worked for several major tour operators, and spent two winters in Borovets, Bulgaria:

I won't be going back. Too many complaints. Clients didn't like their dinner buffet being set out straight after lunch and left all afternoon, unreliable supply of hot water (never available when they came back cold and wet from the slopes), a four-hour wait for their luggage at Sofia airport, etc.

The facilities are better in Romania though there are fewer jobs because there seem to be enough English-speaking ski guides, etc. locally. Working as an aid worker, Tim thought he would return as a ski guide, as he had the relevant BASI qualifications. He went up to Poiana Brasov for the weekend to look around, but decided his conscience wouldn't allow him to take work away from the people who needed it so badly, so he went back to work in Austria.

Many East European countries are dotted with luxurious villas once used as private retreats by the *nomenclatura*. For example in Croatia, many of Tito's villas on the island of Brioni were turned into very attractive villas, where wealthy Americans stayed for $800 a night, until the war frightened tourists away. Ceaucescu is reputed to have had over 160 villas, which are highly suitable for family holidays, provided the families can afford them. Lewis had a tidy nest egg from having worked in the Gulf and so bought a large farmhouse near Arbanassi, Bulgaria, which they intended to rent out to British tourists. For two years they tried to go it alone (by advertising in the UK press in magazines like *The Lady*, etc.) but encountered so many difficulties, chiefly with communication by fax and telephone, that they decided to go in with a UK firm. (Each year more and more villa companies open up as this market is expanding.) Unfortunately Lewis signed a ski tour operator's contract without consulting a lawyer familiar with the industry and ended up out-of-pocket with no bookings. He reverted to operating independently but this time used a telephone answering bureau and employed a local person to operate the fax machine.

HUNGARY

Probably the most sophisticated of the Eastern European countries, with a well-regulated tourism industry. So well-regulated that there are plenty of trained multi-lingual staff locally. Budapest is one of the top destinations for conferences and business tourism. If you contrast that with the countryside of Lake Balaton and the tours to see the horsemen, it is easy to see why this country is one of the top tourist destinations.

Work comes from tour operators and conference companies taking groups to Hungary and obviously, if you speak Hungarian you have a much better chance of finding work. Most work is in the off-season and companies such as Airtours are running popular one-day tours from the UK during the winter. Budapest is very popular with Japanese tourists so if you speak Japanese fluently companies may be interested in you as a tour manager or member of staff for their one day tours. Some coach companies may visit Hungary as part of a larger itinerary. Some companies are:

Arbaster & Clarke Wine Tours, Clarke House, Fernham Road, West Liss GU33 6JQ (01730 893344).

Caravan Tours, 59 Upper Ground, London SE1 9PQ (0171-928 9128). Require experienced tour managers.

Creative Tours, 1 Tenterden Street, London W1R 9AII (0171-495 1775). Japanese speaking staff may be needed.

Limosa, Suffield House, Northrepps, Norfolk NR27 OLZ (01263 578143). Require guides with a specialised knowledge of birds.

Miki Travel, 18 Cannon Street, London EC4M 6XT (0171-398 5211). Need staff who speak Japanese.

New Millenium, 20 High Street, Solihull B91 3TB (0121 7112232).

Page & Moy, PO Box 155, Leicester, LE1 9GZ (0116 2524433).

Prospect, 454 Chiswick High Road, London W4 5TT (0181-995 2151). Require guides with a specialist knowledge of music.

Martin Randall Travel, 10 Barley Mow Passage, London W4 4PII (0181-742 3355).

Robinsons Coach Tours, Park Garages, Great Harwood, Blackburn BB6 7SP (01254 885599).

Also look in the Directory for these entries; *Cosmos, Edwin Doran, Inghams, Saga, Shearings, Solo's, Swan Hellenic, Top Deck* and *Travelsphere*.

POLAND

When the Iron Curtain came down, Poland already had a well developed low budget tourism product. There are several coach companies providing frequent services between London Victoria and various Polish cities like Kraków. At the moment these services do not have hosts/hostesses, but this may change in the future. *Panita Travel* employs people who speak the language for its outgoing groups to Poland and Hungary.

ROMANIA

One of the most beautiful countries in Europe, with a delightfully cultured people, Romania is a country that offers much to the visitor, except the money to build places for them to stay. Many young people have had a stint in Romania as aid workers, a few of whom, like John and Rosemary, fell in love with the country and now organise an annual tour, in their case to see the country's art treasures. They do a 'recce' each Easter to check out hotels and itinerary, use a local agent to cope with the complicated paperwork and hire a coach from a local coach company. By advertising on the company notice board, putting up notices in their local newsagents and distributing homemade leaflets done on their word processor they manage to get about 40 people to book each year. Their biggest problem is the accommodation, with its uncertain plumbing and electrics. They have managed to find enough hotels near the painted churches in Moldavia and the monasteries with their icons in Bulgaria. John and Rosemary are honest with clients about the standard of hotels, and most are not disappointed. They are also wise enough to have a good solicitor, accountant and insurance broker who has arranged for them to be bonded. They make a good profit each year, after costing in their time and expenses. Now that they have established a good client list, they may do more tours when they retire from their jobs.

CZECH REPUBLIC

For companies that might need staff for tours to the Republic, contact the operators listed under Hungary. Unless you speak Czech there would be little chance of finding work in that country's tour companies which include the following:

Cedok, Na prikope 18, 11135 Prague 1 (02-24 19 71 11). Privatised national tourist
   organisation which runs coach tours, resort holidays, etc.
Bohemia Tour, Zlatnická 7, Prague 1.
Doltour, Národni trida 36, Prague 1.
Jama Tour, Mikulandská 9, Prague 1.
Regus Tour, Vodickova 41, Prague 1.

CASUAL WORK

Young people in east European capitals are so eager to embrace western culture that American-style restaurants have sprung up everywhere. In Moscow at least they hire English speakers, as attested by Bruce Collier whose British wife Sharon was hired by La Kantina Restaurant on Tverskaya near the Intourist Hotel and Red Square:

> *There are more and more Western businesses opening in Moscow all the time and the opportunities should continue to grow. This is especially true of the restaurant and entertainment industries. My wife was steered to a job as a waitress in, of all places, a Mexican restaurant (a joint Russian-Irish venture). Her job provided discounted meals (and the standard was equal to that of any Western country) and paid dollar wages.*

Of course as more and more Russians attain a working knowledge of English, there will be fewer jobs for foreigners in this sector.

Such jobs will be heard about by word-of-mouth or possibly advertised in the English-language papers mentioned earlier in the chapter. Turn-over of foreign students is high so if you are staying for a while your chances are reasonable. The trendy area of Moscow is on New Arbat; try the American-style Sports Bar. Irish pubs like Rosie O'Grady's (at Ulnanenka 9) are where expats, including workers, gather. Musicians will find a flourishing jazz and rock music scene; according to Bruce there is even some country-and-western music around.

DIRECTORY REFERENCES

For companies which employ staff in Eastern Europe see Crystal Holidays, FM Recruitment, Neilson Ski, Page & Moy, Panita Travel, Specialised Travel, Steppes East, Top Deck.

AUSTRALASIA

Australia

The Australian government campaign to increase tourism has been phenomenally successful and was crowned by the choice of Sydney for the Olympic Games in the year 2000. Ever since Paul Hogan (aka Crocodile Dundee) threw another prawn on the barbie in the memorable television advertising campaign, people from the northern hemisphere have been flocking downunder. Tourism is Australia's number one growth industry, accounting for more than 450,000 jobs (directly or indirectly) and employing one in every 16 people in the workforce. This popularity has encouraged the giant UK tour operators to feature Australia. Thomson has a weekly flight on its own airline, Britannia, as does Airtours. With prices starting at less than £600 for an inclusive fortnight's holiday, many British holidaymakers are being wooed away from Europe. This has not happened to the same extent in the American market; however, as air fares across the Pacific come down, major US operators will be offering more tours to Australia.

Tourist facilities along the coast of Queensland and the Great Barrier Reef as far north as Port Douglas are being developed at a breakneck rate, especially with an eye to the Japanese market. The Japanese have invested heavily in developments like the Gold Coast Resort Hotels. Anyone who has travelled in Japan or who has a smattering of Japanese will discover that there are some excellent jobs to be had looking after Japanese tour groups. The owner of the Working Holiday Hostel in Sydney reckons that 'people who speak Japanese usually get a job within three hours of landing in Australia.' The Queensland state capital Brisbane is campaigning to turn its airport into an international hub to relieve some of the pressure on Sydney Airport, which will give a further fillip to Queensland tourism.

FINDING A JOB

If you go out to Australia to look for experience of working in tourism, possibly on a working holiday visa (described below), you may be surprised by the amount of competition from others on working holidays. For example, of the 50 replies to an advertisement placed by a company which operates tours of Sydney Harbour for waiting staff and a receptionist, 42 were from Poms. The glut of travelling workers is especially bad before Christmas.

In addition to asking potential employers directly (which is the method used by about one third of successful job-seekers in Australia), there are four main ways of finding work: the Commonwealth Employment Service (Jobcentres), private employment agencies, newspaper advertisements and notice boards. Like job centres anywhere the CES post job details which have been registered with them. Some CESs have separate departments or even separate addresses which specialise in jobs in the hospitality industry, which sometimes produce instantaneous jobs and other times a very disappointing service.

Private employment agencies are not of much use when looking for tourist-related work, though anyone with travel agency experience might contact the specialist Sydney agency Bureau Travel Recruiters (02-9252 2722) or see the entry in the Directory for *Terence Cox & Associates*.

Several holiday cruises depart from Cairns to tour the islands en route to Thursday Island, and take on staff to clean, cook and serve the guests. Ask about openings on the *Atlantic Clipper*, *Queen of the Isles* and the *Nole Buxton*.

The main daily newspapers have job supplements once or twice a week, for example on Wednesday and Saturday in the *Sydney Morning Herald*, the *West Australian* (Perth), *Adelaide Advertiser* or the *Courier-Mail* (Brisbane). The Monday Job Market in the Melbourne *Age* is particularly worthwhile. Remember that these wide-circulation papers generate a lot of competition for jobs, though it is worth checking whenever possible under the specific heading 'Positions Vacant – Hospitality Industry' for bar and restaurant jobs, work on guest ranches, etc. There is often less competition for jobs advertised in local and suburban papers.

Tours

The annually revised *Traveller's Guide* from the Australian Tourist Commission contains the names and addresses of a number of tour operators; a copy can be requested by ringing 0891 070707 (calls at 50p per min).

Specialist wine tours are gaining popularity, although Australia can cater to almost any sporting or special interest. Camping tour operators proliferate in Darwin, most of them featuring Kakadu National Park and Litchfield Park; try Northern Explorer (889-811-633) and Billy Can Tours (889-819-813).

Georgie had always wanted to follow her father into the travel business and studied for the ABTA COTAMM (Certificate of Agency Management). One weekend while talking to one of the grooms who worked for Kerry Packer (the Australian media tycoon) at his polo pony stables at Stedham in Sussex, Georgie came home with an idea. With all her contacts in the world of horse-lovers, she thought there was a niche for specialist tours to Australian events like the Melbourne Gold Cup. She arranged to work at Packer's stables at Ellerston in Australia in order to make contacts. Now she returns twice a year leading groups that go to see the horse scene in Australia and buy polo ponies.

Hotels and Catering

Standards tend to be high in the service industry especially in popular tourist haunts, but anyone with experience as a cook or chef will probably find themselves in great demand and being well rewarded. Jobs in catering can usually be found in the major cities, especially Sydney and Melbourne. Outside ordinary restaurants and cafés, catering jobs crop up in cricket grounds, theatres, yacht clubs and (in Sydney) on harbour cruises.

Australian cooking has come out of the dark ages and is admired internationally for its emphasis on fresh fish and healthy fruit and vegetables. A stint in a well known Australian restaurant is now almost as impressive on a CV as one in France. Harry's catering college had an Australian tutor who helped him to fix up work experience at a top Sydney restaurant:

> *I expected to be laughed at as a Pom, but everyone was very friendly. They didn't even laugh at my accent after I learned how to say a proper 'G'day'. I enjoyed learning how to prepare (and eat) new types of fish, and brought back with me a book full of recipes for when I open my own restaurant.*

Harry had intended to use his savings to travel round Australia after he finished working but instead was offered a step-up in a restaurant in England so returned home with a healthy bank balance.

Diving

The dive industry is a major employer. Although not many visitors would have the qualifications which got Ian Mudge a job as Dive Master on *Nimrod III* operating out of Cookstown in northern Queensland (i.e. qualified mechanical engineer, diver and student of Japanese), his assessment of opportunities for mere mortals is heartening:

Anyone wishing to try their luck as a hostess could do no worse than to approach all the dive operators with live-aboard boats such as Mike Ball Water Sports in Townsville, Down Under Dive, etc. 'Hosties' make beds, clean cabins and generally tidy up. Culinary skills and an ability to speak Japanese would be definite pluses. A non-diver would almost certainly be able to fix up some free dive lessons and thus obtain their basic Open Water Diver qualification while being paid to do so. Normally females only are considered for hostie jobs.

Many of the small islands along the Barrier Reef such as Brampton Island, Great Keppel Island, Dunk Island and Fitzroy Island are completely given over to tourist complexes. The first three are owned by Australian Airlines who recruit staff through their Personnel Department on Dunk Island (off Mission Beach). You might make initial enquiries at CES offices on the mainland for example in Prosperpine, Cannonvale, Mackay or Townsville, though normally you will have to visit an island in person to be interviewed.

Ski Resorts

The Australian Alps have some excellent and expanding ski resorts. Jindabyne (NSW) on the edge of Kosciusko National Park and Thredbo are the ski job capitals, though Mount Buller, Falls Creek, Baw Baw and Hotham in the state of Victoria are relatively developed ski centres too, as are Mount Field and Ben Lomond in Tasmania. Instructors with BASI qualifications can usually fix up work at the ski hiring clinics held in the weeks leading up to the opening of the season (around the 11th of June). The CES offices in Wangaratta and Cooma can advise, though most successful job-seekers use the walk-in-and-ask method. In 'Jindy' try the Brumby Bar, Aspen Hotel, Kookaburra Lodge or any of the dozens of other hotels and pubs.

Henry Pearce's experiences looking for work were not so positive, despite heavy radio advertising by the CES:

When we arrived in Cooma on June 2nd, we enquired about the progress of the applications we had sent in April. We were told that there had been 4,000 applications and two vacancies for bar staff to date. We carried on up to Thredbo and half-heartedly asked around a few chalets and hotels and it seemed most of them had already fixed up their basic requirements. We were told of several definite posts available once the snow fell. In Jindabyne we were hired to work at the 'highest restaurant in Australia' (at the top of the ski lift) for $12 an hour. But accommodation was uniformly expensive in Jindabyne ($100+ a week) as is the cost of lift passes and ski hire.

CASUAL WORK

People on working holidays in Australia pick up an astonishing range of temporary jobs, from acting as a temporary warden in a Tasmanian youth hostel to serving beer at a roadhouse along the nearly uninhabited road through the Australian north-west to serving at an eat-as-much-as-you-can Sizzlers salad bar in the big cities. Casual employees make up 60% of the 140,000 workforce employed in the hospitality industry.

In the major cities, get hold of the excellent free booklets *Australia Travel Planners*, published by TNT Australia, Level 4, 46-48 York Street, Sydney 2000. They carry advertisements and features of interest to job-seekers in their sections on 'Finding Work'.

Hostels

Youth hostels and backpackers' lodges are a goldmine of information for people working their way around the Australian tourist industry. Some hostel managers go so far as to run their own informal job-finding service and try to put backpackers in touch with local employers. You may find employment in the hostels themselves of course, especially along the 'Route' between Sydney and Cairns.

There are about 140 official YHA hostels where employment can sometimes be found on a casual basis, especially at busy periods. In the low season, people are employed as relief managers. Enquiries can be made either directly to the Hostel Manager, or to the YHA state offices (addresses in the *International Youth Hostels Federation* handbook).

One of the most successful groups of non-YHA hostels is VIP Backpackers Resorts of Australia which is especially strong in New South Wales and Queensland. A booklet listing their 130 Australian hostels is widely available after arrival or can be obtained from overseas travel agents. Almost all VIP hostels have notice boards advertising jobs, flats, car shares, etc. and all charge $10-15 a night for a dorm bed. For more information write to VIP Backpackers Resorts, PO Box 600, Cannon Hill, QLD 4170, Australia.

Most Sydney hostels are well clued up on the local job scene, especially in the two main backpackers' areas, Kings Cross (which is becoming increasingly sleazy) and Glebe. One that is recommended is Carole's Place with the promising description 'Sydney's Working Holiday Hostel' (209 Bridge Road, Glebe, NSW 2037; 02-660 0998/0-414 600 998). This small hostel has 15 beds and is about A$100 per week to rent.

Another pleasant area in which to be based is the beach suburb of Coogee (pronounced Cudjee) for example at Coogee Beach Backpackers, 94 Beach St, Coogee, NSW 2034; 2-966-57735) which is regularly contacted for casual workers. The same is true of two other Coogee Beach hostels, Aaronbrook Lodge at 116 Brook St (2-9231-45324), and Aegean Backpackers at 40 Coogee Bay Road.

In Adelaide, try Rucksackers International at 257 Gilles Street which tries its best to direct travellers to relevant jobs, for example at show time. In Perth, one of the best places to head is Cheviot Lodge, 30 Bulwer St, Northbridge (09-227 6817) which Mary Bell heartily recommends:

> *Joe and Diane Lunn, the managers of Cheviot Lodge, get work for residents. Apparently Joe gets rung up each evening with a long list of jobs and gives his residents first chance. Then he rings up other hostels with any left-over work. While I was there all the residents had been found work. Furthermore it is the cleanest and best hostel I have ever stayed in and excellent value.*

Queensland

Queensland is such a popular destination for visitors from overseas that there is a ready pool of people willing to work in these idyllic surroundings for very little money. The pay is generally so low in seasonal jobs in the Queensland tourist industry that the work does not appeal to many Australians, since they can earn nearly as much on the dole. When employers need to fill a vacancy, they tend to hire whomever is handy that day, rather than sift through applications. For example if you phone from Sydney to enquire about possibilities, the advice will normally be to come and see, which can be expensive if you have to pay for the ferry to several islands before you land a job.

If you want a live-in position, you should try the coastal resorts such as Surfers Paradise and Noosa Heads and islands all along the Queensland coast where the season lasts from March, after the cyclones, until Christmas. If Cairns is choc-a-bloc with job-seekers try the huge resort of Palm Cove just north of the city. Here is a list of contacts to whom applications should be addressed to work in specific island resorts:

Fraser Island – Personnel Manager, Kingfisher Bay Resort & Village, PMB Urangan, Hervey Bay, Queensland $655 (008-07 2555).

Heron Island – Assistant Manager, Heron Island Tourist Resort, Heron Island, Via Gladstone, Queensland 4680 (079-78 1488).

Capricorn Coast – Personnel Manager, Capricorn International Resort, Farnborough Road (PO Box 350), Yeppoon, Queensland 4703 (079-39 5111).

Great Keppel Island – Central Recruitment, Australian Resorts, PO Box 1033, Brisbane, Queensland 4000 (079-39 5044).

Be warned that Queensland employers are notorious for laying off staff at a moment's notice without compensation, holiday pay, etc. Emma Dunnage was disillusioned with one of the six backpackers hostels on Magnetic Island where she worked for ten weeks as a catamaran instructor-cum-general dogsbody. She was paid $100 a week, half of what most of the other staff were getting. In fact there is an 'Offshore Islands Award' for workers in isolated places which is a minimum of $350 a week in addition to board and lodging, though it is often ignored.

Caroline Perry was fairly confident that a commercial resort like Surfers Paradise would offer opportunities to work:

> *Jobwise we didn't have much luck in Surfers. We went to every hotel, filling in forms and just waiting for the phone to ring. We both got work in Movie World where they seem to like employing backpackers. Warner Brothers Movie World is similar to Disney World, with lots of coffee shops and restaurants that need staff. I got a job cooking burgers in 'Gotham City' but the pay wasn't that good, especially since we had to spend so much on travel from our backpackers' hostel in town. There is such a high turnover of staff, you are nearly guaranteed a job.*

The address of Movie World is Pacific Highway, Oxenford 4210 (07-55733999). Similar attractions to try along the Gold Coast are Sea World (Sea World Drive, Main Beach, PO Box 190, Surfers Paradise; 07-55882222), Dreamworld (07-58733300), Wet 'n' Wild (07-555532277) and Jupiters Casino (Conrad Jupiters, Broadbeach Island, Broadbeach 4218; 07-55921133).

Cities

Function work is usually easy to come by via specialist agencies provided you can claim to have silver service experience. It is worth applying to catering companies as Fiona Cox did in Sydney, though she was not impressed with the wage of $7.40 an hour (weekly take-home pay of $200).

The best opportunities for bar and waiting staff in Perth are in the city centre, Fremantle and Northbridge, the area around William and James Streets. Rhona Stannage arrived in Perth in November and, having had chalet experience in the French Alps and restaurant experience in Cyprus en route, was in a strong position to find hospitality work:

> *Since there were lots of adverts in the newspapers for bar/restaurant staff we didn't go door-knocking, but we did meet a Canadian guy who had been in Perth one week and who had immediately found work in Northbridge just by asking around in the restaurants, bars and nightclubs. We both got jobs fairly quickly.*

Rhona was also offered a job at the Burswood Resort Casino which often needs staff willing to work shifts (it is open 24 hours). To attract 'permanent' staff, they pay twice the going wage and offer their staff lots of perks such as free meals and a staff gym.

Special Events

As always, special events such as test matches and race meetings are a possible source of employment. If you happen to be in Melbourne in late October or early November for the Melbourne Cup (held on the first Tuesday of November which is a public holiday in Victoria), your chances of finding casual work escalate remarkably. Hotels, restaurants and bars become frantically busy in the period leading up to the Cup, and private catering firms are also often desperate for staff. An application to a firm like Rowlands (which also operates in Sydney) or O'Brien in September or October is quite likely to turn up some casual work. All the major cities have important horse races.

Another major event in Australia's sporting calendar is the Adelaide Grand Prix, also held in early November. Ask at your hostel or at likely looking companies (e.g. Spotless Catering).

Working Conditions

Although there is very little unionism in tourist and service industries, award wages are high both in 5-star hotels and fast food restaurants like Fast Eddy's in Melbourne and Perth. The casual rate for waiting staff is $9-10 an hour, with weekend loadings, although these were recently cut by the Industrial Relations Commission to time and a half on Saturdays and time and three-quarters on Sundays and holidays. Partly because of the tradition of paying high wages in the hotel and catering industry, Australians are not in the habit of tipping much, though this is gradually changing.

REGULATIONS

Working Holiday Visas

British, Irish, Canadian, Dutch and Japanese people between the ages of 18 and 25 (up to 30 in limited circumstances) and without children are eligible to apply for a working holiday visa. More than 25,000 are granted to Britons alone each year. The visa is meant for people intending to use any money they earn in Australia to supplement their holiday funds. Working full-time for the same employer for more than three months is not permitted. The visa is valid for travel within 12 months and allows a stay of 12 months after arrival. Details can be obtained from the High Commission in London (Australia House, Strand, London WC2B 4LA; 0891 600333). The visa is not renewable either in Australia or at home.

The first step is to get the working holiday information sheet and application form 147 from the High Commission's mailing house Australian Outlook, 3 Buckhurst Road, Bexhill-on-Sea, East Sussex TN40 1QF (01424 223111), enclosing an A4 stamped addressed envelope (47p stamp). The non-refundable processing fee in the UK is the sterling equivalent of A$150. Each application is assessed on its own merits, but the most important requirement is a healthy bank balance. The amount currently recommended is £2,000 from which the cost of the airfare may come. In most cases postal applications are processed in between ten days and three weeks.

Obtaining a resident's visa (for permanent migration) is, predictably, much more difficult, though not impossible if you have a skill in short supply or a close relative in Australia. The Application for Migration package including application form 47 explains the points system and is available from the High Commission. Phone the High Commission for details of the fees charged for this as they fluctuate due to exchange rates and changes from the Australian Government. Rhona Stannage was very surprised to learn that three states in Australia recognise a Scottish law degree and considered the seven-month wait and the fee of £250 for a resident's visa worthwhile, although she and her husband were really interested only in a working holiday.

Special Schemes

BUNAC (16 Bowling Green Lane, London EC1R 0QH) features Australia as one of its destination countries. Anyone who is eligible for the working holiday visa may choose to join the BUNAC Work Australia package which costs from £1,500 from London or £1,600 from California. This includes the return flight (departing from August to September), orientation on arrival and back-up from IEP (International Exchange Programme) in Sydney.

Canadian students and recent graduates aged 18-27 can participate in the SWAP programme whereby students qualify for visas lasting six months; ask at any office of Travel Cuts.

CIEE (205 E 42nd St, New York, NY 10017) run a working programme to Australia for **American students** on similar terms as the working holiday scheme for UK students. The quota of 100 may increase in the next few years.

New Zealand

New Zealand is a charmingly rural country where less than four million natives host more than a million tourists every year. With excellent facilities for visitors and lower air fares, more and more tourists, especially older people, are braving the long flight to New Zealand. Air New Zealand consistently wins awards for in-flight service and this helps to spread the message that NZ is a quality destination. It is a wonderfully laid-back country with a refreshing lack of both European snobbishness and North American materialism. Unemployment is falling and the economy is looking less shaky than it was at the beginning of the 1990s. If wages are lower than in Australia, life is comparatively cheap.

The defence of the America's Cup will take place around the turn of the next century, and will no doubt boost the tourism figures yet further, especially since the yacht race will coincide with the Olympics in Sydney. International sporting events like these create many employment opportunities for months beforehand.

FINDING A JOB

New Zealand's tourist industry revolves mainly around the outdoor life, mostly just admiring it but also hiking, sailing, game fishing, rafting, skiing, mountaineering and so on. Anyone who has had experience of working for a rafting company in America or Europe might contact the rafting tour operators (names available from the New Zealand Tourist Office).

Visitors also go to see the bizarre geology of the country with its volcanic hot pools and geysers. Special interest tours go to see the vineyards which have made such an impact on the international market and people interested in agriculture go to visit farms. Many small specialised travel agencies in the UK now organise one New Zealand tour a year for clients. Unfortunately this is usually led by the owner, but those who know the country well might find an opening or even organise their own small-scale tour.

Tours for farmers are an unexpected source of employment. If you have worked as a tour manager, know your lambs from your hogs, and have a pair of wellies, you may be able to take advantage of farmers' interest in seeing the latest farming methods and also some traditional organic ones as well. Companies can occasionally be seen advertising in the farming press like *Valley Farmer*, *Farmers' Weekly* and the *Sheep Farmer*.

Ski Resorts

The main ski resorts in the Southern Alps are Coronet Peak and the Remarkables (serviced by the holiday town of Queenstown), Mount Hutt and Treble Cone (with access from Wanaka), all on the South Island. On the North Island try National Park (for Whakapapa) or Ohakune (for Turoa) on opposite sides of the semi-active volcano Mount Ruapehu. The ski season lasts roughly from April to October. As in Australia, most resorts hold pre-season hiring clinics for instructors. On arrival ring around the resorts to secure a place on a clinic which is a mini-teaching course held at the beginning of July. There is a charge for participating, which is reasonable.

If hired, the work at first will be part-time but you will have your foot in the door and be in a good position to obtain full-time work when it becomes available. Very few people without BASI or equivalent ski instructing qualifications get offered full-time jobs, though the situation for snowboard instructors is more flexible, since they are in heavy demand. Part-timers usually get a ski lift pass (worth about NZ$850) plus instructor training sessions.

If you have a specific skill such as ski instructor, ski patroller, ski hire technician, snowcat/plough driver then your best bet is to apply to the resorts in advance (addresses from New Zealand Consulates).

CASUAL WORK

Despite the recent recession, tourism in New Zealand continues to flourish, and openings for hotel and catering staff proliferate. Waiters and waitresses are usually paid $8 an hour. Remember that tips in New Zealand are virtually non-existent. On the plus side, restaurant kitchens tend to be more relaxed places than they are in Europe.

As in Australia hostels are the best source of job information. There are many adventurous forms of the tourist industry. You might get taken on by a camping tour operator as a cook; perhaps you could find a job on a yacht; or if you're a skier, you should try one of the ski resorts (as described above). Matt Tomlinson accompanied his best mate who has been instructing in Turoa since he was 18 and got two jobs as soon as the summer season started:

> *The first job was as a barman in the ski resort bar which paid $8 an hour plus gave me a ski pass and cheap food and drink in other bars in town. The work was pretty hard, since Kiwi employers like to get their money's worth. My second job was as a waiter in a local restaurant. The trick when you get to town is to chat to as many people as possible and mention what sort of work you're looking for. In small places word often gets around very fast (so don't complain about your boss behind his back). Otherwise a few days spent checking notice-boards in the library or supermarket and just asking in as many places as possible is probably the best way to do it. The season was thoroughly enjoyable, especially being treated as a local rather than a punter (and charged accordingly).*

Queenstown

The lakeside resort of Queenstown is particularly brimming with opportunities. It is a town whose economy is booming due to tourism and whose population is largely young and transient. The central town notice board in the pedestrian mall often carries adverts for waitresses, kitchen help, etc., as do the boards in the Queenstown Youth Hostel and backpacker haunts. One of the favourite drinking establishments for itinerant workers is Eichardts Hotel, while a popular eatery (which also sometimes hires working holidaymakers) is the Cow Pizzeria in Cow Lane. One of the perks of being a worker and therefore an honorary resident (instead of a 'loopy', the local term for tourist), is that often workers can get discounts on local activities like rafting. On the other hand, the town's popularity means that there are often more people (including New Zealanders) looking for work than there are jobs, so it might be advisable to try more out-of-the-way tourist areas. Mike Tunnicliffe landed a job as dishwasher at the hotel at Milford Sound and says that one stands a better chance of obtaining casual work in remote underpopulated places on the tourist trail (of which there are many in New Zealand).

This view is corroborated in the experience of New Zealander Ken Smith:

> *It is accepted practice to phone the resort hotels and ask if they have any immediate vacancies. Good resorts to phone are Milford Sound, Fox Glacier, Franz Josef and Mount Cook. The THC chain of hotels specialise in high-class hotels in remote and scenic locations.*

REGULATIONS

Tourists from the UK need no visa to stay for up to six months, while Americans, Canadians and Europeans can stay for three visa-free months. There is a scheme called the UK Citizens' Working Holiday Scheme whereby a maximum of 500 Britons aged 18-30 are granted permission to work in New Zealand for up to 12 months from date of arrival. When the scheme was introduced in 1993, the quota was 500. That number has now quadrupled, and 2,000 working holiday visas are granted annually on a first come first served basis starting July 1st. To apply, you need the right Application for Work Visa form, your UK passport, the fee of £60, evidence of a return ticket and evidence of NZ$4,200 (about £1,250). Sponsorship from a New Zealand citizen is not considered an acceptable substitute for proof of funds. The scheme has recently been extended to Irish nationals on the same terms, though the allocation is only 250.   A possible alternative for those who have contacts in New Zealand and can obtain a firm offer of employment before leaving the UK is to apply for a temporary work visa (the same non-refundable fee of £60 applies). Your New Zealand sponsor must be prepared to prove to the Immigration Service that it is necessary to hire a foreigner rather than an unemployed New Zealander. The leaflet 'Getting a Work Visa' available from the New Zealand Immigration Service goes into more detail. The work visa does not in itself entitle you to work, but does make it easier to obtain a work permit after arrival. Note that anyone with a substantial amount of money to invest in a tourism project may be welcomed by the government.

It is also possible to apply for a work permit at one of the seven Immigration Service offices in New Zealand even if you arrived in the country as a visitor and landed a job. To be considered for a work permit you must have a written job offer from a prospective employer confirming that the position offered is temporary, a full description of the position, salary, evidence that you are suitably qualified (originals or certified copies of work references, qualification certificates, etc.) and evidence that the employer has made every effort to recruit local people (proof of advertising, vacancy lodged with Employment Service, etc.) As usual there are no hard and fast rules and no guarantee of success, as Ken Smith (a native New Zealander) found when he worked alongside foreigners at Franz Josef resort;

> There was a Northern Irish girl working there who had been granted a work permit to work as a waitress. She was assured of the job over the phone having told them that her application for a work permit was being processed (which it wasn't) and when assured of the job she promptly set about applying for a work permit before arriving at the hotel. The work permit was granted three months later, a week or so before she was due to move on, so she was quite annoyed because it cost over NZ$100. On a previous occasion working at the same resort I remember an English fellow who was working as a barman. His application for a work permit was flatly refused, so I guess it depends on 'Do you feel lucky?'

American students are eligible to apply for a six-month work permit from CIEE (fee $225) to work between April 1st and October 31st. Also Travel CUTS in Canada administers a similar work abroad scheme for Canadian students. All visas expire at the end of October. The point of allowing foreigners to work only during the New Zealand winter is in order to prevent competition with New Zealand students seeking holiday jobs during the summer.

NORTH AMERICA

United States

Air fare wars between transatlantic carriers has made it almost as cheap to take a holiday in Florida as in Europe. The influx of Europeans to popular US destinations like Florida, California and New York combined with the millions of Americans and Canadians who take their holidays in the United States accounts for the staggering statistic from the National Travel & Tourism Awareness Council in Washington DC that there are six million jobs in the American tourist industry. It is the second largest employer in the country after health services and generates hundreds of thousands of interesting job vacancies a year.

There is a catch however, unless you work for a UK tour operator. It is exceedingly difficult to get an immigrant visa or 'green card' (actually it's pink) which allows foreigners to live and work in the US as 'resident aliens'. Nearly all the permanent resident visas which are issued each year are given to close relations of American citizens. Other possibilities are that you can offer a skill which is in short supply and have a US employer willing to sponsor your application for labour certification, or you may be eligible to participate in one of the special schemes for students, trainees, etc.

EXCHANGE PROGRAMMES

Approved organisations such as *BUNAC* and *Camp America* can assist students and some non-students to obtain a special J-1 work and travel visa. A large part of both organisations' programmes consist of placing young people on summer camps (which is described below), but first we will consider BUNAC's more generalised *Work America Programme* which allows full-time university students to do any summer job they are able to find, including jobs in the tourist industry. Obviously the dates of the programme (June to October) do not allow much scope for advancing a career in tourism. However a summer spent doing a seasonal job in an American resort can be useful on your CV.

BUNAC, the British Universities North America Club (16 Bowling Green Lane, London EC1R 0QH; 0171-251 3472) is a student club which all participants on their US work schemes must join (£4). Most UK universities have a BUNAC club which can provide detailed brochures setting out the various and potentially confusing procedures as clearly as possible.

There are around 4,000 places on the Work America Programme for full-time students (university, HND, NVQ4/5 or gap year with a confirmed university place for the following autumn). You must have a job fixed before you go, but this can be done by using BUNAC's own *Work Directory* or the annually revised book *Summer Jobs USA* published in December by Peterson's Guides (202 Carnegie Center, Princeton, NJ 08543) at $16.95 and distributed in Europe by Vacation Work at £12.95. Each employer's entry indicates whether applications from foreign students are encouraged. The categories for each state cover specific job listings in summer camps and theatres, resorts, ranches, restaurants, lodgings, etc.

Internships

Internship is the American term for traineeship, providing a chance to get some experience in your career interest, often as part of your academic course. Several organisations in the UK arrange for students and in some cases graduates to undertake internships in the US. The most important is the Council on International Educational Exchange (CIEE, 52 Poland Street, London W1V 4JQ; tel 0171 478 2000; fax 0171 734 7322; e-mail InfoUK@ciee.org) which helps 1,000 full-time students to arrange work placements in the US lasting up to one year. You (often with the help of an academic adviser) must find the job which has to be related to your course of study, though CIEE offers practical advice on sending speculative applications to US employers. Those who qualify get a J-1 visa. The programme fee is £210-£290 depending on the length of the internship. Applicants in France should apply to CIEE (1 place de l'Odéon, 75006 Paris; 1-44 41 74 74) and in Germany to CIEE (Thomas Mann Strasse 33, 53111 Bonn; 228-98 36 00).

While studying for a leisure and recreational management degree at Thames Valley University, Neil Hibberd arranged a CIEE internship at a Colorado ski resort:

> *The Council's policy is that they need a letter from the employer before giving you the visa. I first went out to Colorado in August. The Steamboat Ski Corporation gave me a written job offer as a lift operator on the condition that I could obtain a work visa. I returned to the UK, obtained the visa through the CIEE and went back to Steamboat in October. Travelling twice to the States and paying for the work visa and insurance came to £650, which exhausted my savings. Looking back on the process, I see that there should be an easier way to obtain such a placement.*

The CIEE also administers a UK/US Career Development Programme for British nationals aged 18-35 with relevant qualifications and/or at least one year of work experience in their chosen field. Part of this programme is designated a Hospitality and Tourism Exchange which is co-sponsored by the Association for International Practical Training (AIPT, 10400 Little Patuxent Parkway, Suite 250, Columbia, Maryland 21044-3510). This exchange is for Britons who have at least one year's experience in industry or UK students who are enrolled in a hotel/catering course and have some experience. Individuals must arrange their own work placement (for a maximum of 18 months), though the Council can provide some assistance. The fee for participants is £65 while the US employer usually pays the $600 to $1,000 processing fee.

Challenge Educational Services (101 Lorna Road, Hove, East Sussex BN3 3EL; tel 01273 220261; fax 01273 220376; e-mail enquiries@challengeuk.com; website http://www.challengeuk.com) offers graduates and undergraduates aged 18-26, a 2-3 month voluntary work placement programme in the San Fransisco area. Internships are tailored to suit each student's requirements and guarantee to provide useful business skills in their chosen field.

The book *Internships* (£16.95) published by Peterson's Guides (202 Carnegie Center, Princeton, NJ 08543; $24.95) lists paid or unpaid intern positions, can last for the summer, for a semester or for a year. The listings of most interest are the ones under the heading 'Museums and Cultural Organisations' which include museums and monuments looking for guides, including well known tourist centres like the Cloisters Museum in New York or the Chicago Academy of Sciences natural history museum. Note that many of these positions are unpaid. The book offers general advice (including a section called 'Foreign Applicants for US Internships'). This annually revised book is available in the UK from Vacation-Work for £16.95 plus £3 postage.

working adventures
WORLDWIDE

Make the most of your long summer holidays or 'year out' with BUNAC's wide range of exciting work and travel programmes. Nobody offers you greater opportunities to explore other countries while gaining valuable work experience!

WE OFFER YOU:

★ BUNACAMP Counsellors and KAMP -summer jobs in the USA

★ Twelve months to work and travel in Canada, Australia, New Zealand or South Africa

★ Summer vacation work in the USA and Canada

★ Three to eighteen month internship with OPT USA

★ Six months to work and travel in Jamaica or Ghana

For further information of BUNAC's programmes, send your name and address on a postcard to William Thrope at the address below.

BUNAC
16 Bowling Green Lane
London EC1R 0QH
e-mail: brochures@bunac.org.uk
Tel: [0171] 251-3472

Tours

Experienced tour managers or people familiar with a popular region of the States should apply to the major UK operators like *Travelsphere, Cosmos* and *Page & Moy*. Typically these companies offer tours of the west coast, California, Florida, the Deep South, the national parks (Grand Canyon, Yellowstone, etc.), plus possibly tours to Hawaii and Alaska too. Having worked two seasons in Europe, Robin wanted to widen her horizons so applied to join Travelsphere. As part of the interview she was videoed giving a commentary which she found somewhat daunting, but was subsequently offered a job taking groups around the States.

People who have worked in Europe for one of the major international coach tour operators based in the States may find work on their employers' domestic tours of the US. Among the most important US operators are:

Globus Gateway/Cosmos Tours, 5301 South Federal Circle, Littleton, 80123-2980 Colorado (800-221-0090). European address: Via alla Roggia, CH-6916 Grancia, Switzerland (091-985 71 11).
Maupintour Inc, 1421 Research Park Drive, 1300 Lawrence, Kansas 66049 (913-843-1211).
Mayflower Tours, 1225 Warren Ave, Downers Grove, Illinois 60515 (708-960-3420/312-960-3430). Continental USA, Hawaii, Alaska, Canada and Mexico.
Tauck Tours, 11 Wilton Road, Westport, Connecticut 06880 (203-226-6911).

Others are included on the list of active members of the National Tour Association, 546 East Main Street, Lexington, KY 40508 (606 226 4236).

Greyhound buses (625 Eighth Ave, New York, NY 10018; 212 971 0492) may require hosts/hostesses for their cross country network.

Special Interest Holidays

Americans are very enthusiastic about outdoor and activity holidays, for which suitably qualified cyclists, hikers and so on may be needed. The best resource for someone with a specialised skill or interest they want to put to use in the American tourist industry is the *Specialty Travel Index* published twice a year (spring/summer and autumn/winter) for $6 a single issue and $10 per annum within North America, $20 abroad. It lists more than 600 companies worldwide, the majority American, including hiking, biking, golfing, winery, cookery, cruising and a host of others from astrology to zoology tours to following in the footsteps of Sherlock Holmes or Count Dracula. All companies are thoroughly indexed according to activity and location, and the book provide an excellent starting place for landing a job. It is available from STI, 305 San Anselmo Avenue, San Anselmo, CA 94960 (415-459-4900).

Camping tours are popular with a younger clientele; try TrekAmerica, 4 Waterperry Street, Middleton Road, Banbury OX16 8QG (tel 01295 256777/e-mail postmaster@trekam.demon.co.uk). Americans are very enthusiastic about outdoor and activity holidays, for which suitably qualified cyclists, hikers and so on may be needed.

Wine tours are gaining popularity not only in California's famous Napa Valley but in other areas as well, often in conjunction with cycling tours.

Ski Resorts

There is plenty of winter work in ski resorts (especially for certified ski instructors), particularly in Colorado and the Lake Tahoe in California/Nevada, between December and May. Aspen, Vail, Steamboat Springs have all been recommended. The best time to arrive is October/November to look for a job on the ski hill, in the hotels and restaurants, etc. Check adverts in the local papers, for example in Steamboat the *Steamboat Pilot* and *Steamboat Today*, and in South Lake Tahoe, the *Tahoe Daily Tribune*. The local Chamber of Commerce can give you the addresses of most local businesses, as well as relocation information, for example the Steamboat Springs Chamber Resort Association (P.O. Box 77448, Steamboat Springs, CO 80444) or the South Lake Tahoe Chamber of Commerce (530 541 5255). Aspen is one of the wealthiest resorts in Colorado and supports a large out-of-town working population. Heavenly is one of the largest resorts in the Lake Tahoe area and sits on the border of California and Nevada. Every year, the Jackson Hole Ski Corporation (address below) holds a job fair in October/ November. Contact them for dates and requirements.

It is common for one company to own all the facilities and control all employment in one resort, and in some cases provide staff accomodation. Here are some of the major resort companies which may be in charge of hiring for all resort jobs:

Aspen Skiing Company, PO Box 1248, Aspen, CO 81612 (970-920-0945).

Breckenbridge Ski Corporation, PO Box 1058, Breckenbridge, CO 80424 (970-453-5000).

Copper Mountain Resort Inc, 209 Ten Mile Circle, Copper Mountain, CO 80443 (303-968-2882).

Heavenly Ski Resort, PO Box 2180, Stateline, NV 89449 (702-586-7000/website www.skiheavenly.com).

Jackson Hole Ski Corporation, PO Box 290, Teton Village, WY 83025 (307-733-2292).

Killington Ski Resort, RR1 Box 2450, Killington, VT 05751 (802-422-3333).

Mammouth Mountain Ski Area, PO Box 24, Mammouth Lakes, CA 93546 (760 934 0654/fax 760 934 0608/e-mail personnel@mammothmtn.com).

Park City Ski Corporation, PO Box 39, Park City, UT 84060 (801-649-8111/website www.pcski.com).

Summer Camps

For anyone who has never worked in tourism, a sideways introduction is to work at summer camps, which cater to a very junior kind of tourist. Summer camps are uniquely American in atmosphere, even if the idea has spread to Europe. Almost every American kid is at some point sent to summer camp for a week or more to participate in outdoor activities and sports, arts and crafts and generally have a wholesome experience. The type of camp varies from plush sports camps for the very rich to more or less charitable camps for the handicapped or underprivileged.

It is estimated that summer camps employ nearly a third of a million people for eight or nine weeks in June, July and August. Each summer thousands of 'counsellors' are recruited in Europe to be in charge of a cabinful of youngsters and to instruct or supervise some activity, from the ordinary (swimming and boating) to the esoteric (puppet-making and ham radio). There is also a massive demand for catering and maintenance staff which may bring less status but more money. Americans seeking listings of summer camps needing staff should see Peterson's *Summer Jobs for Students*.

For Europeans, the two major camp placement organisations authorised to issue J-1 visas are *BUNAC* (address earlier in the chapter) through the BUNACAMP Counsellor Programme and *Camp America*, (37A Queen's Gate, London SW7 5HR; 0171-581 7373/fax 581-7377) which has about 7,000 positions available annually for students and non-students aged 18 and above.

Another programme is arranged by Camp Counselors USA (CCUSA), 6 Richmond Hill, Richmond, Surrey TW10 6QX (0181-332 2952). In 1997, CCUSA placed 6,500 counselors from over 60 different countries in 800 camps in the USA. If accepted, your flight is paid for and then deducted from your wages, leaving you at the end of the nine-week stint with pocket money: $350-$600 with CCUSA, $150-450 with Camp America, $420-$480 with BUNACAMP Counsellors.

Theme Parks & Attractions

Apart from Disney's two major attractions in Anaheim California and Orlando Florida (employment at the latter is described in the next section), the United States boasts some of the most gigantic and innovative theme parks in the world, employing thousands of seasonal staff and many professionals as well. The giant Anheuser-Busch Brewery has a huge investment in tourist attractions including Sea World (1720 S Shores Road, San Diego, CA 92109), Busch Gardens and Adventure Island in Tampa Bay, Florida. The International Association of Amusement Parks and Attractions (1448 Duke St, Alexandria, VA 22314; 703-836-4800) can advise on how to train for specific attractions. There is also a specialist journal *Amusement Business* (BPI Communications, 1515 Broadway, New York, NY 10036) which contains job vacancy information; a subscription costs $129 per year.

Some American attractions employ as many as 3,000 seasonal assistants to work on rides and games, food service, customer services, etc. Here is a small selection of major attractions:

Caesar's Palace Inc, 3570 Las Vegas Blvd S, Las Vegas, NV 89109 (702-731-7110).

Hershey Entertainment & Resort Co, Personnel Office, PO Box 400, Hotel Road, Hershey, PA 17033 (717-534-3156).

Knott's Berry Farm, 8039 Beach Boulevard, Buena Park, CA 90620 (714-220-5170).

San Diego Zoo, PO Box 120-551, San Diego, CA 92112-0051 (619-231-1515).

Hotels & Catering

Hotels in the US are mainly staffed by people who intend to make 'hospitality vending' their career. The lead body for the industry is the American Hotel & Motel Association (1201 New York Ave NW, Washington, DC 20005-3931; tel 202-289-3193/website http://www.ahma.com). The AH&MA's Information Center sends out various leaflets including a directory of hotel/motel companies, training courses and a brief list of placement firms, all of which operate at the executive level.

There are of course many jobs in catering, the majority of which are merely casual work (see section below).

FLORIDA

Despite some recent bad publicity over crime, the state of Florida continues to be in the top ten destinations for European tourists, and a great many UK tour operators feature it. As usual, companies normally send out only those employees who have proved their capabilities in European resorts.

The industry is centred on Orlando, gateway to Walt Disney World, which has a much more user-friendly airport than Miami, where many of the staff speak only Spanish, and holidaymakers are given information leaflets on how to avoid being mugged. A number of UK reps are hired by tour operators to accompany groups of holidaymakers. Tony had worked one summer season in Spain when he applied for a winter job in Florida not expecting to get it. However his availability to fill a last-minute vacancy meant that he flew off to Orlando with a group. On arrival he met his resort manager and the local Disney group tour coordinator who told him that research proves that the longer people queue for a ride, the more their excitement and subsequent enjoyment builds up. Tony was especially grateful for the part of his information pack which listed the top ten attractions for each age group, since he was repeatedly asked for this kind of advice by his clients. He loved his six months in Florida: everyone was very friendly, there were lots of parties around the poolside and (compared to Spain) the plumbing was admirable. Like many Europeans who spend time in the US, his main complaint was that all those 'have a nice days' begin to feel a little synthetic after a while.

Walt Disney World

The Disney Corporation is renowned both in its home country and in Europe for offering a very rigorous training programme, and a stint at Disney enhances the CV of anyone who wants to work in tourism.

The International Staffing Department of Walt Disney World (PO Box 10090, Lake Buena Vista, Florida 32830-0090) hires about 100 extrovert young Britons to work in Disney's World Showcase in the EPCOT Centre which features 11 national pavilions staffed by nationals of those countries. Positions are for six months or a year and the selection is made at two annual recruiting fairs in Britain held in March and October. There is a backlog of applications to attend these fairs, so it will be necessary to wait many months for a chance to show that you can effectively represent the culture and customs of Britain. Paul Binfield from Kent describes the process of being hired by Disney as 'a long and patient' one:

> *I initially wrote to Disney in October and started my contract in January, 15 months later. It was the most enjoyable year of my life, experiencing so many excellent things and making the best friends from all over the world. The pros far outweigh the cons, though some people did hate the work. Disney are a strict company with many rules which are vigorously enforced. The work in merchandising or the pub/restaurant is taken extremely seriously and some-times it can be hard to manufacture a big cheesy Disney smile. There are dress codes (for example men have to be clean shaven every day), verbal and written warnings for matters which would be considered very trivial in Britain, and indeed terminations (which is a very nasty word for being fired). If you go with the right attitude it can be great fun.*

In your first week the induction course will teach you the Disney way of doing things, always smiling. You could be selling British merchandise, selling baked potatoes from a wheeled cart or working in an ersatz English pub. Moving up you graduate to being a waiter and therefore in on the 'tronc' (shared tips). The further you progress the better the money.

Outside the world of Disney, another Florida attraction is Sea World (70077 Sea Harbor Drive, Orlando, FL 32821; 407-351-3600) which looks to hire college graduates and others with animal handling and scuba skills.

Cruise Lines

Miami is the cruise capital of the world which is easy to believe when you see the number of vast white hulls gliding in and out of the harbour. As described in the introductory section *Cruise Ships*, any nationality can work at sea without having to obtain a visa for working in the US. This is not the case if you work on land, though the cruise companies generate a lot of office-based employment. For example *Renaissance Cruises* needs about 100 reservations sales agents, air/sea agents and documentation agents in its corporate offices; applicants must not only have travel training but they must be legally entitled to work in the US. See the section on *Cruise Ships* in the introduction for a list of cruise line offices and concessionaires.

CASUAL WORK

Labour demands in summer resorts sometimes reach crisis proportions especially along the eastern seaboard. However the majority of catering staff are paid the minimum wage of $4.25 an hour, except in tipped positions where the legal minimum is $2.13. An average weekly take in tips for a full-time waiter/waitress might be $120 with possibilities of earning twice that. Bar staff earn much more in tips, as much as $200 a night (but note that bar staff have to be the legal drinking age of 21). Apparently a British accent helps.

Plenty of Brits and Irish people find work in Los Angeles, New Orleans (especially around the time of the Jazz Festival at the end of April) and also in the cafés of Greenwich Village New York, though you'll have to serve a great many generous tippers before you'll be able to afford accommodation in Manhattan. Live-in jobs are preferable, and are often available to British students whose terms allow them to stay beyond Labor Day, the first Monday in September, when most American students resume their studies. After working a season at a large resort in Wisconsin, Timothy Payne concluded:

> *Without doubt the best jobs in the USA are to be found in the resorts, simply because they pay a reasonable wage as well as providing free food and accommodation. Since many resorts are located in remote spots, it is possible to save most of your wages and tips, and also enjoy free use of the resort's facilities. Whatever job you end up with you should have a good time due to the large number of students working there.*

Seaside Resorts

Popular resorts like Wildwood New Jersey near Atlantic City, Virginia Beach (Virginia), Myrtle Beach (South Carolina) and Atlantic Beach (North Carolina) offer thousands of jobs for young Americans. Britons will fare best in April/May or late August when Americans are back at college. Katherine Smith, who got her J-1 visa through BUNAC, describes the range of jobs she found in Ocean City, a popular seaside resort in Maryland:

> *I decided to spend my summer in Ocean Beach because I knew the job scene would be favourable. I found a job as a waitress in a steak restaurant and another full-time job as a reservations clerk in a hotel by approaching employers on an informal basis and enquiring about possible job vacancies. In my case this was very fruitful and I found two relatively well-paid jobs which I enjoyed very much. Other jobs available included fairground attendant, fast food sales assistant, lifeguard, kitchen assistant, chambermaid and every other possible type of work associated with a busy oceanside town. Ocean City was packed with foreign workers. As far as I know, none had any trouble finding work; anyone could have obtained half a dozen jobs. Obviously the employers are*

used to a high turnover of workers, especially if the job is boring. So it's not difficult to walk out of a job on a day's notice and into another one. It really was a great place to spend the summer. I would recommend a holiday resort to anyone wishing to work hard but to have a really fun time.

REGULATIONS

Tourists and visitors entering through the visa-waiver scheme or with a Visitor (B) Visa are prohibited from engaging in paid or unpaid employment in the US. The Visa Branch of the US Embassy (5 Upper Grosvenor St, London W1A 2JB; 0891-200 290) can send a brief outline of the non-immigrant visas available. The J-1 visa entitles the holder to take legal paid employment, normally for a specified period, and is available to participants of government-authorised programmes, known as Exchange Visitor Programmes (EVP). You cannot apply for the J-1 without form IAP-66 and you cannot get form IAP-66 without going through a recognised Exchange Visitor Programme (like BUNAC and Camp America mentioned above) which have sponsoring organisations in the US. In Ireland contact the Irish Student Travel Service, USIT, 19 Aston Quay, Dublin 2.

Apart from the J-1 visa available to people on approved EVPs, there are two possible visas to consider. The Q visa, introduced in 1991, is the 'International Cultural Exchange Visa' (affectionately dubbed the 'Disney' visa, since it was introduced partly in response to their lobbying). After working at Disney World on a Q visa, Paul Binfield concluded that the main difference between the J-1 and the Q-1 was that the latter obliges you to pay more tax. If you find a job in which it can be argued that you will be providing practical training or sharing the history, culture and traditions of your country with Americans, you might be eligible to work legally for up to 15 months. This must be applied for by the prospective employer in the US and approved in advance by an office of the Immigration and Naturalization Service.

In addition, the H-1B 'Temporary Worker' visa is available for 'prearranged professional or highly skilled jobs' for which there are no suitably qualified Americans. All the paperwork is carried out by the American employer. It is exceedingly difficult to get an immigrant visa or 'green card' which allows foreigners to live and work in the USA as 'resident aliens'. Nearly all the permanent resident visas which are issued each year are given to close relatives of American citizens, therefore remaining unavailable to most people.

The penalties and risks of accepting work without the right visa must be carefully considered. Without a visa, you will not be entitled to a social security number for which you will certainly be asked when trying to find a job.

DIRECTORY REFERENCES

The following companies listed in the Directory need staff for the United States, though many large tour operators in Europe do offer tours of the United States as well:

Adventure Alaska, BUNAC, Camp America, Collette Tours, Denali West Lodge, Disney, Gecko Overland, Gunflint Lodge, Renaissance Cruises (Corporate Office), Ski Independence, Ski Scott Dunn, Travelsphere, Unijet Florida

Canada

The Royal Canadian Mounted Police and Niagara Falls have always attracted a large number of tourists (not least from the United States) and, with the heightened value attached these days to pristine wilderness, Canada's tourist industry is booming. Recent statistics from the Department of Tourism at Lausanne University claim that Canada has 1.1 million jobs in tourism, more than twice as many as Austria and three times more than Greece.

Canada has more square miles of land per head of population than almost any other country, yet the vast majority of people live within a few degrees of latitude of the US border, and most visitors confine themselves to the cities and countryside of the southern belt, which includes the three biggest urban areas of Vancouver, Toronto and Montréal. In addition, the Rocky Mountain resorts of Banff, Jasper, Lake Louise, Sunshine Mountain and Waterton are among the most popular tourist destinations. The huge Banff Springs Hotel alone employs 750 people. More and more European skiers are considering Canadian resorts for their winter holiday.

Much investment in the tourist industry comes from Hong Kong and centres on Vancouver where many of Hong Kong's wealthiest Chinese residents have established a colony. This is good news for people working in hotels and airlines.

While the tourist industry of French-speaking Québec is flourishing, it is difficult for non-Québecois people to find work, even if they are French-speaking. For example the French word for old, *vieux*, is pronounced 'voo'. With a French mother and English father, Cecile thought she was in a good position to find work in Québec. She was rather taken aback by the differences between Canadian French and Parisian French, but she did adapt and eventually found a job.

As usual, working for a European tour operator makes it easier to get round the visa difficulties. The regulations make it very difficult to work for a Canadian employer, both because of strictly enforced 'Canada-only' immigration policies and high unemployment. One avenue to avoid the problem is the scheme open to students (see *Regulations* below) with which the British Universities North America Club (BUNAC) can assist. BUNAC produces its own Canadian Job Directory for members, which contains mostly jobs in hotels and tourist attractions in the Rockies. The Directory helped Linda James to fix up a six-month summer job as reception supervisor at Lake Moraine Lodge near Lake Louise. Although she was happy with the job, and found the hours relatively light, she would have preferred a waitressing job in order to earn the excellent tips of $75-100 a night. British university students have an edge over Canadian students in this sphere of employment since they don't have to return to their studies until mid to late September rather than the beginning of September, which means that they are more likely to be eligible for the substantial end-of-season bonuses paid by most seasonal employers.

The Council on International Educational Exchange (Council, 52 Poland Street, London W1V 4JQ; 0171-478 2000/fax 0171-734 7322/e-mail infoUK@ciee.org) arranges for British and Irish students to undertake internships in Canada lasting up to one year. Interns must find their own jobs in their field of study, often with advice from their tutors. Those who qualify get an employment authorisation from the Canadian High Commission. The programme fee is £150.

World Challenge Expeditions' Gap challenge placements offers students in their gap year opportunities to work in high quality family hotels in the Canadian Rockies near and around the town of Banff. Placements begin September,

November or March, last 6 months and cost £1,544 including flights. Students work between 20 and 50 hours a week, earning about £3 an hour. With a twelve month return ticket there is plenty of opportunity to travel independently after the placement.

FINDING A JOB

Many British coach tour operators who have worked successfully in Europe are looking to expand to Canada. The Canadian Tourist Office is working hard to encourage more coach tour visitors to Canada by mounting an advertising campaign and running special marketing exhibitions such as 'Spotlight Canada' at which operators are invited to meet hotel and tourist service representatives who fly into the UK to sell their products. If you are already working in the industry or studying on a tourism course you usually qualify for an invitation.

As usual jobs for staff on British companies' tours of Canada go to experienced UK tour managers who have worked one or more seasons with a big company like Saga, Travelsphere or Titan. Those who already have permission to work in Canada and who have some travel and tourism or hotel experience might investigate the following companies:

British Columbia – Chateau Victoria Hotel (part of the prestigious Chateau Hotels group which operates across Canada), Crystal Lodge, Farwest Adventure, Gray Line, Grizzly Tours, Harbour Towers Hotel, Harrison Hot Springs Hotel, Hotel Georgia, Inbound Canada Tours, Listel Whistler Hotel, Maverick Tours, Ocean Point Resort, Rocky Mountaineer Railtours, Royal Northwest Holidays, Sandman Hotels and Inns, Super Natural Adventure, Westin Bayshore Hotel, Whistler Resort Assocation

Alberta – Banff Park Lodge, Brewster Tours, Canadian Pacific Hotels, Cruise Canada, Ladilaw Transit, Lake Louise Inn, Mountain Park Lodges

Northwest Territories – Touch the Arctic Adventure Tours

Saskatchewan – Fin Feather and Horn Properties, Heart of Canada's Old Northwest, Tourquest.

Manitoba – Frontiers North, Great Canadian Travel Co, North Star Tours

Ontario – Best Western Hotels, Canadian Tours International, Cantours, Commonwealth Hospitality Ltd, Hilton, Hospitality Motels, Niagara Parks, Toronto Convention Association, True North Tours

Québec – Clubtour, Greater Montréal Convention Bureau, Montréal Tower

Nova Scotia – Regal Tours

Most of the upmarket shipping companies offer cruises up the west coast to see glaciers and wildlife. These companies need the usual cruise liner staff but also recruit experts on wildlife.

Ski Resorts

The best known ski areas are in the Rockies of British Columbia and Alberta and include Lake Louise, Banff, Jasper and Whistler (one and a half hours from Vancouver). There are other significant resorts such as Sainte-Agathe and Mont Tremblant in the Laurentian Hills of Québec, and Collingwood in Ontario (which has Canada's biggest skilifts); however these eastern resorts are not much used by European tour operators.

The promotion of North American ski resorts to Britons frustrated by the queues and unreliable snowfalls of the Alps means that more and more companies are looking to the delights of Whistler, Lake Louise and Banff in particular for their clients. A few British ski companies employ their own British ski personnel in Canadian resorts, including *Crystal Holidays, Neilson Ski* and *Thomson.*

At the end of October both the Whistler Mountain Ski Corporation and adjacent Blackcomb Mountain Ski Corporation hold an open weekend at which hundreds of people are recruited for the winter season. The resort of Whistler has its own newspaper *The Whistler Question* which comes out on Thursdays and is available in Vancouver as well as the resort itself. Those considering looking for jobs on-the-spot should be reminded of the vigour with which the Canadian Immigration authorities enforce the rules. In a community as small as a ski resort where everyone knows everyone else's business, it is difficult to keep one's status a secret. Furthermore there is a great deal of competition from all the young Australians and New Zealanders who migrate to Canadian ski resorts with official temporary work permits.

CASUAL WORK

Most temporary jobs in the Canadian tourist industry are found by responding to 'Help Wanted' notices or ads in newspapers. Ana Güemes got one of her two waitressing jobs from the *Toronto Sun* while Vancouver's papers (the *Vancouver Sun* and *Province*) and the *Calgary Herald* contain job adverts, especially for dishwashers, waiting and bar staff. Wages are fairly good in Canada with statutory minimum wages, e.g. $6.85 per hour in Ontario ($6.25 for students) and $5 to $7 in most of the other provinces.

Unfortunately it is much more difficult to find a job in Canada than in the US as Adda Macchich (who had worked at a hotel in Cape Cod) found out one summer:

> *I decided to settle in Ottawa last February and spent five weeks looking for work, with no luck. I filled out about 50 applications; the answer was invariably 'leave it with me; we'll get back to you' and they never did. You never even get to see the manager. I returned to Canada in June, hoping things had improved as the summer approached. I went to Niagara Falls expecting as many summer jobs as in Cape Cod but was disappointed at the total absence of Help Wanted signs or ads in the local paper, so I returned to Toronto. Spent a whole month on an unsuccessful job hunt, constantly being asked to submit resumés for menial jobs in restaurants and cafés and tramping from one end of town to the other merely to fill out more forms. The only available jobs were those paid on commission, which were advertised everywhere.*

Just as Adda was about to give up and fly back to London she stumbled across a commission-only ice cream vending job which was open to virtually anyone willing to man a stationary or bicycle-powered ice cream unit.

Banff is an expensive town in which to job-hunt but if you do land a job it will normally come with accommodation. One traveller to Western Canada reported:

> *While on holiday in Banff, I met a lot of Australians and Britons staying at the youth hostel. All of them were just on holiday visas, and all of them had found work in the height of the tourist season.*

Other popular holiday areas are the Muskoka District of Ontario centred on the town of Huntsville (comparable to England's Lake District) and the shores of the Great Lakes, particularly Lake Huron. Since most holiday job recruitment in Ontario is done through Canadian universities, and the resorts are so widely scattered that asking door to door is impracticable, it is advisable to concentrate your efforts in the west.

REGULATIONS

To work legally in Canada, you must obtain an Employment Authorisation before you leave home. The Canadian government allows a certain number of full-time students to work temporarily in Canada. Participants in the official work exchange must be aged 18-30 years and must have proof that they will be returning to a tertiary level course of study on return to the UK. The programme is open to a number of other nationalities besides British, including Irish, Dutch, Swedish and Australian. The quotas are allocated on the basis of reciprocal agreements between Canada and the partner countries and can fluctuate from year to year. Interested students should obtain the general leaflet 'Student Temporary Employment in Canada' by sending an s.a.e. with a 50p stamp and marked 'SGWHP' in the top right-hand corner to the Canadian High Commission (Immigration Visa Information, Macdonald House, 38 Grosvenor St, London W1X 0AA; website http://www.canada.org.uk/visa-info); or you can use the fax-you-back service by calling 0171-258-6350. The authorisation processing fee is now $120 (approximately £60). Note that anyone with a job fixed up in Quebec must comply with separate and additional Quebec immigration procedures.

Students who already have a job offer from a Canadian employer may be eligible for 'Programme A'. They can apply directly to the High Commission in London for an employment authorisation (reference 1102) which will be valid for a maximum of 12 months and which is not transferable to any other job.

The other and more flexible possibility is to obtain an unspecified employment authorisation which is available only through BUNAC (16 Bowling Green Lane, London EC1R 0QH; 0171-251 3472). Their 'Work Canada' programme offers about 1,300 students (including gap students with a university place and finalists with proof that they will return to the UK) the chance to go to Canada for up to 12 months and take whatever jobs they can find. The only requirements are that applicants have C$1,000 in Canadian funds (or $600 plus either a letter of sponsorship from a Canadian relative or a job offer) and a return ticket. Places are allocated on a first come, first served basis so early application is advantageous (from November). Departure for Canada must be between the beginning of February and the end of August.

All participants of approved student schemes benefit from orientations and back-up from the Canadian Federation of Students' SWAP offices in Toronto, Vancouver and Calgary. Students on work exchanges receive the same tax exemption as Canadian students.

LATIN AMERICA AND THE CARIBBEAN

The South American continent has a great deal to offer the tourist. But there are disincentives too, apart from the long and expensive flights. Street crime, high inflation and a bad environmental record serve to discourage many would-be visitors. Yet the explosion in long haul travel has seen a considerable increase in the number of Europeans joining the throngs of North Americans who have discovered that South America has much more to offer than dictators and drugs.

Many of the national economies of Latin American nations are desperate for the hard currency that tourism can bring. Arguably it is particularly important in the Amazon Basin where only a huge injection of tourist money will persuade governments that the rainforests are worth protecting, just as the demands of tourism are a factor in the protection of wildlife in East Africa. Anyone who conducts a tour into the relevant areas will have to introduce some of these sensitive issues to their group. Most of the head offices of cruise companies which run luxurious tours of the Amazon are in Rio de Janeiro.

FINDING A JOB

If you have spent time in a South American country preferably in a working capacity and can speak some Spanish (or Portuguese for Brazil), you will probably find yourself in demand by tour operators which feature South America. Many of these are based in Spain and Portugal for obvious reasons, and many more operate from the US. Among the best known European operators are Abreu (Abreu House, 109 Westbourne Grove, London W2; 0171-229 9905) and Melia, Kuoni and TUI, whose guides must normally be able to speak Portuguese.

There is a much wider range of tour operator from the United States than Europe; to illustrate the difference, the *Specialty Travel Index* published in the US lists nearly 40 companies active in Ecuador as compared to 11 in the British *AITO Directory*. A high percentage of these are based in Miami, since that is the principal departure airport, including Tara Tours Inc (6595 NW 36 St, Suite 306a, Miami Springs, FL 33166;305-871-1246) and Sol International (13780 SW 56 St, Suite 107, Miami, FL 33175; 305-387-6575). Other major operators include Terra Trails, (PO Box 24, Boulder, CO 80306), Sunny Land Tours (166 Main Street, Hackensack, NJ 07601; 201-487-2150) and Friendly Holidays (1983 Marcus Avenue, Suite C130, Lake Success, NY 11042) which operates primarily in Central America, Mexico and the Caribbean. The region attracts all the companies involved in so-called eco-tourism or environmentally sensitive travel, for example Ecotour Expeditions Inc (PO Box 381066, Cambridge MA 02238).

Brazil is probably the most popular country; most tours take in Rio and Sao Paulo, the Iguazú Falls and a trip on the Amazon. Among the operators of Amazon cruises (based in the US) are International Expeditions (One Environs Park, Helena, AL 35080) and Amazon Tours & Cruises (8700 W Flagler, Suite 190, Miami, FL 33174). The Mardi Gras Festival in Rio has a glamorous image, and British incentive companies often feature the event, so Portuguese-speakers may be needed during February. Brazil also has some sophisticated conference centres and hotels catering for meetings. If you have experience in this field it could be worthwhile contacting member companies of the International Association of Professional Congress Organisers.

Argentina is among the most Europeanised countries in Latin America. It is also one of the top polo playing nations worldwide and guides with horse-related experience might find a tour to lead advertised in the horsy press in the spring. Unlike many other South American countries, Chile's economy is flourishing and its infrastructure much more developed than those of some of its neighbours to the north and east. With wonderful scenery, a healthy climate and good food and wine, Chile is one of the world's up-and-coming destinations. Ski resorts are being developed now that Chile is on the World Cup circuit and European ski instructors might well find an opening. As yet few British ski tour operators go to Chile, though this may change in due course. The wine industry is especially buoyant, recovering some of its lost glory when it is said to have sent 20 million barrels of good red wine to Bordeaux. Wine tour companies are developing tours to this region.

Peru, Ecuador and Bolivia are generally considered to be the most authentic Andean destinations and are particularly targeted by the specialist expedition companies. The major overland companies like *Journey Latin America* offer itineraries which cover the whole continent; applicants for the position of tour leader must be able to communicate in Spanish or Portuguese and be already familiar with the destination countries. Other overland companies offering trips to South and Central America include *Dragoman* and Passage to South America Ltd (Fovant Mews, 12 Noyna Road, London SW17 7PH; 0171-602 9889). South American Experience (47 Causton St, Pimlico, London SW1P 4AT; 0171-976 5511) and *Explore Worldwide* do not themselves run overland tours but are specialist operators in the continent.

Smaller UK companies like Tucan South America (c/o Adventure Travel Centre, 131-135 Earls Court Road, London SW5 9RH; 0171-370 4555) conduct trekking tours of the Andes. Anyone with an interest in this area of tourism might like to join the long established South America Explorers' Club, Av. Portugal 146, Brena, Postal Casilla 3714, Lima 100, Peru (511-425-0142) or Jorge Washington 311 y L. Plaza, Postal Apartado 17-21-431 El Faro, Quito, Ecuador (59-3222-5228) or 126 Indian Creek Road, Ithaca, NY 14850 (607-277-0488). In addition to travel information the club also keeps some information on job opportunities in Peru and Ecuador in the relevant clubhouses. Their mazagine has a classified section which could be useful.

Many of the tour leaders who take tours to the continent work in the office of the tour operator for most of the year but accompany tours when they are booked. Anyone with a background in conservation has an advantage since this is the aspect of South America in which many potential visitors are interested. The celebrated *South American Handbook* (Trade and Travel Publications/Prentice Hall) is an incredible compendium of useful information for people touring the continent. Although pitched at independent travellers, it is useful for everyone.

Tour guides accompanying groups from Europe must not only contend with jet lag (both theirs and their clients') but with the dangers of crime. According to one old hand who has been taking groups to South America for over 20 years, it is essential to deliver a very stern lecture to holidaymakers about safety, not to go out alone, not to wear any jewellery (even the cheapest watch), not to wander off the beaten track in the major cities, not to drink the water, etc.

Foreign guides are sometimes hired by local lodge operators. For example in the Tambopata jungle region of southeast Peru, there are several possibilities. The Tambopata Reserve Society (c/o J. Forrest, 64 Belsize Park, London NW3 4EH) provides details about the resident naturalist programme, offered by several lodges, whereby volunteers (usually biology graduates) over the age of 20 are given free room and board for 3-6 months while acting as guides. The terms and conditions vary between lodges, some of them offer a small gratuity. One of the lodges is the Tambopata Jungle Lodge (PO Box 454, Cusco, Peru; 084-225701/fax 238911; Director Tom Hendrickson), which takes on guides who should speak some Spanish. Andrew James was there in his gap year and reports:

> *We lived in a jungle camp consisting of wooden lodges a four-hour boat trip up the Tambopata River from Puerto Maldonado. I was one of three English guides who took visitors of all nationalities in groups of about ten on dawn walks to explore the rainforest and see the amazing plant life, birds and the occasional animal. I was there for three months and was paid $150 a month for working 20 days a month with the other ten days free to do research, perhaps visit the old Inca city of Cusco.*

In general, however, indigenous companies like Magallanes Travel in Quito (Ecuador) or TrekAndes in Lima (Peru) would be unlikely to hire foreign guides.

Tourism is booming in Venezuela. Although it would be very difficult to break into the world of guiding unless you are semi-resident, there are many expat-style bars and clubs which employ foreigners on a shorter-term basis. Margarita Island in the Caribbean has dozens of places catering to package holiday makers, especially along 4th of May Avenue and Santiago Marino Avenue. The busy seasons are between June and September and again December to March.

Central America'

Moving north to the seven countries of Central America (Panama, Costa Rica, Nicaragua, Honduras, El Salvador, Guatemala and Belize) opportunities to work in tourism are relatively scarce. Belize (formerly British Honduras) is rapidly becoming one of the main centres for eco-tourism. With the second biggest barrier reef in the world, the government has allowed a few outside diving companies to operate under strict control, who occasionally need staff who have studied conservation and have diving qualifications. Specialist companies offering botanical tours are also keen to expand, particularly as there are 95 different orchids in the forests. There are many UK operators who offer tours to Belize, such as *Explore Worldwide*. There are many others in the US, including Travel Belize Ltd (1526 Spruce St, Boulder, CO 80302) and Ocean Connection (211 E Parkwood, Suite 108, Friendswood, TX 77546-5153).

Costa Rica is another country with an impressive record on encouraging tourism which is sympathetic to the environment by protecting vast areas in national parks. For American students, the Council on International Educational Exchange (205 East 42nd St, New York, NY 10017; 1-888-268-6245) runs a working holiday programme in Costa Rica. Participants, who must have intermediate level Spanish, can look for temporary jobs between 1st June and 1st October in hotels and the service industries generally. Wages will be in accordance with local rates, e.g. US$25-50 a week plus board and lodging for a hotel receptionist or kitchen manager (although bear in mind that smaller expenses like daily travel are not included). Catering staff can make $175 plus tips.

Around Acapulco in Mexico the hundreds of hotels earn a large part of their income from incentive conferences. If you speak Spanish it is worthwhile contacting the big companies such as Maritz Travel (10 South Riverside Plaza, Suite 1470,Chicago, IL 60606) to see if they need freelance incentive conference staff. Mexico City is popular for exhibitions, and the companies that handle these sometimes need staff both in the head office for administration and freelance in the field to help set up stands. Again, a knowledge of Spanish is a prerequisite for jobs with companies like Krause in Germany (0211-610730), Show Management Services in the UK (01252 811163), and Interface Group (617-437-1770) in the US.

Between January and March whales migrate from the Bering Sea to the Pacific coast of Baja to bear their young. Each year more tour operators feature trips to see this magnificent spectacle.

Falklands and Antarctica

Remote corners of the globe continue to increase their tourist trade. Although the Falklands and Antarctica still host only a few thousand visitors a year, each of those visitors is paying an average of £4,000. Antarctic tour operators look for conservationists with the appropriate degree. If you have mechanical knowledge and can service a Zodiac engine (the inflatable boats used by most of the passenger carrying ships) this could increase your chance of being hired. Companies such as *Holts' Battlefield Tours* run frequent tours to the Falklands.

THE CARIBBEAN

From icebergs and penguins to rum punches and beaches. Perhaps the easiest jobs to find in the Caribbean are those working on the countless charter yachts, flotilla sailing vessels and cruise ships which ply the West Indian waters each winter and spring. From November until May the Caribbean becomes a hive of marine activity. Since it marks the start of the main tourist season, Christmas is a particularly good time to look for work. The main requirement for being hired is an outgoing personality more than qualifications or experience. Hours are long and wages are minimal, but most do it for the experience. Board and lodging are always free and in certain jobs tips can be high. It would not be unusual to top up a negligible wage with tips of $700.

As mentioned in the Introduction, the world's largest private yacht *Sea Cloud* sails around the Caribbean during the winter with a crew of 60 (see *Activity Holidays: Sailing*). For general information about cruise ship work see the relevant introductory chapter. Contracts are normally for six to nine months and the hours of work are long, often 14 hours a day, seven days a week living aboard the passenger ship with all onboard facilities provided by the ship owner. Most cruise ships active in the Caribbean contract their staff from Florida-based personnel agencies (known as concessionaires), some of which liaise with UK agencies.

The lack of a work permit can be a definite hindrance in the search for local work including with a charter company. Yacht charter companies such as Nicholson Yacht Charters in English Harbour (Antigua) and Caribbean Sailing Yachts in St. Vincent are unwilling to publicise vacancies, both because they have enough speculative enquiries on the spot and also they are forbidden by their respective island governments from hiring anyone without the proper working papers. However once you are on the spot, you will have a better chance of hearing of vacancies, and there may even be a broker who matches up crew with boats, for example Captain and Crews in St. Thomas (US Virgin Islands). For information about where Nicholson Yacht Charters are based contact the US headquarters, 432 Columbia St, Cambridge, MA 02141.

Tim Pask arrived in Boston in August on the look-out for work and soon found day work on a large power boat. After a few weeks he was taken on as a deckhand/steward on a 72ft luxury charter yacht bound for the Virgin Islands:

> *My starting pay was $150 per week, all food and accommodation included. Tips were extra when on charter and could be as much as $400 each. It was very hard work and included long hours, keeping the boat clean, being involved in all aspects of sailing the yacht, maintaining the engine and serving meals and drinks to the guests.*

> *As far as advice for finding work, I suggest simply walking along the docks and asking skippers. This may seem rather awkward at times but it certainly is the best way. If the skipper or owner is unable to offer a position as crew he may well need an extra pair of hands to help out with varnishing, etc. Try to find out when and where boat shows are being held as people are always in a rush to get their boats looking first class. Quite often finding day work such as this can prove financially more rewarding. One can always try the numerous crewing agencies, but usually a fee is required.*

Jobs on Land

Around the Caribbean there is little chance of finding a job unless you or your parents are nationals of the island in question. The upmarket villa companies are strongly represented such as British Virgin Islands Club (10-12 Upper Square, Old Isleworth, Middlesex, TW7 7BJ; 01932 247617) and CV Travel (43 Cadogan St, London SW3 2PR; 0171-581 0851); and in the US, Villas International Ltd (950 Northgate Drive, £206San Rafael, CA 94105;fax 415 499 9491) and Unusual Villas & Island Rentals (101 Tempsford Lane, Penthouse 9, Richmond, VA 23226).

One way of obtaining permission to work in Jamaica (which is notoriously protective of employment for its own nationals) is to join the Work Jamaica scheme run by *BUNAC*, which allows about 30 students to spend up to six months departing June/July or December, working at whatever job they can fix up in Jamaica. Red tape is minimal, but costs are high (i.e. £800 flight and insurance) and wages lower, which probably accounts for the fact that there is not always a full take-up rate of the places available. The deadlines for applications are late March for summer or late October for winter. Andrew Owen hugely enjoyed participating in Work Jamaica, despite being paid a nearly non-existent wage:

> *Despite the high cost it is an experience not to be missed. I worked in the kitchens of a large hotel in Montego Bay. I was provided with three excellent meals a day from the restaurant and my own room 20 yards from the white sand palm beach – PARADISE!*

Some onshore work exists in the duty-free shops operated by companies like Nuance Global Traders (Terminal 4, Heathrow Airport, Airside, Hounslow, Middlesex TW6 3XA; 0181 745 5161 or 1510 S 17th St, Fort Lauderdale, FL 33316/) and Alpha (Fairway House, Greenlane, Hounslow, Middlesex TW4 6BU;0181-577 2555). You may even be able to get some leads on hiring policies, etc. by speaking to the manager of the duty-free shops in UK airports, which are normally part of international chains.

People find work in night clubs and hotels where British staff are considered chic. The Cayman Islands are meant to be one of the best places to look for this sort of work, with over 1,500 Americans alone working there. Without a 'Gainful

Occupation Licence' or work permit (difficult to obtain with hundreds of locals after the same jobs) you should not take for granted that you will be treated fairly. There are plenty of horror stories in circulation concerning maltreatment by employers, such as failure to pay wages and to honour agreements to provide a homeward flight.

One of the most enjoyable jobs in tourism is to work in the Guest Relations department of a resort hotel. These jobs are never advertised; you have to know someone, keep your ears open or make yourself and your suitability known to hotel groups such as Princess. It helps to be able to play tennis, bridge, etc.

MIDDLE EAST

A number of recruitment agencies in Britain and elsewhere act on behalf of companies in the oil states of the Middle East providing a range of trained and experienced personnel. Vacancies are generally advertised in the trade press. There would be little justification in listing agencies here, since vacancies in the hotels and catering industry are so infrequent.

JORDAN

Jordan has recently entered the tourism field in a serious way. Suffering from an adverse trading balance of payments, tourism is seen as a useful addition to the budget and hotels are being encouraged to invest in the country. There are some excellent ground handlers in Jordan, looking for involvement with foreign specialist tour operators. Some of the better ones are based in Amman. Enquire at the tourist information office for details (6-464 2311). Jasmin Tours in the UK are specialists for Jordan (53-55 Balham Hill, London SW12 9DR; 01628 531121). They use the ground handler UTA, based in Amman (PO Box 35241, Amman 11180; 6-4641959) who may be willing to hire Arabic speaking staff.

Petra has always been an attraction and is now becoming so popular that people will probably have to walk or be bussed in instead of taking the picturesque donkey ride, which is a source of great anxiety to the donkey drivers, who are victims of Petra's success.

The Gulf of Aqaba has some excellent dive schools which sometimes need qualified PADI O/W instructors able to take night dives.

Incentive tour operators are beginning to look at the country for incentives, so anyone who speaks Arabic and knows the country should approach the big companies.

LEBANON

Phoenix-like, Lebanon is rising up from its ashes. At one time it was the most sophisticated Middle Eastern country with visitors coming from all over Europe to see Beirut and the Temple of Baalbek. In 1998 only one of the 150 member companies in the Association of Independent Tour Operators listed Lebanon as a destination, though this is set to change.

Since the troubles ceased, the country has been gearing up again, rebuilding hotels and restaurants. Three airlines now run scheduled flights to Beirut, and tour operators are definitely interested, so keep an eye on the specialist media. At the moment there is probably work if you are in the construction industry.

Israel

Most tour operators to Israel rely on the staff provided by Israeli ground handlers rather than sending their own staff. This is because ground handlers normally have no difficulty finding well qualified multilingual locals to work for them.

Sue is a registered guide in the UK, and wanted a working holiday in Israel:

Knowing that guides can sometimes find opportunities while travelling in other countries, I thought there might be work in Israel meeting people at airports or working at conferences on reception. When I arrived with a friend we found that there was no tourism work available at all. Guides have to be licensed by the Ministry of Tourism. The only possibilities for work we could find were in restaurant kitchens and in the fields. So I went to work in a kitchen, feeling frustrated because I knew that I could have done a good job looking after visitors. But there was no chance.

The oldest established tour operator to Israel is *Pullman Holidays* (see entry) and other specialists include All Abroad (26 Temple Fortune Parade, London NW11 0QS) and Superstar Holidays (UK House, 180 Oxford St, London W1N OEL). A major exception to the rule of employing only Israeli guides is made for Christian and pilgrims' tours. Companies such as Inter-Church Travel (part of *Saga Holidays*) have made the case to the Israeli authorities that their clients insist on being guided by people trained in customer care in the UK. Rather than lose all the business such companies bring to the country, the authorities allow them to bring in their own tour managers, though the truce between local staff and visiting guides is often an uneasy one. The other principal companies in this market are Mancunia Travel Ltd (Peter House, 2-14 Oxford St, Manchester M1 5AW) and Tangney Tours (Pilgrim House, Station Court, Borough Green, Kent TN15 8AF).

New hotels continue to spring up along the Red Sea coast, most of which employ trained locals for all but the lowliest jobs.

CASUAL WORK

The best places for finding casual tourism work on-the-spot are Eilat, Tel Aviv, Herzliya (a wealthy resort north of Tel Aviv) and, to a lesser extent, Haifa and Jerusalem. There is a plethora of hostels around Israel, almost all of whom employ two or three foreign young people to spend a few hours a day cleaning or manning the desk in exchange for a free bed and some meals. If you prove yourself a hard worker, you may be moved to a better job or even paid some pocket money.

The Youth Hostel Association of Israel (PO Box 1075, 3 Dorot Rishonim, Jerusalem (02-6758400) can send a list of about 30 hostels around the country which may be in a position to offer free accommodation, meals and pocket money in exchange for six hours of work a day.

Casual work in cafés, restaurants, bars and hotels is also easy to find. As in Greece, these jobs are much easier to get if you're female. The pay is usually low and sometimes non-existent, but you will get free food and drink, and tips. There is no accepted minimum and, as throughout Israel, the price of a day's work has to be negotiated. Most working travellers also recommend collecting your wages on a daily basis to prevent aggravation later. The places that do pay wages on a monthly basis tend to make pay-day about the tenth of the month, so that is a good time to look for a job because lots of people move on after collecting their wages.

Jobs in fast-food restaurants are bound to increase since recently McDonald's and Kentucky Fried Chicken opened their first outlets in Tel Aviv. Burger King has 35 branches in Israel and intends to open 16 more in Israel in 1999.

Eilat

Eilat is the main holiday resort on the Gulf of Aqaba, with several large seafront hotels, numerous smaller establishments and more being built. Virtually all aspects of Israeli culture have been killed off, but it is still an established haven for the working traveller despite a general tightening of immigration rules. The foreign tourist season lasts from late October to March. (Although some Israelis take their holidays in the extreme heat of the summer, workers will be expected to speak Hebrew.) There is such a ready supply of workers desperate for any excuse to stay on that some employers try to get away with offering exploitative wages and working conditions. An additional problem for women is the level of hassle they must endure from male tourists from various countries who are attracted to Eilat on account of its thriving escort business.

The rendezvous point for hopeful workers (mostly men) in Eilat is the Peace Café on the edge of town, though recently it has been filled with Romanians willing to work for even lower wages than other nationalities.

Clean-cut looking women and couples do find work in tourist-related places by making the rounds of the hotel personnel managers as early in the season as possible. The Tourist Center near the Youth Hostel has lots of bars, restaurants and sandwich bars worth trying. Laura O'Connor describes the range of jobs she did in two months in Eilat:

> *I had a variety of jobs: sold tickets for a boat cruise and handed out fliers for a restaurant, waitressed in a fish restaurant, worked in Luna Park amusement park and cleaned in my hostel (Fawlty Towers).*

Eilat is an important yachting and diving centre. Vacancies are sometimes posted on the gates to the Marina, but work as crew or kitchen staff, cleaners or au pairs is usually found by asking boat to boat. According to Xuela Edwards, the atmosphere among working travellers is friendly and a 'welcome relief from the rougher Peace Café crowd'. Anyone with a background in diving should approach Eilat's many dive schools and dive cruise firms.

Tel Aviv

Although not as easy to find as in Eilat, there is plenty of work in Tel Aviv, mostly for women in bars, restaurants and beach cafés. It is a common practice for cafés not to pay any wages and to expect their staff to exist on tips, which are enough to live on providing the restaurant is sufficiently popular.

Many of the dozens of hostels are good sources of job information or casual work itself such as the Hotel Josef at 15 Bograshov St which receives daily phone calls from employers needing workers for casual work. Hostels along Hayarkon St and Ben Yehuda St are worth trying. Cafés along the seafront such as Cherry's Café offer a good chance to earn high tips.

Jerusalem

Jerusalem is also reported to be a good centre for hotel and bar work, and girls may be offered jobs while wandering round the bazaars. Work is much easier to find in the Jewish rather than the Arab areas, though hostels in the Old City do employ people on a free-bed basis. Some good sources of information on jobs in Jerusalem are Ritchie's Pizza Shop on King George St with a good notice board, the New Swedish Hostel at 29 David St and the Lemon Tree Hostel also in the Old City, and finally the Palm and the Fiasel, both Christian hostels. Also check out the notice board in the Goldsmith Building which houses the overseas students union just outside the campus.

REGULATIONS

Having previously had one of the most lenient immigration policies in the world, the Israel Interior Ministry has now tightened up on working travellers. It is much more difficult to obtain a work permit and virtually impossible for the kind of casual work most travellers do in Israel. People do work on tourist visas which have to be renewed every three months. Some people cross into Egypt and get a new visa on returning. If you are counting on receiving some wages owed to fund the trip, be warned that wages are often slow to come and you might find yourself trapped with a visa due to expire and no money to make the trip.

AFRICA

Africa has so much to offer the tourist, not despite of but because large parts of the continent are undeveloped. The past 25 years have seen an explosion in the number of overland and expedition companies offering adventurous travels with a frisson of danger to people from all backgrounds. Longer term possibilities are available with the overland companies like *Truck Africa, Africa Explored, Guerba* and some of the others mentioned in the introductory chapter *Overland Expedition Leaders*.

Now that South Africa is once again on the tourist map, there is already a tourist boom in the Cape with a knock-on effect in other southern African nations like Namibia. There are tremendous new possibilities for tour operators. The main tourism areas in Africa are the Mediterranean resorts of North Africa, Egypt, Kenya and East Africa, and South Africa.

South African Airways (SAA) is one of the world's expanding airlines, and has been offering special promotions to tour operators to encourage them to add South Africa to their brochures, and also cooperating with surrounding countries to offer two or three country holidays. As long as political problems are kept at bay, the tourist industry in this region will expand for the forseeable future. One problem at present is the fact that, for historical reasons, the majority of international flights to Johannesburg and Nairobi (from North America and elsewhere) are routed through Heathrow. However as more direct flights come on-stream cutting diagonally across the Atlantic, a holiday in this part of the world will seem more appealing and more visitors will arrive.

Travellers' hostels are one of the few providers of casual work in the developing nations of the African continent. People who stay any length of time at a hostel, especially in remote places, may be asked to assist the warden or even take charge temporarily while they are away on holiday or getting supplies. It is something that many independent trans-Africa travellers do for the odd week.

NORTH AFRICA

The popular resorts of Tunisia and Morocco are normally incorporated into the Mediterranean programmes of major European tour operators. Companies like *Airtours* need French-speaking reps for resorts like Monastir in Tunisia and Agadir, Morocco. Try also the *Panorama Holiday Group* which also needs French-speaking reps in Tunisia. *Club Med*, as its name might suggest, is a major operator here with vacancies for French-speaking GOs (*gentils organisateurs*) and other positions.

Morocco

The traditional destinations for tourists in Morocco (Tangier, Fez, Marrakesh) now enjoy a year-round season, with Europeans flying in for weekend breaks. Better communications are opening up in the south and in the High Atlas Mountains where there are more hiking and expedition-style holidays available each year. Experienced managers and reps who have spent time in Morocco agree that it is a fascinating country though it can be frustrating. French is widely spoken, at least it is until you are in trouble.

Most of the adventure holiday operators in Morococo are looking for well-trained personnel, as Andrew Dow discovered. When he applied to expedition companies, they all asked for qualifications, so the next winter he obtained an RSA Diploma for Tour Guides. His tutor suggested he contact *Explore Worldwide*:

> *I've just done my first tour with 11 people in Morocco. The company seems to be highly regarded here, and the tour went well, although it was very hard work. I was amazed my books balanced at the end.*

There may also be casual job opportunities in resort hotels and bars. K. McCausland reports on what he found in Morocco one winter:

> *Agadir is a serious winter hotspot for European tourists and as such there are lots of opportunities in hotels, bars and discos. A little further north on the coast is a beautiful and friendly town called Essaouira. It's rapidly making a name as a major windsurfing centre and a service industry is starting to gear up. There seemed to be jobs for receptionists in some of the new hotels. As you would expect, wages are considerably lower than in Europe, but as the cost of living is extremely low, it's not such a problem.*

Tunisia

Tunisia is a very sophisticated country in which the French influence is apparent at every turn. From the beginning the Tunisian government developed the infrastructure in a sensible fashion, for example not allowing hotels to be built any higher than palm trees. Because of the mild winter climate, there are two main seasons, summer for families and winter for 'golden oldies' and others taking short breaks. Tunisia is one country that will gain because clients will be able to buy duty free goods.

Hotels are of a high standard, and there is an excellent hotel school just outside Tunis. The major chains such as Hilton and Sheraton have properties here, and often transfer staff working elsewhere in their network. Banqueting and conference staff are in demand, as the Ministry of Tourism has helped to fund the development of facilities. The Port of El Kantaoui is a purpose-built complex of hotels from three star up to deluxe that thrives on family holidays in the summer and conferences and winter breaks from October to May.

Tunisia is usually a 'second season job' for known reps, though mature French-speaking candidates might be considered in their first season. Most of the work is for reps based at hotels, but some of the big operators such as *Thomson* and *Cosmos* operate short coach tours, usually allied to a week's hotel stay. There are a few villa companies but they mostly employ local staff. Among operators that feature Tunisia are Cadogan (01703 828313), Eclipse Direct (0161-742 2222) and Medward (0171-373 4411).

There are numerous appealing excursions from the resorts, so reps are able to earn well from commission. However the hours worked on these trips are long, involving 5am starts in order to see the desert. Ever since Indiana Jones got up to his tricks filming *Raiders of the Lost Ark* in southern Tunisia, incentive companies have loved this country. During filming, the stars stayed at the spectacular Sahara Palace at Nefta and groups now flock in to follow in their footsteps and ride camels across the desert.

One tour operator specialising in Tunisia is Wigmore Holidays (122 Wigmore St, London W1H 9FE; 0171-486 4425). Since many European birds migrate here for the winter, birdwatching tours with companies like Branta Birdwatching Holidays (0171-635 5812) go to Tunisia in January. Cultural tour operators take groups to see the fantastic Roman Amphitheatre at El Jem and the ruins of Carthage (in a suburb of Tunis). Sports enthusiasts come to play tennis and golf, and many of the top hotels pride themselves on their sports facilities so need staff with appropriate qualifications. If you have marine and sailing qualifications, skippers in the yachting marinas at Port El Kantaoui, Sousse and Monastir may be interested in hiring you.

French is widely spoken, though of course Arabic is a bonus. Although the people are very easy-going and welcoming, women should remember that Tunisia is a Muslim country: Kairouan, with its Great Mosque, is the fourth holiest city in the Islamic world. Another possible drawback is the great heat of the summer. Groups will be fascinated to see cave dwellings in the south, built as a refuge from the desert heat. Unlike the locals, tour groups resemble Noel Coward's mad dogs and Englishmen who go out in the mid-day sun in order to cover all the venues promised in the brochures. A supply of water and wide-brimmed hats is essential.

EGYPT

The two main types of holiday which Egypt can offer are cultural tours (which centre on the famous sites along the River Nile) and diving holidays on the Red Sea (which have survived the vicissitudes of political problems in the region). Kathleen is one of the 'old hands' who has been looking after tours to Egypt for 20 years:

> *I love working here. Egypt gets to you. I prefer the small groups, often families, because then I have enough time to do things like teach them to read some hieroglyphics. The big groups are fun too but you can't get so involved. Usually they travel by Nile steamer for part of the tour and that can be a bit of a problem as people get bored, and there is nowhere to escape.*

The Nile cruise business is booming and it may be possible to find a job after arrival in Egypt, though it appears to be easier for men than women.

Kathleen's advice to those who want to get started is to try to find work with a major tour operator which has an Egypt programme. Once you have worked well for a season, start asking tactfully but persistently for a transfer. If they don't have vacancies leading to Egyptian tours then your experience will assist your application to specialist operators. Some tour operators which occasionally need specialists with experience include:

Bales Tours, (see entry).
British Museum Traveller, (see entry)
Connections, 93 Wimpole Street, London W1 (0171-408 4416).
Cosmos Holidays (see entry).
Goldenjoy Holidays, 36 Mill Lane, London NW6 1NR (0171-794 9818). Also runs tours to Morocco, Jordan and Israel.

The organisation *Wind Sand and Stars* takes on expedition leader and assistant leaders each summer to assist with youth expeditions involving local project work in Sinai. Applicants must have travel experience, knowledge of first aid and preferably an acquaintance with Arabic.

At the other end of the market companies like Goodwood Travel Ltd (St Andrews House, Station Road East, Canterbury, Kent CT1 2WD; 01227 763336) offer very special tours by Concorde or to hear opera in the Temple of Karnak. One of the *British Museum Traveller's* main tour destinations is Egypt. Museum curators usually lead these tours but tour managers or lecturers with an Egyptian specialization would be considered.

Diving Holidays

Anyone with a diver's certificate might be able to find work at Red Sea resorts like Sharm el Sheikh and Ras Muhammad. Many of the companies that offer diving holidays are small specialist companies; divers should check on their club notice boards for leads. The Egyptian diving firm *Emperor Divers* (working through Regal Diving in Cambridgeshire) employs British diving instructors who are willing to stay for at least a year. Also try Ounas Divers (01323 648924). You can sometimes get free diving lessons in exchange for filling air tanks for a sub-aqua club. It is possible to be taken on by an Egyptian operator (especially in the high season December/January); however the norm is to be paid no wage and just earn a percentage of the take.

Preparation

The biggest problem in Egypt is maintaining good health. It is not unusual for more than half the members of a touring group to be struck down by upset stomachs from the change in water and diet. A doctor must be summoned immediately if any client falls ill. Kathleen is adamant that you must ignore the advice of the Egyptian Tourist Board which says that there are no compulsory health precautions and consult a private health clinic about jabs, etc. well before departure (see introductory chapter *Preparation*). Also, malaria protection is needed around the Nile between June and October, and meningitis jabs if you are going to be there between November and May.

Note that tourists in Egypt have been targetted by terrorist groups in the past two years; recorded information on the situation produced by the Foreign & Commonwealth Office may be heard by dialling 0171 238 4503.

EAST AFRICA

The countries of Kenya, Tanzania and Uganda have traditionally been countries which provided superb experiences rather than just holidays. Two recent developments have damaged their tourist industries: the crisis in Rwanda (though it has had no impact on the normal East African tourist destinations) and the spread of a vicious drug-resistant malaria mosquito. Malaria is indeed a big problem for visitors and even worse for those working in the tourist industry who spend long periods of time in the country. When the brother of Simon Hughes the MP died from the disease a few years ago after honeymooning in Kenya (even though he had been taking the usual anti-malarial prophylactics), the public was alerted to the gravity of the disease. The most up-to-date expert advice must always be sought (see *Preparation* in the Introduction). Any company which offers work should be well informed. (If they don't show any interest in what inoculations you have had or should get, don't work for them. Ideally they will pay for all jabs and pills since these can come to hundreds of pounds)

Nevertheless thousands of visitors want to visit these beautiful countries. Most fall into three categories: those who go for sun, sand and sea, those who want a combination beach and safari holiday and thirdly serious wildlife lovers and photographers. It is difficult to find work with any of these groups. Safari tour operators and game wardens in national parks are inundated every year with undergraduates wanting to work in their vacations. As described above in the section on Egypt, those wanting to make a serious career of working in East Africa should first work for a European tour operator which features East Africa and apply to move when they have enough experience.

An increasing number of companies are offering honeymoon packages in this part of the world, typically involving a beach ceremony with the couple flying away in a balloon possibly to a safari lodge. These operators need efficient staff to handle the formalities and it is tempting to wonder whether there are openings for vicars and priests.

Specialist safari tour operators include:

Okavango Tours and Safaris, Gadd House, Arcadia Avenue, London N3 2TJ (0181-343 3283).

Somak Holidays, Somak House, Harrovian Village, Bessborough Road, Harrow on the Hill, Middlesex HA1 3EX (0181-423 3000).

On the Spot

People travelling through East Africa have noticed that diesel mechanics are in great demand to work as drivers for overland companies and suitably connected people might be able to run their own safaris; but in her whole year of volunteer nursing in Uganda, Mary Hall met only one foreigner who had found work on the spot and without a work permit. This woman was asked to manage a tourist lodge in the middle of nowhere and jumped at the chance since it was such a beautiful nowhere.

Working Conditions

If you are working for a European operator, you will have the same type of accommodation as your clients. However staff who are hired locally (such as drivers) often live in very basic conditions. Those 'great white hunter' safari suits of beige cotton do not just belong in the movies. They are practical since the colour is the least likely to attract animals and the long trousers keep off mosquitoes.

SOUTHERN AFRICA

With the political changes of the 1990s, the Republic of South Africa is set to become the next great holiday destination, something of which the new government is keenly aware. The South African Minister for Tourism has said that the industry now has the potential to create 200,000 new jobs, thereby substantially reducing unemployment. Not only will new hotels be built and facilities upgraded, but new tourist boards will have to be created and tour operating companies started up. Already specialist tour operators are offering interesting tours concentrating on game viewing, wine tours, trips along famous rail routes, etc.

The South African Tourism Board in London produces a handy one-page list called 'Contacts' listing about 60 tour operators offering fully inclusive tours, operators of special interest holidays and ground handlers. Some UK operators to try are:

Acacia Expeditions, Lower Ground Floor, 23a Craven Terrace, London W2 3QH (0171 706 4700).

Accompanied Cape Tours, Hill House, Much Marcle, Ledbury, Herefordshire HR8 2NX (01531 660210).

Carrier Tours, 31 London Road, Alderley Edge, Cheshire SK9 7JT (01625 582006).

Designer Travel, Suite 5D, Parsonage Chambers, 3 Parsonage, Manchester M3 2HP (0161-839 5158).

Grenadier Safaris, 11 West Stockwell St, Colchester, Essex CO1 1HN (01206 549585).

Peltours, Sovereign House, 11-19 Ballards Lane, London N3 1UX (0181-346 9144).

Titan Travel, High Tours House, 26/30 Holmethorpe Avenue, Redhill, Surrey RH1 2NL (01737 760033).

Fortunately South Africa's economy is not impoverished like that of some other nations and so it is less likely to allow foreign tour operators too much latitude in spoiling the breathtaking scenery and wildlife the country has to offer at present. The transition to black majority rule has not resulted in the 'brain drain' which some anticipated. Furthermore the policy of affirmative action which is in place to redistribute labour means that there will be plenty of competition for all these new jobs. Yet for some time to come there will be employment for people who know the country, and most work for tour leaders will come from the country of origin of the tour.

Ostrich farms often need linguists

Brigitte Albrech from Germany managed to get a job in her career field with the South African Tourism Board and came away believing that anyone could find a job in the tourist industry. She recommends that on arrival job-seekers should check adverts in the Monday edition of the main dailies, the *Argus* in Cape Town, and the

Star and *Citizen* in Johannesburg. People who can speak more than one language may find that hotels will not only hire them but help them to obtain a work permit. Brigitte also suggests that people who want to be tour guides should head for the Oudtshoorn region where ostrich farms often need linguists for the summer season. The local Backpackers Resort (the Oasis) should be able to advise.

Casual Work

Apart from the difficulties with work permits in South Africa, casual work is relatively accessible. Cape Town is the tourist capital of South Africa for backpackers as for everyone else; there are now about nine youth hostels in the city. The Backpack has been recommended for its notice board and Oak Lodge on Breda Street for its willingness to give free accommodation to people who do some work around the hostel.

Everyone who has looked for a tourist job in Cape Town recommends Seapoint, a beach suburb lined with cafés, ice cream kiosks, snack bars and other places which have high staff turnovers. (Ice cream is also sold from cycle carts; find out whom to contact for work by asking the sellers.) Also try using the door-to-door approach in the flashy new Waterfront development, Camps Bay and the beaches along the famous Garden Route. J. M. Rapp from California describes his job hunt:

Anyone arriving in Cape Town in the last week of November should have absolutely no trouble finding restaurant/bar work. I found a full-time waiting job in 27 minutes. I was promoted to head waiter just after the Christmas rush (even though I'd never waited on table in my life before). I moved on in March with US$1,000 saved.

Although not as popular a tourist destination as the Cape, Johannesburg offers casual work possibilities, especially in Rosebank, Santom and the Yeoville area of town where bars, restaurants and travellers' hostels like Rocky Street Backpackers on Regent St and the Pink House are located. Try also the Backpackers Ritz which takes on long-term residents at favourable rates. According to Iona Dwyer, Tekweini Backpackers in the Morningside area of Durban employs foreigners for free rent and a small wage.

The east coast stretching from Cape Town to Port Elizabeth or even as far as Ciskei provides lots of opportunities for resort jobs. George, Knysna, Jeffreys Bay, Plettenburg Bay and Port Elizabeth are crowded with tourists during the season (November to March) but especially in December and January. Short-term casual work is available during the fortnight long Arts Festival in Grahamstown in the East Cape in June/July.

Casinos are another possibility for anyone with experience as a croupier as well as for others. The situation is unstable at the moment with casinos opening and closing frequently (apart from those run by Sun International) but if you are hired, the pay is good.

Red Tape

Not surprisingly, the new government has tightened up on foreign workers as the high unemployment rate means it is hard enough to find jobs for its own citizens. It is still not too difficult to extend a three-month tourist visa, but increasingly difficult to get a work permit.

One solution to the problem is *BUNAC'S* (see entry) work exchange. Full-time students may be eligible for a working holiday permit. Another organisation which may be of help is Foreign Placements CC (Box 912, Somerset West 7129; 04457 7677/fax 04455 32680) which helps people looking for casual work.

If you choose not to apply through a scheme, it is probably a good idea to indicate that you are considering permanent residency, when you are job-hunting. In order to obtain a work permit, you will need a letter from an employer and proof that the job has been advertised. A further requirement is that you must must deposit a security bond of R6,000 into a bank account (and even then there is no guarantee that an application will succeed). This will be returned to you (in rands of course) only when you leave the country. Key tourist places are regularly raided by the Department of Home Affairs, and employers caught employing foreigners without permits are fined heavily, while the workers are likely to be deported. At the time of writing there was talk of bringing in a version of the American green card to stem the flow of illegal immigrants, mostly from other African nations.

DIRECTORY REFERENCES

Companies listed in the Directory which employ staff on the African continent include: Africa Explored, African Portfolio, Airtours, Bales, Backroads, British Museum Traveller, Cosmos, Emperor Divers, Encounter Overland, Explore Worldwide, Guerba, Kumuka, Panorama Holidays, Kumuka, Thomson, Top Deck, Tracks, Truck Africa, Wind Sand & Stars, Voyages Jules Verne.

ASIA

Exotic destinations are becoming more accessible with each passing year The Asian continent stretching from India to Japan, taking in the ever-popular destinations of Thailand, Singapore, Malaysia, Hong Kong and China, is visited by millions every year. Many UK tour operators include these countries in their programmes. Charter airlines such as Airtours are beginning to take an interest in Thailand. Brittania Airways (part of Thomson) operate a charter flight to Thailand and Airtours are investigating the possibility of operating charter flights to Asian airports. If new charter routes are established, other tour operators will use them and the number of jobs for reps and tour managers will increase. Of course such a sudden increase in tourist traffic can harm a place as has happened to Goa since the Dabolim Airport was opened; one of its nicknames is now 'the Benidorm of the East'. The rate of tourist development in places like Goa and Bali has been too fast and too careless of environmental and other local concerns, so anyone hoping to work in a developing country should be aware of these issues.

For the present, companies employ senior tour directors and representatives. In countries where communications may be poor and transport and contractors unreliable, the tour leader must take full responsibility and have the authorisation to change plans and improvise solutions. It is helpful if the person who has arranged the tour is the one to lead it; hotel and other bookings are less likely to get 'lost' if the individual who has made prior contact is the same individual present. This means that only people who are established in the industry with appropriate qualifications and introductions stand much chance of working for a UK or US tour operator. A further source of competition for jobs comes from the thousands of Asian nationals who come to Britain each year to study tourism often in combination with English as a foreign language.

FINDING A JOB

Tours

As mentioned above, there is little chance of finding work until you are very experienced. Asian economic problems mean less work for those looking for jobs locally, but more for those with top qualifications leading groups from the US, Europe and Britain. Prices of tours to this area are tumbling and companies look for staff with degrees in Oriental studies, history, history of art, etc. to lead groups. Probably the easiest way to break in is to do the least popular tours, i.e. the multi-centre tours which purport to give tourists a brief taste of Japan, Thailand, Malaysia and Hong Kong (though the taste they give is mostly of in-flight cuisine). Old hands do not relish the prospect of suffering permanent jet lag, so the tour operators sometimes encounter difficulties in finding staff.

Annabel White was an experienced tour manager in Europe, with a degree in European History. She wanted to take groups to Asia but discovered that most companies wanted somebody with experience. Applying to Jules Verne, they took her on to look after a group on the Trans Siberian Express:

> *The tour is a long one: experienced tour managers know that passengers get*
> *bored, frustrated and argumentative. But still, I needed this tour for my CV so*
> *that I could tell operators I had been to the region.*

The strategy worked and now she takes up-market but shorter tours to Asia. Others work for tour operators taking groups to Europe and ask personnel departments to put them on the list for Asia. Eventually experience counts. Work well for an operator and when someone falls out, they look for reliable staff and promote them. Annabel says operators employ local guides; you are there to act as tour administrator, so it is more important to have experience dealing with problems. She says she was a long way from the office and had much more responsibility. One compensation for the jet lag and the heat is that most tour leaders are very well looked after in Asia where service is a way of life.

Elderly travellers are surprisingly adventurous and there are numerous Asian tours aimed at people of retirement age. One of the first tour operators to take advantage of the freedom to visit Vietnam when it opened its frontiers was *Saga Holidays* which is patronised only by people over 50. Saga like more mature tour leaders (in fact they accept fit people up to the age of 75) and are keen on candidates with a nursing qualification. Another company catering to an older clientele is Elderhostel (75 Federal St, Boston, MA 02110; 617-426 8056). A UK specialist in Southeast Asia is Thai Adventures (PO Box 82, High Street, Alderney, Channel Islands GY9 3DG: 01481 823417). *The China Travel Service* (see entry in the Directory) also specialises tours to China and Hong Kong.

Despite the fact that there is still easy entrance into Hong Kong for those seeking work, the Chinese takeover has meant that obtaining casual work is no longer as easy as it once was. The influx of Chinese jobseekers has seriously lowered the number of jobs available and some businesses will now only recruit Chinese employees. Your best chance is to go with a tour operator from outside.

Malaysia is spending mega-bucks on improving and building new resort hotels. Thailand has suffered recently from adverse publicity about sex tourism, which should force the Thai authorities to clean up the situation in order to entice back tour operators.

The major adventure tour companies like *Explore Worldwide*, and *Encounter Overland*, have tours in Asia. Intrepid Travels (c/o The Imaginative Traveller, 14 Barley Mow Passage, London W4 4PH; 0181-742 8612) specialises is Southeast Asian destinations. Australians can try companies in Australia like Intrepid Travels (03-948 60460) and Odyssey (03-9381 2088) both in Melbourne, and World Expeditions in Sydney (02-9264 3366). First aid qualifications are usually mandatory to lead tours off the beaten track.

American companies which specialise in adventurous tours to Asia include:

Asian Pacific Adventures, 826 South Sierra Bonita Avenue, Los Angeles, CA 90036 (323-935 3156).
Asia Trans Pacific Journeys – (800) 642-2742.
Backroads, (see entry in Directory).
Geographic Expeditions – (415) 922-0448.
Mountain Travel-Sobek, 6420 Fairmount Avenue, El Cerrito, CA 94530 (510-527-8100).
Wilderness Travel, 801 Allston Way, Berkeley, CA 94710 (800-368-2794).

Trekking trips in the Himalayas may offer some possibilities. *World Challenge Expeditions* takes on expedition leaders with a relevant background to conduct parties of school pupils in India, Nepal, etc. They also place a few gap year students with a trekking agency in Kathmandu to learn how to lead treks.

A wealth of other special interest tours to Asia is available. Horse sports are popular throughout Asia, particularly in Hong Kong and Brunei (whose Sultan is mad on polo).

Speakers of Japanese normally find it easy to get jobs, particularly working in souvenir shops and hotels. If you lead a group with Japanese clients in it, be prepared to devote yourself 24 hours a day to looking after them. According to Corinna, it is a good idea to ask the hotel switchboard not to put any calls through after 11pm except in an emergency. She is not prepared to have her sleep interrupted at 2am because someone can't remember if a temple was 12th century BC or AD.

Hotels & Catering

Most of the major international chains have properties in Asia. Similarly, the oriental hotel groups such as Taj now have properties in Europe, so transfers may be possible. However be prepared for long waiting lists if you want to work in one of the hotels like the Regent or the Mandarin which are consistently voted best in the world.

Chefs are often attracted to Thailand because of the excellence and current popularity of Thai cuisine. Good catering colleges should have contacts in Bangkok.

Cruises

The itineraries of cruise companies such as Royal Viking Line, Pearl Cruises, Renaissance Cruises, Cunard, Princess Cruises and Seabourn Cruises all include Asian ports. More adventurous companies like P & O Spice Island Cruises use smaller ships to explore less well known ports; the latter specialises in the islands of Indonesia including Bali. Sea Trek run cruises in tall-masted schooners. If you have a mate's qualification or want to work as sail crew or cabin staff, contact them at Herengracht 215, 1016 BG Amsterdam, Netherlands.

Airlines

Many of the mainstream Asian airlines employ British staff such as JAL, Cathay Pacific, ANA, etc. and the Gulf airlines that criss-cross the areas such as Gulf Air and Emirates. Contact their UK or European offices to find out when they will be recruiting. British Airways will also be interested in candidates who can speak an Asian language fluently. Fiona went to an interview with the Japanese national airline JAL and was surprised and delighted to be selected. An intensive course in Japanese ensued before being sent off to Tokyo. The training course was very demanding and she had to bite her tongue repeatedly when her dress and make-up were criticised every day. She discovered that more tongue-biting was a requirement of the job:

> *I kept forgetting that work had to be taken very seriously. My flippant comments (made to relieve the atmosphere during the long Tokyo-Heathrow flights) did not go down well. I found that the cultural differences were too great and after a year the airline and I parted company. My recommendation is that anyone who wants to work for an Asian airline should go and live in the country first to understand the culture.*

Working Conditions

Health concerns should be preeminent and all the necessary precautions taken (see introductory section *Health & Insurance*). Cultural differences are also very important and you should consult a good book about what might unwittingly cause offence such as casually discarding a Japanese business card presented to you, touching people on the head, parading your feet in company, proffering your left hand, etc. But the most important thing to remember is never to lose your temper which causes you to lose face. The best way to tackle a problem is to smile and ask the official what advice they can offer.

Theft is always a possibility so be sure to keep separate photocopies of your passport, visas, credit cards, insurance documents and so on.

PART III

Directory of Placement Agencies and Travel Companies

DIRECTORY OF PLACEMENT AGENCIES AND TRAVEL COMPANIES

Alphabetical listing of 325 companies worldwide which have occasional vacancies for tourism staff. The information given in this section should be checked personally when applying for a job.

Placement Agencies

BLOOMSBURY BUREAU
37 Store St, London WC1E 7BS. Tel 0171-813 4061. Fax 0171-813 4038. E-mail bloomsburo@aol.com
In business since 1995.
Cultural exchange and au pair agency which makes hotel placements in Germany.
Hotel staff (chambermaids/kitchen helps) needed for Bavarian hotels: 20-30. Period of work from June (preferably the beginning) to the end of September or end of October. To work 48 hours per week. Also permanent posts.
Qualifications needed: some knowledge of German required. Minimum age 18 years.
Wages: DM1100 per month, free board and lodging.

BUNAC
16 Bowling Green Lane, London EC1R 0QH. Tel 0171-251 3472. Fax 0171-251 0215.
The British Universities North America Club has been in operation since 1962.
Non-profit organisation which encourages student work exchanges to the US, Canada, Australia, New Zealand, South Africa, Ghana and Jamaica. Cooperates with CFS/SWAP in Canada, SYTO in Ghana, SASTS in South Africa, JOYST in Jamaica and BUNAC's subsidiary IEP in Australia and New Zealand.
Range of programmes for students and non-students to work on American summer camps (see US chapter) or to find their own jobs in the tourist industry or any other field of employment. In all cases BUNAC assists participants to obtain the appropriate short-term working visa.
Qualifications needed: vary according to North American programmes. Work Jamaica programme allows about 50 full-time university/HND students to spend up 3-6 months (between 1st June and 1st December or early December to June) working at whatever job they can find, normally in the resorts along the north coast.

For details of *Work America*, *Work Canada* and *Work Australia*, see relevant country chapters.

Approximate costs: £580 for Work America, £150 for US summer camp programmes (cost of flight is deducted from wages), £520 for Work Canada, £1,000-£1,500 for Work Australia and £800 for Work Jamaica, including flights and (in some cases) insurance. Participants earn local wages, from as little as £10 a week in Jamaican hotels to $400 in the US.

BURO METRO
Freigutstrasse 7, PO Box 626, CH-8039 Zürich, Switzerland. Tel 201 41 10. Fax 202 16 46.
Independent recruitment agency, in business for over half a century. Place people in the hotel and catering industry and on cruise ships worldwide. An application fee of CHF 30 is charged. Can help with interviews, flight and visas. Will send an application form and information on request.

CAMP AMERICA
37a Queen's Gate, London SW7 5HR. Tel 0171-581 7373. Fax 0171-581 7377.
Major summer camp organisation which places thousands of young Europeans on American summer camps.
Camp counsellors are needed for a 9-10 week summer assignment.
Applicants need to have childcare experience and /or the ability to teach activities such as sports, arts and crafts or music/drama.
Students are also required to work on the Campower programme which deals with the kitchen/laundry/maintenance side of the camp. Sports and other instructors, catering and utility staff and nurses needed for 9 weeks in July/August.
Qualifications needed: counsellors must turn 18 (by June 1st) and be free to fly to the states in June.
Wages: free return flight from London to New York and pocket money which ranges from $150-650 (dependant on age and experience). Early application advised.

CAMP COUNSELORS USA (CCUSA)
6 Richmond Hill, Richmond Upon Thames, Surrey TW10 6QX. Tel 0181-332 2952. Fax 0181-332 2956. E-mail 100744.1754@compuserve.com
CCUSA is now a worldwide organisation with up to 30 offices across the globe. In 1997, CCUSA placed nearly 6,500 counselors from over 60 different countries throughout the USA. Positions available are counselors and activity leaders for children aged 6-16. Activities include land and water-based sports, outdoor adventure,programmes, arts and crafts and performing arts. International and domestic transport to camp, J1 visa and insurance provided.
Qualifications needed: minimum age 19. Must be available to work for a minimum of nine continuous weeks from June.
Wages: full board and lodging, pocket money of $350-600, depending on age and qualifications.

CHANGING PLACES
18-22 Hand Court, High Holborn, London WC1V 6JF (0171-222 3444).
Recruitment agency which specialises in making placements in the travel industry. Member of FRES.

EUROTOQUES
European Union of Top Chefs (Germany), c/o Schassbergers Kurund Sporthotel, 73667 Ebnisee, Germany. Tel 07184 232102. Fax 07184 292 138.
In operation since 1986.
Kitchen assistants and waiting staff needed for restaurants and housekeeping staff for hotels throughout Germany. Minimum period of work 3 months at any time of year.
Qualifications needed: knowledge of German.
Wages: none, but free room and board.

FM RECRUITMENT
Hedges House, 153-155 Regent Street, London W1R 7FD. Tel 0171 287 5400. Fax 0171 287 5411
In business since 1985.
Specialist recruitment service for financial management within the international hotel, catering and leisure industry. Clients comprise hotels, restaurants, event and industrial catering, casino, timeshare, resort operators, etc. looking for permanent or temporary accounting and finance staff. Opportunities worldwide though majority of recent appointments in Russia and Eastern Europe.
Qualifications needed: positions normally require graduate education, language skills and relevant technical and professional training and qualifications.

GATWICK JOB CENTRE
Ashdown House, Gatwick Airport, West Sussex RH6 0NP. Tel 01293 728 100. Fax 01293 728 101.
Job centre which handles over 3,000 vacancies per year for cabin crew, passenger service, reservations staff, operations staff, airline reps, tour operators, pilots, etc. Seasonal work available April to October.
Qualifications needed: cabin crew must be EU nationals and should have knowledge of a European language.

HEATHROW JOBCENTRE
Building No. 1154, Newall Road, Heathrow North, Hounslow, Middlesex TW6 2AP. Tel 0181 2504700.
Jobcentre which handles thousands of vacancies for airport and airline staff. Some seasonal work available over summer.
Qualifications needed: must be EU nationals. Knowledge of languages preferable for some jobs.

INTERNATIONAL SERVICES
Tour C.I.T., 3 rue de l'Arrivée, 75749 Paris, France. Postal address: B.P. 23, 91250 St. Germain-les-Corbeil Cedex, France. Tel 33(1) 60 75 95 95. Fax 33(1) 60 75 97 97.
In business since 1991.
Recruitment agency for Caribbean cruise ships, including RCI/Disney Cruise Line. Commis de Rang (250) and chef de rang (250) recruited for Miami-based cruise ships on 6 month contracts starting throughout the year.
Qualifications needed: must speak fluent English. Catering qualification or 2 years of experience needed. All nationalities welcome.

JULIANA'S LEISURE SERVICES
15-17 Broadway, West Ealing, London W13 9DA. Tel 0181-567 6765.
Agency which places disc jockeys worldwide, mostly in luxury hotels and resorts.
Experienced disc jockeys needed for contracts worldwide.
Qualifications needed: must have good presentation skills. Applicants should submit CV, demo tape (including mixing and voice overs) and photograph.
Wages: small wage paid in addition to free flights, accommodation, food and records/CDs.

NEW FRONTIERS
Lion House, 23 Islington High Street, London N1 9LQ. Tel 0171-833 9977. fax 0171-833 9995. Website www.newfrontiers.co.uk/E-mail info@newfrontiers.co.uk
In business since 1993.
Major recruitment consultancy for travel industry. Temporary and permanent positions in retail travel, business travel, tour operations, airlines and hotel sectors at all levels. Visit website for the latest vacancies, career advice and training at competitive prices. Recruitment service free.

QUEST RESORT RECRUITMENT
Binning House, 4-6 High St, Eastleigh, Southampton, Hants. SO50 5LA. Tel 01703 644933. Fax 01703 618827. E-mail info@questhotelstaff.co.uk
Member of FRES. Formerly a recruitment agency for cruise ships but now deals more with hotel staff in South Africa, Caribbean, Middle East, USA. Staff required: hotel management, supervisory personnel, chefs, chefs de rang, sommeliers, guest services and reservation staff.
Opportunities only available for personnel who can demonstrate relevant experience within hotels of 4/5 star quality.

STEINER TRAINING LTD
The Broadway, Stanmore, Middlesex HA7 4DU. Tel 0181-9546121. Fax 0181-9547980.
Concessionaire to run spas and salons on 52 cruise ships.
Beauty therapists, nail technicians, hairdressers, massage therapists and fitness instructors needed throughout the year (8 month contract). Free full board.
Qualifications needed: minimum age 19. Must be qualified, professional and highly motivated.

T&T TRAVEL RECRUITMENT AND RESOURCING PLC
113 Southwark Street, London W1N 7LB. Tel 0171-463 0106. Also T&T Travel Training, address as shown. Tel 0171-463 0107.
In business since 1983.
Specialist recruitment agency for permanent and temporary jobs in the travel industry.
Only agency to offer in-house training on British Airways Fares and Ticketing plus Galileo CRS. Courses available full-time or part-time (Saturdays). Placements made within UK and Europe in the field of business travel, retail travel, tour operations, conference and incentives, and sales and marketing. All levels of positions available.

TERENCE COX & ASSOCIATES LTD
PO Box 60229, Titirangi, Auckland 7, New Zealand. Tel 09-817-8019/8777. Fax 09-817-3033.
In business since 1985.
Recruitment consultancy within the hospitality industry active in New Zealand, Australia, the Pacific Islands (including Papua New Guinea, Fiji, etc.). Specialise in the placement of chefs. Assistance given with work permits.

UKOH (UK OVERSEAS HANDLING)
26 Bruton Place, London W1X 7AA.
In business since 1991/2.
UK recruitment company for the French-owned tour operator and accomodation management company, Eurogroup. Operate mainly in the French Alps in the winter and in coastal resorts on the south and west coasts in the summer.
Staff required: 65-75 hotel and restaurant staff, including, waiting, bar and kitchen staff, chefs, chambermaids, receptionists, handymen, and DJs. Winter season is December to May, summer season is May to October.
Qualifications: Minimum age 18. Must hold EC passport. Experience not necessary but must be bright and enthusiastic with plenty of stamina. Must speak good French.
Eurogroup also runs a Management Trainee scheme for graduates or year-abroad candidates studying French. Hands on training in all aspects of hotel work, such as dispensing wine and spirits, meeting and greeting, and marketing given on site.
Wages: Basic and commissioned salaries, depending on position. All food and shared accomodation provided. One day off per week except peak times.

VIP INTERNATIONAL
VIP House, 17 Charing Cross Road, London WC2H 0EP. Tel 0171-930 0541. Fax 0171-930 2860. E-mail vip@vipinternational.co.uk
International recruitment consultancy for the hospitality industry, including cruise lines.
Head waiters, chefs, hotel managers, food and beverage managers, pursers, housekeepers, controllers and all department heads.
Qualifications needed: minimum 3 years experience with 4 or 5 star operations. Must be aged 21-40 and have good command of English.
Wages: some posts pay up to $2,500-5,000 per month tax free.

WORK EXPERIENCE USA (WEUSA)
6 Richmond Hill, Richmond Upon Thames, Surrey TW10 6QX. Tel 0181-332 2952. Fax 0181-332 2956. E-mail 100744.1754@1754compuserve
WEUSA organises work placements for full-time students aged 19-30 in the USA. The package includes international transport, visa and insurance, together with an extensive job directory detailing available placements for applicants to select work from. Areas include hotels, restaurants, tour operators, work on ranches or national parks and performing arts centres. Average wages are between $4.50 to $8 per hour but this is dependant upon the placement.

WORLD CHALLENGE EXPEDITIONS LTD
Black Arrow House, 2 Chandos Road, London NW10 6NF. Tel 0181-961 1122. Fax 0181-961 1551.
Gap Challenge placements offers students, aged 18-25 and taking a Gap year, the

opportunity to work in high quality, family hotels in the Canadian Rockies, near and around the town of Banff.

Placements begin in September, November and March, last 6 months and cost £1,544 including flights. Students work between 20 to 50 hours a week, for approximately £3 per hour. The 12 month return ticket gives plenty of time for independent travel after the placement.

Travel Companies

ACADEMIC TRAVEL (LOWESTOFT) LTD.
The Briar School of English, 8 Gunton Cliff, Lowestoft, Suffolk NR32 4PE. Tel 01502 573781. Fax 01502 589150.
Holiday language courses on the Suffolk coast for foreign language learners.
In business since 1958.
English teachers and sports instructors needed. Minimum period of work 3 weeks between February and September. Teachers must be British, and have a BA or teaching certificate, or be a university student. TEFL qualification/experience preferred. Sports instructors should have Lawn Tennis Association Part 1 certificate and general knowledge of sport.

ACIS (AMERICAN COUNCIL FOR INTERNATIONAL STUDIES))
38 Queen,s Gate, London SW7 5HR. Tel 0171-590 7474. Fax 0171 590 7475.
Educational travel company, part of the American Institute for Foreign Study (AIFS) based in Connecticut.
Tour managers recruited to lead groups of North American high school students on educational tours around Europe. Tours are between 9 days and 2 weeks in length and run principally at Easter and in the summer. Recruitment starts in October - contact office for details.
Qualifications needed: must be fluent in English and at least one other European language. Be familiar with the relevant country (particularly its capital city), have a university degree or be studying for one. Minimum age 21. Previous experience preferred but not essential. Applicants should be able to communicate a genuine interest in the people and places of Europe.

ACORN VENTURE LTD
22 Worcester Street, Stourbridge, West Midlands DY8 1AN. Tel 01384 378827. Fax 01384 378866. E-mail topstaff@acorn-venture.com
In business since 1982. Members of BCU, RYA, ABTA, AALA, BAHA.
Activity holiday company offering groups multi-activity camping holidays in North Wales, the Lake District, France, Spain and Italy.
250 seasonal opportunities: instructors, maintenance staff, administrators, catering staff and nurses needed mid-April to September (some shorter contracts are available). Activities include sailing, canoeing, kayaking, climbing, abseiling and caving. Send a CV from October onwards; interviews in January.
Wages: living allowance of approximately £50, plus supplement. Bonus subject to qualifications and experience.

ADVENTURE & COMPUTER HOLIDAYS
PO Box 183, Dorking, Surrey RH5 6FA. Tel/fax 01306 730716.
Children's activity day camps in Surrey and residential camps in Cornwall.
Camp leaders needed: 2. Period of work Easter and school summer holidays.
Qualifications needed: training/experience with children. Minimum age 21 for day camps.
Wages: £130-£160 per week for day camp leaders, £160 for residential camp leaders.

ADENTURE ALASKA TOURS
PO Box 64, Hope, Alaska 99605, USA. Tel 907 782 3730. Fax 907 782 3725.
In business since 1987.
Operate tours in Alaska, Yukon, Northwest territories.
Multi day tour guides (6) and housekeeping interns (2) needed. Contract lasts from early June to late August. Applications welcome in winter/spring.
Qualifications needed: previous experience of guiding. Knowledge of French or German is preferred.

AFRICA EXPLORED
Rose Cottage, Summerleaze, Magor, Newport, Gwent NP9 3DE. Tel 01633 880224. Fax 01633 882128.
In business since 1983.
Overland camping expedition organiser in Africa. Trips last 5 weeks to 6 months.
Trainee expedition leaders required (10-15).
Qualifications needed: Must be qualified diesel mechanics and hold HGV or PCV licence. Minimum age 23. Knowledge of language not essential.

AFRICAN PORTFOLIO
225 East 79th Street, New York, NY 10021, USA. Tel 212 737 0144. Fax 212 737 6730.
Tours operators to Southern and East Africa, Seychelles, Mauritius, Madagascar, Mozambique.
May require staff for sales and itinary planning with clients, etc. Contracts for 1-2 years. Languages not necessary but ablity to pay attention to detail is. Must have residency and work permit for Zimbabwe.

AIR 2000
Cabin Crew Recruitment, 7th Floor, Commonwealth House, Chicago Avenue, Manchester Airport MP0 3DP.
Winners of the 1998 Golden Globe Award for best UK charter airline
Cabin crew required.
Qualifications needed:Must hold EC passport. Qualified to GCSE standard. Be able to swim a minimum of 25 meteres. Aged 21-40. Minimum height 5ft 3in, with weight in proportion and excellent standard of personal presentation. Must be friendly, caring and have a realistic view of what the job entails.

AIRTOURS HOLIDAYS LTD
Wavell House, Holcombe Road, Helmshore, Rossendale, Lancs. BB4 4NB. Tel 01706 909 027. Fax 01706 232328.
Giant UK tour operator to worldwide destinations.
Staff needed: approximately 300 holiday services executives, 100 children's club

leaders, 50 holiday services assistants, 30 escapades reps, 30 entertainers and 30 overseas administration executives needed April to October, mostly for Mediterranean resorts. Staff sometimes taken on in the resorts.

Qualifications needed: reps should have GCSE in English and maths, and have an efficient track record of working with the public. 12 months customer service experience is required for all positions. Knowledge of a foreign language is not essential. Minimum age 20-21 and 19 for holiday services assistants. Children's reps must be at least 19, with experience of working with children, a childcare qualification and boundless energy.

ALPINE TRACKS
40 High Street, Menai Bridge, Anglesey LL59 5EF. Tel 01248 716550. Fax 01248 716616.
Organisers of skiing and mountain biking trips in France (Morzine), Canada (Whistler).
3 chefs, 5 chalet girls and 4 guides needed. Winter season is 5 months, summer season is 3 months. Interviews for winter take place in June and in January for summer season. Sometimes employ people on location.
Qualifications needed: knowledge of French preferred. Good sense of humour.

ALPOTELS
17 High Street, Fretton, Northants NN17 3DE. Tel 01536 771150.
Associated with Jobs in the Alps (see separate entry). Have opportunities for waiters, waitresses, chambermaids, porters, chefs and kitchen staff in German and French owned hotels. Applications by 15th September for winter, 15th April for summer.
Qualifications needed: must be alert, intelligent, hardworking, responsible and pleasant. Hotel experience valuable but not esential. Knowledge of language needed for French jobs, less so for German. Applicants must be EU nationals.
Wages ca. £500 per month France, £400 Germany, plus free food and lodging.

ALTERNATIVE TRAVEL GROUP
69-71 Banbury Road, Oxford OX2 6PE. Tel 01865 315679. Fax 01865 315697/8/9.
Upmarket independent tour operator organising walking and cycling tours in Europe. Member of AITO.
Tour leaders needed to look after individual clients and groups in Italy and France. Extended training given (company has won National Training Awards).
Bonuses paid for good performance.

AMSTERDAM TRAVEL SERVICE
Bridge House, 55-59 High Road, Broxbourne, Herts EN10 7DT. Tel. 01992 456056. Fax 01992 444554.
Travel service to, Stockholm, Copenhagen, Paris, Brussels, Bruges.
Need 6 telesales and reservations staff. Other staff recruited as and when needed.
Qualifications needed: a good level of standard education as training is given on the job.

ANGLO CONTINENTAL PLACEMENT AGENCY
21 Amesbury Crescent, Hove, Sussex BN3 5RD (tel/fax 01273 705959/e-mail anglocont@applied-tech.com).
Established 1985

Place staff in hotels in UK; chefs, waiting staff, chamber staff, housekeepers, bar staff, receptionists and porters, for 6-12 month period.
References essential. Send CV plus 4 international reply coupons. Live-in accomodation provided.

ARDMORE LANGUAGE SCHOOL
Berkshire College, Burchetts Green, Maidenhead SL6 6QR. Tel 01628 826699.
Multi activity and English language camps mainly in London and region.
Tour guides occasionally needed. Must speak a European language. Group leaders and centre directors also needed.

ASTONS HOLIDAYS
Clerkenleap, Broomhall, Worcester WR5 3HR. Tel 01905 829200. Fax 01905 820850.
Ski tour operator, mainly to Austria and Switzerland.
Ski tutors/guides required 1-7 weeks through winter season, particularly New Year, February, half-term and Easter holidays. Applications processed all year. Some vacancies filled abroad with people who are qualified and already working with local ski school.
Qualifications needed: BASI/National Ski School/Alpine Ski Leader award and proven track record as a ski guide. Preferred minimum age 21. Current first aid certificate linked to outdoor education environment needed. Knowledge of foreign languages not essential.

BACKROADS
801 Cedar Street, Berkeley, CA 94710, USA. Tel 510 527 1555 ext. 560. Fax 510 527 1444. Website www.backroads.com
In operation since 1979.
Leading activity travel company to worldwide destinations.
15 office staff and 60 trip leaders needed. Recruitment takes place in early spring.
Qualifications needed: minimum age 21. Languages preferred. Must have ability to relate to people of different ages and backgrounds, have clean driving record, good public speaking skills, be capable of solving problems independently and professionally.
Wages: $55 per day for inn trips, $73 per day for camping trips. Meals, lodging and transportation included. Bonuses and wage increases awarded annually.

BALES WORLDWIDE LTD
Bales House, Junction Road, Dorking, Surrey RH4 3HL. Tel 01306 885991. Fax 01306 740048.
In operation for 50 years. members of ATOL and ABTA.
Tours to worldwide destinations (not Europe).
Recruit permanent staff only. Need reservations executives (2-3).
Advertise vacancies in trade journals and agencies throughout the year. Travel and tourism qualifications or experience necessary.

BECKS HOLIDAYS
Southfields, Shirleys Ditchling, Hassocks, West Sussex BN6 8UD. Tel 01273 842843. Fax 01273 842849.
In business since 1982.
Specialise in campsite holidays in France. Campsite couriers required from May-

September, May-July or July-September. Usually recruit through *En Route* (Caravan Club magazine).
Qualifications needed: mature couples with own caravan preferred. Knowledge of French essential. Must be reliable and friendly.

BELLE FRANCE
15 East Street, Rye, East Sussex TN31 7JY. Tel 01797 22377. Fax 01797 223666.
Walking and cycling tour operator through rural France.
Member of AITO.
Bike reps needed: 7. To maintain bikes, transport luggage, collect customers, etc. May to September. Applications welcomed around Christmas.
Qualifications needed: must be well organised, capable of working independently and like the country. Minimum age 21. Driving experience required.
Wages: £300 per month plus caravan accommodation, utilities, insurance and travel by Belle France car.

BIKE RIDERS TOURS
PO Box 130254, Boston, MA 02113, USA. Tel 617 723 2354. Fax 617 723 2355.
Bicycle tour holidays in Italy, Ireland, Spain and Portugal.
Recruit 20 tour guides for full and part time work from April-October. Recruitment begins January, interviews in February.
Qualifications needed: appropriate language for each country, Must be well-travelled and organised individuals with good ability in customer service.

BOURNE LEISURE GROUP
Normandy Court, Wolsey road, Hemel Hempstead HP2 4TU. Tel 01442 241658. Fax 01442 219031.
In business for over 35 years,
Operates holiday parks throughout Britain.
Recruits over 500 staff, including receptionists and holiday sales supervisors. Full and part time positions available from January onwards.
Qualifications needed: knowledge of languages not necessary. Must have outgoing personality, be customer orientated, have computer skills.

BOWHILLS LTD
Mayhill Farm, Swanmore, Southampton SO32 2QW. Tel 01489 877627. Fax 01489 877872.
Farmhouse and villa holidays in France.
Sometimes need reservations and admin staff.

THE BRITISH MUSEUM TRAVELLER
46 Bloomsbury St, London WC1B 3QQ. Tel 0171-323 8895.
Specialist tours for people interested in art, archeology, history and culture to worldwide destinations. Although the majority of guides are curators from the British Museum, highly qualified guides may be needed.

CANVAS HOLIDAYS
12 Abbey Park Place, Dunfermline, Fife KY12 7PD. Tel 01383 644018. Fax 01383 620481.
Self-drive tour operator with 34 years experience. Operates 70 campsites in France,

Spain, Italy, Germany, Austria, Switzerland and Luxembourg.
Area supervisors, campsite couriers, children's couriers, wildlife guides and warehouse assistants needed. Season lasts from April to October with some high season positions available from July to September. Recruitment takes place from October to March, in Dunfermline, Manchester and London.
Qualifications needed: must be hard-working, flexible, enthusuaistic and level-headed. A good working knowledge of a European language is preferred but not essential. Children's couriers and wildlife guides must have relevant experience. Minimum age 19 (21 for area supervisors and warehouse assistants). Applications are invited from mature couples and individuals.
Wages: £95 per week (paid into UK bank account), return travel to and from UK port of entry. Uniform and tented accomodation provided.

CARISMA HOLIDAYS
Bethel House, Heronsgate Road, Chorleywood, Herts. WD3 5BB. Fax 01923 284235.
In business since 1979. Specialises in mobile homes and tents on their own private beaches on the west coast of France and Brittany. Couriers/reps required. Candidates should have friendly personalities, be flexible, outgoing and have the ability to get on with people. It would be advantageous to speak French. Children's courier/rep and maintenance manager also required.
Full season couriers/reps work from May 1st to mid September and high season workers are required from July 1st to mid September. When applying, state whether applying for full or high season work.Wages: up to £100 per week.

CASTERBRIDGE TOURS
Casterbridge Hall, Bowden Road, Templecombe, Somerset BA8 0LB. Tel 01963 370753. Fax 01963 371220.
In business since 1979.
European tour company.
Tour guides needed: 25 to escort groups in Britain and Europe, mainly France, Spain and Italy, between March and July. Residents of destination countries could be considered for tours in that country.
Qualifications needed: knowledge of languages preferred but not always required. Guides must attend Casterbridge training course in January, February or November (see entry in Training chapter). Applicants should be well travelled and have good standard of education.
Wages: from £200 per week plus board and lodging.

CHINA TRAVEL SERVICE AND INFORMATION CENTRE
124 Euston Road, London NW1 2AL. Tel 0171-388 8818. Fax 0171-388 8828.
Tours to China and Hong Kong.
Need staff for ticketing, incoming tour administration and assistant accountancy.
Qualifications needed: fluent English and writen/spoken Chinese is essential. Candidates with knowledge of both Mandarin and Cantonese are preferred. Must have knowledge of Chinese culture and history. Experience in travel trade, office administration, customer relations and computer literacy is required.

CICLISMO CLASSICO
13 Marathon Street, Arlington, MA 02474, USA. Tel 800 866 7314. Fax 781 641 1512. E-mail info@ciclismoclassico.com

Established 1988.
Leading specialists in bicycle and walking educational tours around Italy.
Need 5 bilingual guides (Italian/English) with experience of cycling or walking in Italy, to work for 2-8 months between April and November. Recruitment takes place December to February. Sometimes employ people on location.
Qualifications needed: minimum age 23. Must speak Italian, have leadership skills, knowledge of Italian culture, cycling and bike repair skills.

CITALIA
Marco Polo House, 3-5 Lansdowne Road, Croydon, Surrey CR9 1LL. Tel 0181-686 5533. Fax 0181- 0328.
In business since 1935.
UK's leading Italian specialist. Member of AITO.
Reps and support staff needed. Interviews held in London, though people who are based in Italy are also required.
Qualifications needed: fluent Italian. French or Flemish also useful. Minimum age 23. Should have driving licence.

CLUB 18-30
81 Farringdon Street, London EC4A 4EJ. Tel 0171-583 8300. Fax 0171-583 5608.
Leading specialist in youth holidays for over 30 years. Staff contribute to an atmosphere that turns 'an ordinary holiday into a fortnight of Saturday nights'.
Reps and resort staff are needed throughout the Mediterranean.
Qualifications needed: large personality, stamina, initiative and plenty of common sense.

CLUB CANTABRICA HOLIDAYS LTD.
Holiday House, 146/148 London Road, St. Albans, Herts. AL1 1PQ. Tel 01727 833141. Fax 01727 843766.
In business since 1975. Member of AITO.
Camping tour operator to France, Italy, Spain and Corfu.
Campsite couriers needed: 70. Season lasts May to October. Applications processed from January.
Qualifications needed: knowledge of languages preferred. Minimum age 21.
Work also available for children's couriers and drivers with B.C.V licence.

CLUB MED
106 Brompton Road, London SW3 1JJ. Tel 0171-225 7710. Fax 0171-589 6086. Employment hotline in the US: 212-755-6458.
In business since just after World War II.
Runs over 100 Club Med villages around the world which employ thousands of staff.
Excursion guides, nannies, sports instructors, hostesses, GOs (*gentils organisateurs*), boutique assistants, receptionists, and cashiers needed: 40 in winter, 100 in summer. Work is seasonal, from 3 weeks to 6 months.
Recruitment takes place August to November for winter season and December to May for summer season. Applicants must send CV and covering letter to London office.
Qualifications needed: varies depending on position applied for. Minimum age 20. Applicants must speak fluent English and French (for some positions a third language is required).EU nationality. Sports instructors must have relevant

qualifications and experience to teach sailing, water-skiing, scuba diving, tennis, windsurfing, golf and archery. Hostesses and guides should speak three European languages including German. Nannies must have childcare experience.

COLLETTE TOURS
162 Middle St, Pawtucket, Rhode Island 02860, USA. Tel (401) 728-3805. Fax (401) 728-1380.
In business since 1918.
Deluxe motorcoach tour wholesaler to 100 destinations worldwide.
Staff needed: reservationists and inside sales (telemarketing), tour guides, sales reps. Sales and reservation personnel recruited year round, tour guides in spring.
Qualifications needed: knowledge of languages preferred (German, Spanish, French, Russian, Greek, Italian).

CONTIKI HOLIDAYS
Wells House, 15 Elmfield Road, Bromley, Kent BR1 1LS. Tel: 0181-290 6777. Fax 0181-313 0063.
In business since 1961 (founded by a New Zealander).
Coach and camping tour operator to Europe catering for 18-35s market.
30 Tour managers, drivers and site representatives needed. Contracts are for 30 weeks March to October/November. Interviews take place between October and January. 10-day training seminar held in February and then a 45-day training trip in Europe.
Qualifications needed: tour managers must have European experience, excellent organisational skills and interest in history, politics, etc. Tour drivers must have coach licence. Reps must be people-oriented. All must be over 23 and prepared to work hard. Knowledge of languages not necessary. Must have European passport or right to work in UK.
Wages: from £80 a week plus incentive bonuses (from £1.20 a day).
Work also available for cooks, bar staff and cleaners at sites throughout Europe. Minimum period of work 4 months. Applications to Contiki Services Ltd.

COSMOS AIR PLC
Representatives Recruitment, Overseas Operations Dept, Tourama House, 17 Homesdale Road, Bromley, Kent BR2 9LX. Tel 0181-464 3444.
Tour operator for UK clients.
Overseas reps and children's reps required.
Qualifications needed: Minumum age 21 (19 for children's reps). Second language is desirable. 5 GCSEs including Maths and English.

COSMOS COACH TOURS
Via alla Roggia, PO Box 6916 Grancia, Switzerland Tel. 91-985 7111.
Tour reps, shuttle hosts and other staff needed during the season (April-October).
Qualifications needed: Minimum age 23. second language essential and qualifications in higher education. Calm but assertive personality.

COUNTRY WALKERS
PO Box 180, Waterbury, VT 05676, USA. Tel 802 244 1387. Fax 802 244 5661.
In business since 1979.
Tours to Europe, South and Central America, USA, Canada.

Need 20 tour guides with appropriate languages. Work is for 10 one-week tours per year. Recruitment takes place all year. Must have detailed knowledge of the country with multi-tasking skills.

CROSS-CHANNEL CATERING COMPANY
Waterloo International Terminal, London E1 7LT. Tel 0171-928 7090.
Has franchise which runs service and food arrangements on Eurostar.
Stewards and catering staff needed for Channel Tunnel rail services between UK, France and Belgium, on permanent basis. 16 staff needed for each train to serve more than 200 first-class passengers (breakfast or a hot meal) and 500 standard class travellers (snacks).
Qualifications needed: must be bilingual (English, French) and have customer care skills. Dutch, German, Spanish, Italian, Japanese, etc. useful. Must also have relevant experience with an airline, restaurant, etc.

CRUSADER HOLIDAYS LTD.
Crusader Business Park, Clacton-on-Sea CD15 4HP. Tel 01255 425453. Fax 01255 222683.
In business since 1969.
Coach tour operator to European cities.
Tour escorts and tour managers needed: 20 (extra). For both summer (May to September) and winter (October to March) seasons. Staff recruited via adverts in trade press in February.
Qualifications: experience in customer care and knowledge of languages preferred. Staff sometimes hired on location.

CRYSTAL HOLIDAYS
Crystal House, The Courtyard, Arlington Road, Surbiton, Surrey KT6 6BW. Tel 0181-241 5128. Fax 0181-408 4848.
In business since 1981. Owned by Thomson.
UK's leading ski chalet holiday operator to France, Austria, Switzerland, Italy, Andorra, Romania, Bulgaria, Slovenia, Norway, Lapland, Canada, USA.
Resort reps (200), chalet reps (500), hotel staff (300) and nannies (80) needed, late November to end of April to work in ski resorts throughout Europe. Applications welcomed between June and November. Seasonal work is 6 months; December-April or May-September. Interviews held June to November.
Qualifications needed: reps must speak appropriate language, be able to ski, have stamina, patience, tact and organisational abilities. Chalet staff must be able to cook for up to 14 people on strict budget. Nannies must have NNEB or equivalent. All staff much hold UK or EU passport, or have valid work permit with national insurance number to work in EU.
Basic salary and all expenses (plus commission for resort reps).
Work may also be available in company's multi activity and water sports programme in Austria, Italy and France. Limited number of places for non-EU passport holders.

CV TRAVEL
43 Cadogan St, London SW3 2PR. Tel 0171-591 2800.
In business since 1971.
Well established upmarket villa holiday company in Corfu and Paxos, Greece.
Vacancies for Greek speaking reps in the summer season (May-October). Also require experienced cooks for either ad hoc apointments or seasonal vacancies. Must drive.

DELTA TRAVEL
University Precinct, Oxford Road, Manchester M13 9RN.
Travel agents to worldwide destinations.
Occasionally require travel consultants for permanent contracts.

DENALI WEST LODGE
PO Box 40, Lake Minchumina, AK 99757, USA. Tel/Fax 907 674 3112.
In business since 1986.
Holiday resort in Alaska. Need domestic staff and may occasionally need guides. Contracts for varying lengths between March and September. Recruitment takes place in January. Candidates should have relevant experience but mostly an initiative spirit.

DISCOVER LTD.
Timbers, Oxted Road, Godstone, Surrey RH9 8AD. Tel 01883 744392.
Fax 01883 744913.
In business since 1978.
Field study and personal development courses for students in the Cevennes mountains of France.
Staff needed: general kitchen assistant, assistant housekeeper, 2 cooks and handy person. Season lasts April to October though assistants can work for shorter periods. Interviews held in January/February.
Qualifications needed: cooks must have relevant qualifications/experience. General help must be willing and have likeable personality. No knowledge of French needed. British nationals preferred.
Work also available for bricklayer/builder for 1 month working holiday.

DISCOVER BRITAIN
International House, Pierpoint Street, Worcester WR1 1YD. tel 01905
613746. Fax 01905 613747.
UK tours company require 20 reservations staff. Seasonal work for varying lengths between April and October. Recruitment takes place between February and May.
Qualifications needed: knowledge of languages and office skills are useful.

DISNEYLAND PARIS
Service du Recruitement-Casting, Euro Disney SCA, BP 110, F-77777
Marne-la-Vallée Cedex 4, France.
The biggest theme park in Europe with 12 million guests per year, situated 30km east of Paris. The Disneyland Paris Resort consists of 7 hotels, 2 convention centres, and the Theme Park with 42 attractions, 61 restaurants, plus 54 shops and boutiques.
Permanent or seasonal staff (known as cast members) are required to work in Animation (attractions, entertainment), Guest Services (reception, parking, ticketing), Food and Beverage (kitchen, table, bar and banqueting service), cleaning, fast food restaurants and shops. Seasonal positions available between March and October, minimum contract 3 months, open ended contracts are also available. Monthly gross wage is approximately £700 (F 6798,00) for a 39 hour week. Staff contribute towards and are covered by French social security during their contract. Assistance is provided to help find accomodation and travel expenses wil be reimbursed providing the contract is successfully completed.
Qualifications needed: minimum age 18. Must be of European nationality or have a valid work permit to work in France. Candidates must be friendly, cheerful

and outgoing as the work involves a good deal of contact with visitors. It is also necessary to be able to communicate well in French and English and knowledge of a third European language is an asset. Applicants should send a covering letter, CV and photo, including contact details and availability, quoting Reference TOU98 to the above address.

DISNEY WORLDWIDE SERVICES INC
International Recruiting, PO Box 10090, Lake Buena Vista, FL 32830. Tel 407 828 2696. Fax 407 934 6878. E-mail sue–sharpe@wda. disney.com

Biggest theme park in USA with a keen scope for international recruitment. Require people to feature in their Cultural Representative Program at the World Showcase at Epcot. Activities may include selling British merchandise or working in an English pub.

Send CV to address above. Recruitment takes place twice a year in United Kingdom (March and October). For details of other countries, contact office in Florida.

Qualifications needed: Minimum age 18. Must be flexible, outgoing, willing to share a room with someone from a different country.

DRIVELINE EUROPE
Greenleaf House, Suite 9, Darkes Lane, Potters Bar, Herts EN6 1AE. Tel 01707 222307. Fax 01707 649126.

Driving tours through Europe.

Require telephone reservation clerks, preferably for long term contracts. Applications should be made June/July. Experience in a retail outlet is preferable.

DUVINE ADVENTURES
635 Boston Avenue, Somerville, MA 02144, USA. Tel 781-395-7440. Website www.Duvine.com
In operation for 4 years.

Operate cycling, food and wine tours to France.

Recruit 5 staff for summer season. Apply in winter.

Qualifications needed: French and knowledge of wine, food and biking.

EDWIN DORAN MUSIC TRAVEL
9 York St, Twickenham, Middlesex TW1 3JZ. Tel 0181-288 1000.

Organises tours in Europe (mainly Austria Germany and the Netherlands) for British school choirs and bands.

Tour guides needed.

Qualifications needed: minimum age 25. Knowledge of German preferred. Should be familiar with countries on itinerary and able to organise excursions, arrange quiz nights and solve problems.

Wages: £30 a day.

EDWIN DORAN SPORTS TRAVEL
9 York Street, Twickenham, Middlesex TW1 3JZ. Tel 0181-288 1000.

Organisers of sports tours (rugby, lacrosse, field hockey, athletics). Good knowledge of geography and languages preferred. Good administration skills and self motivation needed.

EMPEROR DIVERS
c/o Regal Diving, 22 High St, Sutton, Ely, Cambridgeshire CB6 2RB. Tel 01353 778096. Fax 01353 777897.
In business since 1986.
Diving holidays on the Red Sea in Egypt.
Diving instructors needed to teach holidaymakers in Egypt, for a minimum of one year.
Qualifications needed: minimum PADI OWI plus BSAC A1 if possible. Knowledge of German, French, Italian and/or Spanish would be useful.
Wages: by arrangement plus 20% commission on each course (which normally cost US$600-800 per person). Accommodation available.

ENCOUNTER OVERLAND
Wren Park, Shefford, Beds. SG17 5JD. Tel 01462 811470.
Overland expedition and adventure holiday operator to Africa, Asia, South and Central America.
Full-time solo expedition Leader Drivers required. Minimum commitment three years.
Qualifications needed: must have some distinct leadership skills mechanical aptitude and travel exerperience within the developing world be aged 25-35 and be single. Applicants must have or be prepared to obtain a British PCV licence. Training in the UK and overseas in all aspects of expeditioning prior to first solo deployment .

ENGLISH WANDERER
6 George Street, Ferryhill, Co. Durham DL17 0DT. Tel 01740 653169. Fax 01740 657996. E-mail EnglishWanderer@btinternet.com
Specialises in tour holidays in UK.
Need walking guides and part time staff. Applications welcomed all year, interviews held in January. Sometimes hire people on location if knowledgeable about folk culture.
Qualifications needed: German or French preferred. MLTB certificate (starting or completed). Current first aid certificate essential. Prefer to recruit candidates of the same nationality as the country where the tour operates.

EQUITY LTD.
Dukes Lane House, 47 Middle Street, Brighton BN1 1AL. Tel 01273 886 878. Fax 01273 203212. E-mail travel@equity.co.uk
In business since 1991. Leading independent direct-sell tour operator. Organise all-inclusive ski holidays for adults and school groups to 25 resorts in Italy, 7 in France, 4 in Austria, as well as summer educational tours and courses primarily in France and Germany.
Ski resort reps, ski guides/technicians, chalet staff and hotel staff (100+) needed for 5 month winter season (December-April). Applications welcome between May and October.
Summer reps/interpreters (5+) needed for various periods (1 week-1 month) between April and October. Aplications welcomed from December to June.
Qualifications: fluent language essential for reps, useful for others. Experience of working with adults or children abroad is useful. Outgoing, confident personality more important than qualifications. Skiing ability an advantage for ski reps.
Wages: £200-450 per month, depending on position, plus bonus, board, accomodation, ski pass, insurance, uniform and transport. Summer - £100-150 per course, plus board and accomodation, travel expenses, uniform and insurance.

ESPRIT HOLIDAYS LTD.
Oaklands, Reading Road North, Fleet, Hants. GU13 8AA. Tel 01252 625177. Fax 01252 811243.
Ski tour operator to France and Switzerland. Also alpine summer holidays.
Resort reps needed: 15. Chalet boys/girls: 35. Nannies: 40. Snow rangers: 25. All needed from December to the end of April. Recruitment takes place year round. Some hiring takes place in the resorts.
Qualifications needed: knowledge of language essential for reps, useful for others. Reps should have overseas and supervisory experience and preferably a degree in languages. Nannies should have NNEB, BTEC or RGN qualification or equivalent. Chalet boys/girls should have City & Guilds 7061/7062 or relevant catering experience. Must be British passport holder.

EUROCAMP
Overseas Recruitment Department, Canute Court, Toft Road, Knutsford, Cheshire WA16 0NL. Tel 01565 625522. Fax 01565 625522.
Members of ABTA and AITO.
Major camping and mobile-home tour operator with more than 250 campsites in Austria, Belgium, France (mainly), Germany, Italy, Netherlands, Spain and Switzerland.
Campsite couriers and children's couriers needed: up to 1,000. Telephone applications are preferred, from October. Interviews are held up until April in Knutsford (Cheshire).
Qualifications needed: knowledge of local language and previous customer service or team work experience. Children's couriers require previous childcare experience. Only employ British, German or Dutch staff.

EUROCAMP - THE COUNTRY SELECTION
Canute Court, Toft Road, Knutsford, Cheshire WA16 ONL. Tel 01565 625 571. Fax 01565 625 553.
In business since 1973. Member of AITO.
Camping tour operator in France with 47 campsites on the coasts and inland.
Operations team members needed to assemble and dismantle company tents at beginning and end of season. 3-4 week contracts: usually 25th April to 25th May or 10th September to 5th October. Interviews usually in January/February.
Qualifications needed: driving experience and knowledge of French both useful. UK nationals only, preferably mature couples .
Wages: couples are paid £110-190 a week, depending on size of the site.
Work also available for operations team leaders (6) and campsite couriers (20).

EUROPEAN ESCAPES LLC
487 2nd Avenue, San Fransisco, CA 94118, USA. Tel 415 386 2633/(freephone) 888 387 6589. Fax 415 386 0477.
Operates tours to all of Europe. Need reservations staff for permanent contract and guides for season (late spring to early Autumn). Sometimes employ people on location.
Qualifications needed: must have broad based European travel knowledge, be fluent in English and at least one other European language.

EUROPEAN WATERWAYS
35 Wharf Road, Wraysbury, Staines, Middlesex TW19 5JQ. Tel 01784 482439. Fax 01784 483072. E-mail Compuserve 103145.1422

Operate luxury hotel barge holidays in France, England, Ireland and Holland. Chefs, stewardesses, deckhands, tour guides and qualified barge captains needed. French employment is in Burgundy, Loire Valley and the South of France. EC nationals only. Some French useful. Driving licence required. Minimum age 21. Salary plus tips, and free board and lodging.

EUROSITES RECRUITMENT
Wavell House, Holcombe Road, Helmshore, Lancs. BB4 4NB.
In business since 1990 (though subsidiary of Airtours plc).
Camping tour operator to France, Spain and Italy; also a few in Austria, Germany, Holland and Luxembourg.
Campsite couriers and children's couriers needed: 175. Must be available to work for whole season (March-October). Group and individual interviews held between October and February.
Qualifications needed: knowledge of more than one European language required. Minimum age 19. Applicants should have liking for outdoor life, be a good communicator, have initiative and have previous experience of working with people. Must have permit for work in Europe.
Wages: £423 per month.

EUROSTAR
Recruitment Department, ESP House, Waterloo Terminal, London SE1 8US.
In business since 1994.
Company which runs Channel Tunnel rail services.
On-board train managers and customer services team members needed for fast trains between London and Paris/Brussels, on permanent basis.
Qualifications needed: must speak English plus French, Japanese or another European language and have experience of working with the public.
(See also Cross-Channel Catering Company.)

EXPLORE WORLDWIDE LTD.
Culdrose House, 1 Frederick St, Aldershot, Hants. GU11 1LQ. Tel 01252 319448. Fax 01252 343170.
In business since 1981. Member of AITO.
Adventure tour operator to Europe, Africa, Asia and the Americas.
Tour leaders needed (approximately 40). Recruit mostly January to February.
Qualifications needed: minimum age 24 years. Must have (or be prepared to obtain) first aid certificate. French or Spanish preferred. Training given.

EXPO GARDEN TOURS
70 Great Oak, Redding, CT 06896, USA. Tel 203 938 0410. Fax 203 938 0427.
Specialises in garden tours in UK, Ireland, Holland, France, Italy.
Hires local guides and tour managers on a freelance basis between April and September. Recruitment takes place July-September. Must be organised, have knowledge about gardens and thier history.

EXTRAORDINARY PLACES
2325 NW Market Street, Seattle, WA98107, USA. Tel 206 784 2761/800891 4706. Fax 206 784 4668. E-mail INFO@EPLACES.COM
In business since 1991.

Organises tours to worldwide destinations. Mostly recruits tour leaders through its own clients (museums, travel agents, etc). Must have experience or relevant academic background to lead tours.

FIRST CHOICE SKI LAKES AND MOUNTAINS
Olivier House, 18 Marine Parade, Brighton, East Sussex BN2 1TL. Tel 01273 677777. Fax 01273 600486.
A division of First Choice Holidays and Flights.
One of the largest tour operators of hotel, chalet and self-catering holidays for individuals, adult and school groups to France, Austria, Italy, Andorra, Canada, Bulgaria. Skibound Hotels Division runs and leases 34 hotels and 68 chalets in ski resorts in Europe.
Winter staff required (850): resort reps, ski technicians, hotel managers and assistant managers, chef and assistant chefs, waiting and cleaning staff, kitchen staff, night porters, bar, staff, handymen, chalet cooks and assistants.
CVs and covering letters are processed from June, group interviews held throughout the UK during September.
Work also available for summer season: see *Travelbound*.

FISHING INTERNATIONAL INC
PO Box 2132, Santa Rosa, CA 95405, USA. Tel 707 542 4242. Fax 707 526 3474. E-mail fishint@cued.eom
Selling agents for fishing holidays. Occasionally recruit agents who speak Spanish, French and English.

FLEUR HOLIDAYS
4 All Hallows Road, Bispham, Blackpool FY2 CAS. Tel 01253 593 333. Fax 01253 595151.
Campsite holiday operators in France.
Need campsite representatives with managerial capabilities. Contracts can be tailored to suit candidate's needs. Eager to take on staff for whom the work experience will form part of a recognised course. Knowledge of languages preferred.

FLUVIALE AUXERROISE
33 Quai National, 21170 Saint-Jean-de-Losne, France. Tel 380 39 24 09. Fax 380 77 94 24. E-mail Fluviale.Auxerroise@wanadoo.fr
In business since 1985.
Hotel barge cruise operator on inland waterways of France.
Chefs, deckhands, pilots, guide/coordinators and stewardesses needed: 20 total. Must be available for whole season (beginning or middle of April to end of October). Candidates are interviewed in London in February. Occasionally staff are taken if crew member leaves mid-season.
Qualifications needed: knowledge of French preferred in all positions and essential for guides and pilots. Chefs must have experience of gourmet cooking. Guide/coordinators must have extensive knowledge of history, architecture, wine, etc. as well as leadership qualities and high degree of responsibility. All staff must have legal right to work in France. Preferred age 21-35.

FRENCH LIFE HOLIDAYS
26 Church Road, Horsforth, Leeds LS18 5LG. Tel 0113 2819 998. Fax 0113 258 4211.
Campsite tour operator in France. Member of AITO.

Campsite couriers needed: 20. Children's couriers needed: 16. Full-season contracts from March to September. Application forms available from December.
Qualifications needed: knowledge of French required and some experience of camping holiday work. Only employ British nationals.
Wages: £380 per month (depending on position) plus tent accommodation.

GECKO OVERLAND TREKKING/TREK AND HIRE
PO Box 402456, Miami Beach, FL 33140, USA. Tel 305 867 2087. Fax 206 374 5547.
In operation since 1993.
Overland tours to South/Central/North America.
Need 3-4 tour leaders to drive clients, negotiate borders and provide general assistance. Also require some office staff.
Qualifications needed: minimum age 25, excellent driving record, preferably a Spanish speaker. Must be 'a people person'. Workers must have a work visa.

GENCTUR
Prof. F. K. Gokay Cad. 21, Denzil Ap. Kat: 1, Hasanpasa, Istanbul, Turkey. Tel 216 336 14 13/216 336 93 94. Fax 216 336 68 78.
In operation since 1979.
Counsellors with experience or enthusiasm needed for summer children/teenager camps. Must have ability in sports, music, art, drama or handicrafts. Native speakers of English, German or French preferred. One assignment in a single camp lasts 2 weeks but it is possible to continue or take more assignments in different camps.
Wages: work is voluntary but return transport, board and excursions are provided.

GETAWAY GROUP
1 Elmfield Park, Bromley, Kent BR1 1LU. Tel 0181-466 0466.
Tour operator for mainly American clients to UK, Europe and Middle East.
Experienced tour reps may be needed.

GLOBUS
Via alla Roggia, CH-6916 Grancia, Switzerland. Tel 091-985 71 11.
Tour operator in Europe for English-speaking clients.
Tour directors may be needed.

GOING ABROAD TRAVEL
417 Hendon Way, London NW4 3LH. Tel 0181 202 2080. Fax 0181 202 3839.
Operate tours to worldwide destinations.
20-25 travel consultants and administration staff needed. Recruitment year round. Minimum length of contract 1 month. Computer skills and good telephone manner required.

GOING PLACES
PO Box 999, Woking, Surrey GU22 7GP Tel: 01483 597 000.
In business since 1993.
Direct sell tour operator, part of Airtours plc.
Sales persons needed annually: 800 to sell package holidays and travel-related products. Full-time, part-time or seasonal (April-October) work in UK. Recruitment carries on year round.
Qualifications needed: minimum 'O' level/GCSE in English and maths or travel

qualification. Knowledge of languages not needed. Must be enthusiastic, sen motivated and enjoy working in a team.

GREEK ISLANDS CLUB
10-12 Upper Square, Old Isleworth, Middlesex TW7 7BJ. Tel 0181 2329780. Fax 0181 5688330.
In business since 1968.
Villa specialist to the Greek islands, part of Sunvil Holidays. Member of AITO.
Reps and other experienced staff needed.

GUERBA EXPEDITIONS
Operations Department, Wessex House, 40 Station Road, Westbury, Wilts BA13 3JN. Tel 01373 826611. Fax 01373 858351.
In business since 1980. Member of AITO.
Camping safari operator to many countries in Africa, lasting 1-27 weeks.
Trainee driver leaders, co-driver leaders and full tour leaders needed: 20 (3 crew members per vehicle). Minimum commitment preferred 3 years; June to December is busiest period. Staff occasionally join in Africa.
Qualifications needed: must have mechanical experience (preferably with Bedford or Mercedes trucks) and hold a PCV or HGV licence. Age range 25-30. Conversational French, knowledge of Swahili and experience of travelling in Africa or developing countries would be advantages.
Wages: trainees receive £35 a week plus all expenses (food kitty, visas, passports, air tickets, etc.). Full expedition leaders (who have worked for the company 8-12 months) receive £60-150 per week.

GUIDE FRIDAY
Civic Hall, 14 Rother Street, Stratford-Upon-Avon, Warwickshire. Tel 01789 294466. Fax 01789 414681.
In business since 1975.
Long established tours to major cities in Britain and Ireland.
Require 200 staff; guides, ticket selling staff, PCV drivers and office staff for summer season (May-October). Knowledge of languages required and relevant experience desired.

GULLIVER'S SPORTS TRAVEL
Fiddington Manor, Tewkesbury, Glos. GL20 7AD. Tel 01684 293175. Fax 01684 297926.
Coordinate and tailor-make tours to world sporting events in Australia, New Zealand, South Africa, india, North America, West Indies.
Need 6 tour managers for 1 year to 18 months period. Sometimes employ staff on location for major sporting events.
Qualifications needed: candidates must hold a degree. Languages are preferred, if not sometimes essential.

GUNFLINT LODGE
143 S. Gunflint Lake, Grand Marais, MN 55604, USA. Tel 218 388 2294. Fax 218 388 9429.
In operation since 1927.
Long established wilderness holiday resort, with fishing and canoeing activities.
Keen to employ overseas personnel for various positions; domestic staff, activities leaders, reception staff. Recruitment and work continues throughout the year, and

contracts are a minimum of 3 months. Staff work 45 hours per week. Workers must have a work visa.
Wages: $1065 per month, plus bonuses. Shared accommodation is available for $115 per month.

HAVEN EUROPE
1 Park Lane, Hemel Hampstead HP2 4YL. Tel. 01442 203 276. Fax. 01442 260 779.
In business since 1974.
Camping tour operator to France (mainly), Spain and Italy.
Seasonal staff needed: 300 including couriers for self-catering mobile home and tented campsites, children's couriers, bar staff, lifeguards, receptionists, general cleaners and entertainers. Season lasts from March to end of September. Recruitment begins in September; staff sometimes employed on location.
Qualifications needed: should be conversant in French. Minimum age 18 years. Tourism or hospitality qualification desirable. Mature couples welcome to apply. Experience of working with people, children, etc. needed. Employees must have a UK bank account and NI number.

HERITAGE TOUR LTD
PO Box 3364, Boulder, CO 80307-3364, USA. Tel 303-494-8329. Fax 303-494-8329.
In business since 1995.
Specialise in tours to Ireland.
Require 3 tour guides and 2 drivers for seasonal work. Recruitment takes place on location.
Qualifications needed: must speak Irish, be seasoned travellers, quick learners and patient. Applicants must be from the USA (for tax reasons).

HEADWATER HOLIDAYS
146 London Road, Northwich, Cheshire CW9 5HH. Tel 01606 813333. Fax 01606 813334.
Activity holiday and ski tour operator mainly to France and Italy but also Spain, Norway and Morocco.
30 Overseas reps needed. Duties include client and hotel liason, transport schedules, moving luggage, bike maintenace and on-the-spot problem solving. 5 walking guides, 5 ski guides, and canoe instructors required. Contracts usually for 3-7 months. Recruitment usualy takes place January-February.
Qualifications needed: for reps, minimum age 21. Must be fluent in Italian or French. Full, clean driving licence essential. For canoe instructors, BCU Instructor qualifications or relevant level of experience essential.
Wages: £105-130 per week plus accomodation.

HOLTS, BATTLEFIELD TOURS
The Golden Key Building, 15 Market Street, Sandwich, Kent CT13 9DA. Tel 01304 612248. Fax 01304 614930.
In business since 1976. Member of AITO.
Tour operator specialising in military historical tours, taking in battlefields worldwide, from Europe to the Falkland Islands.
Expert tour leaders may be needed. Background in military history essential.

HOVERSPEED LTD
International Hoverport, Western Docks, Dover, Kent CT17 9TG. Tel 01304 865000. Fax 01304 865090.
In business since 1981.
Runs frequent cross-Channel service (Dover-Calais, Dover-Ostend and Folkestone-Boulogne) on Hovercraft and SeaCat.
Summer season staff needed: 150-200 including cabin crew (50) to work at sea looking after the safety and comfort of passengers, serving refreshments and selling duty-free goods; retail assistants (15) to work in duty-free outlets; and reservation assistants (25). Staff work various rosters at any time of the day or night, 7 days a week. Season lasts from March or June till the end of September, but some contracts are shorter. Applications accepted from January.
Qualifications needed: some knowledge of French needed; German preferred for some posts. Duty-free shop staff must have previous retail experience and reservations assistants must have keyboard experience. Cabin crew are given 3 weeks' training and must sit an exam. Previous experience of dealing with the public an advantage. Travel and tourism qualifications desirable. Must be EU national or have permission to work in UK.
Wages: £5.25 an hour. No accommodation available.

IAN MEARNS HOLIDAYS
Tannery Yard, Witney St, Burford, Oxfordshire OX18 4DP. Tel 01993 822655.
Campsite tour operator to France.
Campsite representatives (12) and montage/démontage assistants (7) needed. Minimum period of work for reps is 10 weeks between Easter and mid-September. Camps are set up between Easter and early May, and dismantled for 3-4 weeks from the middle of September. Applications from November, giving dates of availability with s.a.e.
Qualifications needed: reps must have good knowledge of French, in good health and able to work without supervision.
Wages: from £90 a week for reps, depending on number of units on site.

INGHAMS
Gemini House, 10-18 Putney Hill, London SW15 6AX. Tel 0181-780 4400.
In business since 1934.
Long-established tour operator, specialising in Austria and Italy, especially Lakes and Mountains holidays for an older clientele. Also ski tour operator to many European resorts plus US and Canada.
Need resort reps, coach reps, train couriers and chalet staff (in winter).
Qualifications needed: Must speak German, Italian or French for rep work. Chalet staff need cooking qualifications or experience.

INSIGHT HOLIDAYS
24-26 Paradise Road, Richmond, Surrey, TW9 1SE. Tel 0181-332 2900.
Escorted coach tour operator to Britain and Europe.
Tour managers needed for coach tours. Seasonal reception staff needed for London office.
Qualifications needed: must be experienced.

INTERLOCKEN INTERNATIONAL SUMMER CAMP
RR2, Box 165, Hillsboro, NY 03244. Tel (603) 478-3166. Fax (603) 478-5260.
In operation since 1961.
One of the first United Nations-inspired summer camps, dedicated to bringing together campers from different ethnic, religious, socio-economic and national backgrounds.
Camp counsellors needed (50) to work for 9 weeks during the summer, starting in mid June. CV and covering letter should be sent October - February.
Qualifications needed: experience working with children in a camp environment, specific skills (art, ceramics, photography, sports, sailing, etc.), creativity and abundant enthusiasm. Minimum age 21.

IN THE LIMELIGHT
PO Box 1612, Bradford-on-Avon, Wilts BA15 1FE. Tel 01225 868671.
Tour operator specialising in concert tours, theatre and theme weekends.
Reps may be needed.
Qualifications needed: should have good knowledge of Europe, preferably a knowledge of languages and common sense.

JOBS IN THE ALPS (EMPLOYMENT AGENCY)
PO Box 388, London SW1X 8LX.
In business since 1972. Opportunities for waiters, waitresses, chambermaids, night-porters, chefs and kitchen staff in Swiss owned hotels (see also Alpotels, an affiliated company).Applications by 15th September for winter, 15th April for summer.
Qualifications needed: must be alert, intelligent, hardworking, responsible and pleasant. Hotel experience valuable but not essential. Knowledge of language needed. Applicants must be EU nationals.
Wages ca. £500 per month plus free board and lodging. Please send SAE.

JOURNEY LATIN AMERICA LTD.
12-13 Heathfield Terrace, Chiswick, London W4 4JE. Tel 0181 567 6765. Fax 0181 742 1312.
In business since 1980. Member of AITO.
Overland tour operator to South and Central America.
Applicants should know Latin America and fluent in Spanish or Portuguese.

KEYCAMP HOLIDAYS
Overseas Recruitment Department, Hartford Manor, Greenbank Lane, Northwich CW8 1HW. Tel 01606 787522.
Member of AITO. Camping tour operator to France, Italy, Spain, Germany, Austria, Switzerland, Luxembourg.
Campsite couriers, children's couriers, activity couriers, senior couriers, site supervisors for *montage/démontage* needed.
Qualifications needed: GCSE English and Maths. Working knowledge of French is an advantage. Customer service experience. Minimum age 18 (21 for site supervisor).
Wages: £105 per week. One full day off per week guaranteed.

KUMUKA EXPEDITIONS
40 Earls Court Road, London W8 6EJ. Tel 0171-937 8855. Fax 0171-937 6664. E-mail sales@Kumuka.co.uk

In business since 1987.
Overland tour operator to Africa and South America.
Expedition leaders and driversoccasionally needed, with appropriate ł

KUONI
Kuoni House, Dorking, Surrey RH5 4AZ. Tel 01306 740888.
Upmarket Swiss-based tour operator to long haul destinations.
Reps needed.
Qualifications needed: only people with overseas or customer experience who can speak French, German or Spanish as well as English should apply.

LOGBRIDGE LTD.
6 Saxon Gate, Back Of The Walls, Southampton SO14 3HA. Tel 01703 631331. Fax 01703 339893.
Recruitment agency for hotel and catering staff for Cunard Lines including the *Queen Elizabeth II.*
Positions all on permanent basis, including silver service waiter/waitress, commis waiter, 2nd commis cook, demi chef de partie, bar staff. Qualifications needed: minimum age ranges from 19 for commis waiters to 23 for demi chef de partie, most are 22. At least 2 years full-time experience in the hotel/service industry needed for most posts. City & Guilds certificates essential for chefs/cooks but only preferred for others.

LOTUS SUPERTRAVEL
Sandpiper House, 39 Queen Elizabeth Street, London SE1 2BT. Tel 0171 962 9931. Fax 0171 962 9965
Ski tour operator specialising in upmarket chalet holidays in the 3 valleys; Val D,Isere, St. Anton, and Zermatt, plus Canadian and American ski resorts.
Resort reps (5), chalet staff (40), nannies (4), carpenters/plumbers, electricians (2) and resort managers needed mainly for Méribel, Courchevel and Val d'Isere.
Qualifications needed: applicants must have EU passports, be over 21 and have cooking or NNEB qualifications. All candidates must have relevant experience. Reps must speak good French or German.

MAGIC OF ITALY/MAGIC OF SPAIN/MAGIC OF PORTUGAL
227 Shepherds Bush Road, London W6 7AS. Tel 0181-748 4999.
In business since 1975. Member of AITO.
Reps needed.
Qualifications needed: must speak relevant language. Clean driving licence useful.

MALTA YOUTH HOSTELS ASSOCIATION
17 Triq Tal-Borg, Pawla, Malta PLA 06 Tel/fax 356-693957.
Independent group of Maltese youth hostels, separate from the International Federation of Youth Hostels.
Volunteers needed to work 21 hours a week in youth hostels. Jobs to be done include administration, decorating, building, office work, etc. Period of work from 2 weeks to 3 months. Work permits must be obtained before beginning work, which can take 3 months. A good faith deposit and an application fee are required. Send 3 International Reply Coupons to the above address for details.
Qualifications needed: ages 16-30.
Wages: free hostel accommodation and breakfasts provided.

ANOS HOLIDAYS
168-172 Old Street, London, EC1V 9BP. Tel 0171-216 8070. Fax 0171-216 8099
Resort holidays in the Mediterranean, India and Sri Lanka.
Need 40 overseas reps from March to October. Interviews held in London, in November. Candidates must have ability to deal with people and solve problems.

MARK WARNER LTD
George House, First Floor, 61/65 Kensington Church St, London W8 4BA. Tel 0171 761 7300 (24 hrs).
Has beachclub hotels in Corsica, Italy, Sardinia, Greece and Turkey.
Staff needed: club managers, receptionists, chefs, bar and waiting staff, watersports and tennis instructors, pool attendants, aerobics instructors, laundry staff, handymen, drivers, gardeners, night watchmen and nannies (but not couriers or resort representatives). Must be available from mid-April to mid-October, though there is a continuous need for replacements throughout the season.
Qualifications needed: minimum age 19.
Wages: £40-150 per week; benefits include use of watersports facilities, travel, medical insurance and the potential for winter work in the Alps.
Work also available in the Alps for winter staff, though these are normally chosen from summer staff.

MATTHEWS HOLIDAYS LTD.
8 Bishopsmead Parade, East Horsley, Surrey KT24 6RP. Tel 01483 284044.
In business since 1968.
Campsite and mobile home holiday organiser in France.
Campsite reps/couriers needed: 40. Season lasts May to September inclusive.
Applications are processed from January.
Qualifications needed: GCSE standard of French minimum requirement. Minimum age 21 years. Must be responsible, enthusiastic and reliable.

MERISKI
The Old School, Great Barrington, Burford, Oxon OX18 4UR. Tel 01451 843125. Fax 01451 844799.
Part of the British Rock Leisure Division.
Own ski resort in Mérribel, France. Need chalet staff (30), drivers (5), nannies (10), managers (5). Season lasts early December to late April.
Qualifications needed: cookery, hospitality, and childcare experience for relevant positons. Languages not necessary for all positions.

NEILSON SKI
29-31 Elmfield Road, Bromley, Kent BR1 1LT. Tel 0181-218 3300.
Major ski holiday company, part of Thomas Cook Group to 80 resorts in Andorra, Austria, France, Italy, Switzerland, Bulgaria, Romania, Canada and the USA.
Chalet staff, resort managers and ski leaders required throughout this programme, in Europe and the US, (about 150 total).
Qualifications needed: should be committed to tourism as a career. Minimum age for chalet staff is 20, for resort reps 21.
Successful winter staff may have chance to work as reps for Sunworld Ltd (also part of Thomas Cook) in Spain, Greece or Turkey. A few positions available in Neilson Lakes and Mountains programme.

NEWMARKET PROMOTIONS
McMillan House, Cheam Common Road, Worcester Park, Surrey RT4 8RH. Tel 0181-330 7111.
Operates weekend breaks in Britain and Europe.
Couriers needed for pick-up points throughout the UK.
Qualifications needed: French an advantage.

NORTHUMBRIA HORSE HOLIDAYS
East Castle, Annfield Plain, Co. Durham DH9 8PH. Tel 01207 230555/235354.
Equestrian tour operator.
Reps needed to take charge of parties of riders on equestrian holidays.
Qualifications needed: must be competent rider and be bright and enthusiastic.

NSS RIVIERA HOLIDAYS
199 Marlborough Avenue, Hull HU5 3LG.
Holiday village between St. Tropez and Cannes in the south of France.
Maintenance couples with DIY skills to act as caretakers of 28 chalets, cottages and mobile homes. Minimum age 45 years. Period of work 4-7 weeks at beginning and end of summer season. In exchange for 3 days of work a week (e.g. joinery, plumbing, electrics, building, decorating), couples receive free self-catering accommodation. Must have own vehicle.

NST
Chiltern House, Bristol Avenue, Blackpool FY2 0FA. Tel 01253 352525. Fax 01253 356955.
In business since 1968.
Children's activity holidays in UK and France. Need 10 group leaders, 40 instructors and senior staff, 10 maintenance workers and 15 catering staff.
Contracts last up to 10 months between February and November, depending on location. Recruitment takes place between September and March.
Qualifications needed: must enjoy working with children, work well in a team. Activity instructors must hold relevant UK qualifications.

NUANCE
84-98 Southampton Road, Eastleigh, Hants. SO5 5ZF. Tel 01703 644599.
Operates shops on cruise ships. Shop staff may be required.

OLYMPIC HOLIDAYS LTD
Olympic House, 30-32 Cross St, London N1 2BG. Tel 0171-359 3030. Fax 0171-359 2686.
In business since 1967.
Specialist package tour operator to Greece, affiliated to Greek national airline Olympic Airways.
Reps needed for many island resorts.
Wages: from £160 per month plus commission.

OPENWIDE INTERNATIONAL
103a Oxford Street, London W1R 1TF. Tel 0171-494 232. Fax 0171-439 2037.
Primarily entertainment suppliers for mainstream leisure and tourism industry.

Recruit over 200 people a year to work on cruise ships and in hotels; dancers, vocalists, technicians, ballroom dancing hosts, children's entertainers, comperes.

For hotel work, positions are available all year but main season is May-Novemeber. For cruise ships, 5-month contracts are available. All applicants must be able to participate in a 1-month training course before commencing their contract.

Qualifications needed: knowledge of French, German, Spanish is useful but not essential. Candidates must have lively, strong personalitiesn with some entertainment experience and excellent public relations skills.

OPERATION EUROPE
52-54 Rosebery Avenue, London EC1R 4RP. Tel 0171-837 7702. Fax 0171-837 6925. E-mail SALES@OPERATIONEUROPE.COM

Tour operator to UK and Europe.

Travel reps needed and office staff in high season. Qualifications needed: must be keen and have a second language.

OXFORD CLASSIC TOUR
Holiday House, Station Road, Didcot OX11 7LZ. Tel 01235 819393. Fax 01235 816464.

Open top bus tours around Oxford. Need 10 staff for ticket selling. Contract for any length between April and October. People often employed on location. Knowledge of languages or previous experience not required.

PAGE & MOY
136-140 London Road, Leicester LE2 1EN. Tel 0116-254 2000.

Worldwide direct sell tour operator. Also run national and regional reader holiday offers and motor racing tours.

Experienced freelance tour leaders needed.

Qualifications needed: minimum age 21. Second language and experience essential.

PANITA TRAVEL
10 Thurloe Place, London SW7 2RZ. Tel 0171-581 5606. Fax 0171-581 2360.

Handles incoming and outgoing groups to Germany, Poland and Iceland.

Staff needed with appropriate languages.

PANORAMA HOLIDAY GROUP LTD
29 Queens Road, Brighton BN1 3YN. Tel 01273 206531. Fax 01273 205338.

Tour operator with long haul, european sunshine, ski and youth programmes.

Overseas representatives needed for Tunisia, Morocco, Malta, Balearic Islands, Canaries, Madeira, Cuba, Andorra, Italy. Summer season: May to October. Winter season: November to April. Ski season: December to April.

Qualifications needed: minimum age 21 years. Customer service experience. Language essential for some positions. Ski applicants must have a minimum of three weeks ski experience.

Wages: £335 per month, plus commission, accomodation, uniform, travel expenses. Seasonal lift pass is included for skiing positions. Contact the Overseas Department for an application form.

PGL ADVENTURE
416 Alton Court, Penyard Lane, Ross-on-Wye, Herefordshire HR9 5NR. Tel 01989 767833. Fax 01989 765451. E-mail recruitment@ pgl.co.uk. Web site www.pgl.co.uk/personnel
In business since 1959.
Europe's largest provider of activity holidays for children at 26 centres throughout Britain, France and Spain. Require 2,500 enthusiastic staff to work between February and October. Oppotunities exist to work directly with children as group leaders or activity instructors. Catering and support staff are also required.
Qualifications needed: previous experience is not essential but a sense of fun and enthusiasm is. Minimum age 18 years or over. Must be able to work between February and May for a minimum of 8 weeks.
Wages: living allowance £50-£70, plus board and lodgings.

PROSPECT TOURS
454-458 Chiswick High Road, London W4 5TT. Tel 0181-995 2151.
Tour operator specialising in cultural tours. Graduate operations staff always needed. Expert tour leaders may be needed to lead tours abroad..

PULLMAN HOLIDAYS (UK) LTD.
31 Belgrave Road, London SW1V 1RB. Tel 0171-630 5111. Fax 0171-976 4928.
In business since 1960.
Long established independent tour operator to Israel.
Reservations assistant needed: 1. Placement lasts 48 weeks (September to July) for university student.
Qualifications needed: telephone and travel experience needed.

RAMBLERS HOLIDAYS LTD
PO Box 43, Welwyn Garden City, Herts. AL8 6PQ. Tel 01707 331133.
Operate walking and sightseeing holidays in Europe and beyond.
Tour leaders are needed to run their programmes of walking holidays. Hours normally 8 per day, 7 days a week. Minimum period of work 8 weeks between April and October.
Qualifications needed: minimum age 24. Should have knowledge of relevant language (French, German, Spanish, Italian or Greek). Must demonstrate leadership qualities, have experience of first aid and enjoy walking and map reading.
Wages: from £450 per month.

REGENT HOLIDAYS
15 John Street, Bristol BS1 2HR. Tel 0117-921 1711. Fax 0117-925 4866. E-mail regent@regent-holidays.co.uk
In business since 1970.
Special interest holiday operator to unusual countries, e.g. Albania, Baltics, CIS, China, Cuba, Turkey, Iceland and Vietnam.
Staff needed: 1 at most (only when permanent vacancy crops up).
Qualifications needed: higher education background in tourism or in destination countries. Knowledge of languages needed.

RENAISSANCE CRUISES INC
PO Box 350307, Fort Lauderdale, FL 35335, USA. Tel (954) 463 0982. Fax (954) 356 0183.
In business since 1988.
Cruise line operating in Asian, African, Caribbean and European waters.
Bar staff, silver service waiters, cruise directors, stewardesses, maitres d'hotel and cooks needed: about 650. 6 month contracts starting throughout the year. All staff employed through Fort Lauderdale Fleet Personnel office.
Qualifications needed: fluent English needed. Previous shipboard employment or comparable experience in field necessary. All nationalities accepted.
All travel from home to ship (return) are paid to those who fulfil their contract.
Work also available for reservations sales agents, air/sea agents and documentation agents in corporate offices. Applicants should have travel school certificate or diploma, and be legally eligible to work in the US.

ROMANIA TRAVEL CENTRE
Clayfield Mews, Newcomen Road, Tunbridge Wells, Kent TN4 9PA. Tel 01892 516901. Fax 01892 511579.
Newly established tour operator to Romania. Need reservation and administration staff occasionally. Candididates should have a good education and some experience in the travel industry.

S&S Tours
865 El Camino Real, Sierra Vista, AZ 856 35. Tel 800 499 5685. Fax 520 458 5258.
Small operator of naturalist tours in Mexico and Costa Rica.
May need a Spanish speaker for week-long trips throughout the year. A part-time position, ideal for a retired person. Working knowledge of bird, plant and tree identification necessary.

SAGA HOLIDAYS
The Saga Building, Middleburg Square, Folkestone, Kent CT20 1AZ. Tel 01303 771326/771111.
Holidays for those aged 50+, with a very wide range of worldwide destinations.
Reps and coach couriers needed in British tourist areas and on the continent.
Qualifications needed: ex-nurses especially welcome.
Work also available for London-based reps (0171-828 1954).

SANDPIPER HOLIDAYS
Sandpiper House, 19 Fairmile Avenue, Cobham, Surrey KT11 2JA. Tel 01932 868658. Fax 01932 860535.
In business since 1989. Member of AITO.
Family-run camping holiday operator to west coast of France.
On-site campsite couriers needed: 12. Full season May to September or part season (May to July or June/July to September). Most applications are processed between October and December.
Qualifications: good French required. Enclose CV and SAE with application.

SCANTOURS
47 Whitcomb Street, London WC2H 7DH. Tel 0171-839 2927. Fax 0171-839 5891.
In business since 1964. Member of AITO and ABTA.

Tour operator to Scandinavia and the Baltics.
Administration clerk needed: 1 (temporary) in London office.
Qualifications needed: previous experience in travel industry and knowledge of Scandinavia.

SELECT FRANCE
(JA 99), Murcott, Oxon OX5 2RE. Tel 01865 331350. E-mail selectfrance@sol.co.uk
Member of AITO.
Small family camping holiday operator to west coast of France.
On-site campsite representatives/couriers needed. Duties include; hosting company clientele, small amount of paperwork, organising activities for adults and children and preparing the accomodation.
Qualifications needed: must be cheerful, careful, pragmatic, responsible, self-reliant and, above all, honest. Knowledge of French is preferred and applicants over 23 are at an advantage. Must have a clean driving licence and be available to work mid-May to end of September.
Wages: approximately £390 per month, plus accomodation on site and bonuses.

SHEARINGS
Miry Lane, Wigan, Lancs. WN3 4AG. Tel 01942 244246.
Established coach touring company in UK and tour operator in Europe.
Resort reps needed (Austria, France, Italy and Spain), coach tour guides and TGV couriers for France.
Qualifications needed: minimum age 21. Languages and experience preferred..

SIESTA INTERNATIONAL HOLIDAYS
103 High St, Erdington, Birmingham B23 6SA. Tel 0121-384 5111. Also offices in Middlesbrough, Newcastle, Hull, Leeds, Nottingham and Liverpool.
Low budget tour operator with many departures from northern England to Spanish resorts plus French Riviera, Disneyland Paris and Lido di Jesolo, Italy.
Resort reps, kiddies' club organisers, stewards for coaches and couriers needed.

SILVER SKI HOLIDAYS
Conifers House, Grove Green Lane, Maidstone, Kent ME14 5JW. Tel 01622 735544.
In business since 1984.
Ski chalet operator in French resorts (e.g. Val d'Isère, Méribel, La Plagne, Courchevel).
Two-person teams needed to look after chalets and cook for clients for whole season. Applications from May.
Qualifications needed: mature couples preferred. Must be able to drive, cook and have proven ability to run a household. Should be good skiers. Knowledge of French helpful but not essential.
Wages: pocket money, lift pass, plus all expenses and commission.

SIMPLY TRAVEL
Chiswick Gate, 598-608 Chiswick High Road, London W4 5RT. Tel 0181-995 3883. Fax 0181-995 5346.
In business since 1979.
Tour operator to Greece (Crete and Ionian Islands), Italy (Tuscany and Umbria),

Corsica, Turkey, Spain and Portugal. Also ski tour operator to France (Courchevel, La Plagne, Meribel, Val D,Isere and Chamonix), Switzerland (Verbier) and Austria (St. Anton).

Resort reps needed: 70. Season lasts from April to October/November. Interviews held in London from December to February.

Qualifications needed: must be fluent in English. Knowledge of other languages preferred. Minimum age 25. Must have previous experience in a customer services role. Full training provided.

Work also available for chalet staff, handymen, nannies, chefs for winter season.

SKI ACTIVITY
Lawmuir House, Methven, Perthshire PH2 OLD. Tel 01738 840888. Fax 01738 840079.

Ski tour operator to France, Switzerland, USA and Canada.

Need chalet staff, resort reps and office staff. Contracts last approximately six months (December-April) with possibility of permanent work after. Recruitment takes place from July to December.

Qualifications needed: reps should have a knowledge of languages, customer service and skiing experience. Chalet staff must have catering and customer service experience

SKI AMIS LTD
Alanda, Hornash lane, Shadoxhurst, Ashford, Kent TN26 1HT. tel 01233 732187. Fax 01233 732769.

Ski tour operator to resorts in France. Need 7 chalet staff for 5 month contract (December-May).

Qualifications needed: preferable minimum age 25. Candidates should be well-presented, be able to communicate well, have cooking and skiing experience. French is useful but not essential.

SKIBOUND
see First Choice Ski, Lakes and Mountains

SKI CHAMOIS
18 Lawn Road, Doncaster DN1 2JF. Tel 01302 369006. Fax 01302 326640.

In business since 1980.

Small ski tour operator which specialises in chalet holidays in France (Morzine).

Chefs, ski guides, coach courier/skiguides, nannies, chalet girls and bar staff needed. Applications welcomed from June.

Qualifications needed: fluent French speaking bar staff and chalet girls.

SKI ESPRIT
see Esprit Holidays

SKI INDEPENDENCE
Broughton Market, Edinburgh, Scotland EH3 6HU. Tel 0990 550555. Fax 0990 502020.

Upmarket ski chalets in USA and Canada. Require 9 chalet staff for season lasting from end of November to end of April. Sometimes employ people on location.

Qualifications needed: languages not necessary. Catering qualification or experience required.

SKI MIQUEL
33 High St, Uppermill, Nr. Oldham, Lancs. OL3 6HTS Tel 01457 820200. Fax 01457 872715.
In business since 1981.
Ski tour operator to France (Alpe d'Huez, Serre Chevalier), Austria (Badgastein), Switzerland (Lauterbrunnen) and Spain (Baqueira), Canada (Whistler).
Resort managers (5), bar person/ski guides (4), chalet people (10) and chefs (4) to work 4¹/₂-5 months for winter season.
Qualifications needed: chefs must have City & Guilds 706/1/2; resort managers need to speak appropriate language and have 2 years repping experience (minimum age 23); chalet assistants and barmen/ski guides need bubbly personalities and staying power.
Wages: chalet staff and barmen earn £60 per week, chefs £110 and resort managers £120-£140.

SKI OLYMPIC
PO Box 396, Doncaster DN5 7YS. Tel 01709 579 999. Fax 01709 579 898.
In business since 1987.
Ski tour operator to France (Courchevel, Val d'Isère, Tignes, La Plagne, La Rosiere and Val Thorens).
Winter season staff needed: 35 out of total of 70 (10 ski guides, 5 chefs, 15 chalet girls, 2 nannies, 3 bar staff. 5 month contract (1st December to 28th April). Applications are processed from August. Unexpected vacancies are somtimes filled in France.
Qualifications needed: minimum age 22 for all positions. Knowledge of French preferred but not essential. Ski guides must have BASI III (or equivalent); chefs must have good qualifications and extensive experience in restaurant or hotel; nannies must have NNEB. All must have EU passport.

SKI SCOTT DUNN LTD
Fovant Mews, 12 Noyna Road, London SW17 7PH. Tel 0181-767 0202. Fax 0181-767 2026.
In business since 1986.
Ski tour operator to France (Courchevel 1850, Val d'Isère and Meribel), Switzerland (Zermatt), USA and Canada.
Winter season staff needed: 5 resort managers, 1 ski guide, 19 chalet cooks, 12 chalet helpers and 10 nannies. Period of work from mid-December to end of April. Applications are processed from end of May; interviews are held at London office.
Qualifications needed: resort managers must be over 25, speak fluent French or German, and have accounting experience. Cooks must be over 21, have completed 6-month cookery course and have experience. Guides must be over 23 and have 25 weeks of skiing experience. Nannies must be over 20 and have NNEB or equivalent. Australians and New Zealanders are not eligible.
Wages: £50-£150 per week depending on job. Staff) receive ski pass, ski and boot hire, and all receive food and accommodation away from their place of work, 1 day off a week, medical insurance, return travel to resort, and ski jacket and trousers.

SKI TOTAL
3 The Square, Richmond, Surrey TW9 1DY. Tel 0181-948 6922. Fax 0181-332 1268.
Ski tour operator to France, Austria and Switzerland..
Winter season staff needed: 6 reps, 30 chalet girls, 8 ski guides and 6 chefs. Period of work December-April. Applications are processed between May and October.
Qualifications needed: catering staff must be qualified and experienced (e.g. cordon bleu, Tante Marie). Fluency in language essential for reps, helpful for other posts. Catering staff must be over 20, the rest must be over 23. Australians and New Zealanders are not eligible; EU nationals preferred.

SKIWORLD
41 North End Road, West Kensington, London W14 8SZ. Tel 0171-602 4826. Fax 0171-371 1463.
In business since 1982.
Ski tour operator to a number of French resorts, plus Switzerland, Italy, USA and Canada.
Approximately 240 staff required: chalet staff, resort managers, resort reps, nannies, maintenance staff and chefs needed to work winter season. Recruitment takes place between June and December. Staff are sometimes hired on location.
Qualifications needed: minimum age 21. Reps and managers must be able to speak French and ski; management work overseas preferred. Chalet staff must be confident cooks and hard-working. Must be UK/EU nationals.
Wages: about £50-£65 per week.

SKYROS HOLIDAYS
92 Prince of Wales Road, London NW5 3NE. Tel 0171-267 4424. Fax 0171-284 3063. E-Mail skyros@easynet.co.uk. Web site www.skyros@easynet.co.uk
Holistic holiday community on Skyros island, Greece, offers over 200 workshops. Eight 'work scholarship' places are available for 3 months, May to July or August to October. Duties involve the overall smooth running and cleanliness of the site, flexible 5-7 hours per day in split shifts, 6 days per week.
Qualifications: minimum age 21. Need qualified nurses and chefs. Will consider those with culinary, maintenance or musical skills or those fluent in Greek. Must be hardworking, fit, exceptionally caring and thrive in a community environment.
Wages: full board, course tuition fees, plus approx £40 pocket money.

SOBEIR AGENCY
Avenue Louise 396, 1050 Brussels, Belgium. Tel 02-640 12 20. Fax 02-647 28 97.
Recruitment agency which specialises in the placement of hotel and catering personnel in Belgium and Luxembourg.

SOLAIRE HOLIDAYS
1158 Stratford Road, Hall Green, Birmingham B28 8AF. Tel 0121-778 5061.
Camping and mobile home tour operator to France (Brittany, Normandy, Paris region, Loire, Vendée and Mediterranean coast) and Blanes (Costa Dorada, Spain). Campsite couriers needed: from 30 to prepare camps at beginning of season (May) and look after clients until end of season (September). Details available in January.
Qualifications needed: knowledge of French or Spanish preferred but not essential.

Wages: £75-100 per week plus on-site accommodation, travel and insurance.
Work also available for children's couriers in France, bar staff (who must be fluent in the language) and cleaners on Solaire's campsites.

SOLO'S
54-58 High Street, Edgeware, Middlesex H7EJ. Tel 0181-951 2800.
Holidays for singles.
Staff must be good at mixing and creating a sociable atmosphere.

SPECIALISED TRAVEL LTD
12-15 Hanger Green, London W5 3EL. Tel 0181-799 8300. Fax 0181-998 7965.
In business since 1955.
Specialises in concert tours of Europe. Also incentive tour operator.
Tour leaders needed: 60-80 to accompany choirs, orchestras and bands (including American groups) on concert tours around Europe (including UK and the CIS) between April and August (mainly June/July). Work involves being responsible for all daily events, reconfirming concert arrangements, accommodation, transport and leading sightseeing excursions. Applications accepted in summer and autumn for the following season. Individual contracts for various tours which last between 2 and 3 weeks each.
Qualifications needed: applicants must have excellent organistaions skills, leadership qualities and initiative. A musical background and knowledge of touring are advantages. Languages necessary according to specific tour destination. All nationalities welcome.

SPORTSWORLD
New Abbey Court, Stert St, Abingdon, Oxon. OX14 3JZ. Tel 01235 554844.
Tour operator to sports events including the Olympic Games, etc.
Experienced tour leaders may be needed.

SPRINGBOARD
3 Denmark St, London WC2H 8LP. Tel 0171-497 8654. Fax 0171-4972466. Website www.springboarduk.org.uk.
Anne Walker: Managing Director - E-Mail AnneW@springboarduk.org.uk.
General information - E-Mail Info.london@springboarduk.org.uk
A free specialist careers advice centre providing details on training courses, CV advice, qualifications and the various career paths into hotels, catering, leisure and tourism.

STEPPES EAST LTD
Castle Eaton, Swindon, Wiltshire SN6 6JU. Tel 01285 810267. Fax 01285810693.
In operation since 1979.
Tour operators to worlwide destinations including Russia, the Far East, India and the Middle East.
Occasionally require sales staff with detailed knowledge of locations for UK office. Previous work in tour operations preferred.

AYS

, 7 St. John's Road, Isleworth, Middlesex TW7 6NA.

in Spain and Portugal.

ort reps for seasonal work April to October. Part season short term contracts also possible.

Qualifications needed: languages preferred but not essential. Driving licence and EU passport needed. Customer service experience, initiative, teamwork, problem-solving skills and sense of humour required.

SO WHEN ARE YOU GOING TO GET A PROPER JOB?

Come now. It's high time you stopped messing around with that dull desk job. And what *do* you do at weekends? Now then, what about a nice trip abroad? Come with us next summer to the Algarve, Costa Blanca or the Balearic Islands and join the overseas rep's team known as the best in the business. As well as first class personal performance standards, you'll need an undying commitment to customer satisfaction, loads of enthusiasm, heaps of initiative, bags of stamina and a sense of humour! Oh, and you must be a great team player. Minimum age is 23, driver's licence and EC passport are essential, knowledge of Portuguese or Spanish an advantage. Previous experience is not necessary, but you must have a face-to-face customer service background.

So – quit commuting and get moving. Life as a Style Rep will never be dull. Challenging, naturally. Demanding, definitely. Rewarding, absolutely. Just another job? You have to be kidding.

Style Holidays, Coomb House, 7 St John's Rd, Isleworth, Middx, TW7 6NA

Tel. Overseas Dept: 0181 568 2344   ABTA V1498   ATOL 3443

SUNSAIL LTD
The Port House, Port Solent, Portsmouth, Hants. PO6 4TH. Tel 01705 219847 or 24-hour ansaphone 214330.
Operate flotilla and bareboat sailing holidays and watersports hotels in Greece, Turkey, Corsica and Sardinia, as well as Thailand, Caribbean, New Zealand and Australia.
Staff needed: more than 300, as flotilla skippers, hostesses, engineers, qualified dinghy instructors, receptionists, chefs, bar staff and qualified nannies. Season lasts from March/April to October/November. Some winter work usually reserved for loyal summer employees.
Qualifications needed: ages 20-35. Knowledge of German an advantage for many positions. Training and experience appropriate to job required, e.g. sailing positions require RYA/AYF/NZYF certification.
Wages: vary from £220 to £400 a month plus return flights.

SUNVIL HOLIDAYS
Sunvil House, Upper Square, Old Isleworth, Middlesex TW7 7BJ. Tel 0181-568 4499. Fax 0181-568 8330.
Villa holiday operator to Greece and Cyprus, plus Fly Drive Islands programme.
In business since 1970. Member of AITO, ABTA, AGTA. Experienced staff needed with knowledge of Greek and tourism experience.

SUNWORLD
29 Elmfield Road, Bromley, Kent BR1 1LT. Tel 0181-290 1111.
Tour operator to Mediterranean resorts (part of Iberotravel Group, see entry).
Property reps needed to look after villas. Also children's reps.
Qualifications needed: minimum age 21 for reps, 19 for kiddies' reps.

SUSI MADRON'S CYCLING FOR SOFTIES
2-4 Birch Polygon, Rusholme, Manchester M14 5HX.
Cycling holiday operator in France.
Company assistants needed. Minimum period of work 2 months between May and September.
Qualifications needed: must speak French and be at least 20. Non-smokers only.
Full training on bicycle maintenance given.
Wages: fixed wage plus bonus.

SWISS TRAVEL SERVICE
Bridge House, 55-59 High Road, Broxbourne, Herts. EN10 7DT. Tel 01992 456143. Fax: 01992 448855.
In business since 1950.
Tour operator to Switzerland.
Resort representatives needed: 16 for summer season (April-October/November), 10 in winter (December-April).
Qualifications needed: Graduates preferred. Must be at least 21, have a smart appearance and a responsible and friendly attitude. No Australians or New Zealanders. Applications accepted year round. Interviews in UK.
Wages: £350-400 per month plus free board and accommodation.
Work also available for scenic tour guides to guide rail tours in 4 or 5 Swiss resorts.

TALL STORIES
67a High Street, Walton-on-Thames, Surrey KT12 1DJ. Tel 01932 252002. Fax 01932 225145.
In business since 1991.
Adventure sports tour operator in Austria, Spain and France.
Reps needed: 2 in Spain, 1 in France and 1-2 in Austria, to host small groups of adult clients doing multisport holidays, to work with suppliers of all sports and activities, hoteliers, etc. 17 week season in Spain and Austria (May-September) and 12 weeks in France (July-September). Applications processed from February; occasional last-minute opportunities but all interviews in UK.
Qualifications needed: knowledge of French, Spanish or German needed. Minimum age 23, and must have driving licence (PCV an advantage) and outdoor sporting interests. UK passport holders only.
Wages: £100 per week plus perks.
Work also available for 1 chalet chef in France.

TANA TRAVEL
2 Ely Street, Stratford-Upon-Avon, Warwickshire CV37 6LW. Tel 01784 414200. Fax 01784 414420.
Tour operator to Australasia, Africa, South Pacific, Costa Rica, specialising in tailor-made holidays.
Require 2 permanent travel consultants.
Qualifications needed: languages preferred. 2 years travel experience and knowledge of destination points.

TAPESTRY HOLIDAYS
24 Chiswick High Road, London W4 1TE. Tel 0181-742 0144. Fax 0181-235 7500.
In business since 1991.
Small upmarket tour operator to Turkey.
Experienced staff sometimes needed.

THOMAS COOK HOLIDAYS
12 Conningsby Road, Merlin Business Park, North Bretton, Peterborough PE3 8XP. Tel 01733 417000. Fax 01733 417784.
One of the biggest tour operators in ABTA.
Experienced tour directors occasionally needed for long haul and other destinations. Normally won't consider anyone until they have had 5 years' industry experience.

THOMSON HOLIDAYS
Human Resources Overseas, Greater London House, Hampstead Road, London NW1 7SD. Tel 0171-387 9321.
Giant tour operator to worldwide destinations. Also extensive ski programme. Skytours and the Luton-based charter airline Britannia Airways are owned by Thomson.
Overseas and children's representatives needed to work in European and worldwide resorts for summer season April to October, with the possibility of winter employment. Applications for summer work preferred in preceding September. Possibility of winter work for chalet reps and ski rangers (applications should be sent in June). Entertainment staff neede to organise a varied programme of daytime and evening events.
Qualifications needed: applicants must have a high degree of patience, tact and diplomacy, a pleasant outgoing nature, initiative and a strong sense of responsibility. Fluency in English plus one of Spanish, Greek, German, Italian or Portuguese needed.
Representatives need minimum of 1 year's experience in a customer service role along with an empathy with all kinds of people. Minimum of 5 GCSEs including Maths and English, and the ability to converse in another European language is desirable. Minimum age 23 years.
Children's representatives should have an NNEB or similar childcare qualification along with at least 6 months practical work experience with children. Minimum age 19 years.
Entertainment staff must be educated to minimum GCSE level and have previous experience of entertaining an audience in a similar role in the leisure industry. Minimum age 21 years

TOP DECK
131-135 Earls Court Road, London SW5 9RH. Tel 0171-244 8641. Fax 0171-373 6201.
In business since 1972.
Youth tour operator in Central and Eastern Europe, Russia and Scandinavia, Turkey and Morocco.
Coach drivers needed: 10-20. Most work available March-October.
Applications processed November-February. Occasional on-site opportunities in July.
Qualifications needed: full PCV coach licence (will help promising candidates to get their licence). Knowledge of languages an advantage (must be fluent in English).
Work also available for overland drivers/reps for London to Kathmandu trip, and for ski resort staff in Andorra, Austria, Switzerland and France.

TRACKS
The Flots, Brookland, Romney Marsh, Kent TN29 9TG. Tel 01797 344 164. Fax 01797 344 135.
In business since 1971.
Overland camping tour operator in Europe and Africa.
Tour leaders in Europe needed: 30. Employed tour by tour in summer season. Applicants must show apptitude and be EU nationals.
African expedition driver/leaders needed: 10. Period of work 2 years. Must be aged 23-28, have a British PCV or LGV (HGV) licence and be technically-minded. Must also have the ability to mix with groups of all ages and nationalities. Trainees are based in UK for 3-6 months in the first instance.

TRAFALGAR TOURS
9 Bressenden Place, London SW1E 5DD. Tel 0171-828 4388.
Major tour operator in Europe, Ireland and the UK.
Meet and greet staff needed to work at London airports and hotels. Seasonal vacancies.

TRANS SURE (UK) LTD.
c/o 8 Cour de Chateau, 44430 Le Loroux-Bottereau, France. Tel 40 03 74 720.
LGV drivers required to work in Europe for the UK camping industry. Job involves loading and delivering camping equipment from central depots to campsites at the beginning of the season. This equipment is then picked up and returned to the depots at the end of the season. Often hard work but sociable. Periods of work from March 15 to May 15 and September 10 to October 30.
Qualifications needed: must have Class 1 or 3 LGV licences and at least one year's driving experience. Applicants must have initiative, commitment and a sense of adventure. Wages: £30 a day (5 days a week) plus accommodation when not working.. Outward and return travel paid for.

TRAVELART LTD
Imperial 0661, Puerto Varas, Chile. Tel 65 232 198. Fax 65 234 818.
Handle clients for German and North American tour operators, as well as individual clients. Require tour guides (3-5) and office staff. Minimum contract for 1 year, preferably longer. Guides work seasonal period between October and April on a freelance basis for daily wage. No special time of recruitment.

:eded: fluency in German and English is essential. Knowledge of
irable. Office staff should a qualification or practical experience in
;try and see tourism as a career, not just a vacation job. Knowledge
needed. Guides should have experience, knowledge of geology,
nd Chile.

TRAVELBAG PLC
12 High Street, Alton, Hampshire GU34 1BN. Tel 01420 541441. Fax 01420 82133.
Specialist travel consultants, selling tailor-made itineries to long-haul destinations including; Australia, Asia, Far east, South Pacific, South Africa, USA, South America.
Require 200 staff for mostly permanent staff (some 1 year contracts available for students). Benefits include high level of training and travel concessions.
Qualifications needed: sales, customer service and travel experience/knowledge. HND leisure and Tourism (or equivalent).

TRAVELBOUND
Olivier House, 18 Marine Parade, Brighton, East Sussex BN2 1TL. Tel 01273 677777. Fax 01273 600486.
A division of First Choice Holidays. Activity/Educational tour operator to Austria and France (Alps and Normandy). ?
Summer staff needed: 250 including resort reps, chalet and hotel staff (chefs, waiting staff, chamber staff, kitchen, night porters).
Full season in Austria and French Alps lasts May-September, in Normandy February-October. Flexible contract lengths available. CVs and covering letters processed in January and June.
Qualifications needed: minimum age for hotel positions: 18, resort reps: 21. Must have EU passport and National Insurance number. Salary package from £200-300 per month plus food, accomodation, insurance and travel to and from the resort.
Winter work also available for ski season: see First Choice Ski, Lakes, Mountains.

TRAVELCOAST LTD
First floor, Fraser House, London Road, Twickenham, Middlesex. Tel 0181 8912222. Fax 0181 8929588.
In business since 1986.
Resort holidays in Cuba, Cayo Largo, Cayo Coco.
Need 3 resort repsfor Cuba for 1 year contract. Interviews take place March-August. Sometimes employ people on location.
Qualifications needed: minimum age 21. Fluency in Spanish and experience in customer service necessary. Candidates must be self-reliant. EU nationals only.

TRAVELSPHERE LTD
Compass House, Rockingham Road, Market Harborough, Leics. LE16 7QD. Tel 01858 410456.
Major coach tour operator in Europe, UK, North America and worldwide, specialising in older adults.
Couriers needed to escort groups throughout Europe, including Belgium, Italy, France, Germany, Spain, Portugal, Austria, Switzerland, Czech and Slovak Republics, Poland and Norway. To work long hours for a minimum of 4 months.
Qualifications needed: ages 20-55. Previous courier experience not essential but must have a friendly outgoing personality and an ability to deal with people.

Experience of travelling in Europe useful.

Wages: daily rate plus commission on excursions sold. Half-board accommodation usually provided plus full insurance, travel costs and training.

Work may also be available for people familiar with long haul destinations.

TRAVELWORLD INTERNATIONAL LTD
1 Beal Road, Ilford, Essex 1G1 4QF. tel 0181 5544545. Fax 0181 5184992.

Run business travel, conference and incentive trips.

Occasionally recruit staff in early winter. Candidates must speak western European languages and have minimum 3 years business travel experience.

TRUCK AFRICA
37 Ranelagh Gardens Mansions, Fulham, London SW6 3UQ. Tel 0171-731 6142. Fax 0171-371 7445.

In business since 1988.

Overland tour operator in Africa.

Drivers needed. Must be diesel mechanics with HGV licence. Also work for couriers. Must have first-hand knowledge of travel in Africa or be prepared to train for at least 3 months with no guarantee of work afterwards.

UNIJET TRAVEL LTD.
'Sandrocks,' Rocky Lane, Haywards Heath, W. Sussex RH16 4RH. Tel 01444 459100. Fax 01444 417100.

In business since 1981.

Part of the First Choice Group since 1998. Tour operator to Europe, USA, the Caribbean and worldwide.

Resort reps and children's couriers needed for Mediterranean resorts (including Spain, Portugal and Malta in winter too). Seasonal ticketing, May to October,

VENTURE ABROAD
Arc House, 1 Coalhill Lane, Farsley, Leeds LS28 5NA. Tel 01483 273027.

Tour operator for UK youth groups to Europe especially Switzerland.

Group leaders needed to meet and guide youth groups around Gstaad, Grindelwald, Interlaken and several other Swiss resorts.

Qualifications needed: minimum age 19. University students who know French or German are acceptable provided they can prove that they have leadership qualities.

Wages: £90 per week, self-catering accommodation and insurance provided.

VENUE HOLIDAYS
21 Christchurch Road, Ashford, Kent TN23 7XD. Tel 01233 642505. Fax 01233 634494.

In business since 1985.

Camping tour operator to Italy (Venetian Riviera, Lake Garda, Tuscany), France (Vendee, Dordogne, Roussillon) and Spain (Costa Brava).

Resort reps needed: 17. Season lasts April to end of September though minimum period of work is May to August. Applications are processed from October to April.

Qualifications needed: knowledge of languages advantageous. Should be hard-working, resourceful, fit and have experience of working with the public.

Wages: £350 per month, with accommodation provided.

Work also available for 1 children's courier.

VFB HOLIDAYS LTD.
Normandy House, High Street, Cheltenham, Glos. GL50 3HW. Tel 01242 235515. Fax 01242 570340.
In business since 1970. Member of AITO.
Activity holiday operator in France (la Clusaz, Morzine, les Deux Alpes and Samoëns in the French Alps and Corsica).
Resort reps needed: 20 (4-6 senior reps) for French Alps and 3 for Corsica. Season in Alps from end of June to 1st September; season in Corsica from May to October. Applications are processed from December to April, training session mid-June.
Qualifications needed: fluent French essential. Knowledge of France and French lifestyle important. Age 20-35. British or French nationals. Must have sports/outdoor activity background with a confident and enthusiastic personality.
Wages: £350-420 per month in Alps, £450-600 in Corsica.

VIGVATTEN KLUB
Aptdo 3253, 01002 Vitoria Gasteiz, Spain. Tel 945-281794. Fax 945-281794.
In business since 1994. 3 multi activity children's camps in rural Spain (the Basque country, Pyrenees and Sierra de Urbion).
Camp staff needed: 15 monitors, 12 support staff in kitchen and for maintenance, 3 cooks and 3 camp nurses. Minimum period of work 2 weeks during summer. Applications welcomed in February and March, but accepted until end of June.
Qualifications needed: minimum age 18. All staff must speak English; knowledge of Spanish desirable. Monitors must have previous experience of working with children, and instructors must have necessary qualifications/experience. Certificate

of food hygiene useful for support staff.

Wages: £150 per fortnight plus full board and accommodation (Cooks about £250).

VILLAGE CAMPS
c/o rue de la Morache, 1260 Nyon, Switzerland. Tel 22 990 9405. Fax 22 990 9494.

In business since 1972. Multi-activity language camps for children in Switzerland (Anzere, Leysin, Morgins, etc.), Austria (Zell-am-See), France, Netherlands, Spain and England. Most are summer camps, but also winter camps in ski resorts.

Children's counsellors, EFL teachers, sports instructors, nurses and domestic staff needed. Minimum period of work is 4 weeks.

Wages: pocket money for counsellors SFr275 for ten days and SFr325 for 14 days plus food, accommodation and insurance.

Work also available for ski counsellors (up to 100) and other staff in ski season.

VOYAGES ILENA
1 Old Garden House, The Lanterns, Bridge Lane, London SW11 3AD. Tel 0171-924 4440. Fax 0171-924 4441.

Tour operators to Corsica and Sardinia.

Occasionally recruit selling, ticketing, administration staff, programme managers.

Qualifications needed: French and Italian speakers desired. Candidates must have a degree and preferably experience in the travel industry.

VOYAGES JULES VERNE
21 Dorset Square, London NW1 7SD. Tel 0171-723 5066.

Upmarket tours to unusual destinations, train tours, art and culture tours, etc.

Experienced tour directors only.

WEXAS INTERNATIONAL
45-49 Brompton Road, London SW3 1DE. Tel 0171-589 3315. Fax 0171 589 8418.

Telesales consultants for travel and related products to worldwide destinations.

Require 12-20 travel consultants. Candidates must be well-travelled, educated to minimum 'A' level standard, have knowledge of SABRE GDS and have experience in retail travel. Knowledge of languages preferred.

WIND, SAND & STARS
2 Arkwright Road, Hampstead, London NW3 6AD. Tel 0171-433 3684. Fax 0171-431 3247.

In business since 1991.

Special interest tours to the deserts and mountains of Sinai for adults and students.

Leaders needed for student and school expeditions (from 8 days–4 weeks).

Qualifications needed: Wilderness experience or relevant academic expertise, remote first aid, leadership or youth experience.

Wages: according to background. Free board and lodging.

WORLDWIDE JOURNEYS
243 Euston Road, London NW1 2BU. Tel 0171-383 3898. Fax 0171-383 3848.

Travel agency in business since 1985.

Reservations sales agents needed: 5. Administration and ticketing agent: 1. Permanent positions available as vacancies occur.

Qualifications: 5 GCSEs or 2 years job experience. No restriction on nationality.

COACH TOURING COMPANIES

The following coach tour companies might have occasional vacancies for tour managers and guides. Most of them are too small to be able to cope with an influx of written applications, so the best plan is to ring round the ones in your part of the country to find out what their hiring procedures are:

Abbey Hove, Lincoln – 01522 720683
Appleby Coaches, Lincolnshire – 01522 537799
Arvonia Coaches, Carnarvon – 01286 675175
Bebb Travel, Pontypridd – 01443 204211
Bennets Coaches, Newbury – 01635 248423
Bere Regis Coaches, Dorset – 01305 262992
Big Bus Company, London – 0181 944 7810
Black Prince Coaches, Leeds – 0113-253 2305
Blubird Coaches, Weymouth – 01305 786262
Bowens, 101 Cotterills Lane, Alum Rock, Birmingham B8 3SA (0121-327 5921).
Harry Brown, St Albans – 01582 831153
Peter Cartwell, Burneley – 01282 456351
Chambers Coach Hire, Co. Londonderry – 01648 748152
Channel Coachways, London – 0181 985 8888
Circle Line, Gloucestr – 01452 526662
Clarksons Coaches, W.Yorks – 01977 642500
JD Cleverly Ltd, Gwent – 01633 872424
Colwill Coaches, Swansea – 01792 850320
Cooks Coaches, Westcliffe-on-Sea – 01702 344702
Continental Connection, Clwyd – 01244 281606
Crusader Coaches, Yorkshire – 01226 293566
De Courcy Mike Travel, Coventry – 01203 302656
Director Travel, Yorkshire – 0113 2326262
Eavesway Coaches, Wigan – 01942 727985
Enterprise Travel, PO Box 1, Bradford BD1 2QE (01756 710501)
Erringtons of Evington, Leicester – 0116 2592131
Euroview Holidays, Dereham – 01362 698667
Excelsior Holidays, Bournemouth – 01202 309555
Facts Travel Ltd, London – 0171 603 1246
Fareway Coaches, Liverpool – 0151 5491289
Fargo Coaches, Essex – 01376 321817
Farthing Holidays, Holiday House, Weir Road, Kibworth, Leics. LE8 0LQ (0116-279 6060). Readers' offer holidays.
Fords Travel, Callington – 01579 84307
Gain Travel – 01274 603224
Galloway Travel – 01449 767778 (readers' offer holidays)
Garretts, Devon – 01626 66580
Grays Travel, Yorkshire – 01226 743109.
Grimsby Transport, Grimsby – 01472 358207
Guideissue, Stoke-on-Trent, 01782 522101
Hays Coaches, Aberdeenshire – 01446 740283
Heards Coaches, Devon – 01237 441233

Hookways, Devon – 01837 810257
Hudson, Cleveland – 01429 860860
Hutchinsons Coaches, Lanarkshire – 01698 372132
Independent Coach Travel, 45 Marris Road, London E14 6PA (0171-538 4627). Coach tour wholesaler.
Johnsons, Solihull – 01564 792325
Jones Motors, North Wales – 01509 267131
Jeff Lamb, Stockport – 01625 426463
Leger Travel, Sunway House, Canklow Meadows, West Bawtry Road, Rotherham S60 2XR (01709 839839) (readers' offer holidays).
Leiston Motor Hire, Suffolk – 01728 830358
Andrew McDade, Glasgow – 01698 818509
DR Macgregor, Essex – 01206 212932
K. Mackie, Birmingham – 0121 3275921
Macpherson Coaches, Midlands – 01530 270216
Ian Mactavish, Clydebank – 0141 9520064
Monetgrange, Nottingham – 01159784088
Motts Travel, Aylesbury – 01296 613831
National Express – 0121-456 1122, Need hostesses/stewards for their countrywide Rapide services. Phone for list of coach companies offering this service locally.
Norman Allen Group Travel, 13 Commercial St, Hereford HR1 2DB (01432 277666). Wholesale coach tour operator.
David Ogden Travel, Cornwall – 01744 20977
Oates Travel, Cornwall – 01736 995 343
OK Motor Services, Co. Durham – 01388 450000
David Palmer Coaches, Normanton – 01924 895849
Paramount Leisure, Midlands – 01438 861192
Paterson & Brown, Ayrshire – 01505 683344
Priory Coaches, Gosport – 01705 580522
Redby Coaches, Northumberland – 0191-514 2294
CW Riddler, Angus – 01241 873464
Robinsons Coaches, Bedfordshire – 01525 2402624.
Seamarks Coach & Travel, Luton – 01207 232976
Shalder Coaches, Shetland Islands – 01595 880217
E. Shaw & Son, Peterborough – 01778 342224
Skills Motor Coaches, Nottingham – 0115 978 4645
Leslie J. Smith, Braintree – 01376 321817
Stanley Taxis, Co. Durham – 01207 232976
Stones Coaches, Bath – 01225 422267
Tims Travel, Kent – 01795 663884
Trans Euro – 0181 784 0100 for coach shuttle work
Trathens Travel Service, Devon – 01752 790565
Travel Care – 0104 548025 for coach shuttle work
Edward Watts, Taunton – 01460 281213
Whites Travel, Yorkshire – 01246 276666
Wilfreda Beehive, Yorkshire – 01302 330330
Willing Bros Mini Coaches, Middlesex – 0181 8900882
Wood's Coaches, Leicester – 0116-278 6374
Woods Travel, Sussex – 01243 868080
Yorkshire Coachline, Huddersfield – 01484 519915
Yorkshire Traction – 01226 202555

Appendix 1

Tourist Offices in London

ANDORRA: Andorran Delegation, 63 Westover Road, SW18 2RS (0181-874 4806).

AUSTRALIA: Australian Tourist Commission, Gemini House, 10-18 Putney Hill, Putney, SW15 6AA (0181-780 2229).

AUSTRIA: Austrian National Tourist Office, 14 Cork St W1X 1PF (0171-629 0461).

BELGIUM: Belgian National Tourist Office, 29 Princes St, W1R 7RG (0171-629 3977).

CANADA: Tourism Section, Canadian High Commission, Macdonald House, 1 Grosvenor Square, W1X 0AB (0171-258 6600).

CYPRUS: Cyprus Tourist Office, 213 Regent St, W1R 8DA (0171-734 9822).

DENMARK: Danish Tourist Board, 55 Sloane St SW1X 9SY (0171-259 5958).

EGYPT: Egyptian State Tourist Office, 170 Piccadilly, W1V 9DD (0171-493 5282).

FINLAND: Finnish Tourist Board, 52-55 Pall Mall, SW1Y 5LP (0171-839 4048).

FRANCE: French Government Tourist Office, 178 Piccadilly, W1V 0AL (0891 244123).

GERMANY: German National Tourist Office, 65 Curzon St, W1Y 7PE (0891 600100).

GIBRALTAR: Gibraltar Tourist Board, Arundel, Great Court, 179 Strand, WC2R 1EH (0171-836 0777).

GREECE: Greek National Tourism Organisation, 4 Conduit St, W1R 0DJ (0171-734 5997).

HUNGARY: Hungarian National Tourist Board, PO Box 4336, SW18 4XE (0891 171200).

ICELAND: Icelandic Tourist Office, c/o Icelandair, 172 Tottenham Court Road, W1P 0LY (0171-388 5599).

INDIA: Indian National Tourist Office, 7 Cork St, W1X 2AB (0171-437 3677/8).

IRELAND: Irish Tourist Board/Bord Fáilte, 150 New Bond St, W1Y 0AQ (0171-493 3201).

ISRAEL: Israel Government Tourist Office, UK House, 180 Oxford Street, W1N 9DJ (0171-434 3651).

ITALY: Italian State Tourist Office, 1 Princes St, W1R 8AY (0171-408 1254).

JAPAN: Japan National Tourist Organisation, 120 Saville Row, W1X 1AE (0171-734 9638).

LUXEMBOURG: Luxembourg National Tourist Office, 122 Regent St, W1R 5FE (0171-434 2800).

MALTA: Malta National Tourist Office, 36-38 Piccadilly, W1V 0PP (0171 2924900).

MONACO: Monaco Tourist & Convention Office, The Chambers, Chelsea Harbour, SW10 0XE (0171-352 9962).

NETHERLANDS: Netherlands Board of Tourism, 25 Buckingham Gate, (PO Box 523), SW1E 6NT (0891 200277).

NEW ZEALAND: New Zealand Tourism Board, 7th Floor, New Zealand House,

80 Haymarket, SW1Y 4TE (0839 300900).

NORWAY: Norwegian National Tourist Office, Charles House, 5 Regent St, SW1Y 4LR (0171-839 6255).

PORTUGAL: Portuguese Tourist Office, 2nd Floor, 22/25a Sackville St, W1X 1DE (0171-494 1441).

SOUTH AFRICA: South African Tourism Board, 5-6 Alt Grove, Wimbledon, London SW19 4DZ (0541 550044).

SPAIN: Spanish Tourist Office, 57 St. James St, SW1A 1LD (0171-486 8077).

SWEDEN: Swedish National Tourist Office, 11 Montagu place, W1H 2AL (0171-724 5868).

SWITZERLAND: Swiss National Tourist Office, Swiss Centre, Swiss Court, New Coventry St, W1V 8EE (0171-734 1921).

THAILAND: Thailand Tourist Office, 49 Albemarle St, W1X 3SE (0171-499 7679).

TURKEY: Turkish Information Office, 170-3 Piccadilly, W1V 9DD (0171-355 4207).

UK: British Tourist Authority, Thames Tower, Black's Road, Hammersmith, W6 9EL (0181-846 9000).

USA: United States Travel and Tourism Administration, PO Box 1EN, London W1R 1EN (0897 508911) or Visit USA (a private non-profit organisation; 0891 600530) .

Appendix 2

Embassies/Consulates in London and Washington

AUSTRALIA: Australia House, The Strand, London WC2B 4LA (0171-379 4334/0891 600333).
1601 Massachusetts Ave NW, Washington DC 20036-2273 (202-797-3000/3145).
AUSTRIA: 18 Belgrave Mews West, London SW1X 8HU (0171-235 3731).
3524 International Court NW, Washington DC 20008 (202-895-6767).
BELGIUM: 103 Eaton Square, London SW1W 9AB (0171-470 3700).
3330 Garfield St NW, Washington DC 20008 (202-333-6900).
BRAZIL: Consular Section, 6 St. Alban's St, London SW1Y 4SG (0171-930 9055).
3009 Whitehaven St NW, Washington DC 20008 (202-745-2828).
CANADA: 1 Grosvenor St, London W1X 0AB (0171-258 6601).
501 Pennsylvania Ave NW, Washington DC 20001 (202-682-1740).
CHILE: 12 Devonshire St, London W1N 2DS (0171-580 1023).
1732 Massachusetts Ave NW, Washington DC 20036 (202-785-3159).
CHINA: 31 Portland Place, London W1N 3AG (0891 880808).
2300 Connecticut Ave NW, Washington DC 20008 (202-328-2517).
CZECH REPUBLIC: 26-30 Kensington Palace Gardens, London W8 4QY (0171-727 4918).
3900 Spring of Freedom St NW, Washington DC 20008 (202-363-6315/6).
DENMARK: 55 Sloane St, London SW1X 9SR (0171-333 0200).
3200 White Haven St NW, Washington DC 20008 (202-234-4300).
EGYPT: 2 Lowndes St, London SW1X 9ET (0171-235 9719).
2310 Decatur Place NW, Washington DC 20008 (202-234-3903).
FINLAND: 38 Chesham Place, London SW1X 8HW (0171-235 9531).
3216 New Mexico Ave NW, Washington DC 20016 (202-363-2430).
FRANCE: 21 Cromwell Road, London SW7 2DQ (0171-838 2000).
4101 Reservoir Road NW, Washington DC 20007 (202-944-6200/6215).
GERMANY: 23 Belgrave Square, London SW1X 8PZ (0171-824 1300).
4645 Reservoir Road NW, Washington DC 20007 (202-298-4000).
GREECE: 1A Holland Park, London W11 3TP (0171-221 6467; Labour Counsellor's Office 0171-221 6774).
2221 Massachusetts Ave NW, Washington DC 20008 (202-232-8222).
HONG KONG: 6 Grafton St, London W1X 3LB (0171-499 9821). c/o Chinese Embassy.
HUNGARY: 35b Eaton Place, London SW1X 8BY (0171-235 2664).
3910 Shoemaker St NW, Washington DC 20008 (202-362-6730).
ICELAND: 1 Eaton Terrace, London SW1W 8EY (0171-590 1100).
2022 Connecticut Ave NW, Washington DC 20008-6194 (202-265 6653).
INDIA: India House, Aldwych, London WC2B 4NA (0171-836 8484).
2536 Massachusetts Ave NW, Washington DC 20008 (202-939-9839/9850).
IRELAND: 17 Grosvenor Place, London SW1X 7HR (0171-235 2171).
2234 Massachusetts Ave NW, Washington DC 20008 (202-462-3939).
ISRAEL: 15 Old Court Place, London W8 4QB (0171-957 9500).

3514 International Dr NW, Washington DC 20008-3099 (202-364-5500).
ITALY: 14 Three Kings Yard, Davies St, London W1Y 2EH (0171-629 8200).
1601 Fuller St NW, Washington DC 20009 (202-328-5500).
JAPAN: 101-104 Piccadilly, London W1V 9FN (0171-465 6500).
2520 Massachusetts Ave NW, Washington DC 20008 (202-939-6800).
KENYA: 45 Portland Place, London W1N 4AS (0171-636 2371/5).
2249 R St NW, Washington DC 20008 (202-387-6101).
LUXEMBOURG: 27 Wilton Crescent, London SW1X 8SD (0171-235 6961).
2200 Massachusetts Ave NW, Washington DC 20008 (202-265-4171/2).
MALAYSIA: 45 Belgrave Square, London SW1X 8QT (0171-235 8033).
2401 Massachusetts Ave NW, Washington, DC 20008 (202-328-2700).
MEXICO: 8 Halkin St, London SW1X 7DN (0171-235 6393).
2827 16th St NW, Washington, DC 20009-4260 (202-736-1000).
MOROCCO: Diamond House, 97-99 Praed St, London W2 (0171-724 01719).
1601 21st St NW, Washington DC 20009 (202-462-7979).
NETHERLANDS: 38 Hyde Park Gate, London SW7 5DP (0171-584 5040).
4200 Linnean Ave NW, Washington DC 20008 (202-244-5300).
NEW ZEALAND: New Zealand House, Haymarket, London SW1Y 4TE (0171-973 0366/0891 200288).
37 Observatory Circle NW, Washington DC 20008 (202-328-4848).
NORWAY: 25 Belgrave Square, London SW1X 8QD (0171-235 7151).
2820 34th St NW, Washington DC 20008-2799 (202-333-6000).
PERU: 52 Sloane St, London SW1X 9SP (0171-235 6867/1917).
1700 Massachusetts Ave NW, Washington DC 20036 (202-833-9860).
POLAND: 73 New Cavendish Street, London W1M 8LS (0171-580 0476).
2224 Wyoming Ave NW, Washington, DC 20036 (202-8339860).
PORTUGAL: Silver City House, 62 Brompton Road, London SW3 1BJ (0171-581 8722/4).
2125 Kalorama Road NW, Washington DC 20008 (202-332-3307).
RUSSIA: 5 Kensington Palace Gardens, London W8 4QS (0171-229 8027).
1825 Phelps Place NW, Washington DC 20008 (202-939-8907/8911/8913).
SINGAPORE: 9 Wilton Crescent, London SW1X 8SA (0171-235 8315).
3501 International PLace NW, Washington, DC 20008 (202-537-3100).
SLOVAKIA: 25 Kensington Palace Gardens, London W8 4QY (0171-243 0803).
2201 Wisconsin Ave NW, Suite 380, Washington, DC 20007 (202-965-5164).
SOUTH AFRICA: South Africa House, Trafalgar Square, London WC2N 5DP (0171-839 2211).
3201 New Mexico Ave, Washington, DC 20016 (202-966-1650).
SPAIN: 20 Draycott Place, London SW3 2SB (0171-581 5921).
2700 15th St NW, Washington DC 20009 (202-265-0190/1).
SWEDEN: 11 Montagu Place, London W1H 2AL (0171-914 6413).
Suite 1200, 600 New Hampshire Ave NW, 1200, Washington DC 20037 (202-944-5600).
SWITZERLAND: 16/18 Montagu Place, London W1H 2BQ (0171-723 0701).
2900 Cathedral Ave NW, Washington DC 20008 (202-745-7900).
THAILAND: 29/30 Queen's Gate, London SW7 5JB (0171-589 0173).
2300 Kalorama Road NW, Washington DC 20008 (202-234-5052).
TURKEY: 43 Belgrave Square, London SW1X 8PA (0171-235 5252/3/4).
1714 Massachusetts Ave NW, Washington DC 20036 (202-659-0742).
UK: 19 Observatory Circle NW, Washington DC 20008 (202-986-0205).
USA: 5 Upper Grosvenor St, London W1A 2JB (0891 200290).
ZIMBABWE: 429 Strand, London WC2R 0SA (0171-836 7755).

1608 New Hampshire Ave NW, Washington DC 20009 (202-332-7100).

See *The London Diplomatic List* published frequently by the Foreign & Commonwealth Office and held in most public libraries in Britain.